Evolution of Italian Enterprises in the 20th Century

Contributions to Economics

www.springer.com/series/1262

Further volumes of this series can be found at our homepage.

Wojciech W. Charemza/Krystyna Strzala (Eds.)
East European Transition and EU Enlargement
2002. ISBN 3-7908-1501-1

Natalja von Westernhagen
Systemic Transformation, Trade and Economic Growth
2002. ISBN 3-7908-1521-7

Josef Falkinger
A Theory of Employment in Firms
2002. ISBN 3-7908-1520-9

Engelbert Plassmann
Econometric Modelling of European Money Demand
2003. ISBN 3-7908-1522-5

Reginald Loyen/Erik Buyst/Greta Devos (Eds.)
Struggeling for Leadership: Antwerp-Rotterdam Port Competition between 1870–2000
2003. ISBN 3-7908-1524-1

Pablo Coto-Millán
Utility and Production, 2nd Edition
2003. ISBN 3-7908-1523-7

Emilio Colombo/John Driffill (Eds.)
The Role of Financial Markets in the Transition Process
2003. ISBN 3-7908-0004-X

Guido S. Merzoni
Strategic Delegation in Firms and in the Trade Union
2003. ISBN 3-7908-1432-6

Jan B. Kuné
On Global Aging
2003. ISBN 3-7908-0030-9

Sugata Marjit, Rajat Acharyya
International Trade, Wage Inequality and the Developing Economy
2003. ISBN 3-7908-0031-7

Francesco C. Billari/Alexia Prskawetz (Eds.)
Agent-Based Computational Demography
2003. ISBN 3-7908-1550-0

Georg Bol/Gholamreza Nakhaeizadeh/Svetloza T. Rachev/Thomas Ridder/Karl-Heinz Vollmer (Eds.)
Credit Risk
2003. ISBN 3-7908-0054-6

Christian Müller
Money Demand in Europe
2003. ISBN 3-7908-0064-3

Christina Nardi Spiller
The Dynamics of the Price Structure and the Business Cycle
2003. ISBN 3-7908-0063-5

Michael Bräuninger
Public Debt and Endogenous Growth
2003. ISBN 3-7908-0056-1

Brigitte Preissl/Laura Solimene
The Dynamics of Clusters and Innovation
2003. ISBN 3-7908-0077-5

Markus Gangl
Unemployment Dynamics in the United States and West Germany
2003. ISBN 3-7908-1533-0

Pablo Coto-Milián (Ed.)
Essays on Microeconomics and Industrial Organisation, 2nd Edition
2004. ISBN 3-7908-0104-6

Wendelin Schnedler
The Value of Signals in Hidden Action Models
2004. ISBN 3-7908-0173-9

Carsten Schröder
Variable Income Equivalence Scales
2004. ISBN 3-7908-0183-6

Wilhelm J. Meester
Locational Preferences of Entrepreneurs
2004. ISBN 3-7908-0178-X

Russel Cooper/Gary Madden (Eds.)
Frontiers of Broadband, Electronic and Mobile Commerce
2004. ISBN 3-7908-0087-2

Sardar M. N. Islam
Empirical Finance
2004. ISBN 3-7908-1551-9

Jan-Egbert Sturm/Timo Wollmershäuser (Eds.)
Ifo Survey Data in Business Cycle and Monetary Policy Analysis
2005. ISBN 3-7908-0174-7

Bernard Michael Gilroy/Thomas Gries/Willem A. Naudé (Eds.)
Multinational Enterprises, Foreign Direct Investment and Growth in Africa
2005. ISBN 3-7908-0276-X

Günter S. Heiduk/Kar-yiu Wong (Eds.)
WTO and World Trade
2005. ISBN 3-7908-1579-9

Emilio Colombo/Luca Stanca
Financial Market Imperfections and Corporate Decisions
2006. ISBN 3-7908-1581-0

Birgit Mattil
Pension Systems
2006. ISBN 3-7908-1675-2

Francesco C. Billari/Thomas Fent/Alexia Prskawetz/Jürgen Scheffran (Eds.)
Agent-Based Computational Modelling
2006. ISBN 3-7908-1640-X

Renato Giannetti · Michelangelo Vasta
(Editors)

Evolution of Italian Enterprises in the 20th Century

With 21 Figures and 99 Tables

Physica-Verlag
A Springer Company

Series Editors
Werner A. Müller
Martina Bihn

Editors
Prof. Renato Giannetti
Università di Firenze
Dipartimento di Studi Storici
e Geografici
Via San Gallo 10
50129 Firenze
Italy
E-mail: giannetti@unifi.it

Prof. Michelangelo Vasta
Università di Siena
Dipartimento di Economia
Politica
Piazza San Francesco 7
53100 Siena
Italy
E-mail: vasta@unisi.it

ISSN 1431-1933
ISBN 10 3-7908-1711-2 Physica-Verlag Heidelberg New York
ISBN 13 978-3-7908-1711-9 Physica-Verlag Heidelberg New York

Physica-Verlag is a part of Springer Science+Business Media GmbH

springer.com

Typesetting: Camera ready by editors
Cover: Erich Kirchner, Heidelberg
Production: LE-TEX, Jelonek, Schmidt & Vöckler GbR, Leipzig

SPIN 11685876 Printed on acid-free paper – 88/3100 – 5 4 3 2 1 0

Preface

The research which has given rise to this volume concerns the nature of Italian industrial capitalism, a theme which has attracted much attention in Italy among economists and economic historians, but is not well represented in international comparisons, due to language problems as well as to the difficulty of categorizing it. Indeed, the few who have tried to include Italy in a comparative framework end up generally with a negative view, as a result of the distance of the Italian case from the classical ones - Britain first and then US. However, since at least Gerschenkron it should be clear that there is no single model of capitalism, but several, sharing basic components like investment and technology, but differing institutionally and also organizationally.

The line taken by the group of researchers, coordinated by Renato Giannetti and Michelangelo Vasta, contributing to this volume is that of dissecting Italian capitalism in its inner features, to examine strengths and weaknesses without preconceptions, using existing tools of analysis, but trying to resort to new ones capable of revealing more original dimensions.

Indeed, Italy, after having been leader of the modern market economy between the XII and the XVI centuries, plunged into a decline and belatedly faced industrialization as a *follower*, though a special one, exempt from a number of features characterizing underdeveloped countries: it kept good trade relations with Europe, especially for the export of silk; it had Universities and Academies; it boasted a cultivated elite, who shaped the new Kingdom institutionally after Unification (1861) according to the most advanced models of the time[1]. The process of *catching up* was somewhat slow at the beginning, but by the turn of the XIX century was well in place and continued in the XX century, unabated by two World Wars and the Great crisis, becoming particularly rapid in the post-Second World War period and slowing down considerably only in the past decade. This *catching up* is well portrayed in this volume by the sectoral distribution of the first 200 manufacturing firms analyzed in Chap. 5 by Vasta, a distribution that started from a traditional pattern of the disproportionate presence of textiles and moved by the end of the century to a pattern similar to that of the US.

However, the sectoral convergence hides profound differences in the organization of Italian enterprises, with no evidence so far of such differences evolving over time. We have an example here of path dependence, that throws light on the limits of the Gerschenkronian theorization. The exclusive attention by Gerschenkron on *take-off*, which according to him can be based on different factors due to the process of substitution, has tended to hide the fact that differences are often there to stay well after *take-off* and a turn is likely to be produced only when such differences become a stumbling block to the continuation of growth, not however without major difficulties.

---

[1] The interested reader could follow the development of all these arguments in V. Zamagni, *The economic history of Italy 1860-1990*, Oxford, Clarendon Press, 1993.

It is precisely on the illustration of the peculiarities of Italian enterprises that the essays appearing in this volume insist, making use of new datasets. The most important of these datasets, Imita.db (see Appendix), derives from the digitalization of a publication collecting basic data on Italian joint stock companies which was issued between 1911 and 1984 (there are other sources that can be linked to the present one for the following period). It was possible through successive inter-University research projects to digitalize all available data from that publication for 8 benchmark years and the balance sheets data for all the years of the period for a universe of companies ranging from 787 in 1911, 3,072 in 1921 to 11,783 in 1972, covering some 90 per cent of the capitalization of all joint stock companies at each date. All the large and medium size companies are included, while the tail of small companies, already quite substantial in our dataset, was at all times far thicker, given the exclusion from the publication that has been digitalized of the very small joint stock companies and of companies that were not incorporated (all small). From this dataset it was possible to extract the first 200 corporations active in manufacturing, for the purpose of including Italy within the Chandlerian comparative analysis developed in *Scale and Scope* for US, Great Britain and Germany (see Chap. 5 by Vasta).

The second source is less new, being made up of the industrial censuses administered in Italy since 1911. However, in the present volume the original data have been processed for the period 1911-2001 with the aim of standardizing them along the lines previously laid[2], but with the ATECO-ISTAT 1991 classification, to allow for diachronic comparisons without the distortions produced by changes in classification from one census to the next. The results are commented in Chap. 2 by Giovanni Federico. Finally, an effort to collect more qualitative data on the largest enterprises was accomplished through the creation of file cards with entries to be filled from material made available by existing company histories. As many as 142 of these cards were compiled and the conclusions deriving from this original, though numerically limited, data bank are discussed in Chap. 8 devoted to strategies by Federico and Pier Angelo Toninelli. The method is available for the inclusion of other company cases in the future.

The presentation of the three main sources on which the essays of this volume are constructed is already enlightening about its originality: not many countries have comparable datasets on the evolution of enterprises encompassing almost a century. But the elaborations made in the book on such basis are also valuable, as they make use of the most up to date statistical techniques and of categories and concepts developed by business history at the international level. Of the innovative conclusions reached, I will bind myself to comment here only on the most distinctive ones, with the hope of stimulating the readers to resort to Chaps.

The first main conclusion points to an established feature of the Italian productive system and can be found spelled out in the Chap. 3 by Giannetti and Vasta: the level of concentration of the Italian manufacturing system is low, as a result of

---

[2] See V. Zamagni, "A Century of change: trends in the composition of the Italian labour force 1881-1981", *Historical Social Research*, 44, 1987: 36-97, republished in G. Federico (ed.), *The economic development of Italy since 1870*, Aldershot, Elgar, 1994: 210-271.

the joint effect of low sectoral concentration levels (at the exception of rubber and means of transport) and of the modest weight that sectors with higher concentration have on the aggregate. It is not however possible to conclude from this that we are in presence of nearly perfect competitive markets, because often the low concentration index is produced by the existence of a large number of very small enterprises together with one or few large corporations. In this case we have imperfect monopoly or oligopoly markets, where the small enterprises live in the shadow of the large ones. But there is more to be said. As the very innovative Chap. 6 by Leonardo Bargigli and Vasta shows, Italian capitalism is highly collusive. The exploitation of the dataset of members of the boards of directors points quite clearly to the existence of extensive *interlocking directorates*, with some key figures performing the role of *big linkers* within the system. These *big linkers* have been individually characterized in the Chap. 9 by Alberto Rinaldi, who has selected the first 20 directors most present in boards in the benchmark years covered by the dataset. The networks built up through the *interlocking directorates* encompass most of the Italian corporations (as can be seen in Table 6.2), leaving only a few companies isolated, and they include also most of the small companies. On the basis of this result, it is possible to rebuild concentration indices, calculated normally at face value, and higher values are uniformly obtained (see Table 3.5): the Italian corporate milieu is more compact than it superficially seems, because of the existence of vast networking, through the building up of groups.

Very interesting is the confirmation that networks are built around the *central* role of the financial sector (banks and insurance companies), showing multiple links within and without, not only in the years of the *universal banks*[3], but also later, with links put in place by more banks than was usually maintained. After the financial sector, the next central sector is electricity, before nationalization (that took place in 1963), as a result of the electrical companies being public companies, namely companies the shares of which were held widely by other companies, beside private individuals. Moreover, after the birth of state-owned corporations in 1933[4], networks include both private and state-owned corporations, without appreciable differences. The grouping analysis developed by Bargigli and Vasta is a

[3] Italy moved from a nearly specialized financial system to a *universal banking* system after the banking crisis of the early 1890s and the foundation of the Bank of Italy in 1893. But the solution of the 1929 crisis brought about a new state-owned long-term investment bank (IMI founded in 1931) and a new banking bill (1936), which put an end to the *universal banking* practice and inaugurated another version of the specialized banking system, where all the long-term investment banks were state-owned and the former three major *universal banks* were downgraded to short-term banks. This system remained in place up to the 1993 banking bill, when privatizations started and the *universal banks* were once again recalled into existence.

[4] Istituto per la Ricostruzione Industriale (IRI), born in January 1933 as a State holding to rescue *universal banks* from the burden of joint stock companies shares in their hands, did not change the legal status of the corporations acquired, which kept their private legal incorporation and sometimes remained quoted on the stock exchange, while most, but often not all, of their shares became state-owned.

preliminary approach, because the source does not allow going any further. What would be needed is a dataset of the distribution of share ownership, similar to the one built for the beginning of the 1990s by a Bank of Italy research project. In the latter, it was possible among other things, to compare the percentage of capital of the corporations quoted on the stock exchange that was in the hands of other corporations, banks and insurance companies and of the State. The total reached in Italy was 62 per cent as against 66 per cent in Germany and 58 per cent in Japan, but only 5 per cent in the US and 24 per cent in the UK[5], where pension funds and families held most of the shares.

Indeed, the analysis of groupings is likely to give more results in the future, as it will be possible to complement its quantitative basis with qualitative information on the nature of groups. There are in fact *spurious* groups, like the SIR led by Nino Rovelli in the 1960s and 1970s, which was made up of more than 100 companies kept legally separate for fiscal reasons, but forming a few technical and organizational units. There are *classical* groups, made up of companies controlled by one single owner, but active in different though related fields, with administrative autonomy and the presence of partners. There are conglomerates, under the same holding (like Montedison, to quote a famous one) and there are alliances. In the latter case, more than a group we could speak of a *galaxy*, where members exchange shares (usually minority blocks) and pursue common strategies, but ownership and control remain separate. There are two other forms of networking widely present in Italy which could not be captured by the present data bank until recently: *industrial districts* and cooperative enterprises. In the former case, we are in presence of *informal* links among very small firms, specialized in each single *district* in one line of production (shoes, jewelries, packaging machinery, ceramic tiles, etc.)[6]. More recently, there have been stratification processes taking place in most of the *districts*, with one or a few firms becoming larger and starting the formation of groups. In the case of cooperatives, they too have undergone a process of consolidation in the past 20 years, with the formation of groups. Both cases, therefore, are tending to a homogenization with the group approach typical of the Italian industrial milieu.

Another more well-known feature of Italian capitalism is its family control. It is true that family control is often underrated in many countries, even in the US, where there are very famous and successful cases in which big corporations (like Microsoft) are still under the control of the founder, but in Italy managerial corporations are truly an exception, as Chap. 8 by Federico and Toninelli shows, and this is certainly at the basis of the difficulties Italy shows in having enough trans-

---

[5] F. Barca (ed.), *Assetti proprietari e mercato delle imprese*, vol. II, Bologna, Il Mulino, 1994: Table 5.11, 124.

[6] Recent statistical analysis of the Italian *industrial districts* has fixed their number at around 200, mostly located in the Centre-North of the country. See F. Pyke, G. Becattini and W. Sengenberger (eds), *Industrial districts and inter-firm cooperation in Italy*, Geneva, ILO, 1990; M. Bagella and L. Becchetti (eds), *Evolutionary patterns of local industrial Systems. towards a cognitive approach to the industrial district*, Aldershot, Ashgate, 2000.

national companies and also accounts for widespread intergenerational crises (when the children of the founder are not capable of replacing him successfully).

In Chap. 7 by Vasta there is an answer to another question which so far could never be addressed: how profitable was the investment in Italian industrial corporations? A glance at the ROE series confirms the well-known economic cycles (see fig. 7.2): the slowdown before the First World War, the War peak, the 1921 fall, the slowdown in 1927 after the stabilization of the lira, the 1930 fall and the strong recovery in the 1930s, the boom during the *economic miracle* up to the middle of the 1960s, followed by a slowdown and then by a fall in the 1970s. But the performance of ROE by sectors (see Table 7.2), or by type of product using the Pavitt technological classification (see Table 7.6), or by corporate size (see Table 7.8) is more interesting. An econometric test of profitability is also attempted, which delivers a couple of firm conclusions: a positive relation exists between corporate size and profitability and between corporate age and profitability. In the light of these results it becomes even more difficult to explain the preference by Italian entrepreneurs for the small size on the basis of simple economic logic. Other tests could be tried in the future. For example, an exercise I deem of the utmost usefulness to improve the understanding of the Italian corporate milieu is that of comparing profitability of the corporations quoted on the stock exchange[7] with the profitability of the unquoted corporations. This could shed light on the reasons for the lack of interest of Italian corporations in becoming quoted on the stock exchange[8].

A final distinctive feature that has been analyzed in both Chap. 4 by Giannetti and Margherita Velucchi and Chap. 5 by Vasta is instability: the largest Italian enterprises tend to change size dramatically over time, when they do not disappear altogether. In the period 1911-2001, only 8 of the first 200 enterprises in manufacturing have remained present in each benchmark year. This instability is confirmed by the survival analysis carried out in Chap. 4, suggesting to Giannetti and Velucchi the creation of the nickname *leaping frogs* for those firms that have shown such remarkable instability in performance. The identification of the *leaping frogs* and their characterization through the use of additional sources is the object of further research in progress, but it can already be anticipated that the two World Wars, the intergenerational crises, the low technological content and the industrial policies often unfriendly to large enterprises, when they were not under State control[9], are the candidate causes of the observed instability.

The unique contribution this book gives to the understanding of the character and evolution of Italian industrial capitalism is best summarized as follows: Italian industrial capitalism cannot be categorized with simple indicators like average size of firm and concentration indices. There are formal and informal links among

---

[7] Notoriously, a very small number, which has fluctuated until recently at around 200.

[8] As is well-known, a very good reason comes from having a bank-oriented financial market. This is another feature that ranks Italy together with Germany and Japan.

[9] Among the eight Italian corporations listed in *Fortune global 500* for 2004, six are former state-owned enterprises (of which three are banks) and only two are established private enterprises (Assicurazioni Generali, an insurance company, and FIAT).

firms making them much more coordinated than they appear, through groupings, *industrial districts* and networks of cooperatives. If it could be proved that this co-ordination is today no longer adequate to improve efficiency and productivity, it is from here that industrial policies must start and not from an unrealistic dream of importing the alien form of the Chandlerian multidivisional corporation.

February 2006 Vera Zamagni

Acknowledgments

This volume is the result of a ten-year research project which has required a huge data entry standardization and revision effort. Thus, first of all, we would like to thank Riccardo Benedetti, Andrea Micheletti and Stefano Susini for their precious collaboration in setting up Imita.db, the dataset which is the basis of this research. Many thanks are due also to Cristina Badon, Angela Betti, Lucia Castellucci, Enrico Conti, Paolo Di Martino, Massimo Ferraioli, Alessandro Marucelli, Paolo Raspadori, Paola Susini, Erica Ussi, Maria Teresa Zanella for their helpful contribution in the creation of the dataset. Our gratitude goes also to Emanuele Bernardi, Francesca Pino, Francesca Polese and Giampietro Morreale for their aid in the research of the original sources.

Special thanks are due to Giovanni Federico and Pier Angelo Toninelli for their contribution to the set up of the volume and the numerous suggestions provided at different stages of this project. We owe a special debt to Giorgio Mori for the long discussions and numerous suggestions provided during the years and to Vera Zamagni for her valuable comments on previous versions of the text and her encouragements from the very beginning of this work. Many thanks for their precious comments are also due to Leonardo Bargigli, Martina Cioni and Alberto Rinaldi and, for her econometric assistance, to Michela Baccini.

We would also like to thank all participants at the Workshop *L'IRI e la storia delle imprese italiane nel Novecento* (Rome, February 2003) promoted by the Fondazione IRI, and at the *Incontri di storia dell'impresa* (Milan, May 2003) promoted by the Fondazione ASSI and Bocconi University, where some parts of this research were presented, and in particular Francesco Brioschi, Yousseuf Cassis and Peter Wardley for their valuable suggestions. A special mention is due to Franco Amatori who helped us promote our research and offered precious comments.

Finally, we would like to thank all the colleagues and friends with whom we have discussed the themes of this volume along the years: Alberto Baccini, Carlo Bardini, Beppe Berta, Steve Borgatti, Giovanni Bruno, Luciano Cafagna, Albert Carreras, Valerio Castronovo, Andrea Colli, Leandro Conte, Giuseppe Conti, Augusto De Benedetti, Marcello de Cecco, Martin Fiedler, Paolo Frascani, Andrea Giuntini, Mauro Lombardi, Michele Lungonelli, Giuliano Muzzioli, Claudio Pavese, Giandomenico Piluso, Jaime Reis, Gianni Toniolo, Fabrizio Traù.

The quality of this book has certainly been raised by the valuable language assistance supplied by Serena Rotunno and to the precious and patient editing work of Riccardo Benedetti.

Of course, the editors retain responsibility for any remaining errors.

This research received financial support from the Ministero dell'Istruzione, dell'Università e della Ricerca (MIUR) for a research project *Italian Enterprise in the 20th* developed in collaboration with Bocconi University, University of Bologna and University of Florence, and a research project *Models of enterprise in the*

Italian 20th century capitalism carried out by Bocconi University, University of Bologna, University of Florence, University of Modena and Reggio Emilia and University of Siena. We also received financial support from the Consiglio Nazionale delle Ricerche (CNR).

Florence, January 2006

Renato Giannetti
Michelangelo Vasta

Contents

1. The historiography

Renato Giannetti and Michelangelo Vasta

1.1. Introduction

The historiography of the Italian firm in the 20th is essentially divided into two phases. For the first two-thirds of the century it was centered on the process of industrialization of the leading countries, on the delay in this process and on the ways followed by latecomer countries to catch up. The focus was, therefore, on the processes of imitation or on original experience based on *substitutive factors*. The analysis concentrated on the themes of sectoral structure (modern and traditional sectors) and on comparative performance. In the last part of the century, however, the analysis became decidedly oriented towards microeconomic aspects. Attention was focused on the study of the strategies and the variety of organizational formulas adopted by the single *actors*. The 20th century, thus, ended with an economic debate centered on the market, the enterprise and the entrepreneur. A singular destiny for a century in which the macroeconomic themes of development and the development policies for its maintenance were, instead, largely preponderant. Economic historiography is also characterized by a succession of different views on the nature and dynamics of enterprises. Until the 1970s, in fact, the analysis was concentrated on the firm as an aggregate issue that could be described with a few *stylized facts* such as size, concentration and performance. The main topic of research was the large firm, identified as the *engine* of economic growth. During the last third of the century the firm is no longer seen as a generic subject with simple and well-defined aims, but rather as the result of the complex interaction between the behavior of its owners (stock-holders, families, groups), its management (top and middle) and its workers (qualified and non-qualified).

In the light of this characterization, in the following pages we propose a review of the historiography of the firm in Italy. This review is organized according to the themes that have emerged during the course of time - sectoral composition, size, market power, performance, ownership, strategies and agent - and that constitute the subject of the essays making up this book. In Sect. 1.2 we analyze the first phase, in which the macroeconomic approach prevails, while in Sect. 1.3 we illustrate the historiography of the second phase, characterized by a microeconomic approach. The review concludes (Sect. 1.4) with a brief synthesis on the topic of Italy's industrial *decline*, a theme that has characterized economic debate since the beginning of the new century.

Although the present work was set up by both authors, only Sect. 1.1 is actually co-written. Section 1.2 is to be attributed to Renato Giannetti and Sects. 1.3 and 1.4 to Michelangelo Vasta.

1.2. The macroeconomic approach

In Italian economic historiography the topic of the firm has been tackled, in the first place, in reference to the economic development of the country, through debates revolving around issues such as *financial capital*, *monopolistic capitalism* and *backwardness*. In this literature the enterprise is considered a homogenous *actor* with precise aims and its characterization is so aggregated that, in Marxist inspired literature, the large enterprise coincides with an entire social class, the capitalist class [Grifone 1945; Sereni 1966].

In the considerable historiographical tradition constituted around the notion of *financial capital*, we can differentiate between two trends. The first traces the dynamics of Italian economic development during the Giolittian era to the universal pre-eminence of *financial capital*, which, according to many, is a trait common to several countries in this phase of capitalistic development [Grifone 1945]. The above is linked to the monopolistic character of the large Italian firm - ILVA, Ansaldo, FIAT, Breda, etc. - which by controlling supply, kept profits high, shrinking the market. In this interpretation large Italian firms do not differ from those of other countries. The second trend represents a *reformist* interpretation of the notion of *financial capital*, considered, however, as *parasitic revenue* rather than as the final form of capitalism. The concept of *original weaknesses* can be traced back to this interpretation, a definition of Italian capitalism that, expressed through different points of view, runs through the entire economic history of contemporary Italy. These *original weaknesses* consist in the persistence of traditional agricultural rents [Gramsci 1949; Sereni 1966] and in the weight of speculation alongside the more modern sectors of industry and enterprise [Mori 1977, 1992, 1994]. The interpretation of the peculiar traits of Italian economic growth in terms of *original weaknesses* has important implications regarding the topic of the firm. In this perspective, in fact, the modern large enterprise is an expression of *financial capital*, but it is its industrial component that is considered more efficient and, above all, capable of improving working conditions and raising income levels. At the same time, however, the process of concentration that accompanies the success of the large enterprise reduces the importance of small and medium enterprises, that are less efficient, but that make up the greatest occupational sector. The historiography stemming from a liberal approach is more determined in its monopolistic characterization of the Italian firm; it denotes large enterprise as the *padroni del vapore*, as the major obstacle towards the modernization of the country [Rossi 1955; Scalfari 1963; Scalfari and Turani 1974].

The evaluation of the effective degree of monopolistic power of the Italian system of enterprises is, however, controversial, due to the differences between the periods studied and the sources and methods used for its measurement. A high market power is observed, for example, by Rossi and Toniolo [1992] who show, through a production function for the period 1895-1938, that prices were 40 to 150 per cent higher than marginal costs, namely than the conditions for perfect competition. On the other hand, Boni and Gros Pietro [1967], and Giannetti, Federico and Toninelli [1994] observe a relatively modest level of concentration for two different periods (1951-1961 in the former study and 1908-1940 in the latter) with the use respectively of industrial censuses and the *Notizie statistiche sulle principali società per azioni* (see Appendix).

The themes of the power of monopoly and the *narrowness* of the internal market and its effects on growth are resumed, in the 1960s and the 1970s, following the indications of the theory of economic development worked out during the post-Second World War period [Kuznets 1966]. According to this view the paths towards growth of developing countries are linked to the ability to channel large investments into industrial plants. This entails the availability, through the compression of wage levels, of high savings rates at the expense of domestic consumption. The oligopoly is therefore a *necessary* result of a market limited by the *degree of backwardness*, as, Romeo [1959] for example, strongly argues at the end of the 1950s. Some subsequent works present more articulate arguments. For Bonelli [1978], for example, it is the bottleneck in the balance of payments that hinder the growth of the internal market, and therefore of firms, rather than a deliberate strategy of product containment. Other scholars [Ciocca, Filosa and Rey 1973], attribute the scant capacity for the growth in size of firms in the post-Second World War period to the lack of adequate policies to sustain effective demand, capable of setting in motion the virtuous circle of specialization and economies of scale. This hypothesis is more or less explicitly present in the majority of the literature on the history of the single industrial sectors, such as that of beer [Colli 1997], chocolate [Chiapparino 1997], mineral water [Raspadori 2003] and especially chemical products [Zamagni 1990b], a history in which insufficient development is attributed to the *narrowness* of the internal market. Finally, this element is also referred to the most recent Italian business history, synthesized in the work of Amatori and Colli [1999], in order to explain the oligopolistic character of the Italian enterprise. According to this standpoint the Italian market was too small, due the reasons described above, and could only sustain a few enterprises, of the minimum size to guarantee efficiency, in each of the new sectors. For this reason as from the end of the 19th century the Italian market had been entangled in a network of relations between banks, the State and firms. This network reached its peak in the 1930s, when the economic crisis and the policies subsequently adopted - the bank bailouts and the foundation of the Istituto per la Ricostruzione Industriale (IRI) in 1933 - promoted the further concentration of economic power in the hands of large firms.

According to this historiography, the *narrowness* of the market is therefore, at the root, not only of the monopolistic power of large firms, but also of their weakness. The latter is apparent, firstly, in their smaller size with respect to those belonging to the same sectors in other countries and, secondly, in profit performance. The large firms in modern sectors, in fact, show only modest results and encounter frequent crises in all the phases of Italian modern economic growth, from the bailouts at the end of the 19th century to the great IRI bailout, until the crisis of large enterprise which practically brought about its disappearance from the Italian industrial scene in the last fifteen years of the 20th century [Gallino 2003].

Bonelli [1978] suggests a more complex description of the relationship between *narrowness* of the market and performance. The *narrowness* of the market, according to this author, has hindered the completion of the inter-sectoral matrix limiting the development of the dynamic inter-dependences associated with it. In a closed system in fact, the growth of industries producing mass consumer goods creates a market for machinery and other intermediate goods whose production increases the demand of semi-finished goods such as steel or some chemical products. According to Bonelli, this does not happen in the Italian system, which, consequently, at least until the post-Second World War period, is not aligned with the economic structure of the main European countries. In reality, as Pellegrini [2003] for example, argues, the completion of this matrix does not necessarily require the presence of large firms. Regarding the post-Second World War period Pellegrini also underlines the importance of the flexibility and adaptiveness of the productive structure to changes in demand.

Historiography identifies the main weakness of the large Italian firms especially in their lower capacity to fuel investments in Research and Development (R&D) which, as from the Second Industrial Revolution, represents the most dynamic factor of modern growth [Rosenberg and Birdzell 1986]. This factor was first associated with the weakness of the large Italian firms by Sylos Labini [1970] and was then extensively resumed during the 1980s, when the new growth theory [Romer 1986; Lucas 1988] and the return of Schumpeterian inspired theories [Dosi 1988] placed the role of the growing profits from R&D activities and the externalities created by them at the centre of the analysis. Italian performance in this field is considered in the long-term rather low, especially as regards autonomous innovative capacity [Giannetti 1998; Vasta 1999a]. Italy, according to some scholars, pays for the inefficiency of its institutional system which is little oriented towards technical education and invests few resources in scientific and technological research [Vasta 1999b]. Also according to this interpretation, Italian firms rarely have R&D divisions comparable to those of the more innovative firms in other countries, usually limiting their activities to the adaptation of imported patented innovations.

Alongside the macroeconomic relationships between growth, size, performance and innovative capacity, the historiography of the firm has identified another two *protagonists* with relevant roles in explaining the dynamics of Italian industry: the bank and the State. The former refers to the financial system and its role in economic development. The earliest literature [Grifone 1945] underlines its dominant and *authoritarian* character. In Marxist literature, as mentioned above, Italian industrialization up until Second World War is simply the result of the strategy of *financial capital* which has overtaken industrial capital as the leader in the drive towards capitalistic expansion. The processes of firm concentration derive from *financial capital* strategies that restrict the market in order to guarantee profits. According to this reading, the role of *universal banks*, Banca Commerciale Italiana and Credito Italiano in the first place, is nothing other than the Italian form of the more general process of *financialization* of capitalism that characterized the world economy between the end of the 19th century and the First World War.

The perspective on the role of banks, and particularly of *universal banks*, in the growth of the modern large firm changes radically in the historiography of the 1960s and the 1970s, in accordance with the new paradigm of the theory of development. The reasoning is based on the hypothesis that latecomer countries, such as Italy in the late 19th century, did not have the necessary savings and institutions (the stock exchange) at their disposal to direct resources towards the sectors with the major potential for growth and that therefore, other substitute institutions (banks and the State) had to carry out this function of collection and industrial funding. Gerschenkron [1962], for example, maintains that these banks played a crucial role in the industrial *take-off* of the Giolittian era contributing to the success of firms operating in modern sectors, such as the iron and steel industry, heavy mechanical machinery, shipbuilding construction and electricity.

Gerschenkron's positive evaluation is not however, shared by other studies. Some historians underline how the *universal bank* formula worked worse for Italy than for other continental European countries such as, for example, Germany. It did, in fact, undergo recurrent crises, as in the post-First World War period and at the end of the 1920s; and following the latter crisis, the *universal bank* function was forbidden by the 1936 banking law [Conti 1999]. Furthermore, several case studies do not concur with some of the hypotheses put forward by Gerschenkron. For example, Fohlin [1998, 1999] underlines how the Italian *universal banks* preferentially financed already consolidated firms, rather than firms with a high potential for growth. In the same way, Confalonieri [1974-76, 1982, 1992] argues, that during the *take-off* period, *universal banks* were more interested in standard bank activities than in the development strategies of certain industrial enterprises, and that if the Gerschenkron model is valid, it is so in the period from the 1920s up until the Great Crisis when, in reality, there is a strong openness of banks towards industrial enterprises.

The historiography of the Italian firm generally highlights the trait of the centrality of firm funding through credit. In the post-Second World War period, for example, the financing of the investments of public and private firms - especially in the chemical and in the iron and steel sectors - represented the main instrument of intervention for industrial policy and was carried out through the creation of medium term institutes such as the *credito speciale* branches of some banks, the Mediocredito Centrale and its regional branches: the Istituto per lo Sviluppo Economico dell'Impresa Meridionale (ISVEIMER), the Istituto Regionale per il Finanziamento Industriale in Sicilia (IRFIS) and the Credito Industriale Sardo (CIS). These organisms, moreover, operated through a public credit circuit based on the so-called *double brokerage*, on the basis of which these institutes issued obligations guaranteed by the State, which ended up in the portfolio of ordinary banks [de Cecco 2004].

The other protagonist identified by the historiography of the large Italian enterprise is the State. Its centrality represents a long-term trait in Italian economic development, due to its effects on growth, and for the variety of forms of direct intervention it adopted: public orders, industrial tariffs and policies, the public ownership of a relevant quota of the industrial system from the 1930s to the 1990s, which reached its apex halfway through the 1970s [Amatori 2000;

Toninelli 2003]. The State, in fact, is at the centre of many definitions of the Italian economic development model: Bonelli [1978] speaks of *State capitalism*, Amatori [1997] of *political capitalism*, Gualerni [1982] of the *industrial State*, Zamagni [1978] of a *non-lethargic State*.

The relationship between the State and the firm is generally debated within the models of economic development proposed between the 1950s and the 1960s. In these models the State supplies demand in the new sectors, it finances and protects newly constituted firms, and it favors the creation of economies of scale through the support of concentration processes for existing firms or directly takes over the management of strategic enterprises.

In Italy, the support for demand in new sectors takes place in the first period of Italian growth, both in the liberal and in the more *interventionist* phase [Federico and Giannetti 1999]. In the liberal phase, it essentially takes the form of support for the construction of the railroad system through the system of concessions, in other words the private management of the sector in exchange for a minimum income guaranteed by the same State. In the second phase, it takes the form of public demand for military supplies, which gives rise to the birth of the iron and steel industry in the last decades of the 19th century. For example, at the beginning of the 1880s, the government promoted the construction of a plant for the production of high quality steel for cannons and armor-plating at Terni [Bonelli 1975], thus ensuring orders to naval construction companies such as Ansaldo [Doria 1989; Castronovo, Hertner and Mori 1994-2002]. Protection and financing were the instruments most used during the phase of industrial *take-off*. The new-born iron and steel firms enjoyed a consistent customs protection (1887) against foreign competition, as did the firms involved in vehicle construction. In the period between the two World Wars public intervention became even greater, especially in the 1930s with autarchy and the support for the processes of substitution of imports, as in the case of the chemical sector. In this phase the State also promoted the growth in size of firms through compulsory consortiums and mergers [Petri 2002]. In the post-Second World War period, instead, the most relevant state intervention in the system of enterprises was the diffusion of the public enterprise. In the first phase - that of the Golden age (1950-1973) - the legacy of the IRI, whose origins will be discussed further on, is described in the light of the *Americanization* of the industrial system in the energy sector (ENI) and the iron and steel sector (FINSIDER), while the electric sector comes under state ownership with the institution of ENEL (1962). In the second phase, the 1970s and the 1980s, public intervention is based on the *national champions* namely the support for the concentration of sectors around leader firms, in such a way as to increase the latter's competitiveness on the international market through interventions involving the public sector, the private sector or both [Federico and Giannetti 1999]. The first case regards the iron and steel industry, the second the automobile and FIAT, the third the chemical industry, which develops around the controversial relationship between ENI and Montedison.

While the centrality of the role of the State in the development of the system of enterprises is widely acknowledged by historiography, the evaluation of its effects is less homogenous. Customs policies are probably the most controversial topic of the entire debate on Italian industrialization. Zamagni [1990a] and Sapelli [1992] believe that without these policies Italian industry would not have been able to develop, while Gerschenkron [1962] criticizes the favored sectors arguing that a high labor intensity sector such as the mechanical one would have been a more suitable sector to protect than one with a high intensity of resources such as the iron and steel sector. Fenoaltea [1973] also goes in the same direction arguing that the duty on steel hampered the development of the mechanical sector, which would have been promoted by exports, and that was the most suitable candidate for customs protection. A more recent series of works, however, questions the effective importance of duties in Italy through the estimate of effective and nominal protectionism. Federico and Tena [1998, 1999] for example argue that protectionism was rather low, and even nonexistent for many products. In the absence of protectionist policies, i.e. in the hypothesis of absence of all duties, the quota of industry on GDP would have remained more or less the same, with a reduction in the value added of the iron and steel sector and the mechanical sector and an increase in that of the textiles sector [Federico and O'Rourke 2000].

The assessment of the effects, during the first phase of industrialization, of the different forms of public intervention on the enterprises involved, is also controversial. The enterprises involved never managed to reduce their dependence on public orders, so much so that the State had to intervene several times to save them from bankruptcy. For example, towards the end of the 1880s, the premature bankruptcy of Terni was avoided through advances on future orders. In 1911 the Bank of Italy compelled the main Italian banks to bailout the two main iron and steel firms, the ILVA and the Piombino [Confalonieri 1982]. These problems recur in the post-First World War period, when firms were unable to adjust to the sudden contraction in public orders, for example, the Ansaldo [Doria 1989; Castronovo, Hertner and Mori 1994-2002] and the ILVA, were bailed out by the banks who transformed their bank loans into shares. This was the premise for the even greater bailout, which in 1933, compelled the State to assume direct control of the entire system, subsequently transferred to an agency created *ad hoc*, the IRI, which became permanent by decree in 1937. According to Federico and Giannetti [1999], these results depend on collusive behaviors and on the organizational inefficiencies that public orders necessarily trigger in the firms exempted from operating with market mechanisms. Petri [2002] instead underlines the dynamic effect of this allocation of resources, even though inefficient, which he argues promoted innovation, economies of scale and the modernization of plants and machinery.

The public enterprise represents the crucial point of state intervention during the post-Second World War period and is at the centre of a very broad historiographical debate. In general, historiography evaluates the results of public enterprises in the 1950s positively [Posner and Woolf 1967; Bottiglieri 1984]. The IRI invested enormous resources in the modernization of services (in particular in the telecommunications network) and in the manufacturing sector. The most successful firms were the FINSIDER in the iron and steel sector, with the adoption of the process of continuous fusion based on great production volumes [Balconi 1991], and the ENI, founded in 1953, who's task it was to supply Italy with energy [Sapelli and Carnevali 1992]. These success stories, according to some, were more probably due to the entrepreneurial abilities of single managers, for example Enrico Mattei and Oscar Sinigaglia, than to rigorous industrial policies [Osti 1993; Balconi, Orsenigo and Toninelli 1995]. These managers, in fact, contrived to have their projects approved by the government, thanks to personal relationships with the most important politicians. This virtuous cycle was broken in the 1970s, when the relationship between politics and public enterprise deteriorated and the latter was directed towards more general economic policy objectives, such as the territorial re-equilibrium of growth and occupational support. This severely compromised the public enterprise's organizational efficiency and strategies, also through the political appointment of managers [Amatori 2000; Toninelli 2003].

Historiography's overall assessment of the role of the public enterprise is, however, controversial. This assessment, in fact, depends on the evaluation criteria used. These are linked to indices of statistical efficiency that evaluate accounting profits and losses, or dynamics, and that also take into consideration the externalities generated by the public enterprise in terms of the spread of innovative capacity and therefore of greater productivity of the industrial system. However, even if we limit our assessment to the accounting situation of the public enterprise, some of the estimates suggested for the impact of the latter on the state budget, from the time of its institution to the wave of privatizations in the early 1990s, induce caution in subscribing to the fairly common idea that state ownership was a failure. For example, a raw measure such as the accounting balance of the *entrepreneurial State* registers a credit balance, excluding the value of the RAI (Italian state radio and television broadcasting service), of 81,300 billion lire during the period from 1937-2000 [Mediobanca 2000; Toninelli 2003].

1.3. The microeconomic approach

From the above, it is evident that the historiography of the firm, up until the end of the 1970s, selected the object, the large enterprise, and the categories to describe it - size, market power, performance and innovative capacity - in accordance with the prevalent representation of economic development, and the paradigm of industrial economics expressed by economic theory. This perspective starts changing halfway through the 1970s due to the great changes caused by the oil crisis, the difficulties of large enterprise and its decentralization, and the diffusion of a new *technological regime* less related to largeness in size [Giannetti 1998]. The compared macro categories are substituted by dynamic representations, containing a large amount of details on the micro-behavior of the economic *actors* and their strategic interactions. Generalization is substituted with a focus on the single case, the single problem, the *event*.

In the light of this interpretative context historiography turns its attention to a topic which had so far been relatively little analyzed: the small enterprise and its role in economic growth, its organizational systems and its strategies for expansion [Bagnasco 1977; Becattini 1987]. Until the 1970s, in fact, the small firm had been prevalently considered residual or subordinate to the dynamics of large enterprise and, at any rate, less efficient and innovative [Graziani 1998]. Subsequently, the panorama becomes more varied. Thus, side by side with literature that underlines how smallness in size is one of the main limits to growth in the Italian economy [de Cecco 2001a], because of the positive correlation between increase in productivity and size of the firm [Pagano and Schivardi 2001]; there is another body of literature, that is more interested in the specific characteristics of the small firm and which underlines its dynamic and adaptive capacity, especially if organized in a *district* form [Becattini 1987; Becattini et al. 2001].

The historical enquiry aimed at reconsidering the role played by small and medium enterprises in Italian economic development distinguishes itself in the first place in terms of periodization. On the one hand, economic-oriented literature [Bellandi 1999] sees it essentially as one of the *surprises* of the 1970s when, due to the crisis of large enterprise, the process of industrialization spread to *new* areas of the country, the so-called NEC (North-East-Centre). The proposed model is generally based on the presence in these areas of common values, that guarantee social control, minimizing tensions in the labor market, or at least reducing them through use of the most diverse forms of irregular work contracts [Bologna and Fumagalli 1997; Bonomi 1997]. Other scholars do not see the surprising rise of the small enterprise system in the same virtuous and creative light. De Cecco [2000, 2001a, 2001b], for example, traces its origins to two events in the early 1970s: the collapse of the fixed exchange system based on the Bretton Woods agreements and the petrol crises that greatly increased energy costs for European countries. A vicious circle was thus initiated, characterized by the devaluation of the lira and price inflation that made Italian firms more competitive with regard to their competitors. It was especially the firms with the greatest labor force intensity that manufactured products of a low technological level that gained the most. The strong tensions present within large factories facilitated the beginning of an intense reorganization of the productive structure, which favored decentralization.

Historical research, on the other hand, has searched for the long-term *roots* of the presence of the small firm and the local systems of production of which it is often a part. In the first direction Cafagna [1989] and Federico [1994b] while emphasizing the historically *dualistic* character of the Italian system of enterprises, also highlight the long-term dynamic role of the small firm in traditional sectors, in which it has shown itself capable of exploiting the comparative advantage of a country with a high availability of the labor factor - an example being the case of silk [Federico 1994a]. Within a *dualistic* industrial system [Cafagna 1999], the emphasis is on the ability of the *Manchesterian* component (whose origins go back to the pre-Unification period), to remain competitive without needing fostering from *above*. On the contrary, the other state or oligopolistic component, survives only through state rescues and public demand. More recently a vast body of literature going back to the tradition of local systems of production has tried to show how the small and medium enterprise systems that were so successful from the 1970s onwards, have their roots in that productive humus (urban, town and rural) that is diffuse in vast areas of the Centre-North. This productive humus, even in the remote past, contained many of the elements (entrepreneurial nature, organizational structure, sectoral specialization) that are at the root of long-term competitiveness in these areas [Belfanti and Maccabelli 1997; Fontana 1997].

Alongside the two main veins, other interpretations and periodizations have been suggested for the dualism in size of Italian firms. According to Sapelli [1992, 1997], for example, the specificity of the Italian case resides in the simultaneous presence of large scale macro impulses institutionalized by the State, and of small and medium scale micro impulses institutionalized by the pervasiveness of subcultures and community localism. In this view point the dynamics of small enterprises represent a unique phenomenon of social mobility in the country, because this new industrial *bourgeoisie* is not backed by land property, financial capital or great families. Together with the small enterprise, a new industrial *bourgeoisie* was formed in Italy during the post-Second World War period. This new industrial *bourgeoisie* was capable of extending its activity from the traditional sectors to the more dynamic ones and also of introducing important technological innovation.

The *dualistic* vision that emphasizes the existence of two separate, and in some ways contrasting, worlds has been subjected to a few critical reviews. These emphasize the originality of the Italian model of development, and argue that the plurality of subjects is the foundation of the positive dynamics of Italian economic growth. Bolchini [2003], for example, argues that each of the two subjects had its own golden periods and that, industrial policies favored, depending on the phase, one or the other of the two parts offsetting contrasting forces through a balance of interests. Colli [2002a] too has underlined the relevance, in terms of the overall efficiency of the Italian industrial system, of the interrelations that were created between the different components of the productive system. Finally, yet others suggest that a *dualism* in size corresponds to an *institutional dualism*, which has allowed the two systems to peacefully co-exist, at least until halfway through the 1980s [Arrighetti and Seravalli 1997].

The bipolar model has been called into question by a number of empirical studies. These show how a study of the group organizational structure leads to an at least partial re-examination of the pulverization of the productive system which, in reality, is based on a much smaller number of decisional centers [Barca et al. 1994a, 1994b]. These studies have given rise to some reflections on the existence, at least in the last two decades, of a group of intermediate size that has taken a central role in the industrial structure of the country. These firms, defined as the *new protagonists* [Balloni and Iacobucci 2001] or, using an even broader term, *fourth capitalism* [Turani 1996; Colli 2002b] apparently show considerable dynamism, and constitute a new example of the adaptive capacity of the Italian industrial system [Crepax 2002; Berta 2004]. These studies, however, seem more adept at identifying the existence of hierarchical grading phenomena within the small enterprise system than at identifying the presence of a new entrepreneurial model [Harrison 1997]. The great differences between the subjects studied - there are groups with tens of thousands of employees and firms with little more than 500 employees - do not allow, so far, for a precise delimitation of the boundaries of this phenomenon.

The reconsideration of the themes of the Italian growth model through the view point of the small enterprise and of local systems has also led to a re-visitation of already explored topics, such as those of banks and the State. While, as we have already seen, the bank and the State have been considered two *protagonists* in the dynamics of large enterprise, in the analysis of the small and medium enterprise historiography centers on the examination of the competitive abilities of bank and the State, omitting, at least in part, the active role played also in this segment of the Italian productive structure, by the banking system and public policy.

As far as the bank is concerned the focus is on how this has naturally had a lesser weight, in comparison with the case of large enterprise, in the process of development of the small and medium enterprises, whose limited investment activities are usually carried out through self-financing. Some historians, however, have signaled the long-term presence of a network of local banks, similar to *fractal geography*, capable of sustaining the credit demand of smaller firms as from the first decade of the century [Conti 1999]. The most prevalent hypothesis is that a structure based on small local banks is the most suitable for sustaining local development [Conti and Ferri 1997]. From this point of view, small enterprise systems, especially in the post-Second World War period when demand for credit became more intense, benefited greatly from the proliferation of minor banks capable of sustaining many enterprises and contributing to maintaining the delicate balance between local needs and national economic policy choices. In this context there are also descriptions of the interventions which, during the post-Second World War period, instituted regional medium-term credit and other small and medium enterprise-oriented special credit sections [Conti and Ferri 1997; Piluso 1999].

The studies of the strategies of the *actors* has also led to a reconsideration of the efficiency of the family business, namely of that form of financial allocation that does not distinguish between family finance and firm finance. This commingling is traditionally considered one of the main causes of the durability of the small enterprise. In fact the organization of the financial system, in which, especially in the last thirty years, important intermediaries of a different nature play an important part, is one of the main causes of the *dwarfism* of Italian firms. This is due to a mechanism in which the *actors* involved gain from keeping enterprises small: also because *multiple credit lines* minimize credit risks and risks for entrepreneurs, since the latter can avoid losing control of their firms [de Cecco 2001a]. The new historiographic approach gives a less severe judgment, in the light of the strategic rationality guiding the choices of entrepreneurs [Colli 2003].

Another traditional theme revisited in the light of the centrality of the small enterprise is that of the role of the State. As has already been seen, public policies regarding small and medium enterprises are, according to some [Becattini 1998], nonexistent, at least until recently, and anyhow insufficient compared to those adopted to support large enterprise. This hypothesis, however, is called into question both by those that underscore the fact that these interventions (in terms of labor legislation and fiscal policies), or more often the absence of such interventions (which leaves the possibility for recourse to *informal employment* with almost no risk of being fined), have, in fact, promoted the diffusion and persistence of micro entrepreneurial activities [Zamagni 1994; de Cecco 2001b]; and by those that maintain that the forms of *regime speciale* have contributed to increasing the efficiency of the smaller firms [Arrighetti and Seravalli 1997, 1999], also in the case of unselective interventions, see for example Artigiancassa [Baccini 2002].

Another of the themes reconsidered is that the innovative capacity of the Italian system of enterprises. According to Cohen and Federico [2001] the Italian technological mix is simply the combination of the rational response to the level of relative prices and an optimal use of factors. In a country with a high labor supply and few resources, the selection of a less capital intensive production function necessarily implies the use of less sophisticated technologies. Some scholars [Brusco and Paba 1997; Colli 2002a] criticize the hypothesis according to which Italy has been characterized by a modest innovative capacity compared to other countries with whom it has shared, in a more or less linear way, the same dynamics of economic growth. According to Colli, for example, the production of innovative knowledge in a local system is in reality very high, even though it is not easily measurable because it is characterized by incremental innovations that are usually not patented. Knowledge developed in the local systems of small and medium enterprise is prevalently tacit, i.e. characterized by the absence of any form of codification. Finally, another argument is that Italian specialization in traditional sectors (textiles, clothing, leather) strongly influences the traditional proxy for innovative capacity (patents), because in these sectors there is less propensity for patenting in comparison to other more advanced sectors. This argument is also enforced by Malerba [1993] who, moreover, finds forms of *dualism* in the innovative Italian system. It is characterized by two contrasting systems: one, undergoing a crisis, is founded on large enterprise and the other more dynamic one is composed of small productive units. According to other studies [Vasta 1999b, 2003] these arguments are not sufficient to change the negative assessment on the Italian system of innovation. In fact, in the first place, the innovative dynamics of local systems cannot be extrapolated from the *technological regimes* that have characterized capitalistic systems in the last two centuries. Innovative capacity, over and above the specific problems of the proxies used for its measurement [Vasta 2006], cannot, therefore, be evaluated within closed micro-universes, but must be evaluated within the context of the progress in knowledge at a global level. In the second place, the diffusion of tacit knowledge, the latter notion is not considered to be sufficiently explained [Cowan, David and Foray 2000], does not seem to be exclusive of local enterprise systems, but characterizes the whole set of cognitive processes also in more advanced sectors [Nightingale 1998, 2000; Lombardi 2003]. Finally, there is also a difficulty in defining the relative consistency of innovative small and medium enterprises in Italy in the absence of some form of measurement [Archibugi, Evangelista and Nascia 1999].

Interest in micro-behaviors also implies the extension of the themes comprehensively studied by modern industrial economics, such as that of governance and entrepreneurialism, to the field of the business history. The study of the first topic is in its initial phase and deals with the relationships between ownership, management and institutional context [Teti 1999] and also with micro-organizational topics such as the study of the interaction between staff and intermediate management [Amatori 1999]. The study of the second follows two different approaches. One investigates the ways in which the cultural characteristics and ethnic relationships of entrepreneurial groups affect strategy formation, as in the case of Swiss and Jewish merchants in Lombardy in the 19th century [Bigazzi 1996; Maifreda 2000; Martignone 2001], and the role of the family in orienting these strategies, not only in the case of family businesses in small and medium enterprises, but also in the large entrepreneurial families [Colli 2003]. The other approach is linked to the centrality of the figure of the innovating entrepreneur who accompanies the creation of new *technological regimes*, which have characteristics of greater flexibility with respect to managerial ones or ones that are in the *infant* phase. Examples of this type of entrepreneur are Carlo Esterle for the electrical industry [Pavese 1993] and Giovanni Battista Pirelli for the tire industry [Polese 2003, 2004].

1.4. Industrial *decline*

The debate on the Italian economy has recently concentrated on the existence of a widespread *decline* undermining the competitive capacity of the entire industrial system. The current dynamics of Italian industry, according to this perspective, are characterized by the disappearance, or the heavy downsizing of some sectors (computers, aeronautical, chemical, automobile, etc.) based on technological innovation and on a high capital intensity [Gallino 2003]. In the absence of intersectoral spillover effects generated by the more technologically advanced sectors, the entire industrial sector and more generally, the entire Italian economy is involved in a broad vicious circle. It has therefore been argued that these elements combined constitute the signs of a decline which will be difficult to reverse [de Cecco 2000; Gallino 2003], or even of a rapid regression towards a pre-industrial structure or to a First Industrial Revolution economic environment [Sori 2002]. According to some, the divested, due to the privatization processes in the 1990s, of a nucleus of oligopolistic firms who had followed, albeit with difficulty, the dynamics of the technological frontier ever since the beginning of the process of industrialization, has contributed greatly to the creation of this situation [Affinito, de Cecco and Dringoli 2000]. Italy, it is thus argued, has "come close to being an industrial colony" [Gallino 2003: 78] whose destiny cannot be autonomously determined.

This approach is criticized by those that continue to underline the *creative* ability of Italian industry in cutting out market niches (for a growing series of *light* goods often with a good technological content such as the *made in Italy* sectors), for itself in international competition [Quadrio Curzio and Fortis 2000; Becattini and Bellandi 2002]. In this perspective the *district* form, with its development of a multiplicity of entrepreneurial *life projects*, is still considered the most suitable for resisting the growing competitive forces operating on a global scale.

Finally, other studies have adopted a more moderate vision, emphasizing both the difficulties present in the current phase of economic growth and a number of positive perspectives. Some have underlined how the term *decline* is excessive and that it would be more correct to speak of a *growth problem* that makes this phase similar to other phases that Italy has undergone in the course of its recent history [Ciocca 2003]. In this sense a number of positive aspects characterizing the last decade of the Italian economy have been identified: (i) a greater accumulation of capital; (ii) the higher level of education of the labor force; (iii) the greater degree of openness; (iv) the improvement in the efficiency of the financial system.

Still other scholars have underlined the fact that the Italian *decline* is, in reality, part of a wider process involving the whole of Europe and, in particular, the main continental economies [Berta 2004]. In this case too a number of positive elements have been identified, such as the process of *metamorphosis* that characterizes the industrial fabric of the country, with the emergence of a subsystem of medium enterprises. This subsystem could take a guiding role in Italian economic development thus substituting the local systems which, though important for economic growth in the last decades of the 20th century, have experienced great difficulties in becoming the new center propelling Italian industry and compensating the decline of *industrialism* [Berta 2001].

The debate is still open and new contributions appear daily, however, many aspects are still obscure. Even if we accept the hypothesis that we are facing a widespread *decline* of the Italian economy and particularly of its industrial system, the big question is whether this *decline* is due to the decisions taken in the last decade, or whether the long-term characteristics of the Italian economy have little congruency with the current dynamics of technical progress.

2. Industrial structure (1911–2001)

Giovanni Federico

2.1. Introduction

Industrialization in Italy is quite recent. The process started in the 19th century, although exact dating is still controversial, and reached full development in the 20th[1]. As late as 1911, the secondary sector (including manufacturing, mining, building and utilities) accounted for only 24 per cent of GDP [Vitali 1992: Table 7]. The figure increased to an all-time peak of 42.5 per cent in 1976 [ISTAT 1986: Table 8.16]. As in most advanced countries, the share of industry has declined in more recent times, as a consequence of the growth of the tertiary sector, and nowadays it accounts for 28 per cent of GDP [ISTAT 2002: prosp. 2.11]. In all advanced countries, the growth of industry has been accompanied by substantial structural changes. *Heavy* industries, such as chemicals and engineering, have grown, in terms of GDP and employment, more than the total, while the *light* ones, such as food, textiles or clothing, have declined in relative terms [Hoffmann 1955; Kuznets 1966]. The human and physical capital per worker has increased, the scale of production has grown and the number of hours of work has decreased [Maddison 1995; Huberman 2004]. Most of these changes reflect parallel changes in final demand, brought about by the different income elasticity of consumption - 1.5 for products of *heavy* industries and 1.1 for those of *light* industries, according to Chenery [1979]. The income elasticity of leisure is even higher, and thus the growth in income accounts also for the decrease in hours of work put in by full time workers. But, in the short run, this trend may be offset by the increase in the share of full-time workers on total manpower and, possibly, by an increase in the number of hours put in by seasonal workers. The rise in productivity and wages and the growth of savings in most (but not all) countries have made it profitable to substitute capital for labor. In contrast, physical and human capital were probably complementary [Goldin and Katz 1998; Sanders and ter Weel 2000] and thus the accumulation of the former brought about an increase in human capital as well.

To what extent does the Italian case follow these common patterns? This Chap. deals with these issues by exploiting the industrial censuses. These were held in 1911, 1927, 1937-39 and from 1951 onwards at ten-year intervals[2]. Industrial cen-

[1] For a survey of the literature see Cohen and Federico [2001].

[2] The Ministero dell'Agricoltura, Industria e Commercio (MAIC) published a partial industrial census in 1876 and a series of monographs on industrial conditions by county. Each of these provides much data, but they refer to dates ranging from 1885 to 1903 and thus are almost useless for a comparison over time. See ISTAT [1957], Lungonelli [1987], Missaggia [1988] and Bolchini [2003].

suses are highly suitable for analyzing long-term structural change and indeed Italian scholars have often resorted to them. Some years ago Chiaventi [1987] published data on employment and power by sector from 1911 to 1951, and more recently Cainelli and Stampini [1999a, 1999b] have constructed a database of workers by sector and region, which has been used by Cainelli and Leoncini [1999] and Cainelli and Stampini [2002] to analyze changes in industrial location from 1911 to 1991. Finally, Bolchini [2003] uses censuses to study the change in the size of plants from 1927 to 1991. This chapter improves upon Chiaventi's work as it covers a longer time span (until 2001) and upon Cainelli and Stampini as it uses the most recent ATECO-ISTAT 1991 classification of economic activities instead of the 1951 ISTAT one. It improves upon all previous work as it exploits all the available information. It thus has the ambition to be as comprehensive as possible, obviously within the limitations of the source.

Italian censuses provide data on:

(*a*) employment and composition of the workforce by sex, age, skills and so on;
(*b*) number of plants (under different denominations);
(*c*) distribution of plants by size-class (measured by the number of workers);
(*d*) motive power (total and by source);
(*e*) total working time.

The data are available for Italy as a whole, by *regione* (region), and, sometimes also by *provincia* (county) and for some major towns. Collecting all these data would have been an impossible task, and therefore the article will deal only with national data. The censuses cover the whole secondary sector, including mining, construction and utilities, but this chapter will focus mainly on manufacturing, divided into *light* and *heavy* industries. As a general rule, *light* industries are featured by a (relatively) low capital intensity and by the prevailing orientation towards the final consumer, while *heavy* industries are more capital-intensive and produce mainly inputs for other sectors. The allocation of each sector to either group is unavoidably arbitrary[3]. However, an alternative division between modern and traditional industries seems even more arbitrary, as characteristics of sectors change over time, and a sector which appears modern at a given moment may no longer be so some time later.

Censuses have always been a major source for Italian industrial history: most notably, they have been extensively used for estimates of industrial production [Fenoaltea 1992, 2003; Fenoaltea and Bardini 2000]. As a whole, the data are considered fairly reliable, but surely not flawless. They must be used with caution, especially in comparisons across time, as they are not perfectly homogeneous under four counts - changes in data coverage, changes in the object of survey (including national boundaries), changes in definition (most notably of power) and changes of presentation (especially in the classification of industries)[4].

The next Sect. describes the main changes in the distribution of employment by sector, capital intensity, plant size (unfortunately there are no data by company), composition of workforce and average working time. Section 2.3 decomposes the

---

[3] See the list in Table 2.1.

[4] These issues are dealt with extensively in Federico [2003: Appendix 1].

total changes into within-sector changes and changes in the structure of industry. The two following Sects. extend the analysis to changes in location, using the Cainelli and Stampini database (Sect. 2.4), and to the secondary sector as a whole (Sect. 2.5). Lastly, Sect. 2.6 contains some conclusions.

2.2. The features of Italian industry in the long run

In ninety years, the total workforce of the secondary sector has increased 2.7 times and the number of manufacturing workers 2.2 times. The absolute number peaked in 1981 and then started to decrease, with a slight rebound in the late 1990s. According to the censuses, in twenty years the Italian industry has lost almost a fifth of its employees. This fall might have been spurious, had it been offset by an increase in the number of employees in the grey market. An increase is likely, but not as great as to compensate the fall in the number of registered workers. Some recent works suggest that the grey economy accounts for less than 20 per cent of Italian GDP and its share has not increased in recent years [Bovi and Castellucci 2001]. On top of this, grey labor is notoriously concentrated in agriculture, construction and services, while in manufacturing it is diffuse only in textile and clothing industries.

The total growth of manpower is the outcome of widely different trends by sector. From 1911 to 1981, employment has more than quadrupled in *heavy* industries, while it has increased only by 75 per cent in *light* ones. Since then, *light* industries have declined relatively more than *heavy* ones. Thus, in the long run, their share has fallen from two-thirds to less than two-fifths of total employment in manufacturing (Table 2.1). Consequently, Italy experienced a structural change *à la* Hoffmann, with a lag relative to more advanced countries, which were also better endowed with capital and raw materials[5]. However, it is important to stress the difference by sector, even within each group. For instance, occupation in textiles increased by a third from 1911 to 1951, and since then it has halved, falling below the initial level. In contrast, occupation in other *light* industries, such as food, clothing and leather has grown in the long run, with a very modest decline in the 1990s[6]. Printing and publishing is the exception among *light* industries, as it has grown from 1911 to 2001 also in terms of total workforce. The *heavy* industries also show quite different patterns.

---

[5] Hoffmann [1955: Table XLV] argues that the third stage (i.e. the balanced growth pattern of advanced countries) started in the main European countries in the interwar years, while Italy reached this stage during its *economic miracle* of the late 1950s.

[6] The 1937 figure for the food industry is exceptionally high because the 1937 census, unlike all the others, was held at different dates in order to maximize the number of workers.

Table 2.1. Employment by sector

Sector	1911	1927	1937	1951	1961	1971	1981	1991	1996	2001
Food products and beverages (15)	304,394	322,300	481,662	358,624	397,357	378,563	462,340	457,200	434,515	443,930
Tobacco products (16)	20,344	26,170	48,745	52,496	26,561	21,135	22,607	17,625	11,999	7,834
Textiles (17)	499,746	643,706	607,037	653,107	612,886	539,553	522,915	403,929	345,338	309,487
Wearing apparel (18)	179,088	165,069	250,421	223,414	289,860	393,280	403,360	418,862	346,387	298,241
Tanning and dressing of leather, bags and footwear (19)	137,973	109,876	171,882	215,312	219,597	240,503	333,028	243,543	230,543	206,035
Manufacture of wood and of products of wood (20)	173,752	178,401	213,882	169,275	237,227	194,995	241,157	186,190	170,294	179,313
Pulp, paper and paper products (21)*	28,949	30,676	45,729	52,631	71,302	76,800	98,800	88,598	85,424	84,212
Publishing and printing (22)	49,914	56,128	63,201	71,573	110,472	145,686	187,377	195,407	175,012	173,431
Coke and refined petroleum products (23)*	-	7,879	16,506	17,670	17,244	26,780	35,145	29,057	24,147	24,537
Chemicals and chemical products (24)*	72,995	73,736	112,241	175,793	263,665	287,036	291,876	237,409	209,242	205,153
Rubber and plastic products (25)*	359	8,347	21,427	34,690	63,564	130,477	125,473	179,439	198,401	216,876
Non-metallic mineral products (26)*	217,094	164,995	200,443	195,072	303,737	332,995	337,849	276,359	250,824	253,664
Basic metals (27)*	69,206	99,537	98,466	165,334	239,462	265,105	275,306	170,381	136,123	139,287
Fabricated metal products (28)*	132,123	149,777	112,545	217,662	278,877	379,690	568,244	614,590	621,642	700,984
Machinery and equipment (29)*	74,541	133,693	290,100	300,313	530,869	735,707	642,246	538,947	554,105	597,544
Office machinery and computers (30)*	1,430	1,490	3,095	9,503	22,916	37,492	28,959	25,565	18,609	19,257
Electrical machinery and apparatus n.e.c. (31)*	5,524	10,075	36,884	56,293	115,523	204,107	258,446	207,799	205,797	211,404
Radio, television and communication equipment (32)*	2,837	13,507	48,298	33,189	77,687	134,223	133,837	138,834	103,161	107,578
Medical, precision and optical instruments (33)*	12,933	44,974	48,600	59,901	66,466	58,304	99,277	117,764	129,448	126,004
Motor vehicles, trailers and semi-trailers (34)*	6,734	24,450	65,589	71,461	111,277	243,425	275,306	214,049	185,748	172,932
Other transport equipment (35)*	120,529	137,110	194,620	139,775	140,951	105,700	144,317	136,116	100,780	103,096
Furniture and manufacturing n.e.c. (36)	109,758	166,172	146,212	200,563	287,402	395,977	406,615	309,098	309,911	301,393
Recycling (37)*	805	7,134	3,573	4,205	2,361	-	-	5,512	8,327	13,666
Light industries	1,474,969	1,667,822	1,983,042	1,944,364	2,181,362	2,309,692	2,579,399	2,231,854	2,023,999	1,919,664
Heavy industries	746,059	907,380	1,298,116	1,533,492	2,305,901	3,017,841	3,315,081	2,980,419	2,831,778	2,976,194
Manufacturing	2,221,028	2,575,202	3,281,158	3,477,856	4,487,263	5,327,533	5,894,480	5,212,273	4,855,777	4,895,858
Mining	66,926	98,598	128,381	130,742	113,163	80,528	54,406	48,561	43,604	37,214
Construction	102,669	331,294	556,761	510,920	851,262	925,978	1,192,398	1,332,233	1,341,850	1,528,629
Utilities	28,535	55,176	40,647	80,774	113,739	155,156	171,818	170,206	158,468	125,008
Other, unspecified	49,690	239,023	159,201	29,743	44,844	36,804	35,635	-	-	-
Total	2,468,848	3,299,293	4,166,148	4,230,035	5,610,271	6,525,999	7,348,737	6,763,273	6,399,699	6,586,709

Legend: * *heavy* industries. Source: see text.

The absolute increase from 1911 to 1981, the overall peak, ranges from a sluggish 20 per cent for the production of other transport equipment (i.e. ships and railway stock) to an almost unbelievable 350 times for rubber manufacturing. However, this latter figure in all likelihood overestimates the real increase: a more realistic estimate suggests an increase by only 30 times[7]. Employment also grew a great deal in other modern sectors, which were almost non-existent on the eve of First World War, such as car-making, or the production of electrical machinery and office equipment. Employment in engineering as a whole (including metal-making and the production of means of transportation) increased from 220,000 to 1.6 millions - i.e. from 10 per cent to 34 per cent of the total. Since 1981, occupation has declined in almost all *heavy* industries. The number of workers in metal-making has halved, falling from 5 per cent to 2.5 per cent of the total industrial workforce.

The censuses do not provide data on total capital stock. However, until 1981, they report data on total power and on the number of productive units using mechanical engines. It is thus possible to compute the share of mechanized units (see Table 2.5) and the number of HP per worker (Table 2.6). As expected, both indexes have increased in the long run. The proportion of mechanized plants has risen from a fifth in 1927 to two-thirds in 1981 and the number of HP per worker from 0.5 in 1911 to 6.3 in 1971[8]. The latter is often used as a proxy for capital intensity, but it underestimates the actual growth of the stock. In fact, the technological level, and thus presumably the cost, of equipment has been rising more than the demand for power (computers use very little power).

A joint look at the two indexes highlights interesting differences in the pattern of mechanization by sector. By 1911, the number of HP per worker was only 55 per cent higher in *heavy* than in *light* industries. The figure for engineering was even lower than that for textiles. Modern technologies were indeed more capital-intensive in *heavy* industries, but only a handful of productive units used them. More than 90 per cent of plants in *heavy* industries and 93 per cent in engineering had less than ten workers, and it is highly unlikely that such small workshops used any motive power before the mass adoption of electricity in the 1920s. As is well known, First World War accelerated the process of modernization of Italian industry. From 1911 to 1927 the number of HP per worker increased by 130 per cent in *light* industries and tripled in *heavy* ones. But this rise was concentrated in modern factories and it only marginally affected traditional workshops. By 1927, 79,000 plants out of 113,000 in *heavy* industries and 32,500 out of 47,000 in engineering still lacked any motive power. From 1927 to 1937-39, the number of HP per

[7] The 1911 census registers only 360 workers in the rubber industry. However, in that year, Pirelli, the leading company of the sector, employed 3,382 workers [Confalonieri 1982: Table 65]. Thus, the total workforce employed in the rubber industry must have numbered about 4,000 people - i.e. a thirtieth of the 1981 level.

[8] The 1911 census omits the reserve power, but this omission does not affect the overall results. If the ratio between reserve and working power was the same in 1911 and in 1927, the total HP per worker would be 0.58, instead of 0.49. Anyway, the 1981 figure also undervalues the total power, as it omits non-electrical engines.

worker increased by a further 30 per cent, without changing the basic dualism between a core of modern plants and a vast number of small workshops. Indeed the wide-ranging mechanization of Italian industry started only after Second World War. Both the share of mechanized plants and the HP/worker ratio increased first in the *heavy* industries and later, mainly during the 1960s, in the *light* ones. The traditional gap in capital intensity remained roughly constant until 1961, to shrink very quickly (without however disappearing) in the following two decades and to disappear in the next two decades. Yet, mechanization left behind a substantial number of plants. In 1971, well after the end of the *economic miracle*, 250,000 workshops, with almost 700,000 workers, out of a total of 600,000 (i.e. almost 15 per cent) had no motive power at all. As easily predictable, these workshops were concentrated in *light* industries, with textiles, clothing and leather accounting for about a half of the total. But they were quite common also in *heavy* industries: engineering had some 66,000 of them - i.e. a quarter of the Italian total. In the 1970s, the number of workshops without power fell by 40 per cent. In all likelihood it continued to decrease in the 1990s, although it is impossible to state by how much, as the censuses no longer report this information.

Nowadays, Italy stands out in Europe for the small size of plants. This feature is sometimes considered a product of recent developments, but the census data show it to be a long-term feature. In 1911 there were on average less than six workers per productive unit (Table 2.7), and plants with less than 10 workers employed about four-fifths of the total manpower (Table 2.8.a)[9]. These micro-plants prevailed not only in *light* industries such as food production, clothing and printing and publishing, but also in *heavy* industry as a whole, with a large number of ironmongers. Since then, the average number of workers for productive unit has risen until 1981, but in the last two decades it has fallen again to 8.2. In the long run the share of micro-plants (those with less than 10 workers) on total workforce has decreased in almost all sectors, with the remarkable exception of textiles. Yet the total number of workers in micro-plants has nevertheless increased from 900,000 in 1911 to almost 1.3 million in 1996[10].

The relative decline of micro-plants accounts for the whole increase in the average number of workers by productive unit. In fact the average number of workers in plants with more than 10 workers (Table 2.9) has halved, from 70 in 1911 to 36.2 in 2001. From 1911 to 1937 the average number of workers remained stable in *light* industries and grew by 40 per cent in the *heavy* ones (with a five-fold growth in car-making, from 70 to almost 400). In contrast after 1937 the average

[9] The data for 1911 are corrected for the omission of the workshops with one worker only. The average number of workers in the original (not corrected) figures was about 9.

[10] The data after 1981 undervalue the share of workers in micro-plants as the maximum threshold was lowered from 10 to 9 workers. A rough estimate of the total occupation in micro-plants in 1996 can be made by adding to the recorded total some 85,000 workers (a quarter of the employment in the class from 6 to 9 workers). This operation increases the total employment in micro-plants to 28 per cent of the total workforce.

number of workers in plants with more than 10 workers decreased in all industries, with the one exception of the production of radio and television sets[11].

These results may seem contradictory. How is it possible that the units with more than 10 workers employed proportionally more workers while their absolute size declined? Table 2.8.b provides an answer. Almost all the workers lost by micro-plants were gained by mini-plants, with 10-50 workers[12]. The share of plants with more than 50 workers declined by 10 percentage points from 1927 (no such data are available for 1911) onwards. In 2001 these plants employed only 41 per cent of the total workforce - some 2 million people. Medium-sized factories (51-100 and 101-500) accounted for a constant or even growing share of employment, so the entire reduction was concentrated in large factories, with more than 500 workers. These employed half a million workers in 1927 (a fifth of the total workforce), 1.15 million in 1981 (still a fifth), 560,000 in 1996 (down to a tenth) and only 468,478 in 2001. The share of large factories remained consistently higher in *heavy* than in *light* industries, but by 1996 they prevailed only in car-making, and (almost) in the production of other vehicles and of office equipment (Table 2.8.e). Summing up, the censuses buttress the conventional wisdom about the small size of Italian industry. It is unclear whether the small increase in the average size of plants and in the share of medium-sized ones (50-500 workers) in the 1990s heralds a new trend.

The composition of the total workforce has not changed very much in the long run. The share of non-manual workers (clerks, managers, etc.) has increased somewhat (Table 2.10), while both that of males (Table 2.11) and that of skilled workers (Table 2.12) have remained roughly constant. However, this stability is the net outcome of quite substantial changes in the composition of the workforce by sector and in the sectoral shares of total employment.

The composition by gender is arguably one of the most stable features of each sector in the long run. In 1911, males accounted for the majority of workers in all sectors but three, textiles, clothing and tobacco. The basic distinction between male and female-dominated sectors has remained constant over the entire century, in spite of non-negligible changes within each sector. The share of males has increased in textiles, up to half of the total, and in tobacco, while it has halved in clothing. In contrast, the share of females has risen in several male-dominated sectors, such as leather manufacturing[13]. Furthermore, as said before, the share of textiles and clothing on total workforce has decreased a great deal. As a result, the

[11] The data may even undervalue the extent of the decline. In fact until 1937, the census registered workers according to the sector, dividing a factory in separate units when necessary (e.g. workers repairing machinery of a textile mill were registered as an independent engineering plant). In contrast, since 1951 all workers of the same plant were recorded in the same sector. This change of definition reduced, *ceteris paribus*, the number of units and thus increased the average number of workers per unit.

[12] See, for a similar evolution in Germany, Stockman and Leicht [1994].

[13] This increase reflects changes in composition within the sector - from a prevalence of processing of hides, a typically male-dominated branch, to a prevalence of bags and other accessories, a typically female-dominated branch.

traditionally female-dominated sectors plunged from about two-thirds of total female workforce in 1911 to about one third in 1991. The proportion of non-manual workers has risen in all sectors, with some significant exceptions such as food, clothing and car-making. In spite of a huge growth in textiles, from 6 per cent to 30 per cent, the share has risen less in *light* than in *heavy* industries. The percentage jumped from 28.7 per cent in 1937 to 38.8 per cent in 1951: this increase is somewhat suspicious and may reflect a change in definition.

As said in the introduction, changes in composition of the workforce are the more relevant the more they reflect changes in the stock of human capital. Unfortunately, it is not easy to infer the latter from the available data. As Table 2.12 shows, the share of skilled workers on total workers has increased only slightly from 1951 to 1981 (no data are available for other periods). But the key trend, in this perspective, is the growth in the share of white collar workers on total manpower (Table 2.11). The latter is a residual category, which by 1911 consisted for three-quarters of entrepreneurs and their family members, and by 1981 consisted mainly of clerks and managers. It seems likely that this change has augmented the per capita endowment of capital. In 1911, many entrepreneurs were artisans with some on-the-job training and clerks had some formal education, usually a high school diploma. In that year, only 1.1 per cent of Italian population had a university degree [Zamagni 1993: Table 6]. In the 1980s, this share had increased to 17 per cent and thus the average clerk was much more likely to hold a university degree. As a whole, there is some evidence of an increase in the share of skill-endowed workers. It is also likely that the skill of individual worker grew, as a consequence of the increase in the number of years of schooling. Yet the average level does not seem impressively high. As late as 1981, one third of total industrial manpower (a half in food processing and textiles and clothing) consisted of "unskilled workers and laborers", people who, according to the census definition, could "perform tasks which an average worker could perform after a short training" or "which do not need any particular skill or aptitude" [Industrial census 1976: viii]. This fact tallies well with the large number of non-mechanized productive units. Italy, even at the end of the fastest period of development in its history, was still quite backward, not only in production, but also in the adoption of modern technology.

Finally, Table 2.13 reports data on the number of hours of work per worker. From 1937 to 1981, most notably between 1937 and 1951, it increased by a quarter in all industries and by a third in *light* industries only. These data refer to manual workers only, but they could be representative of the whole workforce if, as seems plausible, other employees worked as much as full-time employees. Thus, the increase in working time may seem in contrast with the world trend towards its reduction. It might reflect a decline in the share of part-time workers, who are not reported separately in any census. However, the censuses do report data on the distribution of hours worked per month by the whole manpower, which can be used to compute a seasonality index for the i-th industry as:

$$S_i=\Sigma(|(L_m/\Sigma L_m)-(1/12)|)/183.33*100$$

where L_m is the number of hours of work in a month. The index is the sum of absolute values of deviations of the actual monthly distribution from a perfectly homogeneous one (the same number of hours in all months), normalized with the maximum possible deviation (all the hours of work in a month). It thus may range from zero to 100. As Table 2.19 shows, the aggregate index is very low[14]. Seasonality has been declining from 1951 to 1971, and this decline might account for the increase in the number of hours per worker in those years. However, this explanation does not seem to hold from 1937 to 1951, when both the total number of hours and seasonality were growing. Nevertheless, the 1937 figures are somewhat suspect: the index for building, a notoriously cyclical industry was only 0.04 (see Table 2.17.m). The data show that seasonal variations in employment were very low in almost all sectors. The highest index, for tobacco in 1937, was only 19, while the index for the major allegedly seasonal industry, food, peaked at 7.7 in 1951. This figure implies that the maximum number of hours of work (in September) exceeded the minimum (in February) only by 60 per cent. Although incomplete, these data suggest that by 1951 Italian industry had already concluded the separation from the primary sector.

2.3. The causes of change: a first approximation

By their nature, industrial censuses only register changes, but they cannot explain them. However, some additional insights can be gained by computing how much the parameters examined so far (HP/worker, share of mechanized plants, etc.) would have changed in the long run had the composition of industry remained constant. In this way, it is possible to decompose the total change into within-sector and across-sector changes (Table 2.2). Different signs in columns (*c*) and (*d*) imply opposite trends: for instance, from 1911 to 1991 the share of males on total workforce rose by 3.6 per cent, while it would have fallen by 8 per cent with constant composition (as said, the percentage of females has grown in many sectors). This opposition, however, features only four parameters out of fourteen, and in all but one (the share of males on total workforce) the within-sector changes prevail. In the ten other cases, within-sector and between sectors changed in the same direction and the within-sector changes are more important in all of them. Therefore, within-sector changes prevailed in thirteen instances. This result might be interpreted as evidence for the effect of some factors common to the whole industry. Such a conclusion, however, would be somewhat hasty. As Table 2.3 shows, the sign of within sector changes differed in the majority of cases.

---

[14] The indexes by industry are aggregated in two different ways. Row (*a*) is computed by adding up all employees in one big sector, while row (*b*) is a weighted average of indexes by industry, using the share on total employment (Table 2.1) as weights. The latter method augments the weight of seasonal industry, which, by definition, had a lower aggregate working time with the same number of workers.

Table 2.2. The causes of change

Parameters	Period	(*a*)	(*b*)	(*c*)	(*d*)
% of plants with motive power	1927-1981	190.9	101.3	0.78	0.22
HP/worker	1911-1981	1,171.8	1,156.4	0.98	0.02
Workers/plant	1911-1996	40.6	32.4	0.80	0.20
Workers/plant >10	1911-1996	-47.8	-45.7	0.95	0.05
Plants by size <10 workers	1911-1996	-33.8	-27.3	0.81	0.19
<10 workers	1927-1996	14.3	13.3	0.90	0.10
10-50 workers	1927-1996	128.5	120.2	0.94	0.06
51-500 workers	1927-1996	-1.5	-1.5	1.02	-0.02
>500 workers	1927-1996	-43.4	-55.0	1.30	-0.30
% males	1911-1991	3.6	-8.0	-2.35	3.35
% white collar workers	1911-1991	59.5	57.1	0.96	0.04
% skilled workers	1951-1981	-8.1	-5.7	0.69	0.31
Hours of work per worker	1937-1971	25.8	31.6	1.17	-0.17
Seasonality	1937-1971	-32.7	-32.3	1.03	-0.03

Legend: (*a*) total change as percentage of the initial year (Table 2.5-2.13); (*b*) within-sector changes as percentage of the initial year; (*c*) contribution of the within-sector change (col. *b*) to total change (col. *a*); (*d*) contribution of the between-sector change to total change (col. *a*).

Table 2.3. The within sector-change

Parameters	Period	(*a*)	(*b*)	(*c*)
% of plants with motive power	1927-1981	101.3	22	1
HP/worker	1911-1981	1,156.4	22	0
Workers/plant	1911-1996	32.4	13	10
Workers/plant >10	1911-1996	-45.7	3	20
Plants by size <10 workers	1911-1996	-27.3	9	14
<10 workers	1927-1996	13.3	10	13
10-50 workers	1927-1996	120.2	20	3
51-500 workers	1927-1996	-1.5	13	10
>500 workers	1927-1996	-55.0	10	12
% males	1911-1991	-8.0	5	18
% white collar workers	1911-1991	57.1	19	4
% skilled workers	1951-1981	-5.7	17	6
Hours of work per worker	1937-1971	31.6	22	2
Seasonality	1937-1971	-32.3	10	13

Legend: (*a*) within sector change; (*b*) number of sectors with positive change; (*c*) number of sectors with negative change.

There were indeed common trends in few parameters, the share of mechanized plants, the HP/worker ratio and so on. However, in most cases, most notably relating to the distribution of employees by size of plants, this was not the case. Furthermore, sectors are themselves quite large aggregates of different industries, whose composition has changed over time. Thus, changes which are currently classified as within-sector would appear as between-sector with a finer disaggregation.

2.4. Additions, I: the location of Italian industry

As said, this research has not collected data by region. It is nevertheless possible to draw a map of the regional distribution of industries with the data provided by Zamagni [1987] and Cainelli and Stampini [2002]. The data (Table 2.15) refer to Italy at its present (1951) boundaries and use the definition of industry from the 1951 census, which differs slightly from that of the 1991 census, which is used in this work. Cainelli and Stampini use industrial censuses, while Zamagni uses population censuses[15]. The latter were based on household surveys and thus include home and part-time workers as well as the unemployed. Therefore, the population censuses were bound to report a higher number of workers[16]. The difference is likely to have been greater for the backward regions and for the traditional industries (food, textiles and so on). This hypothesis is borne out by a comparison of the results of the population and industrial censuses which were held contemporarily in 1911 (Table 2.15).

In spite of the use of different sources, the two works do yield a consistent outlook of the change in the location of Italian industry in the long term. The 19th century industrialization had been featured by a growing concentration in the *Industrial Triangle* (Piedmont, Liguria, Lombardy). As Fenoaltea [2003: 172] puts it "the industrial triangle, so evident by 1911, was not so in 1871: by then, only Lombardy stood out"[17]. In 1871 household production still accounted for a substantial share of manufacturing output, and thus the great Southern cities still had a proportionally high share of employment. It is likely that the share of North on factory occupation was higher, but this hypothesis cannot be proved without an industrial census. The *Industrial Triangle* accounted for 47 per cent of total man-

---

[15] Zamagni relies on a reconstruction by Vitali [1970], who corrects the glaring overvaluation of the number of employees in textiles in 1881 - from 1.3 million to 350,000. In a later work, using a different method, Fenoaltea [2001: 33-34] reaches the higher figure of 600,000 employees.

[16] On the other hand, one cannot rule out that the industrial censuses registered seasonal workers who happened to be working in industry at the time of the survey, but declared to be employed in other sectors in the population censuses.

[17] Fenoaltea's index of relative industrialization for the i-th region is the ratio of its share on Value Added to its share on population aged 15 years or more. He computes the regional Value Added by dividing his own national estimates by the share of each region on industrial employment from the population censuses.

power in 1911 and for 52 per cent in 1927. Its share remained unchanged until 1961, to decline to about 40 per cent thirty years later. In Liguria, the total number of workers fell by two fifths from 1961 to 1991, below the 1911 level. The shift in location benefited mostly the regions of the North-East (Emilia-Romagna and Veneto), but the South's share also rose from 13 per cent in 1961 to 17 per cent in 1991. However, the share of industrial employment in the South was still lower than in 1911 - about 21 per cent.

2.5. Additions, II: the rest of the secondary sector

This chapter focuses, consistently with the rest of the book, on manufacturing, but the industrial censuses provide data also on mining, building and utilities and it seems worthwhile to dwell, albeit briefly, on them (Table 2.16). According to industrial censuses, these activities increased their share of total occupation of the secondary sector from 10 per cent in 1911 to 25 per cent in 1991. This spectacular increase is however dubious, to say the least. In fact, the 1911 industrial census registered only 100,000 building workers, a seventh of the number reported by the population census in the same year. In all likelihood, the industrial census covered only the major building sites, with a relatively high average number of workers (Table 2.16.d). The mistake was progressively corrected so that in 1981 the ratio between figures from industrial and population census was down to 0.62 [Zamagni 1987: Table A.1]. Thus the growth in employment in construction is largely spurious. The bias also affects the other data, such as the number of HP per worker or the distribution of units by size. In other words, for this sector industrial censuses are so unreliable for building as to be almost useless.

The information on mining and utilities seems more reliable. Both sectors were quite small, but trends in employment diverged. Employment increased, both in absolute numbers and as a share of the secondary sector, in utilities, while it declined in mining. Both sectors were relatively capital-intensive and rather concentrated. The number of HP per worker in utilities was between 3 and 6 times higher than in manufacturing and the number of employees per unit roughly double. Both mining and utilities have always been, and still are, largely a male-dominated activity. Finally, the endowment of human capital, as measured by the shares of non-workers on total occupation and of skilled workers on total, has increased more than in manufacturing, albeit starting from a lower level. By 1996, at least according to these two proxies, the manpower in utilities and mining was more skilled than in manufacturing.

2.6. Conclusions

One can sum up the results in seven stylized facts:

(*a*) *heavy* industries have grown more than manufacturing as a whole;

(*b*) the capital per worker has increased a great deal, but has left behind a substantial number of small non-mechanized workshops;

(*c*) the average size of productive units has declined; employment has concentrated in small and medium-size units, while both the very small (below 10 employees) and the very large units (beyond 500) have decreased;

(*d*) during the *economic miracle* the number of hours worked increased and seasonality decreased;

(*e*) the stock of human capital seems to have increased;

(*f*) industry has been traditionally located in the North-West and is still quite concentrated in spite of the development of the Centre and the North-East;

(*g*) last but not least, most of the listed changes can be attributed mainly to within-sector changes, while structural change has had a minor role, at least apparently.

None of these facts are really unexpected. However, there are some important differences from the norm - i.e. the pattern of industrialization of advanced countries in the 19th century. It is possible to interpret these differences as a creative adaptation to factor endowment (the scarcity of capital and coal) or as serious evidence of backwardness. The choice of one of these interpretations is still an open issue, which will need further research.

Table 2.4. Shares on total employment in manufacturing

Sector	1911	1927	1937	1951	1961	1971	1981	1991	1996	2001
Food products and beverages (15)	13.7	12.5	14.7	10.3	8.9	7.1	7.8	8.8	8.9	9.1
Tobacco products (16)	0.9	1.0	1.5	1.5	0.6	0.4	0.4	0.3	0.2	0.2
Textiles (17)	22.5	25.0	18.5	18.8	13.7	10.1	8.9	7.7	7.1	6.3
Wearing apparel (18)	8.1	6.4	7.6	6.4	6.5	7.4	6.8	8.0	7.1	6.1
Tanning and dressing of leather, bags and footwear (19)	6.2	4.3	5.2	6.2	4.9	4.5	5.6	4.7	4.7	4.2
Manufacture of wood and of products of wood (20)	7.8	6.9	6.5	4.9	5.3	3.7	4.1	3.6	3.5	3.7
Pulp, paper and paper products (21)	1.3	1.2	1.4	1.5	1.6	1.4	1.7	1.7	1.8	1.7
Publishing and printing (22)	2.2	2.2	1.9	2.1	2.5	2.7	3.2	3.7	3.6	3.5
Coke and refined petroleum products (23)	0.0	0.3	0.5	0.5	0.4	0.5	0.6	0.6	0.5	0.5
Chemicals and chemical products (24)	3.3	2.9	3.4	5.1	5.9	5.4	5.0	4.6	4.3	4.2
Rubber and plastic products (25)	0.0	0.3	0.7	1.0	1.4	2.4	2.1	3.4	4.1	4.4
Non-metallic mineral products (26)	9.8	6.4	6.1	5.6	6.8	6.3	5.7	5.3	5.2	5.2
Basic metals (27)	3.1	3.9	3.0	4.8	5.3	5.0	4.7	3.3	2.8	2.8
Fabricated metal products (28)	5.9	5.8	3.4	6.3	6.2	7.1	9.6	11.8	12.8	14.3
Machinery and equipment (29)	3.4	5.2	8.8	8.6	11.8	13.8	10.9	10.3	11.4	12.2
Office machinery and computers (30)	0.1	0.1	0.1	0.3	0.5	0.7	0.5	0.5	0.4	0.4
Electrical machinery and apparatus n.e.c. (31)	0.2	0.4	1.1	1.6	2.6	3.8	4.4	4.0	4.2	4.3
Radio, television and communication equipment (32)	0.1	0.5	1.5	1.0	1.7	2.5	2.3	2.7	2.1	2.2
Medical, precision and optical instruments (33)	0.6	1.7	1.5	1.7	1.5	1.1	1.7	2.3	2.7	2.6
Motor vehicles, trailers and semi-trailers (34)	0.3	0.9	2.0	2.1	2.5	4.6	4.7	4.1	3.8	3.5
Other transport equipment (35)	5.4	5.3	5.9	4.0	3.1	2.0	2.4	2.6	2.1	2.1
Furniture and manufacturing n.e.c. (36)	4.9	6.5	4.5	5.8	6.4	7.4	6.9	5.9	6.4	6.2
Recycling (37)	0.0	0.3	0.1	0.1	0.1	0.0	0.0	0.1	0.2	0.3
Light industries	66.4	64.8	60.4	55.9	48.6	43.4	43.8	42.8	41.7	39.2
Heavy industries	33.6	35.2	39.6	44.1	51.4	56.6	56.2	57.2	58.3	60.8

Table 2.5. Share of plants with motive power

Sector	1927	1937	1951	1961	1971	1981*
Food products and beverages (15)	57.7	34.4	68.8	76.3	72.9	66.7
Tobacco products (16)	47.2	20.5	26.9	52.7	62.2	57.4
Textiles (17)	45.7	17.8	21.7	42.6	54.4	69.1
Wearing apparel (18)	2.0	1.0	1.9	5.2	17.2	40.3
Tanning and dressing of leather, bags and footwear (19)	3.1	3.2	9.0	23.9	46.8	76.3
Manufacture of wood and of products of wood (20)	7.7	14.8	39.3	66.5	77.2	73.9
Pulp, paper and paper products (21)	56.4	57.0	78.0	86.7	86.9	76.5
Publishing and printing (22)	51.4	66.4	66.7	74.6	64.9	56.3
Coke and refined petroleum products (23)	47.1	88.8	81.1	85.2	74.9	67.9
Chemicals and chemical products (24)	44.4	24.2	64.7	73.8	74.5	67.6
Rubber and plastic products (25)	64.2	57.4	84.7	81.8	74.0	73.7
Non-metallic mineral products (26)	28.0	30.9	50.5	73.1	75.9	70.8
Basic metals (27)	80.9	36.9	86.9	89.2	85.3	83.7
Fabricated metal products (28)	21.4	2.3	30.8	56.9	70.3	76.5
Machinery and equipment (29)	28.8	0.6	46.5	59.2	61.8	67.4
Office machinery and computers (30)	29.6	1.6	86.0	83.6	66.3	38.5
Electrical machinery and apparatus n.e.c. (31)	49.0	5.2	48.4	40.7	32.3	58.2
Radio, television and communication equipment (32)	54.8	1.4	37.1	33.4	26.2	40.8
Medical, precision and optical instruments (33)	30.8	2.0	51.1	59.3	63.0	60.2
Motor vehicles, trailers and semi-trailers (34)	28.8	18.6	92.9	94.1	85.2	81.3
Other transport equipment (35)	30.5	11.8	43.6	63.0	68.4	65.8
Furniture and manufacturing n.e.c. (36)	20.2	20.3	44.0	63.1	66.0	67.9
Recycling (37)	10.1	9.3	67.0	34.0	0.0	0.0
Light industries	20.9	18.1	27.4	41.7	53.4	64.6
Heavy industries	29.0	10.8	43.5	60.9	63.4	70.2
Manufacturing	23.0	16.8	31.6	47.9	57.6	66.8

Legend: * only electrical engines.

Table 2.6. HP/worker

Sector	1927	1937	1951	1961	1971	1981*
Food products and beverages (15)	0.97	1.87	1.97	4.24	5.26	6.57
Tobacco products (16)	0.12	0.19	0.17	0.28	1.21	1.91
Textiles (17)	0.42	0.99	1.29	1.83	2.53	3.92
Wearing apparel (18)	0.06	0.11	0.06	0.14	0.32	0.68
Tanning and dressing of leather, bags and footwear (19)	0.08	0.36	0.36	0.89	1.06	2.51
Manufacture of wood and of products of wood (20)	0.23	0.50	0.71	1.97	3.07	14.96
Pulp, paper and paper products (21)	1.68	3.11	4.55	7.73	11.52	17.48
Publishing and printing (22)	0.19	0.55	0.72	1.06	1.74	2.21
Coke and refined petroleum products (23)	-	1.75	4.65	6.43	19.28	46.26
Chemicals and chemical products (24)	0.97	2.82	3.85	6.21	10.17	17.58
Rubber and plastic products (25)	0.66	2.07	1.90	4.31	4.50	6.22
Non-metallic mineral products (26)	0.46	1.39	1.91	3.59	5.84	8.94
Basic metals (27)	1.72	4.50	6.81	8.94	12.90	16.38
Fabricated metal products (28)	0.36	1.57	2.72	3.75	4.61	5.70
Machinery and equipment (29)	0.45	1.07	1.58	2.15	2.85	3.02
Office machinery and computers (30)	0.40	0.49	0.85	1.19	1.44	1.72
Electrical machinery and apparatus n.e.c. (31)	0.36	1.11	1.38	1.50	2.02	2.09
Radio, television and communication equipment (32)	0.32	0.97	1.06	0.93	0.91	7.36
Medical, precision and optical instruments (33)	0.34	0.75	0.75	1.58	1.94	2.02
Motor vehicles, trailers and semi-trailers (34)	0.25	0.85	1.95	2.83	6.72	5.57
Other transport equipment (35)	0.45	1.17	1.67	3.27	4.12	4.31
Furniture and manufacturing n.e.c. (36)	0.15	0.56	0.64	1.32	2.13	3.45
Recycling (37)	0.71	0.84	0.85	3.59	2.81	0.00
Light industries	0.40	0.91	1.06	1.86	2.54	4.38
Heavy industries	0.62	1.80	2.44	4.11	5.89	7.80
Manufacturing	0.49	1.22	1.61	2.85	4.26	6.32

Legend: * only electrical engines.

Table 2.7. Average number of workers per productive unit

Sector	1911	1927	1937	1951	1961	1971	1981	1991	1996	2001
Food products and beverages (15)	3.9	3.9	2.0	4.6	7.1	7.8	7.6	6.8	5.8	6.0
Tobacco products (16)	341.0	251.6	78.7	70.8	35.9	53.2	87.6	68.8	72.7	46.4
Textiles (17)	56.8	56.1	15.2	16.0	12.8	10.2	7.6	8.8	9.5	9.7
Wearing apparel (18)	3.5	2.1	1.7	1.9	2.7	4.5	6.1	7.0	7.0	6.4
Tanning and dressing of leather, bags and footwear (19)	2.4	1.9	1.8	2.2	3.3	6.9	9.6	8.8	9.1	8.5
Manufacture of wood and of products of wood (20)	2.7	2.4	2.0	2.5	3.2	3.1	3.1	3.2	3.4	3.6
Pulp, paper and paper products (21)	27.8	27.9	28.4	40.7	34.7	31.6	21.3	18.1	16.2	16.3
Publishing and printing (22)	9.8	8.4	10.0	9.9	11.7	11.1	8.6	7.3	6.2	5.9
Coke and refined petroleum products (23)	-	24.1	36.1	81.2	87.1	65.8	42.7	28.9	29.3	26.9
Chemicals and chemical products (24)	16.3	18.6	9.7	32.1	48.8	55.7	39.6	33.1	27.6	26.6
Rubber and plastic products (25)	15.8	39.7	16.2	17.5	14.8	14.2	12.6	13.5	13.6	14.3
Non-metallic mineral products (26)	11.6	9.8	10.4	11.7	16.4	14.4	12.3	9.4	8.2	8.1
Basic metals (27)	24.2	31.0	38.0	67.4	44.3	43.2	55.3	42.0	33.7	35.0
Fabricated metal products (28)	3.3	3.7	7.5	3.9	5.7	7.0	6.2	6.7	6.6	6.9
Machinery and equipment (29)	7.4	6.0	6.4	5.5	6.3	6.0	9.6	14.6	12.9	12.9
Office machinery and computers (30)	11.4	18.4	25.7	190.1	375.7	451.7	85.7	66.4	31.4	11.2
Electrical machinery and apparatus n.e.c. (31)	15.6	15.3	13.9	20.6	21.0	14.1	17.9	12.6	11.9	10.4
Radio, television and communication equipment (32)	7.1	9.6	5.1	9.0	13.9	12.5	19.7	13.2	10.6	11.1
Medical, precision and optical instruments (33)	6.9	8.0	4.2	10.6	17.6	15.1	7.3	4.5	4.6	4.8
Motor vehicles, trailers and semi-trailers (34)	5.9	9.2	297.3	115.3	210.2	176.7	105.8	92.6	82.2	77.6
Other transport equipment (35)	10.6	9.8	9.1	13.2	30.7	42.5	42.0	32.8	22.3	20.8
Furniture and manufacturing n.e.c. (36)	5.1	5.6	4.3	4.1	6.7	7.0	6.1	5.5	5.2	5.6
Recycling (37)	17.5	6.7	4.5	13.2	5.0	-	-	3.8	4.0	5.4
Light industries	5.1	4.9	3.0	4.2	5.4	6.5	6.5	6.5	6.2	6.2
Heavy industries	8.0	8.0	9.1	9.5	12.1	11.8	13.0	11.9	10.7	10.6
Manufacturing	5.9	5.7	4.0	5.6	7.5	8.7	9.1	8.8	8.2	8.3

Table 2.8. Share of plants by size-class

(*a*) less than 10 workers

Sector	1911	1927	1937	1951	1961	1971	1981	1991	1996
Food products and beverages (15)	69.9	63.0	60.0	51.4	36.9	32.6	34.2	39.6	42.2
Tobacco products (16)	0.3	0.2	1.1	2.1	5.1	3.7	1.5	2.2	1.8
Textiles (17)	5.3	2.9	8.8	9.2	14.0	16.7	24.8	25.8	23.1
Wearing apparel (18)	65.0	70.8	80.6	80.7	60.7	32.0	27.4	29.7	29.3
Tanning and dressing of leather, bags and footwear (19)	80.7	70.1	69.7	61.8	44.5	24.9	24.6	27.6	25.3
Manufacture of wood and of products of wood (20)	73.5	78.4	71.4	67.3	63.5	63.0	61.4	60.5	57.8
Pulp, paper and paper products (21)	10.0	8.0	8.0	6.0	7.7	7.4	11.1	13.7	13.6
Publishing and printing (22)	30.2	31.0	26.2	27.5	26.2	24.8	29.0	34.8	36.0
Coke and refined petroleum products (23)	0.0	8.2	7.6	3.2	3.1	3.6	4.9	7.8	6.7
Chemicals and chemical products (24)	19.1	13.7	19.0	8.1	5.6	4.2	5.7	6.6	7.3
Rubber and plastic products (25)	21.7	5.4	11.7	12.1	17.7	15.0	18.1	18.6	16.5
Non-metallic mineral products (26)	22.8	25.2	21.1	20.3	16.4	17.2	19.2	26.5	28.4
Basic metals (27)	11.9	8.0	5.5	3.4	5.8	5.6	3.8	5.0	5.8
Fabricated metal products (28)	65.9	53.3	21.7	43.0	37.8	29.9	36.1	37.1	35.4
Machinery and equipment (29)	31.5	36.9	25.9	35.1	37.8	36.1	21.1	15.7	16.3
Office machinery and computers (30)	30.2	12.8	7.3	0.9	0.5	0.3	3.1	2.8	9.0
Electrical machinery and apparatus n.e.c. (31)	16.5	16.0	9.5	10.9	12.1	14.7	13.3	18.5	18.2
Radio, television and communication equipment (32)	32.3	27.4	30.7	20.9	16.3	14.9	9.9	14.1	17.2
Medical, precision and optical instruments (33)	35.4	26.8	39.9	18.2	13.7	14.0	27.4	42.3	39.5
Motor vehicles, trailers and semi-trailers (34)	45.2	24.0	0.4	2.0	0.8	1.1	2.0	1.9	2.0
Other transport equipment (35)	23.7	23.5	18.6	13.1	6.0	4.7	4.9	6.4	8.8
Furniture and manufacturing n.e.c. (36)	49.3	39.4	42.6	49.0	37.5	31.1	34.9	40.4	39.9
Recycling (37)	9.4	34.6	47.0	18.4	45.3	-	-	64.6	54.1
Light industries	45.0	39.8	45.5	40.7	36.5	29.7	32.0	35.1	35.0
Heavy industries	30.0	27.7	19.5	20.4	19.7	18.6	16.8	19.6	20.3
Manufacturing	40.0	35.7	35.2	31.9	28.0	23.5	23.4	26.2	26.5

(*b*) 10-50 workers

Sector	1927	1937	1951	1961	1971	1981	1991	1996
Food products and beverages (15)	17.3	12.5	19.1	20.8	23.7	24.3	24.5	24.7
Tobacco products (16)	0.3	6.7	7.3	11.3	9.6	6.9	11.2	12.5
Textiles (17)	7.1	9.8	8.9	16.0	21.8	29.2	36.0	37.0
Wearing apparel (18)	12.0	8.6	7.5	14.6	21.3	36.1	46.2	47.1
Tanning and dressing of leather, bags and footwear (19)	14.1	11.2	14.7	24.7	32.7	40.6	48.6	50.0
Manufacture of wood and of products of wood (20)	13.7	14.2	17.8	20.1	21.9	27.3	28.6	31.1
Pulp, paper and paper products (21)	26.5	24.2	17.3	22.7	25.0	27.7	31.4	33.4
Publishing and printing (22)	36.9	30.0	28.9	28.5	26.9	29.0	34.8	34.1
Coke and refined petroleum products (23)	22.4	18.7	8.8	7.3	13.0	20.8	23.1	22.8
Chemicals and chemical products (24)	19.5	19.0	12.0	12.2	11.3	13.1	16.4	17.9
Rubber and plastic products (25)	4.7	12.0	8.5	23.7	20.9	25.7	38.0	40.3
Non-metallic mineral products (26)	30.9	23.5	26.5	28.8	31.2	32.4	35.6	33.9
Basic metals (27)	12.1	10.9	9.1	13.8	13.2	12.1	17.7	20.5
Fabricated metal products (28)	11.6	14.1	15.2	21.2	26.6	34.3	41.9	43.8
Machinery and equipment (29)	18.7	8.6	15.6	19.2	18.0	22.3	30.1	30.2
Office machinery and computers (30)	18.8	10.9	3.6	2.4	2.2	5.1	13.9	20.5
Electrical machinery and apparatus n.e.c. (31)	17.0	9.1	12.5	17.0	15.8	23.2	28.5	30.3
Radio, television and communication equipment (32)	19.6	8.5	12.7	11.8	10.2	10.1	17.6	18.7
Medical, precision and optical instruments (33)	17.1	10.4	15.4	21.0	21.0	22.3	24.5	23.5
Motor vehicles, trailers and semi-trailers (34)	8.1	3.3	6.5	5.1	4.9	6.6	8.7	9.0
Other transport equipment (35)	6.9	5.1	6.8	7.6	9.6	9.8	11.8	14.7
Furniture and manufacturing n.e.c. (36)	21.5	19.3	21.3	28.9	33.3	36.9	37.9	37.4
Recycling (37)	65.4	53.0	81.6	54.7	-	-	35.4	45.9
Light industries	13.0	12.2	14.0	20.3	25.3	31.7	36.3	36.7
Heavy industries	17.0	12.5	14.3	17.7	17.9	21.6	28.3	30.2
Manufacturing	14.4	12.3	14.1	19.0	21.2	26.0	31.7	32.9

(*c*) 51-100 workers

Sector	1927	1937	1951	1961	1971	1981	1991
Food products and beverages (15)	7.1	6.0	8.7	9.8	9.9	9.6	8.3
Tobacco products (16)	1.4	14.0	9.1	8.7	3.4	10.3	9.4
Textiles (17)	8.5	10.9	8.8	11.0	12.6	12.4	12.9
Wearing apparel (18)	4.2	2.9	3.4	6.3	10.4	11.2	8.6
Tanning and dressing of leather, bags and footwear (19)	6.2	6.4	6.8	11.6	14.6	13.7	10.8
Manufacture of wood and of products of wood (20)	4.0	5.4	5.0	7.1	7.3	6.6	5.9
Pulp, paper and paper products (21)	11.7	15.2	11.9	12.3	12.8	11.1	14.2
Publishing and printing (22)	12.5	13.0	12.3	11.9	11.1	9.0	8.0
Coke and refined petroleum products (23)	15.9	12.2	7.3	5.8	5.8	10.0	8.6
Chemicals and chemical products (24)	13.3	12.9	9.6	8.9	7.8	8.7	10.0
Rubber and plastic products (25)	4.8	8.4	4.2	11.7	11.4	10.3	13.4
Non-metallic mineral products (26)	13.4	16.3	16.0	19.1	15.5	14.4	12.3
Basic metals (27)	6.7	8.3	6.7	9.1	7.6	7.3	10.1
Fabricated metal products (28)	5.0	9.0	7.2	9.9	12.8	9.9	9.1
Machinery and equipment (29)	7.9	5.7	7.4	9.0	7.9	10.3	13.5
Office machinery and computers (30)	4.0	11.8	4.8	1.4	1.1	2.5	6.7
Electrical machinery and apparatus n.e.c. (31)	13.7	7.0	7.1	10.7	9.2	11.0	11.0
Radio, television and communication equipment (32)	10.3	5.4	6.3	8.8	7.0	5.7	8.1
Medical, precision and optical instruments (33)	7.8	7.1	8.0	11.0	13.2	9.5	8.7
Motor vehicles, trailers and semi-trailers (34)	4.8	3.4	4.5	4.1	3.8	3.6	5.7
Other transport equipment (35)	3.7	3.6	4.5	5.7	6.0	4.9	6.0
Furniture and manufacturing n.e.c. (36)	9.5	10.3	9.0	12.6	14.4	12.2	10.2
Recycling (37)	16.4	40.5	24.6	-	-	32.2	35.3
Light industries	7.2	7.8	7.7	10.0	11.7	11.0	9.5
Heavy industries	8.3	8.6	8.3	10.3	9.3	9.3	10.4
Manufacturing	7.5	8.1	8.0	10.1	10.3	10.0	10.0

(*d*) 101-500 workers

Sector	1927	1937	1951	1961	1971	1981	1991	1996
Food products and beverages (15)	8.9	9.9	16.0	21.4	22.2	22.7	20.8	26.2
Tobacco products (16)	6.2	26.9	30.3	26.3	41.0	47.2	49.0	58.6
Textiles (17)	44.3	39.8	32.7	32.9	32.4	26.6	22.2	36.8
Wearing apparel (18)	8.2	5.6	6.5	13.5	25.2	18.6	12.8	20.3
Tanning and dressing of leather, bags and footwear (19)	7.7	10.6	11.5	15.8	21.3	18.5	11.4	22.1
Manufacture of wood and of products of wood (20)	3.8	7.4	8.6	8.7	6.8	4.2	5.0	10.7
Pulp, paper and paper products (21)	30.9	38.2	37.5	36.6	37.8	34.5	30.7	46.4
Publishing and printing (22)	15.6	19.2	18.9	22.6	21.8	18.0	15.0	22.5
Coke and refined petroleum products (23)	37.8	35.7	27.1	37.9	31.4	21.3	24.3	31.9
Chemicals and chemical products (24)	31.4	26.1	23.5	23.3	25.3	30.1	36.4	48.0
Rubber and plastic products (25)	17.7	29.0	17.6	21.7	23.5	18.6	20.0	35.7
Non-metallic mineral products (26)	25.9	30.4	29.4	28.9	27.2	25.7	21.3	32.3
Basic metals (27)	24.4	37.7	21.4	22.6	23.1	24.2	29.6	40.3
Fabricated metal products (28)	14.5	33.2	16.9	19.0	20.3	14.9	10.5	19.5
Machinery and equipment (29)	17.8	14.5	19.6	18.4	18.9	24.1	24.5	38.9
Office machinery and computers (30)	19.3	11.6	13.9	5.2	9.7	19.4	15.1	24.2
Electrical machinery and apparatus n.e.c. (31)	31.6	24.6	26.8	26.1	25.2	27.3	29.1	36.9
Radio, television and communication equipment (32)	24.3	20.2	22.5	20.2	20.9	23.0	24.4	28.8
Medical, precision and optical instruments (33)	23.9	13.3	19.4	26.6	28.7	25.9	18.2	28.7
Motor vehicles, trailers and semi-trailers (34)	11.0	12.1	11.5	14.3	11.6	13.3	18.5	27.7
Other transport equipment (35)	14.2	11.8	14.9	18.3	22.8	20.5	25.0	31.3
Furniture and manufacturing n.e.c. (36)	20.7	18.9	16.2	16.2	17.0	14.0	10.4	21.0
Recycling (37)	15.8	15.1	19.8	0.0	0.0	0.9	0.0	28.2
Light industries	22.5	19.5	19.9	21.0	22.9	19.1	15.5	24.3
Heavy industries	21.0	22.7	21.2	22.0	21.9	22.5	22.0	32.6
Manufacturing	22.0	20.8	20.5	21.5	22.3	21.0	19.2	29.1

(*e*) more than 500 workers

Sector	1927	1937	1951	1961	1971	1981	1991	1996
Food products and beverages (15)	3.7	11.6	4.8	11.1	11.6	9.3	6.9	6.9
Tobacco products (16)	92.0	51.3	51.2	48.6	42.4	34.1	28.2	27.1
Textiles (17)	37.3	30.7	40.4	26.2	16.5	7.0	3.2	3.1
Wearing apparel (18)	4.7	2.3	1.9	4.9	11.1	6.7	2.7	3.3
Tanning and dressing of leather, bags and footwear (19)	1.9	2.1	5.2	3.4	6.5	2.7	1.7	2.6
Manufacture of wood and of products of wood (20)	0.1	1.6	1.3	0.5	1.1	0.4	0.0	0.4
Pulp, paper and paper products (21)	23.0	14.3	27.3	20.7	17.0	15.6	10.1	6.6
Publishing and printing (22)	4.0	11.6	12.3	10.8	15.4	14.9	7.3	7.4
Coke and refined petroleum products (23)	15.8	25.8	53.6	45.8	46.1	43.0	36.2	38.6
Chemicals and chemical products (24)	22.1	23.0	46.8	50.0	51.4	42.4	30.6	26.8
Rubber and plastic products (25)	67.4	38.9	57.7	25.3	29.2	27.3	10.0	7.5
Non-metallic mineral products (26)	4.6	8.8	7.8	6.8	9.0	8.3	4.2	5.5
Basic metals (27)	48.8	37.7	59.4	48.6	50.5	52.5	37.5	33.4
Fabricated metal products (28)	15.5	22.0	17.7	12.0	10.4	4.8	1.4	1.3
Machinery and equipment (29)	18.7	45.3	22.3	15.7	19.1	22.1	16.2	14.6
Office machinery and computers (30)	45.2	58.4	76.8	90.5	86.7	69.9	61.5	46.2
Electrical machinery and apparatus n.e.c. (31)	21.7	48.7	42.7	34.0	35.0	25.2	12.9	14.6
Radio, television and communication equipment (32)	18.4	35.2	37.5	42.9	47.0	51.4	35.7	35.3
Medical, precision and optical instruments (33)	24.4	29.3	39.0	27.8	23.0	14.9	6.4	8.3
Motor vehicles, trailers and semi-trailers (34)	52.1	80.9	75.4	75.7	78.7	74.6	65.2	61.3
Other transport equipment (35)	51.7	60.9	60.7	62.3	56.8	59.9	50.7	45.2
Furniture and manufacturing n.e.c. (36)	9.0	8.8	4.6	4.8	4.3	1.9	1.2	1.7
Recycling (37)	26.0	10.3	0.0	0.0	2.3	10.5	0.0	11.9
Light industries	17.5	15.0	17.6	12.1	10.4	6.2	3.7	4.0
Heavy industries	26.0	36.6	35.7	30.4	32.3	29.9	19.8	16.9
Manufacturing	20.4	23.5	25.6	21.4	22.7	19.5	12.9	11.5

Table 2.9. Average number of workers, plants with more than 10 workers

Sector	1911	1927	1937	1951	1961	1971	1981	1991	1996	2001
Food products and beverages (15)	39.9	37.2	53.2	43.2	50.4	46.3	42.4	39.6	37.1	37.2
Tobacco products (16)	563.2	756.4	157.5	161.7	124.4	144.2	137.5	115.7	117.9	104.9
Textiles (17)	113.5	150.1	118.8	133.2	83.5	59.2	39.7	33.0	33.9	34.8
Wearing apparel (18)	45.1	40.2	40.0	43.4	46.6	50.1	31.6	25.5	25.2	25.8
Tanning and dressing of leather, bags and footwear (19)	37.8	37.6	47.5	45.3	39.7	37.6	30.2	25.2	25.7	26.2
Manufacture of wood and of products of wood (20)	37.3	27.0	35.8	32.7	31.8	27.4	22.8	22.1	21.9	22.4
Pulp, paper and paper products (21)	61.2	61.6	63.0	82.5	66.9	59.0	49.3	43.4	42.1	41.0
Publishing and printing (22)	38.2	34.0	42.8	43.7	44.0	44.0	37.5	30.6	30.1	29.1
Coke and refined petroleum products (23)	-	62.5	79.0	148.3	154.3	111.6	73.6	66.6	64.9	57.1
Chemicals and chemical products (24)	72.5	69.0	68.8	113.6	117.3	121.0	99.5	83.4	78.0	70.8
Rubber and plastic products (25)	37.5	239.0	111.9	165.0	58.7	64.8	50.3	35.8	35.2	36.2
Non-metallic mineral products (26)	48.0	43.4	58.4	51.9	49.9	44.8	41.2	34.2	34.3	33.8
Basic metals (27)	109.3	113.5	121.8	155.2	109.3	110.4	116.4	82.5	73.3	69.2
Fabricated metal products (28)	62.2	66.1	85.4	63.7	49.8	42.6	29.5	24.4	24.1	24.8
Machinery and equipment (29)	65.2	56.1	126.2	68.0	54.1	55.1	54.7	45.7	45.3	43.9
Office machinery and computers (30)	60.9	81.3	123.7	303.0	497.3	539.5	224.5	110.4	71.1	47.6
Electrical machinery and apparatus n.e.c. (31)	81.3	74.1	70.0	110.2	81.7	79.6	56.4	44.4	43.5	38.0
Radio, television and communication equipment (32)	74.2	60.6	58.2	98.8	108.8	115.0	121.1	74.5	70.8	72.7
Medical, precision and optical instruments (33)	58.9	68.9	72.9	91.7	70.0	63.1	49.6	38.2	41.7	43.5
Motor vehicles, trailers and semi-trailers (34)	73.2	139.7	388.9	222.1	272.9	285.0	212.9	164.2	156.4	139.2
Other transport equipment (35)	138.6	157.5	233.7	186.0	179.3	142.1	134.0	111.8	92.3	85.8
Furniture and manufacturing n.e.c. (36)	47.4	47.0	50.5	41.2	38.1	34.5	28.8	26.0	26.4	27.6
Recycling (37)	286.4	53.8	47.9	35.8	36.7	-	-	19.0	21.2	22.6
Light industries	71.8	71.1	70.3	67.9	52.7	44.6	34.0	29.4	29.1	29.7
Heavy industries	67.3	70.0	84.4	90.2	74.6	71.3	59.5	45.7	42.8	41.0
Manufacturing	70.0	70.7	76.6	77.7	63.2	57.4	46.0	37.8	36.5	36.2

Table 2.10. Share of males on total workforce

Sector	1911	1927	1937	1951	1961	1971	1981	1991
Food products and beverages (15)	85.8	78.1	76.1	75.7	69.8	70.6	68.9	67.7
Tobacco products (16)	13.4	18.6	14.1	21.4	33.3	38.7	54.1	65.0
Textiles (17)	26.7	24.9	23.9	28.0	33.5	39.7	40.1	44.4
Wearing apparel (18)	41.8	34.3	39.8	41.0	33.9	24.0	19.7	21.3
Tanning and dressing of leather, bags and footwear (19)	90.2	87.7	84.4	79.1	69.6	59.8	50.3	49.6
Manufacture of wood and of products of wood (20)	91.9	93.7	90.5	89.3	88.3	88.0	85.5	85.7
Pulp, paper and paper products (21)	56.1	56.6	53.0	65.1	64.1	71.2	72.8	75.2
Publishing and printing (22)	82.2	79.3	72.6	73.9	74.6	76.1	62.9	70.1
Coke and refined petroleum products (23)	-	93.7	97.8	91.6	92.3	93.3	92.6	90.3
Chemicals and chemical products (24)	84.2	73.2	72.8	70.2	72.9	75.8	77.7	75.5
Rubber and plastic products (25)	64.4	71.2	51.8	64.1	62.7	70.6	71.2	71.2
Non-metallic mineral products (26)	90.0	88.2	82.6	83.9	85.4	84.2	82.9	82.8
Basic metals (27)	95.3	95.0	93.9	92.7	93.1	93.7	92.8	90.6
Fabricated metal products (28)	93.7	91.5	78.4	88.5	86.6	86.6	86.2	83.6
Machinery and equipment (29)	95.7	91.7	86.9	91.2	91.4	90.9	86.6	84.7
Office machinery and computers (30)	92.3	75.2	85.3	68.9	75.1	76.5	74.3	73.4
Electrical machinery and apparatus n.e.c. (31)	76.3	77.0	72.3	72.6	73.1	74.8	76.7	71.8
Radio, television and communication equipment (32)	81.0	84.1	80.8	75.0	69.3	68.2	58.2	68.3
Medical, precision and optical instruments (33)	88.5	85.7	81.6	75.8	66.0	67.6	68.2	70.5
Motor vehicles, trailers and semi-trailers (34)	97.1	91.0	93.4	90.9	90.7	87.6	84.8	83.7
Other transport equipment (35)	98.6	96.7	94.3	91.4	91.9	84.1	90.9	89.9
Furniture and manufacturing n.e.c. (36)	75.9	66.2	72.6	76.9	74.8	75.3	73.2	72.6
Recycling (37)	29.9	59.6	52.6	59.0	55.1	-	-	80.8
Light industries	55.8	53.5	55.9	55.8	57.3	56.7	54.6	55.2
Heavy industries	91.0	88.4	83.7	84.3	83.9	83.8	82.4	80.7
Manufacturing	67.4	65.8	66.9	68.4	70.9	72.1	70.2	69.8

Table 2.11. Share of white collars on total workforce

Sector	1911	1927	1937	1951	1961	1971	1981	1991
Food products and beverages (15)	42.7	42.3	37.5	46.3	38.4	40.2	43.0	48.7
Tobacco products (16)	6.1	4.5	4.1	12.9	17.5	17.2	20.0	27.0
Textiles (17)	5.8	4.4	8.8	17.8	27.1	30.2	56.9	38.8
Wearing apparel (18)	42.7	37.0	68.8	80.8	68.5	42.4	40.7	40.0
Tanning and dressing of leather, bags and footwear (19)	53.3	50.1	63.1	64.5	54.9	35.2	36.1	38.0
Manufacture of wood and of products of wood (20)	50.4	49.8	59.9	64.1	58.8	53.2	58.4	57.4
Pulp, paper and paper products (21)	10.4	9.1	6.1	19.5	23.6	23.8	27.2	33.9
Publishing and printing (22)	20.9	16.9	16.8	25.4	45.1	47.5	52.6	57.8
Coke and refined petroleum products (23)	-	17.5	15.6	36.0	35.1	41.5	46.5	54.0
Chemicals and chemical products (24)	15.3	18.1	16.8	26.3	30.5	39.8	44.6	55.2
Rubber and plastic products (25)	17.6	15.2	11.2	26.3	34.5	29.3	32.3	35.6
Non-metallic mineral products (26)	15.7	17.2	15.0	25.2	23.7	24.6	30.5	37.3
Basic metals (27)	11.0	10.2	6.6	17.9	20.5	24.6	23.5	27.8
Fabricated metal products (28)	46.0	36.0	18.5	50.5	46.7	39.0	45.6	44.4
Machinery and equipment (29)	23.3	26.4	23.8	44.9	49.6	46.4	41.3	43.3
Office machinery and computers (30)	21.2	16.6	12.1	23.3	29.7	40.3	58.3	64.8
Electrical machinery and apparatus n.e.c. (31)	15.3	18.5	17.1	29.3	32.7	33.8	37.5	42.1
Radio, television and communication equipment (32)	24.8	21.2	30.5	37.9	37.3	35.9	40.0	53.5
Medical, precision and optical instruments (33)	26.1	24.0	34.2	35.1	34.9	36.8	49.7	62.6
Motor vehicles, trailers and semi-trailers (34)	26.7	21.0	8.6	23.3	23.6	21.6	21.8	26.0
Other transport equipment (35)	19.3	19.2	20.9	30.9	25.1	25.1	26.8	36.7
Furniture and manufacturing n.e.c. (36)	31.4	26.1	31.4	53.4	47.1	39.4	45.1	49.0
Recycling (37)	9.6	23.7	38.9	23.7	46.4	-	-	57.7
Light industries	30.0	25.4	35.4	43.3	44.3	38.9	46.8	45.5
Heavy industries	22.1	21.5	18.4	33.2	34.7	34.8	36.9	42.2
Manufacturing	27.3	24.0	28.7	38.8	39.4	36.6	41.2	43.6

Table 2.12. Share of skilled workers on total of blue collars

Sector	1951	1961	1971	1981
Food products and beverages (15)	44.1	41.7	44.8	55.5
Tobacco products (16)	25.4	24.6	23.2	39.7
Textiles (17)	81.8	80.8	78.9	53.3
Wearing apparel (18)	61.5	65.9	65.5	54.1
Tanning and dressing of leather, bags and footwear (19)	66.7	68.6	63.2	55.8
Manufacture of wood and of products of wood (20)	49.2	50.8	53.7	58.8
Pulp, paper and paper products (21)	44.4	49.0	55.7	68.2
Publishing and printing (22)	80.1	72.8	77.5	79.9
Coke and refined petroleum products (23)	66.5	77.7	86.0	77.2
Chemicals and chemical products (24)	49.9	56.0	69.6	72.9
Rubber and plastic products (25)	72.9	49.4	54.5	67.9
Non-metallic mineral products (26)	41.4	43.9	62.1	69.6
Basic metals (27)	47.1	42.8	62.7	80.9
Fabricated metal products (28)	49.5	48.8	57.8	67.8
Machinery and equipment (29)	65.7	61.7	64.5	73.1
Office machinery and computers (30)	45.4	45.3	53.0	93.3
Electrical machinery and apparatus n.e.c. (31)	57.3	49.6	51.8	69.0
Radio, television and communication equipment (32)	53.3	45.5	41.0	57.6
Medical, precision and optical instruments (33)	62.7	54.0	53.6	70.4
Motor vehicles, trailers and semi-trailers (34)	58.0	44.1	48.4	45.1
Other transport equipment (35)	64.6	60.5	68.9	82.0
Furniture and manufacturing n.e.c. (36)	52.5	56.1	56.9	63.6
Recycling (37)	62.1	49.2	-	-
Light industries	66.7	63.9	63.4	59.8
Heavy industries	53.8	51.2	59.5	69.1
Manufacturing	60.5	56.9	61.1	65.4

Table 2.13. Number of hours worked

Sector	1951	1961	1971	1981
Food products and beverages (15)	1,254	1,913	1,803	2,020
Tobacco products (16)	1,887	2,297	3,534	2,147
Textiles (17)	1,841	1,917	1,929	2,011
Wearing apparel (18)	958	1,699	1,743	1,943
Tanning and dressing of leather, bags and footwear (19)	1,396	1,765	1,692	1,868
Manufacture of wood and of products of wood (20)	1,280	1,775	1,855	2,073
Pulp, paper and paper products (21)	1,893	2,237	1,933	2,078
Publishing and printing (22)	1,920	1,750	2,123	2,337
Coke and refined petroleum products (23)	2,157	2,221	2,019	2,255
Chemicals and chemical products (24)	1,716	2,068	1,901	2,031
Rubber and plastic products (25)	1,641	2,010	1,932	1,887
Non-metallic mineral products (26)	1,462	1,971	1,791	2,025
Basic metals (27)	1,803	2,083	1,973	1,940
Fabricated metal products (28)	1,598	2,095	1,983	2,154
Machinery and equipment (29)	1,584	2,071	2,026	2,291
Office machinery and computers (30)	1,920	2,173	1,734	1,912
Electrical machinery and apparatus n.e.c. (31)	1,808	2,033	1,868	2,029
Radio, television and communication equipment (32)	1,654	1,915	1,872	1,910
Medical, precision and optical instruments (33)	1,579	2,064	1,922	2,129
Motor vehicles, trailers and semi-trailers (34)	1,899	2,245	1,763	1,643
Other transport equipment (35)	1,816	2,265	1,961	1,990
Furniture and manufacturing n.e.c. (36)	1,517	2,043	2,002	2,142
Recycling (37)	1,575	1,683	1,814	-
Light industries	1,569	1,908	1,912	2,031
Heavy industries	1,678	2,090	1,919	2,040
Manufacturing	1,619	1,996	1,916	2,036

Table 2.14. Seasonality index

Sector	1937	1951	1961	1971
Food products and beverages (15)	6.15	7.70	6.56	3.75
Tobacco products (16)	18.54	17.83	21.38	9.76
Textiles (17)	3.59	4.63	3.36	3.20
Wearing apparel (18)	5.36	5.99	4.27	2.55
Tanning and dressing of leather, bags and footwear (19)	4.55	6.38	4.65	2.13
Manufacture of wood and of products of wood (20)	3.00	3.49	2.63	2.53
Pulp, paper and paper products (21)	2.97	2.51	2.14	2.40
Publishing and printing (22)	1.75	2.43	2.42	1.99
Coke and refined petroleum products (23)	1.66	2.32	1.29	1.12
Chemicals and chemical products (24)	2.24	2.18	2.43	1.84
Rubber and plastic products (25)	3.59	3.38	3.82	3.21
Non-metallic mineral products (26)	8.18	6.62	4.79	2.33
Basic metals (27)	2.08	2.34	2.54	2.37
Fabricated metal products (28)	1.80	2.51	3.26	2.63
Machinery and equipment (29)	1.85	2.97	3.35	2.69
Office machinery and computers (30)	1.91	5.03	7.72	2.70
Electrical machinery and apparatus n.e.c. (31)	2.68	3.28	3.22	3.10
Radio, television and communication equipment (32)	2.46	3.31	4.10	3.00
Medical, precision and optical instruments (33)	2.11	3.94	3.27	2.98
Motor vehicles, trailers and semi-trailers (34)	2.07	4.07	2.87	2.60
Other transport equipment (35)	2.00	2.90	2.78	2.77
Furniture and manufacturing n.e.c. (36)	2.82	2.87	2.99	2.68
Recycling (37)	4.73	5.94	4.21	-
Light industries	2.87	3.97	2.93	2.28
Heavy industries	2.12	2.84	2.92	2.48
Manufacturing	2.32	2.98	2.92	2.40
Seasonality	4.04	4.55	3.76	2.72

Table 2.15. Localization of manufacturing: shares by region

(*a*) Population censuses

Region	1881 PC	1911 PC	1911 IC	1911 IC/PC
Piemonte	11.8	13.1	15.2	0.71
Liguria	3.3	4.5	5.7	0.79
Lombardia	20.6	23.7	29.5	0.77
Veneto*	12.4	11.2	9.1	0.50
Emilia-Romagna	7.0	7.1	6.4	0.55
Marche	2.9	2.5	2.2	0.54
Toscana	8.8	9.5	7.7	0.50
Umbria	1.1	1.1	1.4	0.80
Lazio	3.7	3.6	2.9	0.49
Campania	9.0	7.9	7.2	0.56
Abruzzi	2.6	1.9	1.6	0.51
Puglia	3.8	3.8	3.6	0.58
Basilicata	1.1	0.6	0.4	0.43
Calabria	3.0	2.3	1.8	0.50
Sicilia	8.0	6.0	4.4	0.46
Sardegna	1.1	1.1	0.9	0.46

Legend: *PC* Population census; *IC* Industrial census. * including Friuli-Venezia Giulia and Trentino Alto Adige.
Source: Zamagni [1987: Table A.2 and A.3].

(*b*) Industrial censuses

Region	1911	1927	1937	1951	1961	1971	1981	1991	1996	2001
Piemonte and V.A.	14.4	15.8	15.0	16.3	15.7	15.1	12.9	11.5	11.1	10.7
Liguria	5.5	5.0	5.0	4.5	3.6	2.9	2.4	2.0	1.7	1.6
Lombardia	27.6	31.1	29.7	32.1	32.2	30.1	26.9	25.9	26.2	24.9
Trentino A.A.	0.0	1.1	1.1	1.3	1.2	1.2	1.3	1.4	1.5	1.5
Veneto	7.4	7.0	7.4	7.6	8.2	9.4	10.5	12.3	13.4	13.6
Friuli-Venezia G.	3.3	3.3	3.0	2.6	2.4	2.5	2.4	2.5	2.6	2.8
Emilia-Romagna	6.4	5.7	6.8	6.0	7.9	8.7	10.2	10.0	10.6	11.0
Marche	2.3	2.0	2.0	1.8	2.0	2.5	3.4	3.6	4.0	4.2
Toscana	7.7	7.7	7.5	6.9	7.9	8.2	8.3	7.8	7.8	7.6
Umbria	1.4	1.2	1.6	1.3	1.1	1.3	1.6	1.5	1.4	1.6
Lazio	3.3	3.4	3.9	3.8	4.0	4.5	4.8	4.9	4.5	4.1
Campania	7.1	5.4	5.7	5.0	4.7	4.5	5.1	4.7	4.4	4.6
Abruzzo and Molise	1.8	1.4	1.4	1.5	1.2	1.3	1.9	2.4	2.5	2.8
Puglia	3.8	2.7	3.4	3.0	2.5	3.0	3.5	4.1	3.7	4.0
Basilicata	0.6	0.4	0.4	0.5	0.3	0.4	0.4	0.5	0.5	0.7
Calabria	2.0	1.5	1.5	1.5	1.1	0.8	0.8	0.9	0.7	0.8
Sicilia	4.7	4.4	3.7	3.5	3.0	2.7	2.8	2.8	2.4	2.4
Sardegna	1.0	0.9	1.1	0.9	0.8	0.9	0.8	1.3	1.1	1.1
Total	100	100	100	100	100	100	100	100	100	100

Source: Cainelli and Stampini [2002: Table 5]; Giannetti and Vasta [2005: Table 2.4].

Table 2.16. The secondary sector

(*a*) Shares on total workforce of the secondary sector

	1911	1927	1937	1951	1961	1971	1981	1991	1996
Other categories	2.01	7.24	3.82	0.70	0.80	0.56	0.48	-	-
Manufacturing	89.97	78.05	78.73	82.22	79.98	81.64	80.21	77.07	75.88
Mining	2.71	2.99	3.08	3.09	2.02	1.23	0.74	0.72	0.68
Utilities	1.15	1.67	0.97	1.91	2.03	2.38	2.34	2.52	2.48
Construction	4.15	10.04	13.40	12.08	15.17	14.19	16.23	19.70	20.97

(*b*) Share of units with motive power

	1927	1937	1951	1961	1971	1981*
Other categories	6.72	3.81	26.67	15.29	20.11	42.53
Manufacturing	22.96	16.78	31.63	47.86	57.60	66.81
Mining	17.67	8.59	31.10	57.45	62.23	41.53
Utilities	61.70	37.52	71.58	52.77	53.09	36.25
Construction	5.95	6.12	21.01	38.86	31.13	27.78
Total	20.31	15.17	31.43	46.60	52.03	53.38

Legend: * only electrical engines.

(*c*) HP/worker

	1911	1927	1937	1951	1961	1971	1981*
Other categories	0.53	0.04	0.32	2.23	3.44	3.75	3.23
Manufacturing	0.49	1.22	1.61	2.85	4.26	6.32	6.21
Mining	0.30	1.18	1.27	3.49	6.78	10.91	11.44
Utilities	2.90	7.98	3.84	15.72	27.31	18.25	20.96
Construction	0.15	0.33	0.29	0.55	0.78	0.63	0.76
Total	0.50	1.16	1.39	2.84	4.24	5.84	5.69

Legend: * only electrical engines.

(*d*) Workers/plant

	1911	1927	1937	1951	1961	1971	1981	1991	1996
Other categories	4.17	4.21	2.11	3.60	3.39	1.96	4.58	-	-
Manufacturing	5.81	5.66	4.04	5.61	7.55	8.72	9.06	8.80	8.21
Mining	13.35	17.09	6.98	15.88	15.42	13.00	8.17	8.47	7.30
Utilities	12.20	17.91	4.56	10.97	13.72	18.29	20.35	28.59	26.55
Construction	11.68	8.69	9.63	14.01	14.13	6.73	3.62	3.43	2.86
Total	6.02	5.90	4.28	6.22	8.20	8.34	7.33	6.82	5.97

Table 2.16. (cont.)

(*e*) Shares of plants by size-class

(*e.1*) less than 10 workers

	1911	1927	1937	1951	1961	1971	1981	1991	1996
Other categories	46.11	73.15	64.87	52.15	55.47	73.32	44.19	-	-
Manufacturing	39.62	35.67	35.24	31.86	27.95	23.50	23.43	26.20	26.45
Mining	24.02	14.29	27.10	15.24	20.48	24.08	32.12	31.12	33.14
Utilities	21.55	15.89	18.49	21.02	18.90	14.82	10.19	7.53	7.18
Construction	18.78	26.66	18.27	18.23	20.72	38.21	58.18	62.54	69.17
Total	38.25	35.85	33.71	29.68	26.77	25.67	28.93	32.92	34.98

(*e.2*) 10-50 workers

	1927	1937	1951	1961	1971	1981	1991	1996
Other categories	13.10	20.84	24.11	14.03	12.19	27.88	-	-
Manufacturing	14.40	12.34	14.12	18.98	21.15	26.02	31.68	32.90
Mining	22.31	16.99	18.88	31.42	34.97	38.51	36.17	37.14
Utilities	27.32	11.61	27.65	27.28	29.43	23.86	22.94	23.67
Construction	29.39	21.77	37.60	44.71	38.57	30.30	27.45	23.71
Total	16.15	14.06	17.35	23.22	23.87	26.76	30.66	30.77

(*e.3*) 51-100 workers

	1927	1937	1951	1961	1971	1981	1991
Other categories	5.25	2.50	6.65	5.14	4.23	8.07	-
Manufacturing	7.54	8.11	8.01	10.14	10.33	10.05	10.00
Mining	8.87	8.41	9.73	10.29	11.90	7.90	6.67
Utilities	13.28	5.30	17.28	17.86	14.56	15.11	16.50
Construction	13.33	12.09	17.35	16.50	9.92	5.77	4.90
Total	8.08	8.40	9.32	11.20	10.35	9.44	9.14

(*e.4*) 101-500 workers

	1927	1937	1951	1961	1971	1981	1991	1996*
Other categories	6.44	5.33	14.43	14.06	6.15	13.24	-	-
Manufacturing	22.01	20.78	20.47	21.52	22.32	20.98	19.22	29.12
Mining	28.13	22.83	23.02	23.09	17.61	15.88	10.59	10.35
Utilities	29.95	23.51	23.62	28.67	34.42	36.87	37.68	53.87
Construction	22.98	23.87	22.61	16.20	11.33	5.11	4.81	6.67
Total	21.57	20.68	20.82	20.82	20.89	18.70	16.78	24.90

Legend: * included in the higher size-class.

Table 2.16. (cont.)

(*e.5*) more than 500 workers

	1927	1937	1951	1961	1971	1981	1991	1996
Other categories	2.06	6.46	2.66	11.30	4.11	6.65	0.00	0.00
Manufacturing	20.38	23.54	25.55	21.41	22.69	19.53	12.90	11.53
Mining	26.39	24.68	33.13	14.71	11.44	5.59	15.45	19.37
Utilities	13.56	41.09	10.43	7.30	6.77	13.97	15.35	15.27
Construction	7.63	24.00	4.21	1.87	1.97	0.64	0.30	0.45
Total	18.35	23.15	22.84	17.99	19.23	16.17	10.50	9.35

(*f*) Workers/plant, plants with more than 10 workers

	1911	1927	1937	1951	1961	1971	1981	1991	1996
Other categories	58.97	34.07	27.62	37.48	52.38	35.38	32.01	-	-
Manufacturing	70.30	70.66	76.60	77.71	63.19	57.40	46.04	37.78	36.49
Mining	56.96	65.98	70.13	72.03	43.67	34.47	27.97	31.29	30.05
Utilities	62.14	54.66	106.76	48.71	49.29	47.74	60.49	64.32	62.11
Construction	51.78	43.27	50.53	37.62	33.59	26.50	22.03	22.02	20.39
Total	68.08	64.24	68.36	66.63	54.46	49.94	41.73	35.44	34.25

(*g*) Shares of males on total workforce

	1911	1927	1937	1951	1961	1971	1981	1991
Other categories	81.78	67.89	82.83	84.52	83.11	84.56	73.10	-
Manufacturing	69.05	65.78	66.91	68.39	70.93	72.06	70.25	69.77
Mining	95.54	97.21	97.66	97.07	97.25	95.96	95.10	90.80
Utilities	98.47	95.20	99.35	93.23	93.83	93.45	92.27	88.89
Construction	98.09	98.64	99.45	98.19	98.72	98.00	96.29	93.09
Total	71.64	70.66	73.14	73.46	76.24	76.61	75.19	75.00

(*h*) Share of white collars on total workforce

	1911	1927	1937	1951	1961	1971	1981	1991
Other categories	34.03	49.64	33.29	35.13	67.35	72.41	63.55	-
Manufacturing	27.42	24.03	28.65	38.83	39.37	36.62	41.22	43.61
Mining	14.67	9.48	19.92	17.21	19.25	26.36	29.04	39.77
Utilities	20.43	28.10	16.09	27.54	39.53	42.67	43.96	53.57
Construction	14.11	17.43	12.80	18.40	18.35	27.99	46.53	51.44
Total	26.58	24.85	26.31	35.45	36.00	35.61	42.16	45.38

Table 2.16. (cont.)

(*i*) Share of skilled workers on blue collars

	1951	1961	1971	1981
Other categories	64.20	62.31	60.68	63.44
Manufacturing	60.50	56.88	61.12	65.40
Mining	39.26	47.41	63.99	70.52
Utilities	57.73	60.23	81.00	90.26
Construction	36.93	42.47	53.63	60.76
Total	56.09	53.95	60.39	64.67

(*j*) Average number of hours

	1937	1951	1961	1971
Other categories	168	1,975	2,048	2,111
Manufacturing	1,619	1,996	1,916	2,036
Mining	1,653	1,811	1,735	1,799
Utilities	1,977	2,428	2,177	1,899
Construction	1,442	1,314	1,328	1,638
Total	1,546	1,893	1,803	1,967

(*k*) Seasonality index

	1937	1951	1961	1971
Other categories	11.93	45.45	2.19	2.37
Manufacturing	2.32	2.98	2.92	2.40
Mining	5.32	3.43	3.09	3.12
Utilities	0.00	1.23	1.11	2.18
Construction	0.04	11.17	9.40	4.99
Total	2.01	3.22	3.05	2.73

3. The concentration of the industrial structure (1913–1971)

Renato Giannetti and Michelangelo Vasta

3.1. Introduction

In Italian economic historiography the topic of industrial concentration has been tackled by focusing on crucial problems for national economic development, such as *relative backwardness* or *monopolistic capitalism*. In the former case, the precocious presence of a small number of large firms is simply the effect of the *relative backwardness* of the country which, in order to catch the economic growth *train* at the end of the 19th century, was compelled to adopt the technology of leading countries (iron and steel, electricity, chemical, etc.) together with the forms of organization (large enterprise) necessary to utilize it in the appropriate way [Amatori 1997]. In the latter case, the presence of few large firms is attributed to the influence of *financial capital*, which in Italy too, takes the form of the large monopolistic enterprise. The oldest and most radical versions of this view can be found in the work of Grifone [1945]. Moreover, it has a solid and lasting tradition exemplified in the work of Bigazzi [1990], Barca [1996] and, in a different theoretical context, in Rossi and Toniolo [1992]. According to this approach the Italian market was too small and could only support a few enterprises, of the minimum efficiency size, in each of the new sectors. For this reason, as from the end of the 19th century, it became entangled in a network of relationships between banks, the State and large enterprises. This network reached its apex in the 1930s, when the economic crises and the ensuing economic policies - bank bailouts and the foundation of the IRI - favored a further concentration of economic power in the hands of the large firms. In both cases the compound effect of *backwardness*, of the monopolistic character of the Italian system of enterprises - organized in groups - and its plotting with political power, limited the possibilities of economic growth well beyond Second World War, through a limitation of market size [Sereni 1966] or of innovative capacity [Sylos Labini 1970]. This last effect, however, is refuted, especially during the 1930s and the 1960s, by a less critical approach toward large enterprise and state intervention [de Cecco 2000; Petri 2002].

Before the 1970s little attention was paid to the small enterprise, which, however, in the long term, represents the vast majority of Italian firms. In this direction Cafagna [1989] and Federico [1994b] have, for example, emphasized the *du-*

The present work was set up by both authors, and Sects. 3.1 and 3.4 were actually co-written. Section 3.2 must be attributed to Renato Giannetti and Sect. 3.3 to Michelangelo Vasta. The authors wish to thank Leonardo Bargigli for his valuable research assistance.

alistic character of the Italian industry, underlining, moreover, the dynamic role played by small firms in traditional sectors. These firms have shown themselves capable of making the most of the comparative advantage of a country with a high availability of the labor factor, especially in the first phase of growth and in the 1990s. More recently the *dualistic* interpretation has been reformulated as the presence of medium and small firms capable of making use of, see Proteo, "technological and product niches", without necessarily reaching large sizes [Colli 2002a].

The greater part of historiography is based on qualitative evidence linked to firm case studies or to the study of single critical episodes, while quantitative studies are scarcer, even though a few examples that can be cited as from the 1920s. Vinci [1918] and Saibante [1926, 1934] are among the pioneers of this research tradition, followed by the extensive and controversial study carried out by the Commissione economica alla Costituente [1945-46] and, subsequently, by the analysis carried out by the Parliamentary Inquiry on the limits on competition [Battara 1965]. These studies argue that the high concentration is essentially due to the large market imperfections linked to the presence of dominant groups. Zamagni [1978] follows the same direction - in a study limited to the 1911 censuses - as do Rossi and Toniolo [1992] - for the period 1890-1990 - who argue the presence of a high degree of concentration due to market imperfections, but also to the presence of economies of scale. These results, however, are not confirmed by the only quantitative study, based on the comparison between the census results of 1951 and 1961, carried out halfway through the 1960s by Boni and Gros Pietro [1967]. The latter study evidences the prevalence of small and medium-sized enterprises, low levels of concentration and a large dimensional gap in comparison to the most developed countries. The same conclusions are reached by a comparative study by Phlips [1971] - based on the industrial censuses of various European countries - which confirms the low level of concentration prevalent in the majority of sectors of the Italian industrial system during the years of the *economic miracle*. Traù [1999] obtains similar results for the post-Second World War period. Finally, the conclusions of a study by Giannetti, Federico, and Toninelli [1994] on firms surveyed by the Associazione fra le società italiane per azioni (ASIPA) for the period 1907-1940, head the same way. The results, in fact, show a relatively low level of concentration for the entire period.

This range of interpretations depends on a variety of factors. Firstly, on the heterogeneity of the sources, the basis on which concentration is measured: census data in the case of Boni and Gros Pietro [1967], the number of employees in Zamagni [1978] and Phlips [1971]; elaborations on historical series compiled by Rossi and Toniolo [1992] on national accounting on capital; the ASIPA data - based on corporate capital-used by Vinci [1918], Saibante [1926, 1934], Giannetti, Federico and Toninelli [1994]. Secondly, the variety of indices of concentration used, from the Gini inequality index [Vinci 1918; Saibante, 1926, 1934; Zamagni 1978], to the share of the first 4 firms [Phlips 1971; Boni and Gros Pietro 1967], to the Herfindhal index [Giannetti, Federico and Toninelli 1994], to the greater or lesser presence of groups [Battara 1965; Barca 1996]. Finally, the periods studied, the sectors considered and the criteria adopted for their classification vary from one study to the other. As far as the choice of the variable used to measure concentration is concerned, historical studies generally use capital, simply because it is the easiest measure to find, while specialist studies on concentration use employees, total assets, turnover and value added. The latter is considered the most appropriate variable by the literature, because it is the only one that permits an undistorted comparison of the sectoral membership of firms. This type of distortion does, however, occur if the turnover and total assets are used. In the first case, for example, a firm that is subdivided into a production division and a commercial division which buys the former's product to resell it, appears in the sample as two firms of a similar size, while in terms of value added the difference is to the net advantage of the former. On the contrary, if these two firms were to merge, their size would double, while the resultant value added from the merger would be decidedly much smaller in size. In the case of the assets, the greatest bias effect lies in the changes in accounting systems and the taxation of accountancy items over time, as in the case of amortization. Assets are nevertheless considered a reliable variable and one of the best among those available in historical perspective [White 2002].

The choice of the concentration proxy poses fewer problems. A large variety of measures can be found in the literature. The two most frequently used being the concentration index C4, which measures the percentage quota of the observed variable for the first 4 firms - in this case the assets - and Herfindhal's index represented by the sum of the squares of the quotas of the assets of each firm. The choice between one or the other is not particularly relevant, given that they are closely correlated (in our case the average correlation index for the entire period is 0.85). In the text that follows, for briefness' sake, we will analyze only the C4 values.

The data used in this Chap. are referred to the manufacturing firms included in the Imita.db, for seven benchmark years and classified by sector of economic activity according to the ATECO-ISTAT 1991 classification. The availability of this database has enabled us to conduct an analysis of concentration which satisfies four very important requisites for overcoming the limits of existent studies: (i) the analysis was conducted for a sufficiently long period (1913-1971); (ii) it makes use of a homogenous source (the *Notizie Statistiche*), classified according to a standard criterion (ATECO-ISTAT classification); (iii) it uses a size variable (total assets) that is considered satisfactory; (iv) a concentration index (the C4) generally accepted in economic literature as particularly reliable. On the other hand, the choice of restricting the survey to those enterprises established as joint-stock companies, and with the threshold adopted in the source (see Appendix), creates some limits to the analysis. Firms falling below this threshold even though they are established as joint-stock companies, are excluded; but above all, the other forms of companies (limited partnerships, *de facto* companies, limited liability companies, etc.) that represent an ample, though unfortunately not measurable quota, of Italian firms are also excluded. It should also be noted that this set includes a good number of medium-large firms not established as joint-stock companies that are present in relevant numbers at least until halfway through the 1950s (see Chap. 7).

This Chap. is organized as follows. In Sect. 3.2 we reconstruct a picture of the concentration of Italian firms for seven benchmark years (1913, 1921, 1927, 1936, 1952, 1960, 1971) within the period considered, chosen so as to be coincident or close to the census surveys described in Chap. 2. In Sect. 3.3 we describe the role of the *group form* as a factor in co-determining market concentration and we present new estimates for this peculiar aspect of Italian capitalism. The results attained are used as the basis for a few conjectures on some of the fundamental characteristics of the Italian system of enterprises (the relatively low concentration and the role of groups, which substantially changes its values) that can contribute to explaining the descriptive categories which pervade the more recent historical and corporate literature, such as *dwarfism*, *technological niches* or *market niches*, *local systems*, the competitive *medium enterprise* that do not want to grow, and *fourth capitalism*. Lastly, Sect. 3.4 contains some concluding remarks.

3.2. Levels of industrial concentration

One of the crucial themes of the historiographical debate on Italian industry is that of the monopolistic power of a few large firms such as, for example, Montecatini (Montedison from 1965) and FIAT. In order to measure this monopolistic power, and the way in which it has evolved over time, a classification has been built on the basis of a measure of competition. To this purpose a number of classification proposed by industrial economics, which distinguish sectors on the basis of quantitative thresholds for some market representative variable [Shepard 1982; Ratnayake 1999], in our case represented by the total assets, have been adapted to the Italian case. On the basis of these thresholds, industries are classified into three groups: *monopolistic*, *semi-competitive*, *competitive*. A sector is defined as *competitive* if it has a concentration index (C4) below 40 per cent and *semi-competitive* if its value is between 40 per cent and 59 per cent; a concentration index over 59 per cent signals the existence of a *monopolistic* industry with *dominant* firms. It is obviously an arbitrary and approximate definition: in order to establish if a monopoly exists or not, other indicators should also be taken into consideration, for example, barriers to entry and price control through various forms of collusion. On the other hand, given the absence of reliable historical series for the abovementioned variables, the proposed thresholds are essential in order to identify the fundamental trends of concentration in Italian industry.

Before examining the sectoral diachronic values of the concentration index, it is necessary to observe the evolution of aggregate concentration, which can be approximated by the quota of assets covered by the first 10, 50, 100, 200 and 500 firms in the different years (see Table 3.1). The quota of assets covered by the major firms (the first 500, 200 and 100) for each year is rather high, which confirms the strongly flattened character of the distribution of Italian enterprises, with few very large firms and many in smaller sizes (see also Chap. 4).

Table 3.1. Percentage of assets of the first 500-200-100-50-10-4 firms per benchmark year

	1913	1921	1927	1936	1952	1960	1971
First 500 firms	97.0	89.9	82.6	86.7	87.2	83.4	75.2
First 200 firms	75.9	71.9	64.9	72.1	75.1	70.8	62.7
First 100 firms	58.7	58.5	51.9	60.1	64.4	60.8	53.3
First 50 firms	43.2	46.3	39.8	48.2	53.3	50.4	44.5
First 10 firms	18.0	25.6	20.3	24.5	30.5	29.9	27.4
First 4 firms (C4)	10.8	16.8	13.9	14.0	18.7	19.9	20.7

Concentration decreases between 1913 and 1927 (even though there is a relevant exception given that the weight of the first 4, 10 and 50 firms increases between 1913 and 1921, and subsequently decreases); then there is an increase between 1927 and 1952, with reflections on the entire size pyramid; finally there is a rapid decrease in the post-Second World War period, coincidental with the most intense phase of industrial development. The Italian economy's post-War *take-off* is distinguished by a decrease in concentration, which can be explained to the proliferation of entrepreneurial opportunities made possible by the expansion of domestic and international markets. As from 1960 there is, therefore, a strong increase in competition, supported mainly by the entry of new enterprises, such as those in the consumer durables sector during the 1960s, led by a new generation of entrepreneurs such as Borghi for Ignis, Merloni for Ariston, and Zanussi for Rex [Amatori and Colli 1999].

This process of opening up, however, occurs to a much greater extent at the intermediate levels of the size pyramid than at its apex. Figure 3.1 clearly shows how the post-War reduction in concentration gradually decreases in intensity as the number of firms taken into consideration decreases. The Golden age of Italian capitalism is therefore a period in which, due to a combination of factors endogenous and exogenous to the national system, the *proliferation of opportunities* through competition is compatible with the reinforcement of an industrial oligopolistic nucleus.

From an examination of the disaggregated values at a sectoral level of the C4 indicator (see Table 3.2) we can observe that C4 always presents values within conditions of competition in the aggregate of the manufacturing firms, although it shows a growing trend in 1960 and in 1971 coherently with the abovementioned observations. If we observe the preceding trend we note a robust growth between 1913 and 1921 that can be attributed to the effects of the First World War, a subsequent and more modest decrease in the period between the two World Wars, and yet again a robust growth, once again attributable to pre-War preparations and Second World War.

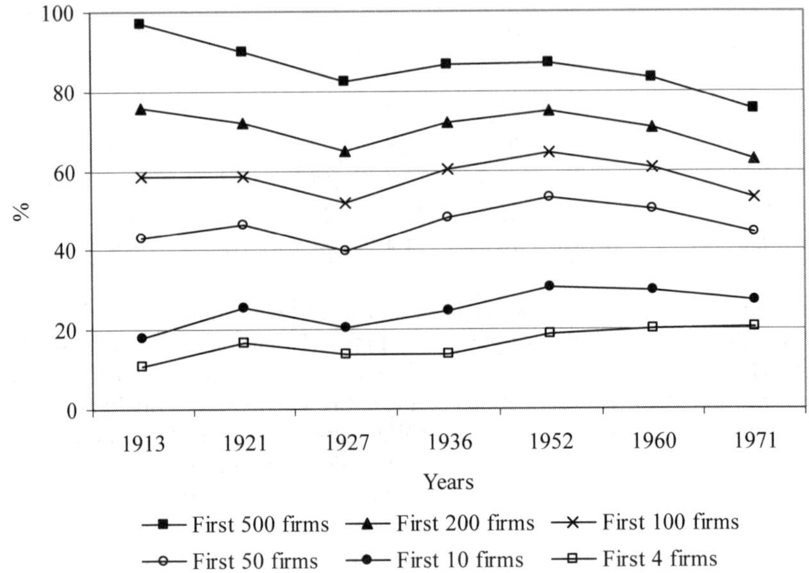

Fig. 3.1. Percentage of assets of the first 500-200-100-50-10-4 firms per benchmark year

However, if we observe the different sectors separately, conditions differ. In particular, the profile of the Italian manufacturing industry does not appear to be very *competitive* on the eve of First World War. In fact 8 sectors out of 14 are *monopolistic* (7) or *semi-competitive* (1). Among these there are also a few *light* sectors such as leather (DC) and wood (DD) or manufacturing n.e.c. (DN) which comprised furniture and other *light* sectors. This apparently implausible result is due to the fact that the only small and medium enterprises taken into consideration were those in the form of joint stock companies while, during that period, the greatest part of the production of consumer goods in the sector was carried out by the other types of small and medium enterprises, while the enterprises surveyed were mainly occupied in the production of intermediate goods. The chemical sector (DG) and the construction of transport equipment sector (DM), which in this phase are still not fully developed, are among the *competitive* sectors. There is no great change in the situation for the period between the two World Wars during which even the abovementioned sectors become *semi-competitive*. It is interesting to note, however, that *monopolistic* conditions give way slightly to *semi-competitive* market conditions: in 1913, 7 sectors are characterized by *monopolistic* conditions, while the number of *monopolistic* sectors is down to 2 in 1921 and in 1927, increasing again to 4 in 1936. On the whole, however, the tendency towards a decrease in competition is present until 1952, when there are 3 *monopolistic* sectors, but 7 *semi-competitive* sectors. Competition increases in 1960 when there are 3 *monopolistic* and 3 *semi-competitive* sectors and also in 1971 when there are only 2 *monopolistic* and 2 *semi-competitive* sectors.

Table 3.2. Concentration (C4) by sectors

Sector	1913	1921	1927	1936	1952	1960	1971
Food products and tobacco (DA)	0.27	0.20	0.17	0.31	0.32	0.24	0.20
Textiles and textile products (DB)	0.15	0.14	0.14	0.15	0.20	0.16	0.13
Leather and leather products (DC)	0.70	0.43	0.43	0.34	0.41	0.37	0.38
Wood and wood products (DD)	0.76	0.49	0.56	0.54	0.43	0.30	0.28
Paper products, publishing and printing (DE)	0.32	0.28	0.28	0.36	0.40	0.26	0.19
Coke and petroleum products (DF)	1.00	0.98	0.82	0.71	0.47	0.44	0.37
Chemicals and chemical products (DG)	0.35	0.36	0.47	0.48	0.58	0.50	0.52
Rubber and plastic products (DH)	1.00	-	0.98	0.97	0.92	0.91	0.62
Other non-metallic products (DI)	0.28	0.34	0.23	0.33	0.40	0.34	0.24
Basic metals and metal products (DJ)	0.51	0.49	0.44	0.46	0.45	0.46	0.47
Machinery and equipment (DK)	0.72	0.88	0.32	0.64	0.28	0.16	0.20
Electrical and optical equipment (DL)	0.67	0.53	0.42	0.35	0.26	0.25	0.27
Transport equipment (DM)	0.33	0.43	0.43	0.53	0.71	0.72	0.70
Manufacturing n.e.c. (DN)	0.73	0.54	0.39	0.61	0.73	0.66	0.33
Manufacturing	*0.11*	*0.17*	*0.14*	*0.14*	*0.19*	*0.20*	*0.21*

Legend:
- (dark shading) *Monopolistic* > 0.59
- (light shading) *Semi-competitive* ≥ 0.40 ≤ 0.59
- (no shading) *Competitive* < 0.40

From the sectoral point of view, the textile sector (DB), the food and tobacco sector (DA), and the paper, publishing and printing sector (DE) consistently remain in the group of *competitive* sectors except in 1952. The sectors with high absolute thresholds for entry and economies of scale have the greatest concentration. The rubber sector (DH) is consistently the most concentrated since 1913, and is made up of only one firm, Pirelli. The same is true for the coke and petroleum sector (DF) which, furthermore, undergoes a constant decrease in concentration over time: it is classified as *monopolistic* between the two World Wars, *semi-competitive* in 1952 and in 1960 and *competitive* in 1971. The chemical sector (DG) is also classified as *competitive* in 1913 and in 1921, after which it is in the *semi-competitive* group. The basic metals and metal products sector (DJ) also belongs to this group and can be constantly classified as *semi-competitive* The only sector whose degree of monopoly shows a constant growth is that of transport equipment (DM), which is classified as *competitive* in 1913, *semi-competitive* between the two World Wars, and *monopolistic* as from 1952, the main firm being the FIAT. This evolution contrasts with the growth in competition experienced by the machinery and equipment (DK), and the electrical and optical equipment (DL) sectors, which are *monopolistic* at the beginning of the period but subsequently become *competitive*.

The results examined above undoubtedly supply relevant information but it raises also some relevant questions. The choice of the level of sectoral detail is, for example, debatable. According to modern industrial economics, in order to measure the degree of market competition correctly it is necessary to accurately define the boundaries of the market by considering advertising costs and the specific characteristics of the technologies employed [Sutton 1998]. In order to define the market and its dynamics, other approaches refer to the interaction between the various subjects (producers, clients and suppliers) that determine its evolution [Saviotti and Krafft 2004]. The information necessary for such a detailed level of analysis is not however, available to historical research at the necessary level of completeness. On the other hand the variation of the values of the concentration index in relation to the greater or lesser level of sectoral disaggregation can give useful indications on the position of firms in various activities, highlighting, for example, the existence of possible niche strategies.

Table 3.3 shows the share of *competitive* sectors for the three main levels of detail of the ATECO-ISTAT classification. For all the years this percentage decreases drastically with the increase in the level of detail: for example in 1971, 71.4 per cent of the subsections are *competitive*, but only 25.3 per cent of the groups of economic activity that make up the subsections are in the same condition.

Table 3.3. Percentage of *competitive* sectors per level of sectoral disaggregation

Disaggregation	1913	1921	1927	1936	1952	1960	1971
Subsections (14 sectors)	42.9	38.5	42.9	42.9	28.6	57.1	71.4
Divisions (23 sectors)	20.0	31.6	36.4	27.3	18.2	50.0	60.9
Groups (99 sectors)	2.6	6.6	11.1	6.7	9.4	13.5	25.3

The first observation deriving from this result is that the level of concentration moves in the opposite direction to the number of active firms in a given sector. This simple interpretation is confirmed by the trend of the index in the post-Second War period, namely the period in which there is a broadening of the Italian manufacturing sectoral matrix [Bianchi 2002; Pellegrini 2003].

From the data in Table 3.2 it could deduced for example, that the machinery and equipment sector (DK) and the electrical and optical equipment sector (DL) showed a tendency towards greater competition in the post-Second World War period corresponding to an intense phase of growth in those sectors. In reality, however, examining these sectors at a greater level of detail (see Table 3.4), the situation changes radically: in the electrical and optical equipment sector (DL) *monopolistic* divisions continue to predominate until recent years, in the machinery and equipment sector (DK) too, growth in competition is delayed as can be seen by the fact that, in 1960, 3 out of 5 groups do not show *competitive* conditions.

Table 3.4. Concentration (C4) for groups of activity in machinery and equipment (DK) and electrical and optical equipment (DL) sectors

	Sector	1936	1952	1960	1971
	Machinery for the production of mech. power (29.1)	0.88	0.54	0.39	0.46
	Other general purpose machinery (29.2)	0.87	0.60	0.38	0.25
DK	Agricultural and forestry machinery (29.3)	0.99	0.79	0.62	0.59
	Manufacture of machine-tools (29.4)	0.73	0.59	0.46	0.39
	Other special purpose machinery (29.5)	0.71	0.58	0.38	0.25
	Office machinery and computers (30.0)	1.00	0.99	0.95	0.91
	Electric motors, generators and transformers (31.1)	0.64	0.94	0.63	0.75
	Electricity distribution and control apparatus (31.2)	1.00	0.60	0.58	0.52
	Manufacture of insulated wire and cable (31.3)	0.90	0.76	0.81	0.66
	Accumulators, primary cells and batteries (31.4)	0.91	0.87	0.80	0.90
	Lighting equipment and electric lamps (31.5)	0.95	0.80	0.87	0.86
	Manufacture of electrical equipment n.e.c. (31.6)	1.00	0.86	0.86	0.70
DL	Electronic valves, tubes and other components (32.1)	1.00	0.90	0.75	0.61
	TV and radio transmitters, apparatus for line tel. (32.2)	0.97	0.76	0.65	0.67
	Television and radio receivers (32.3)	0.97	0.85	0.57	0.68
	Medical and surgical equipment (33.1)	1.00	0.85	0.91	0.77
	Instruments for measuring, checking and testing (33.2)	0.54	0.74	0.66	0.47
	Industrial process control equipment (33.3)	-	1.00	1.00	1.00
	Optical instruments and photographic equipment (33.4)	1.00	0.84	0.89	0.83
	Manufacture of watches and clocks (33.5)	1.00	1.00	0.98	0.93

Legend:

Monopolistic > 0.59
Semi-competitive ≥ 0.40 ≤ 0.59
Competitive < 0.40

In the light of these observations, we could advance the conjecture that the observed result can be interpreted as a confirmation of the greater level of development reached by the mechanical sector (DK) as compared to the electrical equipment sector (DL), which never experienced a real *take-off* phase. By extension, the fact that, even in recent years, only a minority of groups in the manufacturing sector are *competitive*, highlights the structural frailty of the Italian industrial system, whose sectoral matrix is made up of aggregates consisting of few firms. A rather interesting consequence of this line of thought is that in this type of industrial structure the existence of a niche does not depend on an active strategy of leading firms within particular segments of activity, but more simply, on the market's inability to reach the critical size sufficient and necessary to stimulate, not only lively demographic firm dynamics, but also to favor processes of growth and organizational consolidation.

3.3. The role of groups

The diffusion of industrial groups is a common feature shared by Italy, Europe and Japan, where the integrated large enterprise is not the prevalent organizational form, as is the case for the US [Chandler 1962]. Consequently, Italian historiography has attributed this factor an important role in determining the *effective* concentration of the industrial system. According to the prevalent opinion the reconstruction of the map of industrial groups permits a more adequate treatment of the topic of concentration [Momigliano 1975; Battilossi 1999], starting from the implicit hypothesis that the introduction of this level of analysis leads to a rise in concentration indices [Battara 1965], even though this effect, according to some, does not necessarily mean an increase in market power [Encaoua and Jacquemin 1982]. For this reason, notwithstanding the fact that the role of groups in Italian industry is examined in more detail in Chap. 6, the examination of the results of the relationship between groups and concentration is appropriate here. Due to the lack of information on the ownership composition of firms in the Imita.db, in order to estimate the effects of groups on the level of concentration of Italian industry we calculated the C4 index in each sector *consolidating* assets for those firms in the sector reciprocally linked by having the same administrator at the head of each (for the technical details see Sect. 6.6). This measure should offer a good approximation of the real concentration both of the single sectors and of the industry as a whole, in the hypothesis that the links between firms generated by the shared administrators constitute a good proxy for the ownership structure of industrial groups. In our case this hypothesis is not directly verifiable, but must be assumed *a priori*, due to the abovementioned lack of data on ownership composition. On the other hand, an alternative source, capable of directly reconstructing the ownership structure of such a large sample of firms and over such an extended period of time, simply does not exist; nor can the studies conducted on limited samples unrepresentative of the entire national industry be of any use.

Notwithstanding its limits, the analysis presented here is therefore based on the only reconstruction currently possible of the ownership structure of Italian industrial groups during the 20th century. The proposed measure is from now on denoted by the term *consolidated*: this in order to distinguish it on the one hand from concentration calculated on the basis of the articulation of ownership structure (which is unknown to us), and on the other hand from that already calculated for the single firms (see Table 3.2).

The results shown in Table 3.5 considerably modify the setting described previously, confirming the hypothesis that, given the importance of groups in Italian industry, the *consolidated* concentration diverges greatly from that observed at the firm level. The overall concentration of the manufacturing industry, in fact, increases considerably for all the years taken into consideration. In particular, 1960, the year with the greatest increase (+77.2 per cent), also presents the highest *consolidated* concentration (0.35) in comparison with the other benchmark years. The particularity of the period of post-War economic expansion, with a strong growth in the concentration of industry due to the groups formula, is therefore apparent.

The spread registered in 1971 in this regard is striking: in this year not only is the impact of the groups less in comparison to all the others (+ 12 per cent), but the *consolidated* concentration undergoes a real slump as compared to 1960 (- 34 per cent).

The introduction of groups also radically changes the overall picture of the competitiveness of the single industrial sectors. In particular, *competitive* sectors decrease greatly in number during the post-Second World War period, with only textiles (DB), paper, publishing and printing (DE), and machinery and equipment (DK) remaining. Consequently, *monopolistic* and *semi-competitive* sectors prevail: in the former sectors we find those prevalently linked to the Second Industrial Revolution - petroleum (DF), chemicals (DG), rubber and plastic (DH), electrical equipment (DL), transport (DM) - and to the economy of scale - basic metals and metal products (DJ); among the latter we find the majority of traditional sectors - food (DA), leather (DC), wood (DD), non-metallic products (DI). For some of the traditional sectors, such as food (DA) and non-metallic products (DI), this tendency is due to the weight in the sample of firms specializing in economies of scale activities - such as the production respectively of sugar and cement -, which show a high propensity for forming cartels with firms in the same sector. In the period considered, the sugar sector, for example, had state-controlled prices and collusive practices were therefore largely diffused [Tonizzi 2001].

Table 3.5. Index of *consolidated* concentration (C4) by sectors (1913-1971)

Sector	1913	1921	1927	1936	1952	1960	1971
Food products and tobacco (DA)	0.49	0.39	0.39	0.44	0.42	0.38	0.30
Textiles and textile products (DB)	0.22	0.23	0.33	0.28	0.26	0.44	0.27
Leather and leather products (DC)	0.66	0.50	0.54	0.47	0.47	0.55	0.49
Wood and wood products (DD)	0.81	0.49	0.53	0.57	0.47	0.48	0.35
Paper products, publishing and printing (DE)	0.31	0.34	0.31	0.39	0.40	0.63	0.25
Coke and petroleum products (DF)	1.00	0.98	0.62	0.84	0.65	0.91	0.62
Chemicals and chemical products (DG)	0.41	0.61	0.53	0.66	0.71	0.88	0.64
Rubber and plastic products (DH)	1.00		0.97	0.97	0.92	0.96	0.63
Other non-metallic products (DI)	0.30	0.44	0.45	0.61	0.54	0.76	0.34
Basic metals and metal products (DJ)	0.68	0.71	0.66	0.64	0.62	0.79	0.49
Machinery and equipment (DK)	0.81	0.88	0.37	0.65	0.28	0.28	0.30
Electrical and optical equipment (DL)	0.60	0.81	0.42	0.35	0.47	0.67	0.36
Transport equipment (DM)	0.37	0.55	0.60	0.72	0.73	0.85	0.80
Manufacturing n.e.c. (DN)	0.76	053	0.39	0.61	0.72	0.71	0.33
Manufacturing	*0.19*	*0.24*	*0.20*	*0.20*	*0.23*	*0.35*	*0.23*

Legend:

Monopolistic > 0.59

Semi-competitive ≥ 0.40 ≤ 0.59

Competitive < 0.40

Finally, it is interesting to note that the effect of the introduction of groups on concentration is greater primarily in the traditional sectors, and in particular on textiles (DB), paper, publishing and printing (DE) and non-metallic products (DI). The group form is therefore not exclusively linked to the necessity to strengthen the vertical integration between firms, in the context of the *technological regime* of the Second Industrial Revolution, but represents a transversal trait of Italian capitalism, which also has a relevant impact on the most *competitive* traditional sectors, such as textiles, and that also depends on legislative and institutional factors, particularly those connected to company form [Marchetti 1997; Teti 1999]. The Italian regulation of firms governance is in fact characterized by a great delay in the introduction of the fundamental principles of financial transparency for groups (an example: the obligation to keep group balance sheets was only introduced into Italian law in 1994), which has favored the diffusion of this form for purposes different than the mere search for a greater organizational efficiency.

3.4. Conclusions

Concentration values in the aggregate of Italian manufacturing firms consistently show values well within the conditions of competitiveness, while growing in 1960 and 1971. If we observe the preceding trend, we note a robust increase between 1913 and 1921, which can be attributed to the effects of First World War, a successive and more modest reduction in the period between the two World Wars, and once again robust increase, yet again due to the preparation for War and Second World War.

Disaggregating at the sectoral level we can observe how the traditional sectors consistently remain within the *competitive* group of sectors excepting in 1952. The sectors having the greatest barriers to entry and economies of scale show the greatest concentration, for example, rubber and plastic products (DH), coke and petroleum products (DF) and chemicals (DG) which is classified as *competitive* until 1921, and subsequently classified as *semi-competitive*. The only sector which shows increasing levels of concentration is that of transport (DM) which is classified as *competitive* in 1913, *semi-competitive* between the two Wars, and *monopolistic* as from 1952, constantly under the leadership of the main firm, the FIAT. This evolution contrasts with the growth in competition in the machinery and equipment (DK) and electrical and optical equipment (DL) sectors.

The level of concentration moves in the inverse direction to the number of firms active in a specific sector. When we move to a finer level of disaggregation, for example, lower levels of competition emerge, which highlight the structural frailty of the Italian industrial apparatus, whose sectoral production matrix is made up of sectors including relatively few firms. It is therefore evident that the existence of niches does not depend on any active strategy carried out by leading firms within particular segments of activity, but, more simply, from the market's inability to reach the critical size necessary to stimulate demographic dynamics and promote processes of growth and organizational improvement.

As far as the relationship between groups and levels of concentration is concerned, two comments can be made. Firstly, the introduction of the group variable profoundly changes the picture of the competitive structure, both at the aggregate level and at the sectoral level. In particular, *competitive* sectors diminish greatly, while the *monopolistic* and *semi-competitive* sectors prevail; amongst these we find both those sectors linked to the *technological regime* of the Second Industrial Revolution, as also the majority of the traditional sectors.

Secondly, this generalized increase in the levels of concentration leads to the observation that the group form is not exclusively tied to the necessity for strengthening vertical integration between firms but rather represents a transversal and long-term trait of Italian capitalism. This is probably due to legal and institutional factors, particularly those linked to governance rules, which has favored the diffusion of this form for purposes other than the mere search for a greater organizational efficiency.

4. The demography of manufacturing firms (1911–1971)

Renato Giannetti and Margherita Velucchi

4.1. Introduction

As historiography has amply stressed, the size distribution of Italian firms is distinguished, in much greater measure than for other industrialized countries, by the following long-term characteristic: it is extremely skewed to the right, or rather, almost all the firms belong to the smallest size class of the observed distribution, as is evident from the graphs below which represent observed and normal distributions for the benchmark years (see Fig. 4.1).

A similar invariance in size distribution is not particularly satisfactory in historical perspective, in a century that has seen such great changes in the country's industrial structure, and in the technology and organization of firms. In particular, the characterization of the long-term Italian manufacturing firm model as small and medium seems inadequate. With the above in mind, in the following Sects., we will attempt to reconstruct the dynamics leading to the peculiar situation that emerges from the static representation. To this end in Sect. 4.2 we will describe the demography of the Italian firms focusing on the entry and exit of firms and on the *surviving* firms in the four phases of the Italian economic history: 1911-1920; 1921-1936; 1950-1963 and 1964-1971 (Sect. 4.2.1). In Sect. 4.2.2 we focus on a special category of firms, the *leaping frogs*, which are the firms growing in size very fast inside any phase. In Sect. 4.3 we try to explain the causes of the original demography of Italian firms according to a model which explains it considering variables as technology and the life cycle of sectors. Section 4.4 contains some concluding remarks.

4.2. The size distribution and mobility of firms

Usually, to achieve a *more lively* representation of the size distribution the procedure is to divide firms into progressive size classes (generally geometrical). However if, as in our case, we also consider the mobility of firms, the above criterion has important distorting effects, because it renders the size distribution asymmetric. For example, in the hypothesis of a geometric definition with base 2 of the classes, there is a 50 per cent decrease in growth in moving from a higher class to a lower class, whereas a 100 per cent growth rate is necessary to climb to a higher class.

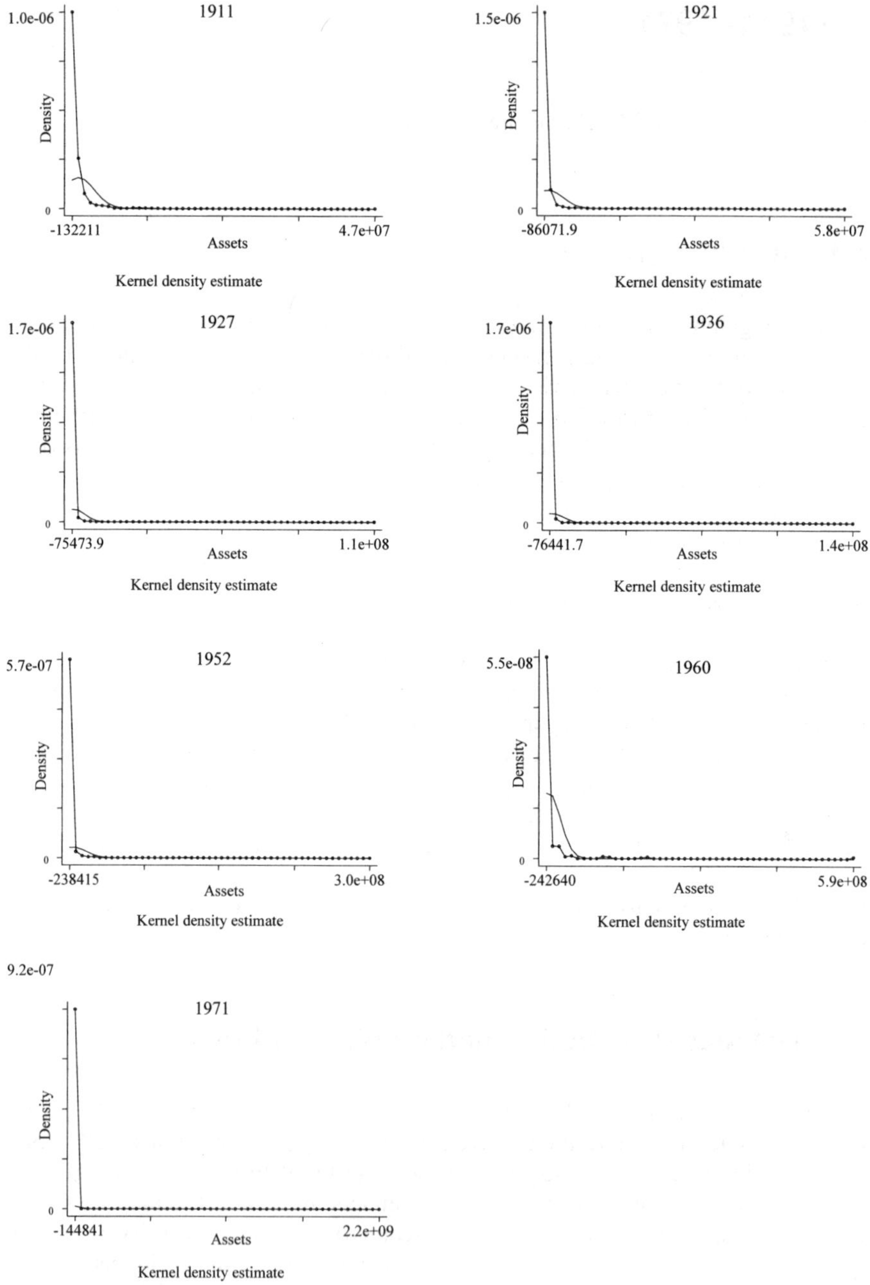

Fig. 4.1. The size distribution of firms for the benchmark years (1911-1971)

To overcome these inconveniences we proceeded to construct classes according to the Fractals Markov chains method which has two advantages over traditional methods: it allows the definition of classes (in this case 8), so as to avoid problems deriving from distribution asymmetry and from the adoption of *ad hoc* classifications, and it is centered on mobility rather than on distribution.

4.2.1. Survival and mobility

In order to observe the dynamics of surviving firms, we adopted a breakdown into periods: the period from 1911-1920, in which Italian industry underwent great transformations due to First World War; 1921-1936, the Fascist period; 1950-1963, the first, most lively part for Italy, of the post-War Golden age; 1964-1971, the period characterized by a decrease in growth and *missed opportunities* [Salvati 2000]. In the last column on the right of Table 4.1, we can observe how the upward mobility of surviving companies was restricted to the first three classes over the entire time span examined (1911-1971), while over 11 per cent remained in their initial class. This result is consistent with the hypothesis of a firm dynamic in which mobility does not follow a life-cycle type path, with a successful firm being born and growing steadily through the various consecutive size classes. Table 4.1, instead, depicts the *successful* Italian firm as one that grows during the first phases, then slows down, and stops short of reaching the higher classes.

Table 4.1. Survival and mobility of firms by phase

	1911-1920	1921-1936	1950-1963	1964-1971	1911-1971
Surviving firms	306	445	1,020	2,500	117
Passage from one class to another (%):					
+1	3.27	24.72	21.57	34.68	24.79
+2	0.98	14.38	28.53	15.24	11.97
+3	0.00	4.27	18.24	4.72	18.80
+4	0.00	2.02	12.06	1.24	11.97
+5	0.00	0.45	3.92	0.44	5.98
+6	0.00	0.00	1.67	0.48	5.98
+7	0.00	0.00	0.20	0.12	0.85
0	26.47	48.99	12.65	36.84	11.11
-1	41.83	4.04	0.88	5.32	6.84
-2	18.30	0.67	0.29	0.60	1.71
-3	7.84	0.45	0.00	0.20	0.00
-4	1.31	0.00	0.00	0.12	0.00
-5	0.00	0.00	0.00	0.00	0.00
-6	0.00	0.00	0.00	0.00	0.00
-7	0.00	0.00	0.00	0.00	0.00

The period that registers the highest growth rate is that from 1950-1963 which shows a significant mobility, in some cases even through four classes, while the lowest growth rate occurs during the first period. In fact, over 60 per cent of the surviving firms drop one or two classes, an obvious indication of the difficulties caused by First World War. The period with the greatest stability (followed by that from 1964-1971) is the one between the two World Wars, during which 50 per cent of the firms remain in their original class. Thus, an evident dependence of size mobility on cyclic dynamics emerges, with a greater mobility during the phases of greater growth. In the Golden age (1950-1963 and 1964-1971) the majority of firms grow in size, while size mobility is lower in downwardly mobile firms (1911-1920 and 1921-1936).

4.2.2. The *leaping frogs*

While the description of surviving firms is consistent with a system characterized by the limited mobility of permanent companies, the profile of the more mobile firms, experiencing 6 or 7 passages of class between the beginning and the end of the period (see Table 4.2).

The first period (1911-1920) shows a very low mobility of firms, only a single firm grows fast (Bacini e Scali Napoletani) in the transport sector. Excluding this first, poorly significant period, the second one (1921-1936) consists of 8 firms belonging to 6 different sectors; the highest number of firms showing the greatest growth can be found in the 1950-1963 period (64 firms) involving 18 sectors.

The period 1964-1971 points out, instead, a decrease in mobility with respect to the previous one: only 24 firms show significant passage of classes, involving 14 different sectors. As to the sectors of activity, the *leaping frogs* are relatively concentrated in high-tech sectors. In the period 1921-1936 there are two transport companies (Moto Guzzi and Società Anonima Airone), while in the period 1950-1963, 13 chemical companies show the highest growth rate like ABET Braidese Estratti Tannici, Antibiotici Lepetit, Cilag Italiana, Azienda Lavorazione Colori Resine ed Affini (ALCREA).

The *leaping frogs* in the final period are three chemical companies (Ajinomoto Insud, Imperial Chemical Industries Italia, Lepetit Sud), four mechanical companies (Macchine e Accessori per l'Industria Grafica Macchingraf, Coster Tecnologie Speciali, F.lli Zanasi, Zanussi Grandi Impianti) and four transport companies (Cantiere Navale Luigi Orlando, Elicotteri Meridionali, Ferrosud and Valeo). Growing fast, however, does not mean stability. In fact, none of the most dynamic firms rank among the most mobile firms over the entire period, assessing the difficulty for the most dynamic firms in maintaining a position attained very quickly. For example, very often the *leaping frogs* in a period become smaller during the next one: Aster, Apice, Cotonificio G. Oliva & C., Electrolux, Bacini e Scali Napoletani; and often they die[1]: Filande e Tessiture Costa, Riseria Italiana, Techint, Cementi Portland, Cotonificio Udinese, Società Ceramica Industriale Cagliari (SCIC).

[1] In this context, the term is referred both to mergers and acquisitions (changes in the ownership of the firm) and to real exit from the market.

Table 4.2. *Leaping frogs* by phase

Company	Sector	Class at the beginning of period	Class at the end of period	Passage of class
(a) 1911-1920				
Bacini e Scali Napoletani	35	1	7	6
(b) 1921-1936				
Società Anonima Airone	35	1	7	6
Cotonificio Udinese	17	1	7	6
Società Anonima Egidio Galbani	15	2	8	6
Industria Nazionale Surrogati di Caffè Frank	15	2	8	6
Moto Guzzi	35	1	7	6
Accumulatori Scaini	31	1	7	6
SCIC Società Ceramica Industriale Cagliari	26	1	7	6
UTET Unione Tipografico Editrice Torinese	22	1	7	6
(c) 1950-1963				
Antibiotici Lepetit	24	1	8	7
Cementi Portland	26	1	8	7
Cotonificio G. Oliva & C.	17	1	8	7
FIAM Fabbrica Italiana Ascensori Montacarichi	29	1	8	7
Filande e Tessiture Costa	17	1	8	7
Industrie Chimiche Italia Centrale ICIC	24	1	8	7
Manifattura di Valle Brembana	17	1	8	7
G.B. Cervesato & C.	20	1	8	7
Sanquirico Industria Petrolifera	23	1	8	7
SICS Società Industrie Chimiche Sintetiche	24	1	8	7
SISAS Società Italiana Serie Acetica Sintetica	24	1	8	7
Techint Compagnia Tecnica Internazionale	29	1	8	7
Vosa	26	1	8	7
A. Sordelli & C.	36	1	7	6
ABET Braidese Estratti Tannici	24	1	7	6
Apice di Carlo Rontani	25	1	7	6
Aspera Meccanica di Precisione	33	2	8	6
Aster Associate Carbonafta Termoimpianti	28	1	7	6
Azienda Lavorazione Colori Resine ed Affini ALCREA	24	1	7	6
Laboratori Cosmochimici	24	1	7	6
Cilag Italiana	24	2	8	6

Table 4.2. (cont.)

Company	Sector	Class at the beginning of period	Class at the end of period	Passage of class
Calzificio F.lli Carabelli	17	1	7	6
Calzificio Milanese Luigi Ciocca	17	1	7	6
Cartiera di Subiaco	21	1	7	6
Cartiere Antonio Sterzi	21	2	8	6
Perego Fabbrica Apparecchiature per Telecomunicazioni	32	1	7	6
Centrale del Latte di Torino	15	1	7	6
Eugenio Carani	26	1	7	6
Compagnia Industrie Saccarifere Sant'Eufemia Lamezia CISSEL	15	2	8	6
Compagnia Tecnica Industrie Petroli	29	2	8	6
Costruzioni Meccaniche Chiesa	28	1	7	6
Dardanio Manuli	25	2	8	6
F.lli Ramazzotti	15	1	7	6
Electrolux	31	1	7	6
Fabbrica Italiana Motori Elettrici Torino FIMET	31	1	7	6
Fabbrica Milanese Conduttori	31	1	7	6
Imballaggi Speciali Asti SISA	25	1	7	6
Industria Fibre & Cartoni Speciali SAIFECS	21	2	8	6
Istituto Chemioterapico Italiano	24	1	7	6
Magneti Permanenti Altre Specialità SAMPAS	31	1	7	6
Manifattura Maglierie Torino	17	1	7	6
Meroni & C. Industrie Metallurgiche	28	1	7	6
Molino e Pastificio F.lli Petrini	15	1	7	6
ORI Officine Riunite Italiane	27	1	7	6
Officine di Seveso	28	1	7	6
Officine Meccaniche Riunite OMR	31	2	8	6
Pagliani & Provenzale	28	2	8	6
Saponerie Italiane SASI	24	1	7	6
Birra Poretti	15	2	8	6
Ravit Società per l'Industria Chimica	24	1	7	6
Riseria Italiana	15	1	7	6
SAGA Acque Gassate Affini	15	1	7	6
SOL Ossigeno Liquido	24	1	7	6
Molini Pastificio Ettore Santi	15	1	7	6
Selezione dal Reader's Digest	22	2	8	6
Serio Officine Meccaniche di Precisione	30	2	8	6
SIAD Italiana Acetilene e Derivati	24	2	8	6

Table 4.2. (cont.)

Company	Sector	Class at the beginning of period	Class at the end of period	Passage of class
SICCET Società Industriale Commerciale Compensati e Tranciati	20	1	7	6
Siderotermica Industria Generale Saldatura Autogena	28	1	7	6
Telettra Laboratorio di Telefonia Elettronica e Radio	32	2	8	6
The Auto Scale & Slicing Machine Co.	29	2	8	6
Torriani & C.	22	1	7	6
V. Gallino	19	2	8	6
Fornaci Valdadige	26	2	8	6
(d) 1964-1971				
Ajinomoto Insud	24	1	8	7
Aulan	19	1	8	7
Cantiere Navale Luigi Orlando	35	1	8	7
Cartiera Vallagarina	21	1	8	7
DEA Digital Electronic Automation	32	1	8	7
Elicotteri Meridionali EM	35	1	8	7
Ermion	17	1	8	7
Ferrosud	35	1	8	7
Imperial Chemical Industries Italia	24	1	8	7
Leonardo da Vinci	17	1	8	7
Lepetit Sud	24	1	8	7
Macchine e Accessori per l'Industria Grafica Macchingraf	29	1	8	7
Valeo Società di Studio e Produzione di Mondovì	34	1	8	7
Compagnia Italiana Nest Pack	25	2	8	6
Coster Tecnologie Speciali	29	1	7	6
F.lli Zanasi	29	1	7	6
Frigodaunia	15	1	7	6
Hudson Italiana	28	2	8	6
Meridionale Cavi Me.Ca.	31	2	8	6
Microel	32	1	7	6
Salumificio Milano	15	1	7	6
Uni.Ma.C.	18	1	7	6
Zanussi Grandi Impianti	29	2	8	6

Legend: Food products and beverages (15); Textiles (17); Tanning and dressing of leather, bags and footwear (19); Manufacture of wood and of products of wood (20); Pulp, paper and paper products (21); Publishing and printing (22); Coke and refined petroleum products (23); Chemicals and chemical products (24); Rubber and plastic products (25); Non-metallic mineral products (26); Basic metals (27); Fabricated metal products (28); Machinery and equipment (29); Office machinery and computers (30); Electrical machinery and apparatus n.e.c. (31); Radio, television and communication equipment (32); Motor vehicles, trailers and semi-trailers (34); Other transport equipment (35).

4.3. Technology, product cycle and firm survival

The above enables us to affirm that a dynamic perspective of the growth of Italian firms *enlivens* the static picture represented by the crushing prevalence of small firms in the long term. We can, in fact, observe a process of growth in size and of convergence towards a medium size, accompanied, furthermore, by a certain difficulty in maintaining stable positions in the highest class. In 1931 a French engineer, Robert Gibrat, proposed an explanation for the appearance of skew size distributions in a number of economic environments starting from biology to income distributions, tracing the origins of his thinking to the work of Jacobus Kapteyn, an astronomer. Gibrat used many examples to motivate his approach and these included the size distribution of firms within manufacturing industries: his book became seminal for the research tradition concerning firm size dynamics in industrial organization. He showed that firms' distributions were well approximated by a Log Normal, hence, he postulated, a firm's absolute rate of growth could be represented by a random variable whose mean was proportionate to the current firm size or, equivalently, that the proportionate rate of growth was represented by a random variable with mean independent of the current firm size. This is the so called Law of Proportionate Effects and it has been a crucial point in the debate concerning firms' size distribution. Since the seminal study by Gibrat, many empirical works, covering different countries and different time periods, provided evidence to derive relationships between firm dynamics and industrial evolution. Even if many scholars have devoted their efforts to empirically verify Gibrat's statement and generalize the results through the Law, the relation that he postulated did not seem to explain the manner in which firms enter into an industry, grow and exit from that industry. More recently, the branch of empirical literature which studies the relation between firm size and growth refuted Gibrat's Law, because the relation between the observable characteristics of the firms and their rate of growth was much more complex than that formulated by Gibrat [Geroski 1995; Caves 1998; Sutton 1998]. Recent empirical studies suggest, for example, that an answer to the observation given by Gibrat could be represented by the fact that, on average, smaller firms have a lower probability of survival, but that those who survive grow proportionately faster than larger firms. This approach proposes a generalization of the problem on the shape of the distribution and allows the expansion of the analysis to other characteristics (age, technological context, etc.) which influence the probability of survival and, consequently, could be relevant for the size-growth relationship. In this view, the typical shape of the size distribution is determined by many factors which interact and may be specific for each industry.

In this Sect. we try to link this theoretical observations to two factors that are considered relevant in explaining the evolution of firms: technological intensity and the life-cycle of the sector in which the firms operate [Agarwal and Audretsch 2001]. The demographical evolution of Italian firms is reconstructed through the description of the phases of the life-cycle of each industry and the relative technological intensity. The procedure used to identify the phases of the life-cycle of a sector is identical to that defined by Gort and Klepper [1982] for determining the life-cycle of a product; the method is a generalization of a standard discriminant analysis. To determine the life-cycle of a sector, we refer to a formation stage and to a mature stage defined on the basis of the positive or negative net entry of firms: a sector is still in a formative stage if the net entry is positive (i.e. if the number of firms born during a certain year is greater than the number that close in the same year) whereas a sector is already mature when net entry is negative. In order to distinguish between the mature stage and the formative stage of the life-cycle of the sectors considered, therefore, the data relative to net entry rates for each year for each sector must be examined (see Annex 4.1).

Table 4.3. Life-cycle and cut-off years for divisions

Sector	Cut-off year
Food products and beverages (15)	Always in mature stage
Tobacco products (16)	Always in mature stage
Textiles (17)	1920
Wearing apparel (18)	1921
Tanning and dressing of leather, bags and footwear (19)	1922
Manufacture of wood and of products of wood (20)	1936
Pulp, paper and paper products (21)	1951
Publishing and printing (22)	1922
Coke and refined petroleum products (23)	1952
Chemicals and chemical products (24)	1952
Rubber and plastic products (25)	Always in formative stage
Non-metallic mineral products (26)	1962
Basic metals (27)	1952
Fabricated metal products (28)	1952
Machinery and equipment (29)	1962
Office machinery and computers (30)	Always in formative stage
Electrical machinery and apparatus n.e.c. (31)	1960
Radio, television and communication equipment (32)	Always in formative stage
Medical, precision and optical instruments (33)	1960
Motor vehicles, trailers and semi-trailers (34)	1965
Other transport equipment (35)	1920
Furniture and manufacturing n.e.c. (36)	Always in formative stage
Recycling (37)	Always in formative stage

As can be seen from Table 4.3 the sectors that remain in the formative stage for the entire period are those that change their structure over time due to subsequent innovation (e.g. sector 32), or those that are *residual*, i.e. made up of firms that manufacture extremely different products (36) and finally, those sectors that undergo the greatest part of their development in the final years of the period examined (30), making it impossible to identify the year of change in the life-cycle.

In order to determine the technological intensity of the sectors, we used the classification proposed by the OECD [Hatzichronoglou 1997]. The lengthiness of the period created the necessity for a further division into two sub periods, separated by Second World War. Some sectors, in fact, are high tech in the period between the two World Wars, for example the construction of transport vehicles (35), but are no longer so in the consecutive period. The criterion for this distinction is essentially qualitative and is based on the number of important innovations introduced in the various sectors. The following Table 4.4 shows the technological level of each division for the period 1911-1950 and 1950-1971.

Table 4.4. Classification of sectors according to technological intensity

	Period 1911-1950	Period 1950-1971
Low technological level	15-16-17-18-19-20-21-22	15-16-17-18-19-20-21-22
Medium technological level	23-25-26-27-28-29-36	23-25-26-27-28-29-33-34-36
High technological level	24-30-31-32-33-34-35	24-30-31-32-35

Legend: see Table 4.3.

In what follows, therefore, we link the survival of firms to their size, the stage of the sector in which they operate and the technological level of the same sector (high technological intensity, medium technological intensity, and low technological intensity). This is necessary in order to verify whether a relationship exists between the size of firms and their survival in sectors with different technological intensities and in different stages of the life-cycle. In order to estimate the probability of survival of Italian firms (large and small) we use *survival rate tables* and Cox Regressions in relation to a number of relevant variables to describe the dynamics of change: the stage of life of the product and the technological level [Agarwal and Audretsch 2001]. All the data relative to firms with 25 or less years of activity were used, considering that, beyond this threshold, the reasons for an exit can be attributed to causes specific to the single firm. Survival rate tables are created separately for small firms (classes from 1 to 5, about 68 per cent of all firms) and large firms (classes from 6 to 8) using the classification already employed together with a between-group homogeneity test (large and small firms). The results of the latter test allow us to evaluate whether inclusion in one of the two macro-classes, within the same context, based on the stage of the sector and its technological level, is significant with regard to the probability of survival, in other words if there is a significant difference in the probability of survival of small and large firms (the null hypothesis of the tests is that the two groups behave in the same way). The results are illustrated in three tables for every sub-period: the first table for each period presents the descriptive statistics of the variables used in the distinct analyses for large and small firms, the second shows the results of the survival rate tables with survival rates listed on the basis of size, stage of the life-cycle and technological level. The last illustrates the results of the Cox regressions, showing the significance of the variables on the hazard function and allowing for the calculation of the risk rate for each variable (see Annex 4.2). The results are organized according to phase.

4.3.1. The phase from 1911 to 1920

In this phase, as can be observed in Table 4.5, the average lifespan of large firms is longer than that of small firms (13.07 years against 9.33 years); almost all the sectors are still in the formative stage; all the sectors exhibit a rather low average technological intensity.

As far as the probability of survival for small and large firms at one year, five years, ten years and fifteen years is concerned, the fact that emerges is that large firms have a higher probability of survival, even though at the five and ten year intervals probability is cut by half practically for all firms. During this period, the medium and high tech sectors are still not mature and therefore, the mature sectors are all low tech.

Small firms show a higher probability of survival if they operate in low tech sectors; in the latter case, they live longer if they belong to a sector in the formative stage rather than a sector in the mature stage, while the probability of survival at five years, for example, is considerably lower for sectors with a high technological intensity in the formative stage. Operating in these sectors is slightly less risky for large firms than operating in medium and low tech sectors; operating in low-tech mature sectors is less risky for large firms than operating in low-tech sectors in the formative stage, while the opposite is true for small firms. In general, homogeneity tests confirm that small and large firms have different dynamics (the tests are always significant): size influences the survival of firms.

A measure of this influence is given by the hazard rate. All the variables are significant but, while size lowers the exit risk (by 6 per cent for small firms and by 28 per cent for large firms), the stage of the sector and its technological intensity increase it (by 12 per cent and by 9 per cent for small firms, by 15 per cent and by 9 per cent for large firms). This means that the exit risk is lower for large firms in mature sectors and in low-tech sectors. The regressions carried out using samples of various characteristics (all the firms operating in high-tech sectors or in sectors in the formative stage, etc.) confirm the positive effect of size on exit risk.

Table 4.5. Descriptive statistics (1911-1920)

(*a*) Small firms

Variables	Number	Average	St. dev.	Min	Max
Survival span	5,290	9.33	7.46	1	66
Product state	5,290	1.20	0.40	1	2
Technological intensity	5,290	1.72	0.80	1	3
Ordinal size	5,290	3.00	1.41	1	5

(*b*) Large firms

Variables	Number	Average	St. dev.	Min	Max
Survival span	3,174	13.07	10.66	1	66
Product state	3,174	1.15	0.36	1	2
Technological intensity	3,174	1.75	0.84	1	3
Ordinal size	3,174	7.00	0.81	6	8

Table 4.6. Survival rate table (1911-1920)

Survival rates (St. Errors) for:	Small firms No.	Small firms 1 year	5 years	10 years	15 years	Large firms No.	Large firms 1 year	5 years	10 years	15 years	Homogeneity tests Likelihood-Ratio (p-value)
All firms	5,096	94.9 (0.3)	63.9 (0.6)	33.6 (0.6)	8.6 (0.3)	2,811	98.1 (0.2)	76.4 (0.8)	41.1 (0.9)	14.8 (0.7)	-
Sector in formation stage	4,046	94.8 (0.3)	63.1 (0.7)	32.9 (0.7)	8.2 (0.4)	2,355	97.9 (0.3)	75.7 (0.8)	39.6 (1)	14.1 (0.7)	94.46 (0.000)
Sector in mature stage (*c*)	1,050	95.7 (0.6)	66.7 (1.4)	36.3 (1.5)	10.1 (0.9)	456	99.1 (0.4)	80.0 (1.8)	48.4 (2.3)	18.6 (1.8)	38.08 (0.000)
Low-tech sectors	2,565	95.4 (0.4)	67.3 (0.9)	37.2 (0.9)	9.6 (0.5)	1,408	98.3 (0.3)	76.7 (1.1)	41.6 (1.3)	15.9 (0.9)	40.02 (0.000)
Medium-tech sectors (*a*)	1,381	95.3 (0.5)	63.9 (1.2)	31.2 (1.2)	7.3 (0.7)	645	97.6 (0.5)	74.6 (1.7)	38.7 (1.9)	12.4 (1.3)	27.67 (0.000)
High-tech sectors (*b*)	1,150	93.6 (0.7)	56.4 (1.4)	28.8 (1.3)	8.0 (0.8)	758	98.0 (0.5)	77.4 (1.5)	42.1 (1.7)	14.7 (1.3)	71.30 (0.000)
Sectors in formation stage, low-tech	1,515	95.2 (0.5)	67.6 (1.2)	37.7 (1.2)	9.24 (0.7)	953	97.9 (0.4)	75.1 (0.7)	38.4 (1.5)	14.7 (1.1)	11.78 (0.000)
Sectors in formation stage, medium-tech (*a*)	1,381	95.3 (0.5)	63.9 (1.2)	31.2 (1.2)	7.3 (0.7)	645	97.6 (0.5)	74.6 (1.7)	38.7 (1.9)	12.4 (1.3)	27.67 (0.000)
Sectors in formation stage, high-tech (*b*)	1,150	93.6 (0.7)	56.4 (1.4)	28.8 (1.3)	8.0 (0.8)	758	98.0 (0.5)	77.4 (1.5)	42.1 (1.7)	14.7 (1.3)	71.30 (0.000)
Sectors in mature stage, low-tech (*c*)	1,050	95.7 (0.6)	66.7 (1.4)	36.3 (1.5)	10.1 (0.9)	456	99.1 (0.4)	80.0 (1.8)	48.4 (2.3)	18.6 (1.8)	38.08 (0.000)
Sectors in mature stage, medium-tech (*d*)	-	-	-	-	-	-	-	-	-	-	-
Sectors in mature stage, high-tech (*d*)	-	-	-	-	-	-	-	-	-	-	-

Legend: (*a*) medium-tech firms are all in sectors in the formation stage; (*b*) high-tech firms are all still in sectors in the formation stage; (*c*) low-tech firms are all in mature sectors; (*d*) there are no medium-tech and high-tech firms in sectors that are already mature.

Table 4.7. The results of the Cox Hazard Regressions (1911-1920)

(*a*) Small firms

Regress.	Variables	Coefficients	Standard error	Hazard (Risk) ratio	Model Chi-Square (p-value)
1	Size**	-0.05	0.009	0.94	57.60 (0.000)
	Stage of the sector**	0.11	0.030	1.12	-
	Technological intensity**	0.09	0.010	1.09	-
2	Size of sectors in formation**	-0.07	0.010	0.92	67.37 (0.000)
	Size of mature sectors (*c*)	0.02	0.020	1.02	0.90 (0.3)
3	Size in low-tech sectors**	-0.04	0.013	0.95	17.06 (0.000)
	Size in medium-tech sectors(*a*)	-0.03	0.180	0.96	3.35 (0.06)
	Size in high-tech sectors**(*b*)	-0.10	0.020	0.90	23.02 (0.000)
4	Size in sectors in formation, low-tech**	-0.08	0.010	0.92	21.91 (0.000)
	Size in sectors in formation, medium-tech (*a*)	-0.03	0.020	0.96	3.40 (0.06)
	Size in sectors in formation, high-tech**(*b*)	-0.10	0.020	0.90	23.02 (0.000)
5	Size in mature sectors, low-tech (*c*)	0.02	0.021	1.02	0.90 (0.3)
	Size in mature sectors, medium-tech (*d*)	-	-	-	-
	Size in mature sectors, high-tech (*d*)	-	-	-	-

Table 4.7. (cont.)

(*b*) Large firms

Regress.	Variables	Coefficients	Standard errors	Hazard (Risk) ratio	Model Chi-Square (p-value)
1	Size**	0.24	0.020	0.78	138.35 (0.000)
	Stage of Sector**	0.14	0.050	1.15	-
	Technological intensity**	0.08	0.220	1.09	-
2	Size in sectors in formation**	-0.23	0.020	0.79	107.98 (0.000)
	Size of mature sectors**	-0.30	0.050	0.73	32.14 (0.000)
3	Size in low-tech sectors**	-0.29	0.030	0.74	96.25 (0.000)
	Size in medium-tech sectors**(*a*)	-0.18	0.040	0.83	16.32 (0.000)
	Size in high-tech sectors**	-0.19	0.040	0.82	21.35 (0.000)
4	Size in sectors in formation, low-tech**	-0.28	0.037	0.75	57.38 (0.000)
	Size in sectors in formation, medium-tech**(*a*)	-0.18	0.040	0.83	16.32 (0.000)
	Size in sectors in formation, high-tech**	-0.19	0.040	0.82	20.66 (0.000)
5	Size in mature sectors, low-tech**	-0.30	0.050	0.74	30.91 (0.000)
	Size in mature sectors, medium-tech (*d*)	-	-	-	-
	Size in mature sectors, high-tech (*d*)	-	-	-	-

Legend: see Table 4.6; ** significance at 1 per cent.

4.3.2. The phase from 1921 to 1936

In this phase, as can be seen from Table 4.8, the average age of firms increases while a net difference remains between small and large firms, half the sectors are still in the formative stage and half are already mature whereas the average technological intensity, while remaining low, grows as compared to the preceding period. Medium tech sectors are not mature.

The probability of survival is constantly lower for small firms: after five years, for example, the probability of survival for a small firm is 60 per cent against 81 per cent for a large firm. Small firms have a low survival probability, even in comparison to those in the preceding period, and survival probability is largely constant with respect to the life-cycle of the sector and technological level. During this period the number of large firms increases as does their probability of survival with respect to small firms; for large firms mature sectors have a slightly higher probability of survival with respect to those in the formative stage, and in particular mature sectors and high-tech sectors, still show a very high probability of survival after five years. Size is significant and the estimated coefficient is negative for both large and small firms: the exit risk is reduced respectively by 29 per cent and 15 per cent. The technological intensity variable, whose coefficient is positive, is significant only for large firms, therefore, for large firms, operating in a high-tech sector increases the risk by 13 per cent. This effect, however, is reversed if the firm is very large (if it belongs to class 8, for example); in this case the risk decreases by 23 per cent. In general, all the hazard rates are very high for this period, which indicates the extreme importance of the size variable for the survival of firms in any context.

Table 4.8. Descriptive statistics (1921-1936)

(*a*) Small firms

Variables	Number	Average	St. dev.	Min	Max
Survival span	14,737	10.6	8.7	1	88
Product state	14,737	1.6	0.5	1	2
Technological intensity	14,737	1.8	0.8	1	3
Ordinal size	14,737	3.0	1.4	1	5

(*b*) Large firms

Variables	Number	Average	St. dev.	Min	Max
Survival span	8,840	17.5	12.4	1	83
Product state	8,840	1.5	0.5	1	2
Technological intensity	8,840	1.7	0.8	1	3
Ordinal size	8,840	7	0.8	6	8

Table 4.9. Survival rate table (1921-1936)

Survival rates (St. Errors) for:	Small firms					Large firms					Homogeneity tests
	No.	1 year	5 years	10 years	15 years	No.	1 year	5 years	10 years	15 years	Likelihood-Ratio (p-value)
All firms	13,875	96.4 (0.2)	60 (0.4)	32.5 (0.4)	16.8 (0.3)	6,794	99.1 (0.1)	81 (0.4)	54.3 (0.6)	33.8 (0.5)	555.70 (0.000)
Sector in formation stage	7,654	96.1 (0.2)	59.6 (0.5)	32.7 (0.5)	17.1 (0.4)	3,243	99.1 (1)	80.3 (0.7)	51.7 (0.8)	30.9 (0.8)	219.43 (0.000)
Sector in mature stage	6,221	96.8 (0.2)	60.6 (0.6)	32.1 (0.6)	16.5 (0.5)	3,551	99.2 (0.2)	81.5 (0.6)	56.7 (0.8)	36.5 (0.8)	332.50 (0.000)
Low-tech sectors	6,672	96.6 (0.2)	59.1 (0.6)	31.1 (0.6)	16.2 (0.4)	3,414	99.2 (1)	80.4 (0.7)	55 (0.8)	34.7 (0.8)	321.90 (0.000)
Medium-tech sectors (*a*)	3,889	96.3 (0.3)	60.4 (0.7)	33.7 (0.7)	18.8 (0.6)	1,442	98.9 (0.2)	80.5 (1)	54.2 (1.3)	33 (1.2)	103.40 (0.000)
High-tech Sectors	3,314	96.2 (0.3)	61.6 (0.8)	33.7 (0.8)	15.8 (0.6)	1,938	99.3 (0.2)	82.2 (0.9)	53.2 (1.1)	32.7 (1.1)	134.80 (0.000)
Sectors in formation stage, low-tech	827	95 (0.8)	51.6 (1.7)	28.2 (1.5)	16.7 (1.3)	292	99.6 (0.3)	77.4 (2.4)	47.6 (3)	32.5 (2.7)	24.20 (0.000)
Sectors in formation stage, medium-tech (*a*)	3,889	96.3 (0.3)	60.4 (0.7)	33.7 (0.7)	18.8 (0.6)	1,442	98.9 (0.2)	80.5 (1)	54.2 (1.3)	33 (1.2)	103.40 (0.000)
Sectors in formation stage, high-tech	2,938	96.1 (0.3)	60.8 (1)	32.8 (0.8)	15.1 (0.6)	1,509	99.3 (0.2)	80.7 (1.02)	50 (1.3)	29.2 (1.1)	92.51 (0.000)
Sectors in mature stage, low-tech	5,845	96.8 (0.2)	60.1 (0.6)	31.5 (0.6)	16.2 (0.5)	3,122	99.2 (0.2)	80.7 (0.7)	55.7 (0.8)	35.2 (0.8)	291.40 (0.000)
Sectors in mature stage, medium-tech (*b*)	-	-	-	-	-	-	-	-	-	-	-
Sectors in mature stage, high-tech	376	97.3 (0.8)	67.5 (2.4)	41.2 (2.5)	21.3 (2.1)	429	99.1 (0.4)	87.4 (1.6)	64.6 (2.3)	45.2 (2.4)	25.60 (0.000)

Legend: see Table 4.6.

Table 4.10. The results of the Cox Hazard Regressions (1921-1936)

(*a*) Small firms

Regress.	Variables	Coefficients	Standard error	Hazard (Risk) ratio	Model Chi-Square (p-value)
	Size**	-0.15	-0.006	0.85	638.26 (0.000)
1	Stage of the sector	0.02	0.230	1.02	-
	Technological intensity	0.01	0.015	1.01	-
2	Size of sectors in formation**	-0.17	0.008	0.84	442.26 (0.000)
	Size of mature sectors**	-0.13	0.009	0.88	210.82 (0.000)
	Size in low-tech sectors**	-0.14	0.008	0.87	254.22 (0.000)
3	Size in medium-tech sectors**(*a*)	-0.15	0.010	0.86	156.22 (0.000)
	Size in high-tech sectors**	-0.21	0.012	0.81	278.85 (0.000)
	Size in sectors in formation, low-tech**	-0.18	0.020	0.83	57.55 (0.000)
4	Size in sectors in formation, medium-tech**(*a*)	-0.15	0.010	0.86	156.22 (0.000)
	Size in sectors in formation, high-tech**	-0.22	0.013	0.81	260.73 (0.000)
	Size in mature sectors, low-tech**	-0.13	0.010	0.88	194.81 (0.000)
5	Size in mature sectors, medium-tech (*b*)	-	-	-	-
	Size in mature sectors, high-tech**	-0.14	0.030	0.87	16.76 (0.000)

(*b*) Large firms

Regress.	Variables	Coefficients	Standard error	Hazard (Risk) ratio	Model Chi-Square (p-value)
	Size**	-0.34	0.010	0.71	679.73 (0.000)
1	Stage of the sector	0.04	0.030	1.04	-
	Technological intensity**	0.12	0.020	1.13	-
2	Size of sectors in formation**	-0.25	0.020	0.77	211.26 (0.000)
	Size of mature sectors**	-0.43	0.020	0.65	509.89 (0.000)
	Size in low-tech sectors**	-0.43	0.020	0.65	511.36 (0.000)
3	Size in medium-tech sectors**(*a*)	-0.25	0.030	0.77	71.98 (0.000)
	Size in high-tech sectors**	0.25	0.030	0.77	111.15 (0.000)
	Size in sectors in formation, low-tech**	-0.63	0.070	0.53	81.52 (0.000)
4	Size in sectors in formation, medium-tech**(*a*)	-0.25	0.030	0.77	71.98 (0.000)
	Size in sectors in formation, high-tech**	-0.17	0.030	0.84	35.96 (0.000)
	Size in mature sectors, low-tech**	-0.41	0.020	0.67	426.45 (0.000)
5	Size in mature sectors, medium-tech (*b*)	-	-	-	-
	Size in mature sectors, high-tech	-0.55	0.050	0.57	94.29 (0.000)

Legend: see Table 4.6; ** significance at 1 per cent.

4.3.3. The phase from 1950 to 1963

As can be seen from Table 4.11, the average probability of survival of firms grows a great deal compared to the previous periods, especially as regards large firms (26.5 years against 15.6 years); the average level of technological intensity and that of the stage of the sector do not change much with respect to the preceding period. In general, the results confirm that after five years the probability of firms' survival is cut by half, especially in the case of small firms. Small firms operating in sectors that are still in the formative stage live a little longer as compared to those operating in mature sectors and those that operate in high-tech sectors have a probability of survival which, on average, is slightly greater than those operating in medium and low-tech sectors.

Large firms have an average probability of survival which is lower compared to the preceding period and they live longer if they operate in sectors in the formation stage, in low-tech sectors; a high technological level allows large firms to survive longer when these sectors are still in formation (78.8 per cent against the 72.7 per cent of sectors in formative stage and with a low technological intensity or 74.8 per cent of the sectors in formative stage and with a medium technological intensity). If we consider the degree of risk, size lowers the risk level for small firms by 14 per cent, the stage of the sectors increases it by 3 per cent, technological intensity increases it by 2 per cent whereas for the large firms size lowers risk by 25 per cent, the stage by 7 per cent and the technological intensity increases it by 16 per cent. This means that the larger the firm the lower the exit risk; if firms are small, the maturity of the sector and a high technological intensity have a negative influence, whereas, if firms are large, it is the maturity of the sector that has the most weight in increasing exit risk.

Table 4.11. Descriptive statistics (1950-1963)

(*a*) Small firms

Variables	Number	Average	St. dev.	Min	Max
Survival span	24,965	15.6	13.8	1	100
Product state	24,965	1.7	0.5	1	2
Technological intensity	24,965	1.7	0.7	1	3
Ordinal size	24,965	3.0	1.4	1	5

(*b*) Large firms

Variables	Number	Average	St. dev.	Min	Max
Survival span	14,981	26.5	18.6	1	110
Product state	14,981	1.72	0.4	1	2
Technological intensity	14,981	1.8	0.7	1	3
Ordinal size	14,981	7,0	0.8	6	8

Table 4.12. Survival rate table (1950-1963)

Survival rates (St. errors) for:	Small firms No.	1 year	5 years	10 years	15 years	Large firms No.	1 year	5 years	10 years	15 years	Homogeneity tests Likelihood-Ratio (p-value)
All firms	19,062	93.3 (0.1)	56.7 (0.3)	36.1 (0.3)	22.6 (0.3)	7,768	97.9 (0.1)	74.9 (0.5)	49.5 (0.5)	29.8 (0.5)	567.7 (0.000)
Sector in formation stage	6,301	93.3 (0.3)	57.3 (0.6)	39.3 (0.6)	24.5 (0.5)	2,166	98.2 (0.2)	75.7 (0.9)	52.4 (1)	35.5 (1)	218.3 (0.000)
Sector in mature stage	12,761	93.3 (0.2)	56.4 (0.4)	34.5 (0.4)	21.7 (0.3)	5,502	97.8 (0.2)	74.6 (0.6)	48.4 (0.6)	27.6 (0.6)	103.4 (0.000)
Low-tech sectors	8,281	93.7 (0.2)	57.9 (0.5)	36.4 (0.5)	22.9 (0.4)	2,767	97.6 (0.3)	75.9 (0.8)	51.4 (0.9)	30 (0.8)	321.8 (0.000)
Medium-tech Sectors	7,226	92.8 (0.3)	53.8 (0.5)	33.7 (0.5)	20.9 (0.5)	3,198	98 (0.2)	75.1 (0.7)	48.6 (0.8)	29.5 (0.8)	293.5 (0.000)
High-tech Sectors	3,555	93.6 (0.4)	59.7 (0.8)	40.2 (0.8)	25.6 (0.7)	1,703	98.4 (0.3)	73 (1)	48.3 (1.2)	30.2 (1.1)	545.7 (0.000)
Sectors in formation stage, low-tech	112	98.2 (1.2)	68.7 (4.3)	49.1 (4.7)	35.7 (4.5)	22	95.4 (4.4)	72.7 (9.5)	45.4 (10.6)	36.3 (10.2)	47.1 (0.000)
Sectors in formation stage, medium-tech	4,829	92.8 (0.3)	54.7 (0.7)	36.6 (0.7)	23.1 (0.6)	1,624	98.2 (0.3)	74.8 (1)	49.7 (1.2)	33 (1.1)	112.7 (0.000)
Sectors in formation stage, high-tech	1,360	95 (0.6)	65.4 (1.3)	48.1 (1.3)	28.2 (1.2)	520	98.4 (0.5)	78.8 (1.8)	61 (2.1)	42.3 (2.1)	65.9 (0.000)
Sectors in mature stage, low-tech	8,169	93.7 (0.2)	57.7 (0.5)	36.2 (0.5)	22.7 (0.5)	2,745	97.6 (0.3)	76 (0.8)	51.4 (0.9)	29.7 (0.8)	225.6 (0.000)
Sectors in mature stage, medium-tech	2,397	92.7 (0.5)	52 (1.02)	27.9 (0.9)	16.3 (0.7)	1,574	97.7 (0.4)	75.5 (1.1)	47.6 (1.2)	25.9 (1.1)	139.6 (0.000)
Sectors in mature stage, high-tech	2,195	92.7 (0.5)	56.2 (1)	35.3 (1)	24 (0.9)	1,183	98.5 (0.5)	70.5 (1.3)	42.7 (1.4)	24.9 (1.2)	347.1 (0.000)

Table 4.13. The results of the Cox Hazard Regressions (1950-1963)

(*a*) Small firms

Regress.	Variables	Coefficients	Standard Error	Hazard (Risk) Ratio	Model Chi-Square (p-value)
1	Size**	-0.15	0.004	0.86	1061.87 (0.000)
	Stage of the sector**	0.03	0.010	1.03	-
	Technological intensity**	0.02	0.009	1.02	-
2	Size of sectors in formation**	-0.13	0.007	0.88	280.39 (0.000)
	Size of mature sectors**	-0.16	0.005	0.85	811.18 (0.000)
3	Size in low-tech sectors**	-0.16	0.007	0.85	542.96 (0.000)
	Size in medium-tech sectors**	-0.15	0.007	0.86	435.23 (0.000)
	Size in high-tech sectors**	-0.15	0.010	0.86	193.87 (0.000)
4	Size in sectors in formation, low-tech**	-0.21	0.070	0.81	10.44 (0.001)
	Size in sectors in formation, medium-tech**	-0.14	0.010	0.87	250.21 (0.000)
	Size in sectors in formation, high-tech**	-0.08	0.010	0.92	24.60 (0.000)
5	Size in mature sectors, low-tech**	-0.16	0.007	0.85	533.81 (0.000)
	Size in mature sectors, medium-tech**	-0.18	0.010	0.84	149.25 (0.000)
	Size in mature sectors, high-tech**	-0.20	0.010	0.82	189.70 (0.000)

Table 4.13. (cont.)

(*b*) Large firms

Regress.	Variables	Coefficients	Standard Errors	Hazard (Risk) Ratio	Model Chi-Square (p-value)
	Size**	-0.28	0.010	0.75	970.97 (0.000)
1	Stage of Sector**	-0.07	0.020	0.93	-
	Technological intensity**	0.15	0.010	1.16	-
2	Size in sectors in formation**	-0.26	0.020	0.77	212.78 (0.000)
	Size of mature sectors**	-0.30	0.010	0.74	715.79 (0.000)
	Size in low-tech sectors**(*a*)	-0.35	0.016	0.70	455.97 (0.000)
3	Size in medium-tech sectors**	-0.26	0.010	0.77	262.77 (0.000)
	Size in high-tech sectors**	-0.26	0.020	0.77	200.54 (0.000)
	Size in sectors in formation, low-tech	-0.15	0.150	0.86	0.93 (0.330)
4	Size in sectors in formation, medium-tech**	-0.27	0.020	0.76	144.90 (0.000)
	Size in sectors in formation, high-tech**	-0.26	0.040	0.77	44.15 (0.000)
	Size in mature sectors, low-tech**(*a*)	-0.35	0.016	0.70	455.76 (0.000)
5	Size in mature sectors, medium-tech (*b*)	-0.24	0.020	0.78	108.02 (0.000)
	Size in mature sectors, high-tech	-0.27	0.020	0.76	115.04 (0.000)

Legend: see Table 4.6; ** significance at 1 per cent.

4.3.4. The phase from 1964 to 1971

In the last period, as can be seen from Table 4.14, the average life expectancy of small and large firms does not greatly differ from that of the preceding period (13.6 years for small firms and 24.3 years for large); almost all sectors are by now mature (1.9) while the average technological intensity is practically constant (1.8, i.e. equal to those of the preceding two periods). Large and small firms show very different survival probabilities and small firms especially show a drop in survival probability after five years. In fact, of the 100 firms present, only 28 are still active after ten years. Small firms have a greater life expectancy in mature sectors (61.5 per cent against 55.5 per cent after five years) and in mature sectors, the probability of survival is higher if the sectors are high- tech (63.3 per cent); in this case there is also a maximum probability of survival at ten years (33.7 per cent). This is the only case in which we can conjecture about the existence of a niche strategy within sectors with large markets, which allow for a high specialization of production. Large firms, instead, have the highest probability of survival if they operate in sectors in formation and with a high technological intensity (81.3 per cent life expectancy after five years).

It is unclear whether the maturity of the sector influences the probability of survival of large firms, but observing the degrees of risk, it can be seen that all the variables are very significant. In particular, the size and the stage of the sector reduce the exit risk for all firms (16 per cent and 25 per cent respectively for the small firms and 25 per cent and 23 per cent for the large firms), while, in this last period too, belonging to a high-tech sector increases the exit risk by 4 per cent for small firms and by 15 per cent for large firms. An indication consistent with the difficulties encountered by firms in, for example, the electronic consumption sector such as Rex, Radiomarelli, Synudine and others, and by Olivetti in the electronic sector.

Table 4.14. Descriptive statistics (1964-1971)

(*a*) Small firms

Variables	Number	Average	St. dev.	Min	Max
Survival span	24,165	13.6	13.60	1	103
Product state	24,165	1.9	0.27	1	2
Technological intensity	24,165	1.8	0.70	1	3
Ordinal size	24,165	3.0	1.41	1	5

(*b*) Large firms

Variables	Number	Average	St. dev.	Min	Max
Survival span	14,497	24.3	19.80	1	118
Product state	14,497	1.92	0.26	1	2
Technological intensity	14,497	1.88	0.75	1	3
Ordinal size	14,497	7.0	0.81	6	8

Table 4.15. Survival rate table (1964-1971)

Survival rates (St. Errors) for:	Small firms					Large firms					Homogeneity tests
	No.	1 year	5 years	10 years	15 years	No.	1 year	5 years	10 years	15 years	Likelihood-Ratio (p-value)
All firms	20,152	96.1 (0.1)	61 (0.3)	28.6 (0.3)	13.1 (0.2)	9,002	98.7 (0.1)	78.4 (0.4)	47.1 (0.5)	25.6 (0.4)	112.8 (0.000)
Sector in formation stage	1,871	95.4 (0.5)	55.5 (1.1)	22.1 (0.9)	8.9 (0.6)	802	99 (0.3)	77.9 (1.4)	45.7 (1.7)	23.4 (1.5)	237.7 (0.000)
Sector in mature stage	18,281	96.2 (0.1)	61.5 (0.3)	29.3 (0.3)	13.5 (0.2)	8,200	98.7 (0.1)	78.4 (0.4)	47.3 (0.5)	25.80 (0.5)	946.1 (0.000)
Low-tech sectors	7,233	96.2 (0.2)	62.4 (0.5)	30.8 (0.5)	14.6 (0.4)	2,873	98.7 (0.2)	77.3 (0.7)	46.2 (0.9)	26.9 (0.8)	376.5 (0.000)
Medium-tech Sectors	9,687	96.1 (0.2)	59.3 (0.5)	25.7 (0.4)	11.4 (0.3)	4,081	98.7 (0.1)	79.5 (0.6)	48.3 (0.7)	25.4 (0.6)	639.2 (0.000)
High-tech sectors	3,232	95.9 (0.3)	62.7 (0.8)	27.7 (0.8)	14.9 (0.6)	2,048	98.8 (0.2)	77.6 (0.9)	46.2 (1.1)	24.1 (0.9)	483.4 (0.000)
Sectors in formation stage, low-tech (*b*)	33	93.9 (4.1)	78.8 (7.1)	30.3 (8.0)	9.1 (5.0)	-	-	-	-	-	-
Sectors in formation stage, medium-tech	1,557	95.3 (0.5)	54.8 (1.2)	21.9 (1.05)	8.7 (0.8)	475	99.2 (0.4)	76 (1.9)	43.8 (2.2)	20.2 (1.8)	110.2 (0.000)
Sectors in formation stage, high-tech	281	96.1 (1.1)	56.6 (2.9)	21 (2.4)	9.9 (1.8)	310	98.7 (0.6)	81.3 (2.2)	48.1 (2.8)	27.4 (2.5)	59.7 (0.000)
Sectors in mature stage, low-tech	7,200	96.3 0.2)	62.3 (0.6)	30.8 (0.5)	14.6 (0.5)	2,856	98.7 (0.2)	77.4 (0.7)	46.1 (0.9)	26.8 (0.8)	330.9 (0.000)
Sectors in mature stage, medium-tech	8,130	96.3 (0.3)	60.1 (0.5)	26.5 (0.5)	11.9 (0.3)	3,606	98.7 (0.2)	80 (0.6)	48.9 (0.8)	26.1 (0.7)	254.8 (0.000)
Sectors in mature stage, high-tech	2,951	95.9 (0.4)	63.3 (0.8)	33.7 (0.8)	15.4 (0.6)	1,738	98.8 (0.2)	76.9 (1.0)	45.8 (1.2)	23.5 (1.0)	957.1 (0.000)

Legend: (*b*) this survival rate table is not comparable to others for large firms due to the low number of occurrences. We can derive the probability of survival at two years [82.3 (9.2)], at ten years [58.8 (1.2)] and at fifteen [41.18 (1.2)] but only with a four to ten year leap due to lack of data. For this reason the results of the section "large firms in low-tech sectors in formation" are not included in the table.

Table 4.16. The results of the Cox Hazard Regressions (1964-1971)

(*a*) Small firms

Regress.	Variables	Coefficients	Standard error	Hazard (Risk) Ratio	Model Chi-Square (p-value)
1	Size**	-0.16	0.004	0.84	1459.29 (0.000)
	Stage of the sector**	-0.28	0.020	0.75	-
	Technological intensity**	0.04	0.008	1.04	-
2	Size of sectors in formation**	-0.10	0.015	0.90	47.73 (0.000)
	Size of mature sectors**	-0.17	0.004	0.84	1227.75 (0.000)
3	Size in low-tech sectors**	-0.16	0.007	0.85	423.16 (0.000)
	Size in medium-tech sectors**	-0.18	0.007	0.83	784.72 (0.000)
	Size in high-tech sectors**	-0.14	0.010	0.87	204.11 (0.000)
4	Size in sectors in formation, low-tech**(*a*)	0.24	0.110	1.27	4.45 (0.003)
	Size in sectors in formation, medium-tech**	-0.10	0.020	0.90	38.79 (0.000)
	Size in sectors in formation, high-tech**	-0.15	0.040	0.86	14.39 (0.001)
5	Size in mature sectors, low-tech**	-0.16	0.007	0.85	430.45 (0.000)
	Size in mature sectors, medium-tech**	-0.20	0.008	0.81	716.05 (0.000)
	Size in mature sectors, high-tech**	-0.14	0.012	0.87	134.65 (0.000)

(*b*) Large firms

Regress.	Variables	Coefficients	Standard error	Hazard (Risk) ratio	Model Chi-Square (p-value)
1	Size**	-0.28	0.010	0.75	933.65 (0.000)
	Stage of the sector**	-0.24	0.030	0.78	-
	Technological intensity**	0.14	0.010	1.15	-
2	Size of sectors in formation**	-0.36	0.040	0.69	94.62 (0.000)
	Size of mature sectors**	-0.27	0.010	0.76	764.16 (0.000)
3	Size in low-tech sectors**(*a*)	-0.30	0.018	0.74	293.70 (0.000)
	Size in medium-tech sectors**	-0.31	0.015	0.73	418.08 (0.000)
	Size in high-tech sectors**	-0.21	0.020	0.81	138.68 (0.000)
4	Size in sectors in formation, low-tech (*a*)	0.08	0.220	1.09	0.15 (0.690)
	Size in sectors in formation, medium-tech**	-0.39	0.050	0.68	60.15 (0.000)
	Size in sectors in formation, high-tech**	-0.34	0.060	0.71	29.29 (0.000)
5	Size in mature sectors, low-tech**	-0.31	0.020	0.73	293.19 (0.000)
	Size in mature sectors, medium-tech**	-0.30	0.020	0.74	343.29 (0.000)
	Size in mature sectors, high-tech	-0.20	0.020	0.82	73.83 (0.000)

Legend: (*a*) number of occurrences too low; ** significance at 1 per cent.

4.4. Conclusions

The dynamic of size distribution highlights three very interesting statistical inter-industrial regularities. Firstly, the dynamic distribution of the major firms shows a convergence towards the bottom of the size distribution, i.e. these firms grow but, the absolute size does not grow much because the firms that reach the highest stages recede. In fact, the entire universe of firms shows an extended series of *leaping frogs*, namely of firms that in the different phases, move many positions forward in the ranking of size classes, but also jump backwards, i.e. they do not remain stable.

Secondly, the analysis of survival, carried out phase by phase for the entire universe of firms with regard to life-cycle and technological regime, presents a few interesting regularities. The first is the major rate of mortality, in general, of small firms, which is higher in mature sectors and in the high tech ones. The major firms also encounter greater risks in high-tech sectors, like, for example, Olivetti, while they have a greater life expectancy in the mature low-tech sectors.

A third interesting characteristic is the fact that, in the Italian system of firms, there are no small and medium size firms in mature, high-tech sectors, and therefore the niche firm described in recent literature is missing. This permits us to exclude the possibility that the phenomenon has deep historical roots and to affirm that it is rather a result of one of the *surprises* of the 1970s.

Annex 4.1: Discriminant analysis for the determination of the product cycle

To determine the cut-off year of the j sector, the series is subdivided into three categories: the first and the third include the years in which the net entry rates are strongly negative or positive, while the second category is that of the t residual years, in which the level of net entry rates is roughly zero or has fluctuating values. The level of net entry rates in the years belonging to this second category is labeled as $x_1, x_2, \ldots, x_i$; the need being to determine a discriminant year i amongst these such that the observations $(x_1, x_2, \ldots, x_i)$ can be classified in the formative stage and $(x_{i+1}, x_{i+2}, \ldots, x_t)$ can be classified as belonging to the mature stage.

In order to identify the cut-off year we use a three step procedure:

(i) For each year i: 1, 2,..., t we calculate the averages relative to the first i years (category 1) and those relative to the following t-$(i$+1$)$ years (category 2):

$$d_1(i) = \sum_{k:1}^{i} x_k / i$$

$$d_2(i) = \sum_{k:i+1}^{t} x_k / (t-i)$$

(ii) The choice of the cut-off year is limited to those values of k for which the following is simultaneously valid:

$$|d_1(i) - \mu_1| \le |(\mu_1 - \mu_2)/2|$$
$$|d_2(i) - \mu_2| \le |(\mu_1 - \mu_2)/2|$$

where μ_1 and μ_2 represent the average rate of net entry in the categories 1 and 2. If no values satisfy the above condition then all observations are classified as belonging to a sector permanently in a formative stage if

$$|d_1(t) - \mu_1| < |d_2(t) - \mu_2|$$

and in a mature stage otherwise.

(iii) If more than one value satisfies the above conditions then we select a value of i that solves the problem

$$\max_{i:1,2,\ldots,t} |d_1(i) - d_2(i)|$$

Step (ii) requires that the mean of the observations classified in each of the two categories (1, 2) be closer to the sample mean of the observations initially classified in those same categories with respect to those observations classified in the alternative category. Step (iii), insures, that among all the values that satisfy point (ii) the choice falls on the one that maximizes the difference between the means of the values classified in the two alternative categories. Finally, since the sectors are composed of many products that interact and that present different life cycles, after having located the cut-off year, we carry out a further check using Chow's test. This type of test is generally used to identify structural breaks in time series; we propose to apply it also in the case of the identification of the cut-off year, because the passage of sectors from the formative stage to the mature stage can be represented as a change in the trend of the net entry of the series; the significance of the test confirms the presence of a break and the corresponding year can be reasonably chosen as the cut-off year.

Annex 4.2: Analysis of duration

The analysis of duration is a developing field of econometrics [Lancaster 1990] which supplies estimates of the time-lapse preceding failure, or in general, the end of all those phenomena that at a specific moment present a conclusion (that analytically represents the disappearance of the phenomenon); examples of duration data are the period of survival of a patient after an operation, the duration of a strike, the period of activity of a firm before its failure. For this kind of data, the analysis of survival allows us to estimate the probability of the appearance of an *end* event in the following period.

The relevant variable in this type of analysis is therefore the duration of the period, from the first occurrence of the phenomenon to its end, and is generally represented by a cross section of survival spans $t_1, t_2, \ldots, t_n \in T$, T random variable (continuous or discrete). The process can begin at different moments in time and its duration can vary; due to these fundamental characteristics the random variable for survival spans T is inevitably *censored* beyond a certain threshold, as is evident, for example from the life-expectancy of a human being. The *probability of survival* is defined as:

$S(t) = 1 - F(t) = \Pr(T \geq t)$ where $F(t)$ is the function of cumulated probability; from which the Hazard Rate:

$$\lambda(t) = \lim_{\Delta \to 0} \frac{\Pr(t \leq T \leq t + \Delta \mid T \geq t)}{\Delta} = \lim_{\Delta \to 0} \frac{F(t+\Delta) - F(t)}{\Delta S(t)} = \frac{f(t)}{S(t)}$$

that is the relationship between the distribution density of the probability of the phenomenon and the probability of survival. This represents the number of elements that fail conditional to their age and constitutes the probability of failure given that the element has survived t years. λ represents the parameter that must be estimated and the estimation method generally used is that of Maximum Likelihood through the Cox Proportional Hazard Regression. The Cox Proportional Hazard Regressions are used to estimate the effect of different regressors on the survival of a phenomenon and to measure the hazard rates of each of the variables considered.

The function Hazard, $h_i(t)$, of the occurrence i of the phenomenon is defined as:

$h_i(t) = h(t,x_i) = h_0(t)\exp(x_i\beta)$, where $h_0(t)$ is a basic unspecified hazard function representing the probability of failure conditional to the fact that the element considered has survived until year t, x_i and the vector of the regressors for the same element i and β is a vector of the parameters that must be estimated in the regression. The negative estimated coefficients (β) indicate a positive effect in the reduction of the risk of failure while the hazard rates measure this effect on the basis of the distance from 1 (a hazard rate lesser than 1 reduces the risk of failure by a percentage equal to the distance from 1).

The *survival tables* are also very useful in this type of analysis. Survival tables use predefined measures to estimate the *survival rate* at moment t of the phenomenon, defining it as the relation between the number of elements that have survived at least t years over the total number of elements. The tables summarize the probabilities of survival at precise moments in time (probability at one year, at five years, at ten years, at fifteen years).

5. The largest 200 manufacturing firms (1913–2001)

Michelangelo Vasta

5.1. Introduction

The study of the largest 200 enterprises in a single national context has its theoretical roots in the literature on monopolies and in the managerial theory of firm organization [Berle and Means 1932]. In historical studies it can be traced back to Alfred Chandler's [1990] imposing comparative study. These studies find that, as from the end of the 19th century, a robust group of firms, now over 100 years old, continues to maintain leading positions in each country. The reasons for this continuity can be explained in two ways. The older literature adopts a critical viewpoint and underlines the monopolistic character of this permanence, linked to the ability to create and maintain high barriers to entry [Bain 1956; Marris 1964]. The more recent literature combines the oligopolistic character of the markets in which the major firms operate and the capacity to accumulate technological and organizational knowledge linked to the *triple investment*: in large plants, in management and in marketing. In this case the barriers to entry and the monopolistic profits that derive from them have the positive function of favoring the accumulation of organizational abilities and of resources. These permit the preservation of competitive advantage through economies of scale and investments in R&D, and the production, within the same firms, of innovations capable of promoting economic growth [Chandler 1977; Teece 1980].

Chandler himself links the birth of the large oligopolistic firms to the presence of the technological innovations generated at the end of the 19th century, the period which, according to him, coincides with the birth of most of the firms found among the top 200. This means that the size and the organization of the firm depend in the first place on the characteristics of the technologies prevalent during a certain historical phase. The large oligopolistic enterprise is a result of the innovations, introduced between the third and the *fourth technological wave*, in the field of electricity, iron and steel, chemistry and in the automobile industry (Table 5.1).

These suggestions have been adopted by the evolutionary theories of industrial organization [Winter 1984; Malerba and Orsenigo 1993]. These link the demography of firms to the prevalent *technological wave*, identified on the basis of the characteristics of the economic potential of the knowledge which it incorporates and to its evolution in time [Dosi 1988; Cohen and Klepper 1991]. This knowledge can be generated and transferred more or less easily, according to the level of dependence connected to the internal skills of the firm which produces it. The higher the level of dependence, the greater the resilience of the existing firms. Among the transfer mechanisms, a key role is also played by the regime of appropriation of innovations both in terms of the intrinsic characteristics of the technology and of the property rights regulating it [Audretsch 1995; Pagano 2003].

Table 5.1. The technological phases of economic development

Period	Industrial Revolution	Technological waves
1770-1830	First	1. Age of industrial mechanization
1830-1875		2. Age of steam power and railways
1875-1908	Second	3. Age of electricity and steel
1908-1970		4. Age of oil, automobiles and mass production
1970-	Third	5. Age of information and communication technologies

Source: our elaborations from Freeman and Soete [1997]; Freeman and Louçã [2001].

A Chandlerian version of this approach, which confirms the stability of the nucleus of large enterprises, has been proposed by Patel and Pavitt [1998], according to which the evolution of the largest 400 enterprises in the world is characterized by an initial turbulence, due to the birth of the *technological wave*, and by a successive long-term stabilization, until the emergence of a new *technological wave*. These same enterprises also explain the change of *wave*, through the diversification of their strategies. This ability is linked to the presence of path dependence in the technological research of enterprises, proof of which is presence of a series of patents, and the building of specific organizational skills capable of creating long-term barriers to entry.

Other empirical studies on the industrial structure and the population of large enterprises in more recent periods [Beesley and Hamilton 1984, for the UK; Invernizzi and Revelli 1993, for Italy; Audretsch 1997; Louçã and Mendonça 2002, for the US] have found that the observed turbulence is greater than that indicated by the Chandlerian tradition. The greater degree of turbulence does not dispute the existence of the *technological waves* and the organizational forms they determine (the economies of scale and large enterprise), but it introduces a variety of agents into the interpretation. These are heterogeneous, and have personal characteristics and different experiences, which condition their selection in the context in which they operate. This means that, when faced with the same type of stimuli, these economic agents adapt in different ways; not so much because of their different abilities, but because their particular experience causes them react in a specific way. The variety of agents determines the variety in the types of enterprises that make up the industrial structure, which in its turn is at the basis of the observed turbulence.

This study is organized as follows: after having described the source and the methodology used to identify the largest 200 Italian firms, and having introduced a few *caveat* (Sect. 5.2), we examine the structural change of the large Italian enterprise system while introducing a few elements of comparison with the main industrialized countries (Sect. 5.3). We then go on to discuss the demographic dynamics comparing, for the different benchmark years, *permanent* firms and *incoming* firms (Sect. 5.4). Particular attention is devoted to the single firms whose evolution is crucial to the understanding of the strong turbulence that, as we shall see, emerges from the observation of this sample. The analysis, furthermore, is centered on intra-sectoral turbulence, with the observation of the dynamics of *incoming* firms (Sect. 5.5). The study ends with a few concluding remarks (Sect. 5.6).

5.2. Source and methodology

The sample selected for the study of the large Italian enterprise, mainly drawn from the Imita.db (see Appendix), includes the top 200 manufacturing firms (sectors 15-37 of the ATECO-ISTAT 1991 classification) ordered in terms of assets for the years 1913, 1921, 1927, 1936, 1952, 1960, 1971 and 1981. For the years 1991 and 2001, for which the Imita.db has no available data, because it ends with the 1984 edition, we made use of the Mediobanca data [1981, 1991, 2001].

The possibility of using a great number of benchmark years, selected in such a way as to be correspondent, or close, to the census surveys, allows us to follow the dynamics of the large Italian enterprise in detail. Notwithstanding the fact that we tried to select benchmark years at a homogeneous distance of about 10 years one from the other, some differences, made necessary by the availability of the sources, prevail. We therefore move from a minimum time span of 6 years between 1921 and 1927, and a maximum of 16 years between 1936 and 1952. The single years, furthermore, occur at different moments of the cycle, thus potentially influencing the comparative static analysis in some ways[1].

The variable used to compile the ranking of the companies is, as in many of the studies on the dynamics of large firms [Berle and Means 1932; Chandler 1990], the assets. This choice is the best possible in the case of Italy, and is at any rate largely agreed upon at the international level [White 2002]. The only possible alternative would have been the use of capital, since data on turnover, employment, value added or market capitalization were not available for the entire period. In the case of market capitalization the reason is that, as is well known, there are relatively few joint stock companies listed in Italy [Baia Curioni 1995; Siciliano 2001]. The use of capital was, however, excluded because it is a less suitable measure than assets for representing the real size of firms, because it varies greatly between different sectors.

Only joint-stock companies are included in the analysis, but this does not substantially alter the picture, even though some even large firms may have adopted other types of company forms, particularly during the first years of the century [see Chap.

[1] For an analysis of the economic cycles in Italy from the Italian Unification to the present, see Delli Gatti, Gallegati and Gallegati [2003]. For a chronology reporting the minimum and maximum of each economic cycle, see ibid. [540].

8]. In the last years, however, some important cooperative societies, which have greatly increased their weight in the Italian economy, could have been excluded[2].

We have, furthermore, not considered the organization into groups of some of the joint-stock companies. These data are in fact available, even though in an incomplete form, only for the last two decades. It was only as from 1994, thanks to the new regulations on financial statements, that it became compulsory for groups of firms to keep a consolidated financial statement of their activities.

The use of such a long time-span poses several problems relative to changes in corporate names, mergers and de-mergers. The criteria adopted to give continuity to a firms are based on a series of qualitative elements obtained from: (i) the brief historical profiles reported by the source for each firm; (ii) the notes found in the Mediobanca volumes [1981, 1991, 2001]; (iii) the historical profiles contained in the digital archive of Mediobanca [R&S Mediobanca various years]; (iv) the information found on the ever more numerous company web sites. Moreover, we also made use of a few Italian traditional sources on enterprises such as the *Guida Monaci, Il Taccuino dell'azionista* and the *Calepino dell'Azionista* and, on some occasions, single case histories and/or essays on the history of firms[3]. Notwithstanding this work of a qualitative nature, the criteria adopted are not exempt from arbitrariness, essentially due to the succession of industrial and financial reorganizations during the course of time.

In general, however, we adopted a very broad continuity criterion in case of changes in corporate name, while in the case of mergers and acquisitions we assigned continuity to a firm on the basis of its localization, ownership structure and sectoral specificity. Finally, in the case of de-mergers, we considered the company that carried on the core business activity of the firm, while the company that branched into different activities was considered a new company[4]. The abovementioned problems, notwithstanding the stratagems adopted to minimize distortions, however, exclude the possibility of a rigorous quantitative analysis. We believe,

---

[2] This last aspect was pointed out to me by Patrizia Battilani and Vera Zamagni who have studied the Italian cooperative movement for many years.

[3] There are several bibliographical reviews on studies on the history of the Italian enterprise. There is the pioneering work of Bigazzi [1990], see also Bigatti [1994, 1999], Carnevali [1998] and Ricciardi [2002].

[4] An example of this is the case of Pirelli which is present in the sample, even though under different names, which are an expression of the industrial activities of the company. During the 1970s, however, the industrial activities were parceled-out and, as from 1981, three companies which can be traced back to Pirelli appear in the sample: Industrie Pirelli (37th position in the ranking), Pneumatici Pirelli (40th), and Cavi Pirelli (54th). In 1991, the situation is again different: Industrie Pirelli disappears from the sample, while Pneumatici Pirelli and Cavi Pirelli are respectively in the 70th and 31st position in the ranking, while in 163rd position we find another company - Pirelli Coordinamento Pneumatici - which can be traced back to the Pirelli Group. In the year 2001, the Pirelli Group has three companies in the sample: Pirelli Pneumatici (79th position in the ranking), Pirelli Cavi e Sistemi Energia (52nd), and Pirelli Cavi e Sistemi Energia Italia (163rd). For this reason we assigned firm continuity to Industrie Pirelli which thus has eight presences in the sample from 1913 to 1981.

however, that the methodology adopted, in line with that used for other countries [Hannah 1976, 1999; Chandler 1990, 1994; Wardley 1991; Carreras and Tafunell 1993; Louçã and Mendonça 2002], nevertheless allows us to furnish useful interpretative notions on the dynamics of large Italian enterprise.

5.3. Structural changes

The first element that must be underlined is that the weight of the large Italian manufacturing enterprise, notwithstanding the prevalent role of small and medium enterprise, has a relevant effect on national wealth during the period considered (see Fig. 5.1). Its dynamics reflect the technological and organizational changes occurring on a global scale. The quota of the assets of the top 200 manufacturing enterprises on Italian GDP shows a rising trend from the beginning of the period and follows the spread of the technologies of the Second Industrial Revolution and the Fordist paradigm. It reaches its apogee, with 38.5 per cent of the total GDP in 1971, in the final phase of the Golden age, when the model of the large enterprise, based on the low cost of raw materials and on economies of scale, undergoes a deep crisis. After the great changes that characterize the 1970s, the weight of the large Italian enterprise decreases, reaching values around 25 per cent in 1981 and 1991.

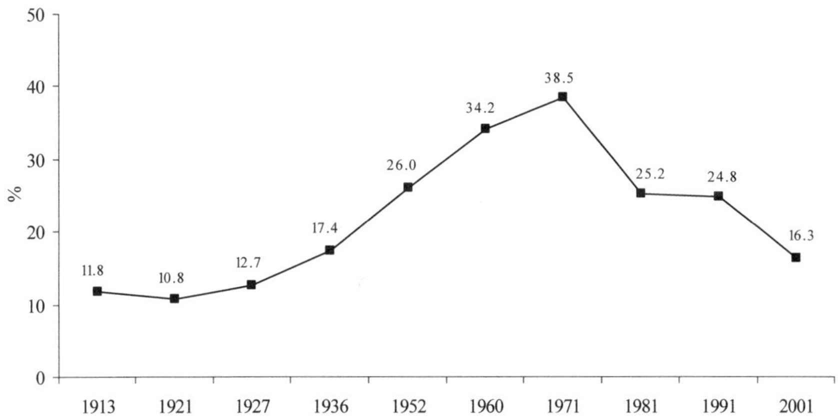

Fig. 5.1. Percentage weight of assets of the top 200 manufacturing firms on GDP

Source: our elaborations on the Imita.db; Mediobanca [1981, 1991, 2001]; Rossi, Sorgato and Toniolo [1993]; ISTAT [2004].

The decline intensifies in the last decade of the century, and it barely exceeds 15 per cent of the total GDP in the year 2001. This is not only due to technological change but also to the important role played by institutional transformations, with the strong impact of the privatization processes [Zanetti and Alzona 1998; Affinito, de Cecco and Dringoli 2000; Gallino 2003].

We now go on to analyze the sectoral changes occurring in the large Italian firms while investigating, also in comparison to the experience of other countries, the manner of diffusion of big business in Italy. If we observe the evolution of disaggregation, at the sectoral level, of the top 200 firms (Table 5.2), we note, firstly, the great relevance, in the first benchmark years, of the textile sector (DB) connected to the technological innovations of the First Industrial Revolution, and also the occurrence of other traditional sectors - leather (DC), wood (DD), manufacturing industries n.e.c. (DN) - not ascribable to the *technological waves* of the Second Industrial Revolution. In 1913 in fact, the four traditional sectors together make up 35.5 per cent of the total occurrences among the top 200 firms. This weight, though in constant decline, is still very high in 1927 with 29 per cent of the total and, once again in 1952, the textile firms (DB) are in second place, overtaken only by metals and metal products (DJ), with regard to the number of occurrences in the sample.

The quota of assets of the textile sector (DB) over the total of the top 200 firms (Table 5.3) also confirms our observations relative to the number of firms: in 1913, this quota tops that of all the other manufacturing sectors, making up over a quarter of the overall total assets of the top 200 firms (26.7 per cent). Regarding the observed weight in terms of the number of firms, the quota of assets of the textile sector (DB) over the total assets decreases more rapidly in the course of time but, in 1927, it still manages to reach 18.2 per cent. This means that within the sample, the firms in this sector recede faster in terms of ranking than in terms of number: the average ranking in fact moves down from the 101st position to the 126th position from 1913 to 1921.

A comparison between the sectoral distribution of the top 200 Italian firms and that of the world's three main industrialized countries gives an understanding of the characteristics of the delay in the spread of new technologies. When we compare the sectoral structure of the large Italian firm on the eve of the First World War with that of the United States, Germany and the United Kingdom (Table 5.4) we can observe, apart from the permanence in the Italian case of the textile sector (DB), substantial differences relative to the reduced presence of basic metals firms (DJ), but also certain similarities regarding the weight of the chemical (DG) and transport equipment (DM) sectors. In both the latter cases, however, even though the number of firms is similar to that of the other countries, the Italian firms carry a different weight with regard to the different technological and productive specialization. In the chemical sector (DG), for example, the Italian firms concentrate their activity on traditional products, especially nitrogenous fertilizers and products deriving from the processing of animal fats, which have little in common with those springing from the innovations of the Second Industrial Revolution [Vasta 1999a].

Table 5.2. Sectoral composition of the top 200 firms by benchmark year (1913-2001)

Sector	1913	1921	1927	1936	1952	1960	1971	1981	1991	2001	Total
Food products and tobacco (DA)	28	35	32	28	22	20	16	16	21	25	243
Textiles and textile products (DB)	64	52	55	41	32	22	10	6	7	4	293
Leather and leather products (DC)	2	3	1	1	1	-	-	-	-	3	11
Wood and wood products (DD)	1	1	1	1	1	-	-	-	-	-	5
Paper products, publishing and printing (DE)	6	5	6	6	7	9	13	11	12	12	87
Coke and petroleum products (DF)	1	2	5	12	23	23	28	19	18	10	141
Chemicals and chemical products (DG)	22	22	30	36	28	33	29	26	35	33	294
Rubber and plastic products (DH)	-	-	2	3	3	4	3	6	5	3	29
Other non-metallic products (DI)	9	5	9	11	7	13	13	12	15	17	111
Basic metals and metal products (DJ)	21	27	23	23	33	31	30	29	18	12	247
Machinery and equipment (DK)	10	3	2	5	6	6	18	28	19	21	118
Electrical and optical equipment (DL)	6	9	5	10	19	22	26	28	36	37	198
Transport equipment (DM)	26	33	28	22	17	16	13	19	14	22	210
Manufacturing n.e.c. (DN)	4	3	1	1	1	1	1	-	-	1	13
Total	200	200	200	200	200	200	200	200	200	200	2,000

Source: our elaborations on the Imita.db; Mediobanca [1981, 1991, 2001].

Table 5.3. Percentage distribution of assets of the top 200 firms by sector and benchmark year (1913-2001)

Sector	1913	1921	1927	1936	1952	1960	1971	1981	1991	2001
Food products and tobacco (DA)	13.2	10.0	9.9	10.0	6.5	5.0	4.1	3.8	7.0	9.9
Textiles and textile products (DB)	26.7	18.7	18.2	10.6	9.1	5.1	2.0	1.7	2.1	2.0
Leather and leather products (DC)	0.6	0.6	0.2	0.2	0.1	0.0	0.0	0.0	0.0	0.8
Wood and wood products (DD)	0.2	0.2	0.3	0.2	0.1	0.0	0.0	0.0	0.0	0.0
Paper products, publishing and printing (DE)	1.7	1.1	1.6	1.9	1.9	1.8	2.4	2.3	2.9	6.0
Coke and petroleum products (DF)	0.2	0.4	1.7	8.5	10.2	9.9	14.3	11.8	9.9	7.5
Chemicals and chemical products (DG)	9.6	8.5	27.0	20.9	19.3	22.2	24.2	9.7	12.3	11.5
Rubber and plastic products (DH)	0.0	0.0	2.3	3.5	3.4	7.4	2.5	3.0	1.6	1.1
Other non-metallic products (DI)	3.0	1.8	2.6	3.1	2.3	4.0	3.4	2.7	4.3	5.3
Basic metals and metal products (DJ)	19.4	21.2	14.6	15.7	23.2	20.3	17.8	18.7	8.6	6.4
Machinery and equipment (DK)	7.6	8.6	0.6	3.5	1.4	1.1	4.6	10.7	7.3	9.1
Electrical and optical equipment (DL)	3.7	5.3	2.3	3.4	5.2	6.1	9.0	15.5	22.5	18.3
Transport equipment (DM)	12.5	22.3	18.4	18.2	17.0	16.8	15.6	20.1	21.4	21.7
Manufacturing n.e.c. (DN)	1.5	1.2	0.4	0.5	0.4	0.3	0.2	0.0	0.0	0.2
Total	100.0	100.0	100.0	100.0	100.0	100.0	100.0	100.0	100.0	100.0

Source: our elaborations on the Imita.db; Mediobanca [1981, 1991, 2001].

As far as transport equipment (DM) is concerned, shipyard and railway production weigh a lot more compared to automobile production. There is a strong discrepancy with respect to the US regarding the occurrence of petroleum firms (DF), but this is due, as for the other European countries, to the difference in the endowment of resources and to the delay in the mass diffusion of the automobile.

Table 5.4. Sectoral distribution of the top 200 firms by country (1913-1917)

Sector	US (1917)	UK (1917)	Germany (1913)	Italy (1913)
Food products and tobacco (DA)	17.5	32.0	13.5	14.0
Textiles and textile products (DB)	4.5	13.0	8.0	32.0
Leather and leather products (DC)	2.0	0.5	1.0	1.0
Wood and wood products (DD)	1.5	-	0.5	0.5
Paper products, publishing and printing (DE)	3.5	4.0	2.0	3.0
Coke and petroleum products (DF)	11.0	1.5	2.5	0.5
Chemicals and chemical products (DG)	10.5	7.0	15.0	11.0
Rubber and plastic products (DH)	2.5	1.5	2.0	-
Other non-metallic products (DI)	2.5	1.0	3.5	4.5
Basic metals and metal products (DJ)	21.0	20.5	27.0	10.5
Machinery and equipment (DK)	8.5	3.5	12.5	5.0
Electrical and optical equipment (DL)	2.5	3.0	4.5	3.0
Transport equipment (DM)	12.0	11.5	8.0	13.0
Manufacturing n.e.c. (DN)	0.5	1.0	-	2.0
Total	100.0	100.0	100.0	100.0

Source: our elaborations on the Imita.db; Chandler [1990].

In general, we can therefore affirm that the strong persistence of firms linked to the technologies of the First Industrial Revolution contributes to creating a greater level of turbulence, as we will see further on (see Sect. 5.4), in the sectoral structure of the large Italian enterprise as compared to that of the US. The comparative analysis shows how, already during the first decades of the 20th century, the sectoral mix of the large Italian enterprise is not too different from that of the two leading countries in Europe, especially that of the UK. In the latter case, in fact, there is an analogous prevalence of firms specialized in the production of consumer durables, although the food products and tobacco firms (DA) prevail. It seems therefore, that even though there is a technological delay, which is however evident only at the finest level of sectoral disaggregation, the diffusion of the high capital-intensive technologies of the Second Industrial Revolution determines, even in follower countries, homogeneity in the pattern of specialization of the large enterprise.

After the Second World War, the structure of the large Italian firm undergoes a change, even though it is not a radical transformation. As already noted, the considerable weight of the textile sector (DB) persists, even though in rapid decline, while the petroleum sector (DF) starts to emerge, owing to the beginning of the diffusion of the automobile and the strong growth in energy consumption. It is, however, the basic metals and metal products sector (DJ) and the electrical and optical equipment sector (DL) that reach the top positions, both in the number ranking and in the quota of assets ranking.

The comparative study of the sectoral structure of the top 200 firms in the early 1950s confirms some of the previous observations. There are high levels of homogeneity in the patterns of specialization with respect to those of the leading countries (Table 5.5). In this case it seems that, even though there is a general convergence, the greater homogeneity of the sectoral structure of the large Italian firm can be compared, also because of the emergence of the petroleum processing firms, to the sectoral structure of the United States. The only relevant exception is the persistence of the textile (DB) firms (16 per cent in Italy versus 4 per cent in the US). The differences in the machinery and equipment sector (DK) and in the electrical and optical equipment sector (DL) tend to compensate each other.

Table 5.5. Sectoral distribution of the top 200 firms by country (1948-1953)

Sector	US (1948)	UK (1948)	Germany (1953)	Italy (1952)
Food products and tobacco (DA)	16.0	29.5	11.0	11.0
Textiles and textile products (DB)	4.0	9.5	13.5	16.0
Leather and leather products (DC)	1.0	-	1.0	0.5
Wood and wood products (DD)	1.0	0.5	-	0.5
Paper products, publishing and printing (DE)	4.0	6.5	1.5	3.5
Coke and petroleum products (DF)	11.0	1.5	3.0	11.5
Chemicals and chemical products (DG)	12.0	9.0	12.5	14.0
Rubber and plastic products (DH)	2.5	1.0	2.5	1.5
Other non-metallic products (DI)	3.0	4.0	3.0	3.5
Basic metals and metal products (DJ)	14.5	16.0	22.5	16.5
Machinery and equipment (DK)	11.5	5.0	14.0	3.0
Electrical and optical equipment (DL)	3.5	5.5	5.0	9.5
Transport equipment (DM)	14.5	10.5	9.0	8.5
Manufacturing n.e.c. (DN)	1.5	1.5	1.5	0.5
Total	100.0	100.0	100.0	100.0

Source: our elaborations on the Imita.db; Chandler [1990].

As shown in Tables 5.2 and 5.3, in the phase of the Golden age, which ends in 1971, the weight of the traditional sectors decreases, this time in a substantial way: the textile sector (DB) shrinks from 32 to 10 firms and its quota of assets also decreases considerably (from 9.1 per cent to 2 per cent of the total); the food products sector (DA) also becomes less important and the leather (DC) and wood product (DD) sectors disappear from the ranking of the top 200 firms. There is considerable growth in the paper products (DE) and non-metallic products (DI) sectors, both in terms of firms and in overall quota of assets. This growth is ascribable to the extensive development of the firms that exploit economies of scale, as in the production of paper and cement. Strong growth dynamics can also be found in the machinery and equipment sector (DK) and in the electrical and optical equipment sector (DL). In this case an extension of the productive matrix that characterizes the large Italian firm can be observed, with the emergence of the companies connected to the production of electrical appliances in the first case and with the *entry* of the first multinational computer companies in the second.

In the last thirty years of the century, the phase of development of the Third Industrial Revolution related to Information and Communication Technologies (ICT), the sectoral structure of the large Italian enterprise seems to adapt fairly rapidly to the technological changes taking place, even though there are some rather relevant peculiarities. There is in fact, a substantial growth in the number of firms belonging to the electrical and optical equipment sector (DL), within which we find all the ICT firms. This latter sector becomes first in order of importance as far as number of firms among the top 200 is concerned, while it takes second place behind that of transport equipment (DM), which is characterized by a greater capital intensity. The transport equipment sector (DM) is the other sector which shows a considerable growth, and in fact, the number of firms among the top 200 in this sector increases from 13 in 1971 to 22 in the year 2001. Minor progress can also be noted in the machinery and equipment (DK) and in the non-metallic products (DI) sectors, while the food products sector (DA) shows intense growth dynamics: from 16 companies, with a quota of 4.1 per cent of the total assets, in 1971, to 25 companies, with 9.9 per cent, in the year 2001. The *reappearance*, after a 50 year absence, of the leather products sector (DC) with the occurrence in the year 2001 of three firms (Prada, Gucci and Tod's), part of the *made in Italy* brand, among the top 200 Italian companies is also worthy of note. The petroleum product firms (DF) decrease in number (down from 28 to 10 in the period 1971-2001) as do the metal products (DJ) ones (down from 30 to 12 during the same period). For both sectors the reduction is also confirmed by the quota of assets held, which in the first case decreases from 14.3 per cent to 7.5 per cent and, in the second, from 17.8 per cent to 6.4 per cent. In the case of the leather sector (DC), the *re-entry* is due to the rise of hierarchical production systems, with the consolidation of a number of leader trademarks within the local systems specialized in traditional products [Harrison 1997]. As far as the petroleum products (DF) and the metals products firms (DJ) are concerned, the main causes are the processes of company reorganization linked to the privatization campaigns of the 1990s and, in some cases, the transfer, presumably for taxation purposes, of company headquarters abroad, as for example, in the case of Europa Metalli.

Although we have no homogeneous comparative data for the UK and Germany, it is still necessary to analyze the structural change that occurs during the last decades of the century concurrently with the diffusion of the ICT. The comparison between the sectoral structure of the top 200 Italian firms in the year 2001 and that of US firms in this case shows a considerable degree of homogeneity (Table 5.6) if we disregard the greater occurrence of the paper sector (DE) and of the manufacturing n.e.c. (DN) in the US. Italy instead shows a greater specialization in the non-metallic products (DI) and in the machinery and equipment sector (DK).

Table 5.6. Comparison Italy-US of the sectoral distribution of the top 200 firms (2001)

Sector	US	Italy
Food products and tobacco (DA)	12.0	12.5
Textiles and textile products (DB)	3.0	2.0
Leather and leather products (DC)	-	1.5
Wood and wood products (DD)	-	-
Paper products, publishing and printing (DE)	9.5	6.0
Coke and petroleum products (DF)	5.5	5.0
Chemicals and chemical products (DG)	20.0	16.5
Rubber and plastic products (DH)	-	1.5
Other non-metallic products (DI)	2.0	8.5
Basic metals and metal products (DJ)	3.5	6.0
Machinery and equipment (DK)	6.0	10.5
Electrical and optical equipment (DL)	21.0	18.5
Transport equipment (DM)	13.5	11.0
Manufacturing n.e.c. (DN)	4.0	0.5
Total	100.0	100.0

Source: our elaborations on Mediobanca [1981, 1991, 2001]; Fortune [2002].

From the long-term analysis, as can be seen above, we can observe a progressive homogeneity in the sectoral specialization of the large Italian firms compared to that of the most industrialized countries, as Cassis [1997] has already shown in a comparison between the firms of the three main European countries. At the same time it seems useful to supply a few comparative elements also regarding firms' size. This is not a simple aim, given the extreme lack of homogeneity of the proxies adopted by the literature and the fact that the sources are not always readily available. Table 5.7 however, shows, for only a few benchmark years, the position that the 200th US, UK and German firm would have held in the ranking of large Italian firms. As far as the US is concerned we can note how the 200th firm always ranks among the top 20 Italian firms. The lowest placing (19th) occurs in 1971 concurrently with the size apogee reached by the main Italian firms among the top 200. The comparison with the 200th UK firm also shows a placing which is not too different from that of the US. The comparison between Italy and Germany, however, shows a different situation: if in fact in the years preceding the Second World War there is an advantage, which is however less evident than that registered for the US and the UK, in favor of the German firms, in 1953 the position of the 200th German firm in the Italian ranking is lower than 300. This is presumably due to the effects that the Second World War had on the German economy.

Table 5.7. Position in the ranking according to assets of the Italian firms of the 200th firm of some countries

Year	US	UK	Year	Germany
1917	7	25	1913	67
1930	14	27	1929	108
1948	11	6	1953	335
1971	19	-		
1991	11	-		

Source: our elaborations on the Imita.db; Fortune [1972, 1992]; Chandler [1990]; Maddison [1991]; Cassis [1997].

Note: data calculated in 1985 US$ (PPP), see Maddison [1991]. Given that Chandler's ranking [1990] for the UK makes use of the value of the stock market, to obtain a comparable unit of measurement it was necessary to calculate the value of the assets. This was obtained by assuming that the relationship between the two measures (value of the stock market and assets) was equal to the average relationship observed for the main UK firms [Cassis 1997].

5.4. Stability *versus* turbulence

The population of the large Italian manufacturing firms in the 20th century is characterized, in contrast to the predictions of the Chandlerian hypothesis, by strong turbulence. Only 8 firms, in fact, are present in all the benchmark years and only another 4 remain in the ranking as from 1921. There are an additional 2 firms present in the initial year (1913) and in the final year (2001), but they are not among the top 200 in all the years. As can be seen from Table 5.8 and Fig. 5.2 overall the dataset contains 877 firms for a total of 2,000 available positions (200 firms for each of the 10 years selected). A total of 449 firms, more than half of the entire sample, appear only once in the list, while 168 firms are present for two benchmark years.

Even though the continuity criteria adopted were rather broad, the change in population has a great relevance, considerably superior, for example, to that observed for the US [Louçã and Mendonça 2002]. In the American case the authors argue, on the basis of the permanence during the period from 1917 to 1997 of 28 firms among the top 200, the existence of a strong turnover at the apex of American capitalism.

Table 5.8. Frequency of occurrence among the top 200 manufacturing firms (1913-2001)

Number of occurrences	Number of firms
10	8
9	9
8	13
7	13
6	26
5	30
4	70
3	91
2	168
1	449
Total	*877*

Source: our elaborations on the Imita.db; Mediobanca [1981, 1991, 2001].

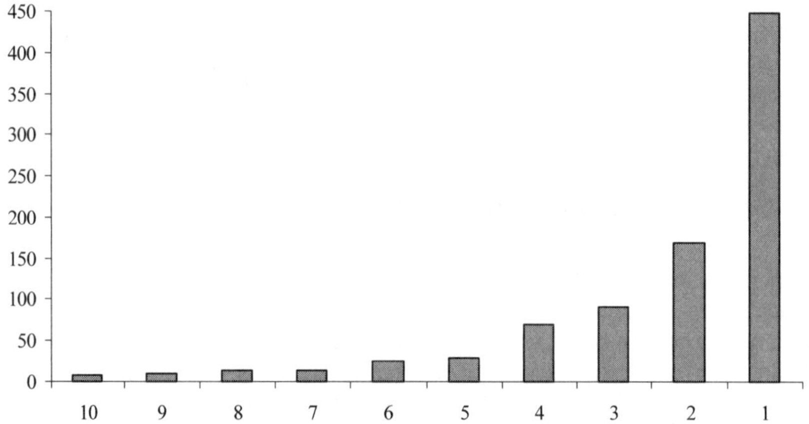

Fig. 5.2. Frequency of occurrence among the top 200 manufacturing firms (1913-2001)

Source: our elaborations on the Imita.db; Mediobanca [1981, 1991, 2001].

As can be seen from the list in Table 5.9, the 8 Italian firms present in all the years do not necessarily represent the top of Italian industry. Only FIAT, and ILVA, whose path is, at any rate, rather troubled, remain constantly in the top positions in the ranking, while the remaining cases display different paths. There are two food products firms (DA), Birra Peroni and Cirio-Del Monte Italia which appear in all the years, but almost always in positions lower than the 100th. Other firms, though they represent the elite of Italian capitalism, appear in the ranking in different positions according to their phases of development. The Breda (identified with the name Ansaldobreda, the last name used), for example, remains at the apex until 1936, when it is the leading Italian railway construction firm, and then moves rapidly downward. It re-emerges in 30th position in the year 2001 when the Ansaldo's railway division is turned over to Breda and the firm adopts the new denomination. See-saw patterns can also be observed in the cases of Eridania and Italcementi. The former registers a peak between the 1930s and the 1960s concurrently with the great growth of the high energy intensity firms founded on economies of scale, while in the remaining periods it settles in positions far from the top of the ranking. Italcementi, instead, even though it follows the same path as Eridania, regains a relevant position as from the 1990s, reaching 15th position in the year 2001. Finally, Manifattura Lane G. Marzotto, another firm present in all the benchmark years, shows a peculiar pattern of growth. It originates as a wool firm and in the year 1913 it has an intermediate position in the sectoral ranking. Subsequently, thanks to a widespread and difficult acquisitions campaign, it diversifies its activities to include the processing of cotton and the manufacture of clothing, becoming the most important Italian textile firm and reaching the 68th position in the ranking in the year 2001.

There are two types of firms among those with 9 occurrences in the dataset. The first is represented by companies that maintain a constant presence in the dataset until 1991, for example, mechanical firms like Ansaldo, at the centre of the recent processes of reorganization of state-owned enterprises, or iron and steel companies such as La Magona d'Italia, which in 1998 became part of one of the sector's main European groups. The other type consists of firms that enter the top 200 in 1921 and remain there until the year 2001, such as Piaggio and SKF.

Of the 13 companies with 8 occurrences in the dataset, 10 are already present as from 1913. Some are firms belonging to traditional sectors, for example the textile sector (DB) - Lanerossi, Cantoni, Olcese - or ceramics (Richard Ginori) which progressively lose importance, thus causing the egress of many firms from the top 200. In other cases such as Cartiere Italiane Riunite or Italiana Industria degli Zuccheri there is a backward slide due to the dynamics of the mature sectors founded on economies of scale. There are other cases that stand out, such as that of AGIP (a state-owned enterprise, founded in 1926), which rapidly rises to the summit of the ranking and consolidates in the top positions; and that of Cartiere Burgo which, as from 1927, is constantly among the top 50 Italian firms.

The *delayed* entry or *early* exit phenomenon present even among the firms with a high number of occurrences in the dataset reflects, as we have already seen, the structural change in Italian industry. The firms that persist in the first benchmark years represent those *success* stories which, despite the technological change which promotes the Second Industrial Revolution sectors, are capable of remaining among the top 200 firms at least until the 1960s.

Table 5.9. Ranking of the firms with more than 7 occurrences in the benchmark years (1913-2001)*

	1913	1921	1927	1936	1952	1960	1971	1981	1991	2001
10 occurrences										
Ansaldobreda	21	5	8	15	75	164	111	157	77	30
Birra Peroni industriale	190	173	192	148	84	119	107	146	104	166
Cirio Del Monte Italia	200	144	117	56	131	118	146	152	118	114
Eridania	16	35	53	5	10	18	14	33	23	88
FIAT Auto	19	3	3	3	1	1	2	2	1	1
ILVA	4	1	4	2	4	4	3	1	3	4
Italcementi - Fabbriche Riunite Cemento	87	46	19	17	17	16	20	36	19	15
G. Marzotto & F. - Manifattura Lane	132	37	52	106	14	25	61	104	43	68
9 occurrences										
ABB Sace	60	48	42	59	83	91	92	100	186	-
Acciaierie Ferriere Lombarde Falck	42	23	27	10	13	12	17	24	41	-
Ansaldo	2	2	5	7	11	5	51	11	9	-
Dalmine	-	30	32	43	18	21	16	16	46	63
Europa Metalli LMI	18	12	21	24	63	49	67	69	60	-
La Magona d'Italia	49	54	66	49	81	136	90	126	140	-
Montefibre	-	78	7	27	25	28	18	43	39	136
Piaggio & C.	-	123	129	36	59	50	64	49	97	53
SKF Industrie	-	138	122	61	26	22	25	46	78	117
8 occurrences										
3M Italia	-	130	197	133	69	76	46	57	53	-
AGIP Petroli	-	-	28	11	9	9	4	4	5	3
Alcan Alluminio	-	43	87	92	113	172	-	199	192	200
Cartiere Burgo	-	-	30	18	19	26	40	47	20	16
Cartiere Italiane Riunite	80	107	165	103	94	120	142	134	-	-
Ceramica Italiana Pozzi Richard-Ginori	55	153	163	159	139	131	120	109	-	-
Cotonificio Cantoni	26	50	55	58	68	75	72	120	-	-
Cotonificio Olcese - Veneziano	51	76	90	87	35	68	105	197	-	-
ELSAG	115	52	85	31	52	-	-	27	87	135
Gruppo Lanerossi	14	17	10	32	34	42	60	42	-	-
Industrie Pirelli	9	6	6	6	7	3	8	37	-	-
Italiana Industria degli Zuccheri	11	60	34	20	21	23	35	59	-	-
SNIA Fibre	-	4	1	8	6	8	6	64	90	-

Source: our elaborations on the Imita.db; Mediobanca [1981, 1991, 2001].

* The name used here is that used during the last year in which the company is present in the dataset.

A further element which reinforces the hypothesis of turbulence among the large Italian firms comes from a comparison between the average ranking of the initial and final year of the firms which survive for two years (Fig. 5.3). In general, the firms which survive are incapable of improving their ranking. On the contrary, until 1981, their position worsens, which seems, for example, particularly relevant between 1921 and 1927, when a backward slide takes place from the 85th position to the 97th position. The only exception occurs between 1927 and 1936, when, however, there is only a slight improvement in the ranking of surviving firms, which move up four positions. As from 1991 the situation is reversed: the *permanent* firms improve their ranking both as compared to the 1981-1991 period and to the 1991-2001 period. This phenomenon, as we shall see further on, coincides with the increase of turbulence among the large Italian firms.

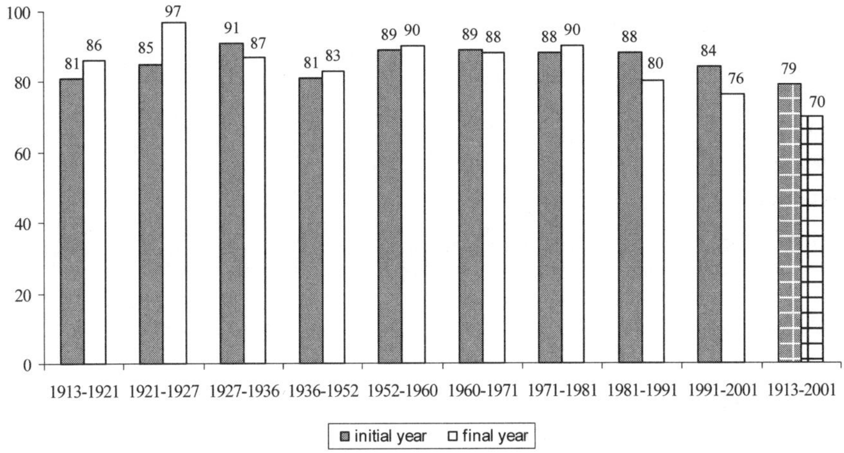

Fig. 5.3. Comparison between the average positions in the ranking of the *permanent* firms for two benchmark years (1913-2001)

Source: our elaborations on the Imita.db; Mediobanca [1981, 1991, 2001].

The comparison between the average ranking of the *permanent* firms and the *incoming* firms (Table 5.10), namely those that are not present in the previous year's sample, confirms earlier affirmations. If, in fact, as expected, the *permanent* firms show a better average position for the entire period as compared to that of the *new entries*, this could be ascribable to the scanty and slow capacity for growth in size of all Italian firms and not to the consolidation of the *permanent* firms. The observation of the transition between the single benchmark years allows us to verify whether the periods of greater turbulence correspond to the change from one technological phase to the next.

As Table 5.11 shows, on average, over the entire period, there is an entry of approximately 41 per cent of firms in each benchmark year, a value slightly greater than that registered for the US, where it is around 35 per cent [Louçã and Mendonça 2002]. The periods of greatest turbulence occur between 1981 and 1991 and between 1991 and the year 2001: it is only in these periods in fact that the rate of permanence falls below 50 per cent. It is plausible therefore, that, as we have seen with structural change, and analogously to the US [Louçã and Mendonça 2002], this phenomenon could be attributed to the technological discontinuity of the Third Industrial Revolution, which causes a general reduction in the size of firms belonging to the Second Industrial Revolution and the rise of some of the new sectors such as those related to the ICT.

Table 5.10. Comparison between the average position in the ranking of the *permanent* firms and the *incoming* firms (1913-2001)

Period	*Permanent* position	*Incoming* position	Difference
1913-1921	86	120	34
1921-1927	97	109	12
1927-1936	87	121	34
1936-1952	83	126	43
1952-1960	90	137	47
1960-1971	88	120	32
1971-1981	90	116	26
1981-1991	80	117	37
1991-2001	76	121	45

Source: our elaborations on the Imita.db; Mediobanca [1981, 1991, 2001].

Table 5.11. *Permanent* and *incoming* firms between benchmark years (1913-2001)

Period	Number of *permanent* companies	%	Number of *incoming* companies	%
1913-1921	114	57.0	86	43.0
1921-1927	134	67.0	66	33.0
1927-1936	121	60.5	79	39.5
1936-1952	119	59.5	81	40.5
1952-1960	154	77.0	46	23.0
1960-1971	122	61.0	78	39.0
1971-1981	120	60.0	80	40.0
1981-1991	89	44.5	111	55.5
1991-2001	92	46.0	108	54.0
1913-2001 (average)	*118.3*	*59.2*	*81.7*	*40.8*

Source: our elaborations on the Imita.db; Mediobanca [1981, 1991, 2001].

The periods of greatest stability occur during the 1920s (67 per cent), even though in this case the data could be partially altered by the shortness of the time-span considered, and above all in the 1950s (77 per cent). These are two phases, especially the second, in which the consolidation of the large firms founded on the Fordist paradigm prevails. In the course of the 1950s the high rate of stability can also be ascribed to the favorable economic trend.

The hypothesis according to which the periods of greater stability of the system of large Italian enterprises coincide with the evolution of *technological regimes* seems therefore confirmed, while the discontinuities in technical progress offer greater opportunities for the new firms, which in turn determines a redefinition of the hierarchies. In order to better distinguish between the different phases, an analysis of the characteristics of the *incoming* firms is now necessary.

5.5. Intra-sectoral turbulence: the dynamics of the *incoming* firms

The change in the sectoral structure of the top 200 firms, presented above (see Sect. 5.3), is determined by the balance between the number of *incoming* firms and *outgoing* firms for each sector between two benchmark years. In order to determine in what measure, during the different phases, the turbulence depends on technological discontinuities, which produce opportunities for growth in the new sectors, or on other factors (ownership arrangements, fiscal regime, industrial policies) not directly linked to the dynamics of technical progress, it is advisable to focus on the *incoming* firms at the sectoral level in each benchmark year. The study of this type of data permits a greater understanding of intra-sectoral turbulence, underlining the characteristics of change, even in the presence of structural stability. The use of an example will better illustrate the difference between structural change and intra-sectoral turbulence: between 1971 and 1981, the food sector (DA), as can be seen from Table 5.2, remains stable with 16 occurrences and does not cause structural changes within the system of large Italian firms. This result, however, is determined by the exodus of 7 firms from the top 200, subsequently replaced by 7 *incoming* firms (see Table 5.12). The strong intra-sectoral turbulence thus underlines the creation of new opportunities, while the weight of the sector on the system of large Italian enterprises remains constant.

Table 5.12 illustrates, for each interval, the sectoral disaggregation of the *incomers*, highlighting in bold type when the flux is equal to, or greater than, 10 units. The absolute value of the intra-sectoral changes, in fact, permits us to underline the breadth of the dynamics in the most important sectors of the Italian industrial structure. For the first interval, that between 1913 and 1921, which, as we have seen, is on the whole characterized by high levels of turbulence, there are 5 sectors which have more than 10 *incoming* firms. These consist in 2 traditional sectors, such as food (DA) and textiles (DB), 2 sectors linked to the innovations of the Second Industrial Revolution, the chemical (DG) and the basic metals (DJ) sectors, and finally the transport equipment sector (DM) whose evolution is linked to the *fourth technological wave* of oil, the automobile and mass production. When we examine the characteristics of the new firms belonging to this latter sector, however, we observe the large number of companies specialized in railway and shipyard products, while there are only 3 automobile companies which appear in the list for the first time in 1921. The strong turbulence therefore, seems linked to the evolution of the *technological waves* of the Second Industrial Revolution rather than to the effects of a new technological discontinuity. The automobile companies which remain among the top 200 reinforce their positions in the ranking - FIAT, for example, moves up from 19th position to 3rd position and Itala moves from 78th position to 39th position - on the other hand, and the same also happens in the UK and Germany, the *incomers* are few, also due to the high levels of concentration which already characterized this sector. The causes of the turbulence are, however, also ascribable to the great transformations in the industrial structure of the country brought about by First World War.

Table 5.12. Number of *incoming* firms by sector (1913-2001)

Sector	1913-1921	1921-1927	1927-1936	1936-1952	1952-1960	1960-1971	1971-1981	1981-1991	1991-2001
Food products and tobacco (DA)	**17**	**12**	**11**	5	4	9	7	**11**	**14**
Textiles and textile products (DB)	**14**	**14**	9	9	1	3	-	5	1
Leather and leather products (DC)	1	-	-	1	-	-	-	-	3
Wood and wood products (DD)	1	-	-	-	-	-	-	-	-
Paper products, publishing and printing (DE)	1	2	3	4	3	5	1	**10**	7
Coke and petroleum products (DF)	2	4	9	**14**	3	**11**	5	**11**	2
Chemicals and chemical products (DG)	**15**	**17**	**13**	**12**	9	9	**10**	**20**	**22**
Rubber and plastic products (DH)	-	1	2	1	1	1	3	3	-
Other non-metallic products (DI)	-	5	6	-	6	4	5	7	7
Basic metals and metal products (DJ)	**14**	5	9	**15**	6	**10**	**16**	8	6
Machinery and equipment (DK)	2	1	2	3	2	**11**	**12**	**11**	**10**
Electrical and optical equipment (DL)	5	1	5	**12**	8	7	**12**	**21**	**24**
Transport equipment (DM)	**14**	4	9	5	3	8	9	4	**12**
Manufacturing n.e.c. (DN)	-	-	1	-	-	-	-	-	1
Total	86	66	79	81	46	78	80	111	108

Source: our elaborations on Imita.db; Mediobanca [1981, 1991, 2001].

The 1920s and 1930s are characterized by a lesser level of turbulence: 3 sectors gain more than 10 *incomers* between 1921-1927 and only 2 between 1927 and 1936. Over and above the dynamics of the textile sector, which are also determined by the high number of occurrences in the sample, there is also an intense sectoral turbulence in the chemical sector (DG), which, moreover, has high barriers to entry. It seems therefore, that the 1920s and the 1930s are distinguished by the existence of new technological opportunities. This could be due to the delay with which the chemical sector develops in Italy [Zamagni 1990b] and, analogously to the US [Louçã and Mendonça 2002], to the development of new products like, for example, the cracking to obtain synthetic fuels [Petri 1998]. The considerable turbulence which can be observed in the food sector (DA) is in large part due to the consolidation of the sugar companies. Notwithstanding the fact that the sugar industry is controlled by only a few industrial groups, the single firms maintain an independent name to that of the controlling company [Tonizzi 2001].

The turbulence that can be observed between 1936 and 1952, which is also influenced by the fact that it is one of the longest intervals among all those examined, is essentially ascribable to the organizational changes that pervade Italian industry after the Second World War. The basic metal sector has 15 new entries, but the better part of these are long standing firms which reorganized in the early post-Second World War period following the Piano Sinigaglia [Balconi 1991]. As far as the petroleum sector (DF) is concerned, the rise in consumption leads to a first phase of growth for the firms in this sector, which are characterized, on average, by a very low age and by positions in the last quartile of the ranking, for example, the Industrie Chimiche Italiane del Petrolio (ICIP) or the Aziende Petrolifere Riunite Italiane (APRI). The chemical sector (DG) also shows a rise of firms with a very low average age, usually born during the fascist period, as in the case of Liquigas (1936), or in the *reconstruction* years, such as Laboratori Palma (1946). The high number of *incomers* in the electrical sector (DL) can, instead, be explained as the first phase of development of the sector, which doubles its weight within the sample with the entry of a number of branches of great multinational companies such as IBM and Marconi.

The 1950s, or the interval between 1952 and 1960, are characterized by a greater stability: all sectors have less than 10 *incomers*. The chemical sector (DG) is still characterized by the greatest degree of turbulence (9 *incomers*) which seems to be due to the growth of some of the petrol-chemical firms, such as Sincat or Sicedison, born in the years immediately after the Second World War.

The 1960s present some peculiar characteristics. The consolidation of the growth in consumption produces the high levels of turbulence which can be seen in the basic metals sector (DJ) and in the petroleum sector (DF). In the former case, however, though there is only a slight increase in the number of occurrences, the turbulence is also caused by the growth in the production of special alloys and aluminum. As far as the petroleum sector (DF) is concerned, the high number of new companies is essentially determined by the entry among the top 200 firms of a number of multinational petrol companies (Amoco, Chevron, Gulf, Texaco and Total) and by the development of some companies, specialized in petrol refinery, in Southern Italy (Saras and Mediterranea Raffineria Siciliana Petroli). The strong dynamics of private consumption explanation for the turbulence is also valid for the machinery and equipment sector (DK), in which companies such as Zoppas, Ignis and Indesit, for the production of electrical appliances, emerge.

The 1970s show a strong turbulence in the basic metals sector (DJ), the machinery and equipment sector (DK), in the electrical (DL) and the chemical (DG) sectors. While the change in this latter sector can be attributed to the crisis involving the chemical sector (DG), which is compelled to redefine ownership arrangements [Marchi and Marchionatti 1992; Giannetti 1996], the basic metals (DJ) is instead characterized by a reduction in firms' size and by numerous de-mergers, which determine the *entry* of 16 new firms. Nevertheless there is stability in the occurrences among the top 200 - which move from 30 to 29 (see Table 5.2). The data for the machinery and mechanical sector (DK) - 12 new *entries* - are caused both by the spin-offs carried out by the FIAT group, with the creation of FIAT Trattori, FIAT Allis and FIAT Carrelli Elevatori, and by the growth in size of some companies, both Italian and foreign, born in the early 1950s. As far as the electrical sector (DL) is concerned a few new firms specializing in telecommunications emerge.

The 1980s, characterized by a general and pronounced turbulence, register 6 sectors with 10, or more, new *incomers*. One of these sectors, the electrical sector (DL), goes beyond the threshold of 20, and another, the chemical sector (DG), reaches that threshold (20). For these two sectors the turbulence is essentially determined by the *fifth technological wave* linked to the ICT sectors. In the electrical sector (DL), which includes the firms which produce computer systems, radio and television equipment and telecommunication instruments, new national firms are born, such as Italtel Telematica and Alenia Spazio, and there is also the rise of the great multinational firms such as Digital, Siemens Data, Motorola and Sony. Finally, the restructuring of the Ansaldo carries some weight, with the entry of 4 firms deriving from the de-mergers carried out by this Genoese firm in the early 1980s [Castronovo, Hertner and Mori 2001, 2002].

This phenomenon can be ascribed to two reasons: on the one hand the growth of private consumption of ICT goods, on the other the development of the demand for more complex products destined to support the pervasive diffusion of ICT. The situation for the chemical sector (DG) is only partly explained by the above. If on the one hand, also in this case, there is the *entry* into the sample of a few multinational firms, especially in the pharmaceutical sector - Abbott, Boehringer and DOW Italia -, on the other hand, there are also the effects of the widespread process of restructuring of the Italian chemical industry with, for example, the numerous spin-offs carried out by Montedison. Finally there is also the weight of the rise of a few *historical* pharmaceutical firms for example Bracco and Caffaro.

The high intra-sectoral turbulence registered during the 1980s in the chemical (DG) and electrical (DL) sectors is also confirmed in the last decade of the century, when they register 22 and 24 new *incomers* respectively. As far as the chemical sector (DG) is concerned, the phenomenon is ascribable to the *entry* of numerous multinational firms such as Basell poliolefine, Roche, Pharmacia & Upjohn, Pfizer, Merck & Sharp, Lever Fabergé, etc. In the electrical sector (DL), the *incomers* are mainly Italian previously state-owned enterprises or parcel-outs of private firms, even though there are also foreign companies, such as Schneider electric and Hewlett Packard. It seems, therefore, that the dynamics of the two sectors are substantially similar, even though in the case of the chemical sector (DG) there is a greater entry of multinationals in the 1990s, while in the electrical sector (DL) it is concentrated during the 1980s, also because some foreign computer firms entered, as we have already seen, in the 1970s. The *entry* of the Third Industrial Revolution firms seems to be faster in the ICT sector than in the chemical sector (DG).

The observation of intra-sectoral turbulence confirms some of the hypotheses formulated previously and, at the same time, suggests further observations. The phases of technological discontinuity are accompanied by strong turbulence which tends to concentrate in the new sectors with the opening up of new opportunities. As is typical of follower countries, the technological changes occur with a certain amount of delay, which has repercussions on the growth dynamics of the large firms. This aspect however, seems to have different features in the different phases: the evolution of the technologies of the Second Industrial Revolution, in fact, though they determine a strong turbulence already from the first interval studied (1913-1921), continues to have effects also during the fascist period with the development of the chemical sector. In fact, in 1913 there is already a conspicuous occurrence of chemical companies in large Italian enterprise, even though they specialize in low intensity technological products [Vasta 1999a]. The *fourth technological wave* that of oil, the automobile and mass production takes place, analogously to the other European countries, with an even greater delay and its effects are manifest only as from the 1960s. On the contrary, the Third Industrial Revolution sectors, also due to the strong growth of the foreign companies, spread a great deal more rapidly with dynamics that do not differ much from those of the leader countries.

As we have already seen, the phases of technological maturity are instead characterized by minor turbulence in absolute terms, which however, with the exception of the 1950s, continues to have significant values at the intra-sectoral level. This could be ascribable to two causes: the first is the very small size, which makes the entry of new firms easier; the second is represented by the large presence of state-owned enterprises whose financial instability causes continuous restructurings, through de-mergers and reunifications, of the organizational arrangements, especially during the 1970s [Federico and Giannetti 1999].

5.6. Conclusions

This study has reconstructed the experience of the largest 200 Italian manufacturing firms during the entire span of the 20th century as regards their evolution in relation to the prevalent *technological wave*. The period studied includes two phases linked to the *technological waves* of the Second Industrial Revolution and the phase of the Third Industrial Revolution, which starts at the beginning of the 1970s (Table 5.1). The first phase of the technologies linked to the Second Industrial Revolution is that of the development of the iron and steel firms and the introduction of electricity; the second is that of mass production - which only spreads in Europe during the post-Second World War period - characterized by the development of the oil industry and the diffusion of the automobile.

As far as change in structure is concerned, the dynamics of the large Italian enterprise clearly display the sequence of the *technological waves* described, with the addition of two original characteristics. The first, which can be ascribed to the dynamics of a follower country, is the delay in the implementation of the technologies of the Second Industrial Revolution and the consequent persistence of the firms linked to the technologies of the First Industrial Revolution. The second is the decrease in the delay which can be observed in the spread of firms active during the second phase of the *technological wave* of the Second Industrial Revolution which is already well represented in the benchmark of 1960. The *technological wave* of the Third Industrial Revolution, instead, appears in Italy at the same time as in the leading countries, already as from the 1980s, and is also favored by the presence in Italy of multinational firms especially in the computer and pharmaceutical sectors.

As far as the size of the main firms is concerned, the Italian case is characterized by a smaller size of firms, as is evident from the comparison with the more advanced countries, but at the same time, a period of growth is clearly visible up to 1971, though there is a subsequent decrease in the last three decades of the century. Both these characteristics are common in the historical experience of developed countries; concurrently with the *technological waves* of the Second Industrial Revolution there is an increase in average size due to high barriers to entry and economies of scale, and there is subsequently a consistent reduction with the advent of the ICT characterized by a high degree of flexibility.

The Chandlerian literature on large enterprise underlines its stability in time linking it to the capacity for creating barriers to entry, for making greater profits and for diversifying the technologies which follow each other thanks to the skills accumulated [Chandler 1990; Patel and Pavitt 1998]. This result is not confirmed by the Italian case: only 8 firms are continuously present in all the benchmark years, while those present only once are 449. The *entry* of new firms is thus also correspondingly high and this determines a high level of turbulence, as can be seen also for the US [Louçã and Mendonça 2002]. Finally, we do not observe any ability on behalf of consolidated firms either to diversify into new sectors or to substantially improve their own position. The firms that do show an ability to take advantage of the new technological opportunities are for the most part new firms. It must be considered, however, that this result could depend on the habit of Italian firms to diversify through the creation of new firms belonging to groups, rather than diversifying existent firms.

Finally two other original traits which distinguish Italian firms should be mentioned. The first is the uncertainty in the trajectory of growth: linear trends are rare, while sizeable fluctuations in the position held over the various years surveyed are more frequent. The second is the strong intra-sectoral turbulence: there is a frequent turnover of firms operating within the same industrial sector. This phenomenon can be given both a positive and a negative interpretation, in the former case it could be interpreted as due to the existence of considerable entrepreneurial liveliness, in the latter as a difficulty of large Italian enterprise in consolidating its position.

6. Ownership and control in Italian capitalism (1911–1972)

Leonardo Bargigli and Michelangelo Vasta

6.1. Introduction

There has been a broad debate on the issue of the separation between the ownership and control of companies, starting with the intuitions of Berle and Means [1932], the successive observations by Galbraith [1967] up until the definition of a managerial approach to the theory of the firm [Baumol 1959; Marris 1964]. On the other hand, this theme had already been dealt with in the Marxist formulations on the influence of financial capital on the control of industrial enterprises [Hilferding 1910]. This last approach underlines how the separation between ownership and control is in reality only apparent, and that the different mechanisms adopted only represent processes of adaptation to different institutional contexts [Stigler and Friedland 1983]. More recently, the analysis of the institutions and the nature of the rules, which determine the processes of reallocation between ownership and control in various countries, have led to the identification of different models of capitalism [Aoki 1990; Franks and Mayer 1990; Albert 1991; Scott 1997]. In a long run perspective, new contributions have underlined how, on the one hand, the changes in capitalistic systems are strictly connected to the discontinuities imposed by the different phases of technological change [Posen 2002; Siebert and Stolpe 2002]; on the other, how the transformations in the regulation of ownership rights can also model national systems, redefining hierarchies [Pagano 2003].

Italian capitalism, as historiography has amply documented, presents mechanisms of allocation and ownership control of companies characterized by a few peculiar traits. These have determined the consolidation of organizational formulas - the large diffusion of holdings at the head of pyramidal groups, the great diffusion of family ownership and of the state-owned enterprise, and firms with a comparatively small average size, in contrast with other developed countries - whose efficiency has been greatly criticized [Barca 1996, 1997]. This theme has pervaded the different seasons of Italian economic historiography from Grifone's formulations [1945] on the centrality of financial capital, to Bonelli's arguments [1978] on the role of State capitalism, from the neo-Chandlerian readings of the same phenomenon proposed by Amatori [1995], up until Barca's observations

---

The present work was set out by both the authors, however, Sects. 6.2, 6.3 and 6.5 were written by Leonardo Bargigli, and Sects. 6.1, 6.4 and 6.6 by Michelangelo Vasta. The conclusions are a combined effort.

[1997] on the existence of an *extraordinary compromise* between the different concepts of the State.

This study, on the basis of the observation of the connections between firms through the presence of directors in the board of directors, intends to reconstruct a number of long run characteristics (1911-1972) of the structure of Italian capitalism and, at the same time, advance a few interpretative hypotheses on the dynamics of groups of firms. The organization of economic activities through groups of firms, in fact, involves several functional specificities typical of the Italian capitalistic system.

If on the one hand microeconomic theory has rarely supplied interpretative models to contribute to the understanding of the phenomenon, analogous difficulties arise from the point of view of industrial economics. The latter, in fact, is modeled on the Anglo-Saxon institutional configuration, in which the firm owns all its activities and has no ownership links to other firms. Many studies have, conversely, evidenced the variety of the forms of ownership and control, commenting on the centrality of the influence of firm groups in the different economic systems. Granovetter [1998], for example, has underlined how this theme has become the invisible problem of analyses on economic organizations, which prevalently adopt micro or macro perspectives, neglecting the *meso* level represented by groups of enterprises.

In accordance with the Chandlerian vision of the structure of economic systems, it has been suggested that company groups represent an answer to the market imperfections characterizing the more backward countries [Trento 1994]; the permanence of company groups also in the more advanced countries being only a residue of the past [Chandler 1982]. Another perspective, more attentive towards institutional contexts, on the other hand, explains the existence of company groups in the more developed countries as an attempt to find forms of organizational efficiency [Encaoua and Jacquemin 1982; Goto 1982].

Even though a number of interesting studies exist on groups, and particularly on the company interlocks which characterize them, the extreme complexity of the sources - the full understanding of which requires the use of techniques rendered possible only by the recent evolution of computers - has greatly limited, also for Italy, the possibility of studying the phenomenon as a whole[1]. There is, however, a consolidated body of literature on the subject, which has its origins in the pioneering contributions of Zorzini [1925] and Luzzatto Fegiz [1928] in the 1920s and continues with the studies by Rienzi [Zerini 1947a, 1947b, 1947c; Rienzi 1947-48; Radar 1948] and Benedetti and Toniolli [1963], who showed how a small number of great capitalistic groups exercised a great predominance over the national econ-

[1] The rapid development of the theoretical bases of network analysis, already as from the 1980s, has multiplied the studies on the connections between *actors*, within which the analysis of company interlocks has become decidedly relevant. These developments have not, however, been accompanied by an analogous growth in the availability of software capable of managing huge datasets. The attention has, therefore, been concentrated on small subsets - for example, large firms or the main banks - which do not allow a complete vision of the phenomenon.

omy after the Second World War. Subsequently, Ragozzino's works [1969] analyze the discontinuity generated in the control structure of the Italian economy by the nationalization of electricity, which caused the return of great family capital to central positions; while Chiesi's studies [1982, 1985] propose, on the one hand, the existence of a financial elite transcending the existence of groups and, on the other, the existence of two distinct poles, one public, the other private, in which the great banks have no place. More recent works, conversely, tend to emphasize, amongst other things, a long run continuity in the role of banks within the Italian capitalistic system [Baccini and Vasta 1995; Ferri and Trento 1997; Rinaldi and Vasta 2003, 2005][2]. Finally, the weight of company groups in the structure of Italian capitalism has been discussed in far-reaching studies, which have used datasets permitting the reconstruction of the dynamics of the ownership structure of firms [Brioschi, Buzzacchi and Colombo 1990; Barca et al. 1994a, 1994b; Capra et al. 1994; Bianco and Pagnoni 1997]. These studies, however, have limited their analysis to the 1990s.

The source used for this study does not permit the reconstruction of the dynamics of ownership participation, but it allows the use of company interlocks as control signals. In this sense these interlocks represent an appropriate proxy for the reconstruction of the workings of a capitalist system but, as suggested by the literature [Pennings 1980], they cannot be used in a mechanical manner to reconstruct the dynamics of ownership structure. The aim of the study, therefore, is to furnish a number of empirically founded *stylized facts*, capable of representing an overall survey of the workings of Italian capitalism in the long run. The source used does not consent the precise identification of the boundaries of the single groups of firms, for which data relative to shareholding portfolios would be necessary. It does, however, permit us to verify, through quantitative surveys, a few hypotheses relating to the size of groups, to the workings of inter-group interlocks, and to the mechanisms which have guaranteed its consolidation and the defense of control arrangements. As far as this last aspect is concerned, in fact, the determination of the weight and influence of the relationships between groups of firms and the financial system seems particularly relevant, also in the light of the important discontinuities of the 1930s, the 1936 banking law and the incorporation of *mixed banks* into the IRI.

This essay is organized as follows: in Sect. 6.2 we describe the source used and illustrate the essential aspects of the methodology employed in the analysis; in Sect. 6.3 we reconstruct the long run dynamics of the structure of Italian capitalism through the use of network analysis techniques; in Sect. 6.4 the attention is focused on types of sectors and sizes of the groups of firms; while Sect. 6.5 examines the evolution of the core of the system analyzing the characteristics of the single firms which make it up. The essay closes with some concluding remarks (Sect. 6.6).

---

[2] For a review of existing studies see, for the period preceding the Second World War, Baccini and Vasta [1995] and, for the post-Second World War period, Rinaldi and Vasta [2003, 2005].

6.2. Sources and methodology

The electronic version of the ASIPA archives (Imita.db) contains, as explained in more detail in the Appendix, data on a broad sample of Italian joint stock companies. In particular, in this essay we analyze the information relating to the composition of the board of directors. The members of the boards of auditors, whose names are available in the Imita.db, are therefore excluded due to their limited function as far as the management of the companies is concerned [Chiesi 1985]. The analysis was conducted over eight benchmark years: Table 6.1 shows the consistency for each of these in terms of companies, positions within the boards of directors[3].

Table 6.1. Imita.db: essential data

Year	Companies	Positions	Board of directors
1911	788	5,808	3,576
1913	1,242	8,348	5,263
1921	3,080	20,803	12,526
1927	4,476	27,246	16,204
1936	4,243	20,882	12,613
1952	6,180	27,424	17,371
1960	6,371	28,813	17,917
1972	11,802	45,543	30,180

As mentioned above, the relationships between the firms in the sample have been reconstructed on the basis of the existence of company interlocks determined by the existence of interlocking directorates (ID). By ID we intend those interlocks that are formed between two firms when the same person is a member of the board of directors of both. The analysis of these interlocks - originally used in the US in the antitrust policies field - has had a significant diffusion only from the 1980s onwards, when a number of comparative studies appeared, carried out using social network analysis software [Mintz and Schwartz 1985; Stokman, Ziegler and Scott 1985]. This approach has been used both in the sociological and in the economics field, in accordance with different theoretical models. However, its usefulness has also been emphasized in a more pluralistic perspective [Scott 1985], according to which it is important firstly to establish the existence and the characteristics of the ID phenomena, and only subsequently to consider the causes. These can include a broad list of themes relevant to the analysis of the firm, with control and strategy problems in the first positions. In particular the presence of ID allows for the identification of informal groups, as also the relationships between different groups or between independent firms.

[3] The information found in the archives, despite numerous controls, can include a margin of error - estimated at around 1.5 per cent - as is also the case with other datasets [Mintz and Schwartz 1985]. This can be due to a coincidence of names, typographical errors in the source or during data entry.

In the more general sphere of the study of social networks, the analysis of ID can make use of a vast set of proxies and analysis techniques, which can be applied to networks with different characteristics - binary or weighted, symmetrical or asymmetrical[4]. For the purposes of the present analysis the relations between the companies present in the Imita.db are represented by binary and symmetrical adjacency matrixes[5], referred to each of the 8 years considered[6]. The elaborations were carried out with *Ucinet 6.0* [Borgatti, Everett and Freeman 2002]. Starting from this data the attention is focused on two fundamental measures:

(i) Density (D), defined as the relation between the number of connections between unit couples and the possible number of connections: D = L(r)/L(p), where L(r) is the number of real connections and L(p) - defined as n(n-1)/2 - indicates the number of possible connections of the network studied. The D index thus defined represents a measure of the degree of cohesion between the firms in the system varying between 0 and 1 respectively for L(r) = 0 and L(r) = n(n-1)/2, which refer to extreme cases of the absence of any interlock and of the fulfillment of all possible interlocks in this order.

(ii) The degree of centrality of a network actor - which in this case corresponds to a firm -: in a binary and symmetrical matrix the number of network actors directly connected to a given actor is said to be the degree of that vertex. In particular, here we adopt a normalized measure [Freeman 1979], composed of the percentage of the relationship between the effective degree of the single actors and the maximum possible value that the degree of an actor can assume in a given

---

4 For a description of the methods and techniques which can be applied in this field, see Scott [1991] and Wasserman and Faust [1994].

5 An adjacency matrix is a square matrix, with as many rows/columns as the elements of the network. In each cell of the matrix we find values corresponding to the presence, and eventually the strength, of a direct relation between each element of the network.

6 The adoption of binary values (1 = presence of a relation; 0 = absence of a relation) means that, in the elaboration of quantitative measures, the differences due to the presence of more than one person in two different boards of directors are not taken into account. The strength of the interlocks between two firms could, in fact, be weighted in respect to the number of ID which connect them; giving them a score equal to the number directors they share. The exclusion of this possibility allows a more extensive and linear use of quantitative measures in the analysis. In particular, the normalized measures of the degree of centrality and *betweeness* (see Sect. 6.5) can be adopted only in this case [Wasserman and Faust 1994: 177-192]. Furthermore, the density of the weighted matrixes is represented by the average of the strength of the interlocks [Wasserman and Faust 1994: 143]. In this case the measure depends on the size of the directorates, which in its turn is conditioned by sectoral biases which hamper inter-sectoral comparisons. If the exclusion of weighting was mainly due to technical reasons, that of the direction of relations depends, on the other hand, mainly on merit considerations. The generally adopted solution [see Lomi, Corrado and Sandri 1997] of assigning the direction of the relations on the basis of the position held - so that the direction in an ID goes from the most important (president, vice-president, managing director) to the least important (director) - does not, in fact, seem sufficiently supported neither theoretically nor empirically. The exclusion of the directionality of relationships makes the adjacency matrix of the network subjects symmetrical.

network[7]. The proxies described above are used here to furnish a picture of the evolution of the structural characteristics of the network of Italian companies in the course of time and to identify the most important firms in the system for each year. The examination of these measures is, however, preceded by the attempt to paint a picture of the degree of cohesion of the system of relations formed by the enterprises present in the sample. To this end we resort to other instruments, which allow us to subdivide the sample into groups of firms which are reciprocally distinct and internally linked by a multiplicity of interlocks. In particular two types of analyses were carried out:

(*a*) the network was partitioned into components, i.e. the maximum subsets of a network which are connected[8]: two members of the same component are always directly or indirectly connected by a *path* through one or more intermediaries, while there is no *path* between any of the members of the component and other members of the network; through this analysis it is possible to identify different *regions* of the network, which are at the same time internally connected and reciprocally separate, as shown in Fig. 6.1;

(*b*) the partitioning of the network into bi-components, i.e. all those components that are robust as regards the removal of a cut point, i.e. of a member of a network whose elimination causes the increase of the number of components of the network; therefore, in Fig. 6.1 the removal of one of the two cut points entails an increase in the components from two to three, and therefore these *new* components are two bi-components of the network[9].

The great advantage of these indicators is to create a univocal partitioning of the sample, without the overlapping in the composition between different groups which characterizes the procedures used to identify the so-called cohesive subgroups, such as cliques and other derived procedures[10]. The analysis of components is adopted in literature as a measure of the degree of centralization, because it allows for the identification of the more or less extended group of firms around which network relations are concentrated [Stokman and Wasseur 1985; Mac Canna, Brennan and O'Higgins 1999].

---

[7] In symbols: $C_D(n_i) = \dfrac{d(n_i)}{g-1}$, where $d(n_i)$ is the degree of a given actor n_i, and g is the number of actors present in the network.

[8] A network can be *connected* or *disconnected.* In the former case there is a path-way uniting every couple of elements in the network, which is therefore made up of a single component which coincides with the same network. In the latter case there are more than one connected subsets. Each of these represents a component of the network.

[9] Further attempts have been made to obtain a partitioning of the network on the basis of k-cores, i.e. sub-graphs connected with a minimum degree (the smallest degree among members of the sub-graph) equal to K; and other indicators, such as lambda-sets. The results, however, do not greatly differ from those obtained by calculating components and bi-components, and were therefore excluded from the analysis.

[10] A cliques is a graph whose elements are all reciprocally connected. Further indicators were derived from this measure, such as n-cliques, n-clan, k-plex. For an in-depth study, see Wassermann and Faust [1994: 249-273].

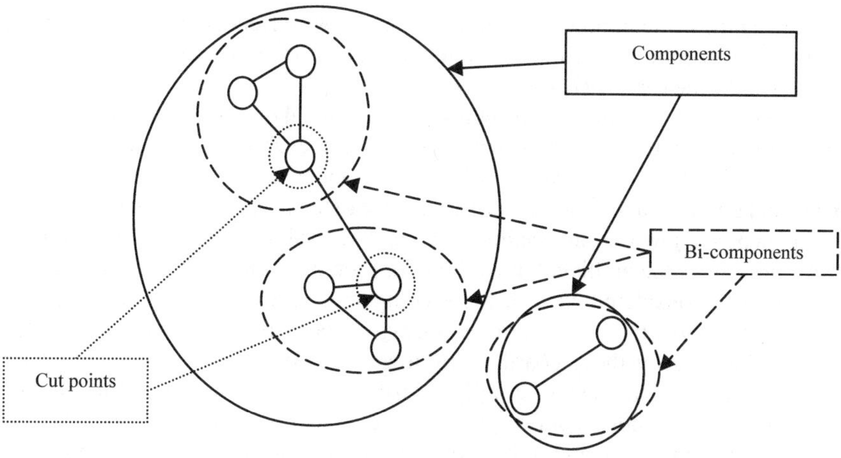

Fig. 6.1. Examples of components and bi-components

6.3. Extension of the relations and collusive mechanisms

As mentioned in the introduction, the debate on the Italian specificity in ownership structures and in the mechanisms of control of firms represents one of the most controversial aspects in the evaluation of the Italian economic system and of its development. In particular, a great number of studies [Radar 1948; Chiesi 1985; Brioschi, Buzzacchi and Colombo 1990; Barca et al. 1994a, 1994b; Barca 1997] has shown the persistent diffusion of control mechanisms based on the group form, together with the relevant extension of inter-group interlocks. The hypothesis that Italian capitalism is based on a highly collusive structure has therefore been consolidated. In substance this term defines a situation in which the coordination mechanisms between typical market agents are only partially operative, and are replaced by forms of coordination based on trust interlocks or power relationships. The negative consequences of this structure have often been emphasized, and consist mainly in the limited competition in the ownership of firms - which entails inefficiencies in the management of these firms - and the absence of competition on goods and services markets, also due to the effect of state intervention.

The abovementioned studies are usually based on indicators regarding reciprocal participations, which are not available in the Imita.db. On the other hand these studies are limited to the examination of the restricted group of top companies. While the analysis of ID allows only an indirect reconstruction of ownership and control structures, subject to significant limits - in the first place due to the impossibility of distinguishing the interlocks within one group from those among different groups -, nevertheless the extension of the source, both from a diachronic point of view and for the number of companies involved, offers an extremely representative cross-section of the Italian capitalist system from the beginning of the 20th century until the early 1970s.

In this regard, the study of the components of the network of Italian firms offers an extremely significant representation. Table 6.2 shows, for each benchmark year, the distribution of firms within the components with a different extension. The fundamental fact which emerges is the existence, in all the years, of a large component - known as the main component -, which comprises the majority of firms present in the archive. Given the definition of component, this means that in all the years considered each of these companies is in the condition to influence the board of directors of the same majority, in some measure - and to be reciprocally influenced by these boards -, through a chain of individual interlocks between directors. This result strongly corroborates the collusive nature of Italian capitalism, once more confirming the abovementioned hypotheses, and even strengthening them, given the extraordinary extension of the phenomenon which emerges from the data just observed.

Table 6.2. Components of the network of Italian companies (1911-1972)

Year		In the main component	In medium components*	In small components**	Isolated	Total
1911	no.	700	-	9	79	788
	%	88.8	-	1.2	10.0	100.0
1913	no.	1,053	-	30	159	1,242
	%	84.8	-	2.4	12.8	100.0
1921	no.	2,699	-	53	327	3,079
	%	87.7	-	1.7	10.6	100.0
1927	no.	3,603	20	159	693	4,475
	%	80.5	0.4	3.6	15.5	100.0
1936	no.	3,021	76	221	923	4,241
	%	71.2	1.8	5.2	21.8	100.0
1952	no.	3,793	102	480	1,790	6,165
	%	61.5	1.7	7.8	29.0	100.0
1960	no.	3,983	134	517	1,733	6,367
	%	62.6	2.1	8.1	27.2	100.0
1972	no.	6,224	459	1,272	3,845	11,800
	%	52.7	3.9	10.8	32.6	100.0

Legend: * Components (excluding the main component) with 4 or more elements; ** Components with 2 or 3 elements.

As further support for this thesis, moreover amply shared by the literature, we must underline how the structure of the network remains robust even with the introduction of more stringent criteria for the identification of the interlocks. If we calculate the distribution of firms in bi-components as we did for the components (see Table 6.3), it is true that the size of the main element of the network is greatly reduced; however, this reduction occurs in favor of the weight of the firms connected in small components, while the existence of medium sized bi-components is not very relevant.

This last piece of evidence seems to reinforce the hypothesis of a high concentration of relations around a core of dominant firms, around which there is also an aggregation of small groups, while there seems to be no sign of the existence, often mentioned in the literature, of a plurality of poles. This element is due to the considerable importance of the inter-group interlocks which do not permit the definition of precise boundaries between the main Italian groups. In particular, it is interesting to note that the data do not show a strong separation between private and state-owned firms [Chiesi 1985]; the analysis in fact does not show two corresponding components, but a sole component comprising the firms of the public pole and those of the private pole, which attests to an extremely strong cohesion of the system, apart from the ownership structure of firms.

Table 6.3. Bi-components of the network of Italian companies (1911-1972)

Year		In the main component	In medium components*	In small components**	Isolated	Total
1911	no.	601	-	97	90	788
	%	76.3	-	12.3	11.4	100.0
1913	no.	867	-	201	174	1,242
	%	69.8	-	16.2	14.0	100.0
1921	no.	2,250	17	449	363	3,079
	%	73.1	0.6	14.6	11.8	100.0
1927	no.	2,866	53	792	764	4,475
	%	64.0	1.2	17.7	17.1	100.0
1936	no.	2,232	137	847	1,025	4,241
	%	52.6	3.2	20.0	24.2	100.0
1952	no.	2,662	178	1,362	1,963	6,165
	%	43.2	2.9	22.1	31.8	100.0
1960	no.	2,764	219	1,489	1,895	6,367
	%	43.4	3.4	23.4	29.8	100.0
1972	no.	3,933	558	3,108	4,201	11,800
	%	33.3	4.7	26.3	35.6	100.0

Legend: * Bi-components (excluding the main component) with 4 or more elements; ** Bi-components with 2 or 3 elements.

As far as the evolution of the distribution of components in the course of time is concerned (see Table 6.2), in 1911 the main component comprises 88.8 per cent of all the companies; this quota remains above 80 per cent until 1927, even though it shows a tendency to decrease; in 1936 it is equal to 71.2 per cent; in 1952 and 1961 it is slightly higher than 60 per cent; and in 1972 slightly higher than 50 per cent. By contrast, in the same period, the weight of the isolated companies increases progressively - from 10 per cent to 32.6 per cent - as does that of companies in small components - from 1.2 per cent to 10.8 per cent. Even though there is a progressive tendency towards a decrease in the weight of the main component (see Fig. 6.2), it should be noted that this is above all a consequence of the broadening of the sample, which progressively includes smaller sized firms which are characterized by a lesser propensity to generate interlocks with other firms, and are often in a peripheral position with respect to the core of the system. By contrast, it is interesting to note, in the first place, that the decrease is a great deal smaller, in proportion, with respect to the increase in the number of companies included in the sample; and, in the second place, that in the course of time the main component grows considerably in absolute terms, till, in 1972, it encompasses over 6,000 companies. The number of the firms in the main component decreases only between 1927 and 1936, from 3,603 to 3,021, as a consequence of an overall contraction in the cohesion of the system already observed in previous studies [Vasta and Baccini 1997].

The great tendency towards *collusion* of Italian firms seems, therefore, to extend well beyond the top companies to include a number of small firms. The largest companies undoubtedly form the nucleus of this network: suffice it to say that in 1972 at least 195 of the top 200 companies by capital - 328 among the top 500 - are included in the main component; among these we find all the main state-owned enterprises (IRI, ENI, Italsider, Ansaldo) and private companies (FIAT, Pirelli, Olivetti, Zanussi). However, the main component includes the entire size spectrum of the companies present in the sample: in 1972 there are in fact 206 companies which rank among the last 500 in terms of capital. From a comparative point of view, the tendency of national networks of companies in the main industrialized countries to concentrate around a large component had already been pointed out in previous studies [Stokman and Wasseur 1985], which, however, make use of very small samples - the top 250 firms by size. The data found in the Imita.db dataset clearly show that the main component in the Italian case extends well beyond the top companies, generating a capillary web of interlocks.

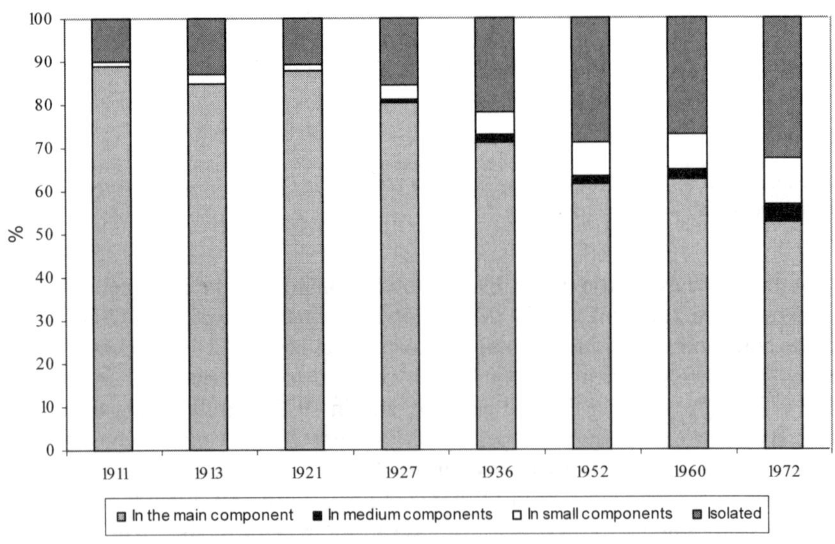

Fig. 6.2. Percentage distribution of companies in the components (1911-1972)

In the absence of homogeneous comparative data it is impossible to determine in what measure this structure of the network represents an Italian peculiarity, or if analogies are to be found also in the economies of other industrialized countries. Nevertheless, the size of the main component is indeed impressive, extending well beyond the limits of the groups of firms which can be determined on the basis of ownership participations. These interlocks are therefore a multidimensional phenomenon, in which the relationships determined by reciprocal participations among companies are accompanied by others of a different nature. Even though it is not simple to formulate a hypothesis as to the factors at the root of this complex phenomenon, generally speaking we can hypothesize that a prominent role is played by the necessity of the firms to control their environment, which is mainly represented by the other firms [Pennings 1980; Lomi 1997], with regard to a few strategic variables (for example, productive coordination and vertical integration, market control of input and output, access to capital, investment decisions). From this view point the results displayed supply only a general indication (the broad extension of the relationships between companies in Italian capitalism), while in the rest of the essay we propose some interpretative hypotheses through the restriction of proxies and the adoption of a few restrictive hypotheses.

6.4. Sectors and size

In this Sect. we intend to carry out an in-depth study of the role of a few factors which contribute to shaping the structure of the extended system of relationships mentioned in the preceding Sect. The indicator on which the analysis is based is that of density which is used to examine the structural characteristics of the network of firms in relation to a few fundamental variables such as sector and size. The crossing of the density values with the variables which characterize the firms is carried out through a block-model, namely an adjacency matrix between the firms which is divided into groups on the basis of the relevant characteristics of the firms; subsequently we calculate the average intra- and inter-block densities. For the purposes of sectoral analysis the density values were subsequently *dichotomized* in order to generate a new binary adjacency matrix referring to the sectors. In particular, the final matrix was calculated, starting from the one containing the density values, assigning a value equal to one unit to every cell whose density value was greater than the average (and a value of zero if it was less). The eight matrixes thus obtained allow us to immediately identify which sectors, in each benchmark year, were the greatest catalysts of relationships. Thanks to this procedure, furthermore, the inter-sectoral relationships emerging from the adjacency matrixes between sectors can be illustrated graphically. The data presented in Figs. 6.3.a-h show, firstly, how the relationships within the network of Italian firms tend to concentrate on a limited number of sectors with respect to the potential ones; and, secondly how the set of key sectors remains relatively stable in the course of time. In particular, the predominant role of the financial sector (65.1, 65.2, 66-67), which is locked to a broad number of sectors with strong internal interconnections in all the years, becomes evident. Until 1960, the mining industry (C) also occupies one of the central positions, and locks stably with a number of manufacturing sectors, such as the chemical sector (DG) and the petroleum products (DF). More generally, as from half-way through the 1920s, the sectors linked to the Second Industrial Revolution occupy the central positions among the manufacturing sectors, while the traditional sectors - food products (DA), textiles (DB), leather (DC), wood products (DD) and manufacturing n.e.c. (DN) - occupy the peripheral positions.

The role of the three different components in which the financial sector is subdivided - banks (65.1), holding companies (65.2), insurance companies (66-67) - varies considerably in the course of time: the banking companies (65.1) occupy a central position during the period 1911-1913 together with the insurance companies (66-67); the former are in a more backward position in 1927 and in 1936, when the insurance component (66-67) takes the leading position, developing interlocks with an ample number of sectors, while the banks (65.1) are only connected to the other two financial sectors and to the utilities (E). Finally the banking sector (65.1) progressively regains centrality as from 1952 until 1972, when - as can be seen from Fig. 6.3.h - it is the financial sector as a whole (65.1, 65.2, 66-67) which occupies the crucial position.

The apparently paradoxical result of the minor centrality of banks in the period in which the great *mixed banks* play a fundamental role in the structure of Italian capitalism can be explained by starting from the high level of concentration reached by the financial system in those years. As we will see in more detail later on (see Sect. 6.5), in fact, the role of the *mixed banks* is confirmed by the data. On the other hand, it should be considered that it is exactly the centralizing of relations around a small number of subjects which can entail a lesser overall density of the network. Conversely the existence from 1927-1936 of a considerable number of insurance companies (66-67), generally a great deal smaller than banks (65.1), but with a thick network of interlocks, pushes the density values for this sector up, as has been observed in previous studies [Baccini and Vasta 1995]. In the same way the analysis presented in Sect. 6.5 shows that the greater centrality of the banking sector after the War is due to the relations developed by a greater number of banks, among which there are also smaller entities, which however, manage to carry out the mediation function typical of the banking sector (65.1) fully [Rinaldi and Vasta 2005]. One of the key roles also belongs to the utilities (E). The electrical firms are particularly relevant in this sector, and occupy an ever more central position in the inter-sectoral relations side by side with the financial sectors (65.1, 65.2, 66-67), with whom they have strong ties. The utilities (E) reach their apogee in 1960 when, as can be seen from Fig. 6.3.g, they are at the core of the system together with the financial sector companies. The subsequent historical passage linked to the nationalization of the sector is evident from the representation of the relations of 1972 (see Fig. 6.3.h), due to the fact that the position of the utilities (E) changes radically, and this sector - as a consequence of the disappearance of the larger private electrical companies - abandons the centre of the system in favor of the financial companies.

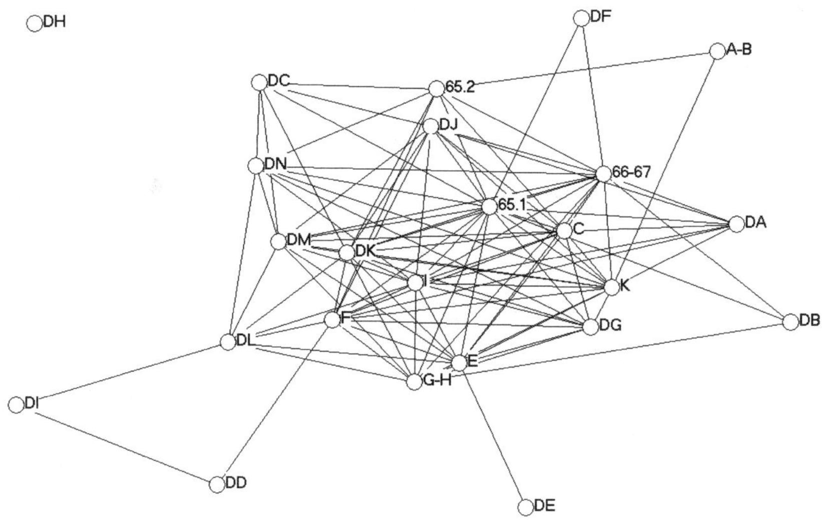

Fig. 6.3.a. Diagram of inter-sectoral relations, 1911

Legend: Agriculture, forestry and fishing (A-B); Mining and quarrying (C); Food products and tobacco (DA); Textiles and textile products (DB); Leather and leather products (DC); Wood and wood products (DD); Paper products, publishing and printing (DE); Coke and petroleum products (DF); Chemicals and chemical products (DG); Rubber and plastic products (DH); Other non-metallic products (DI); Basic metals and metal products (DJ); Machinery and equipment (DK); Electrical and optical equipment (DL); Transport equipment (DM); Manufacturing n.e.c. (DN); Utilities (E); Construction (F); Trade, hotels and restaurants (G-H); Transport, storage and communication (I); Banks (65.1); Holding companies (65.2); Insurance (66-67); Real estate, renting, business activities (K).

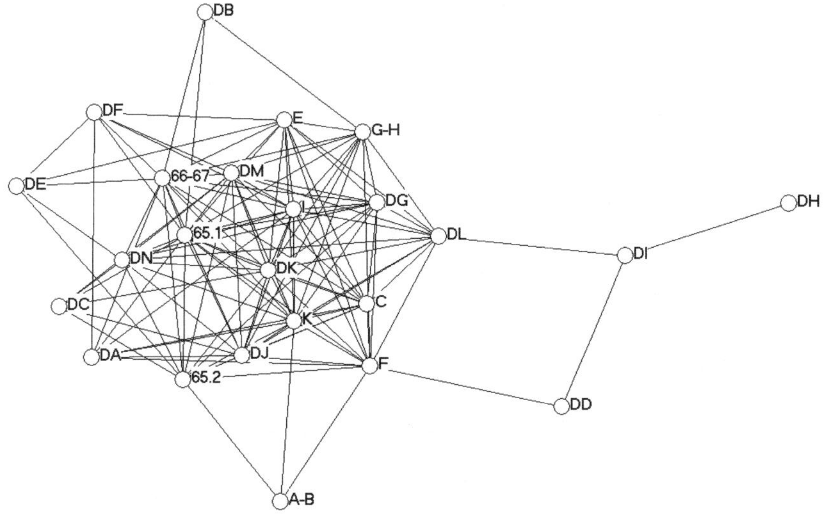

Fig. 6.3.b. Diagram of inter-sectoral relations, 1913

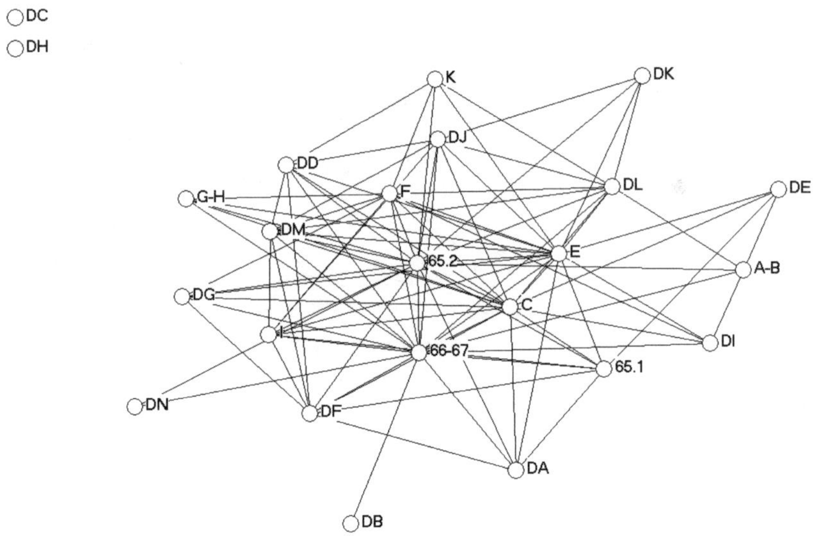

Fig. 6.3.c. Diagram of inter-sectoral relations, 1921

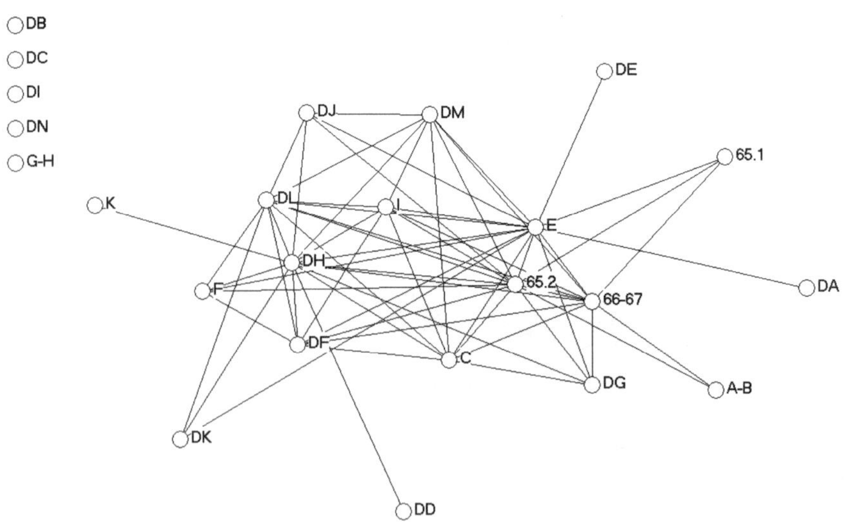

Fig. 6.3.d. Diagram of inter-sectoral relations, 1927

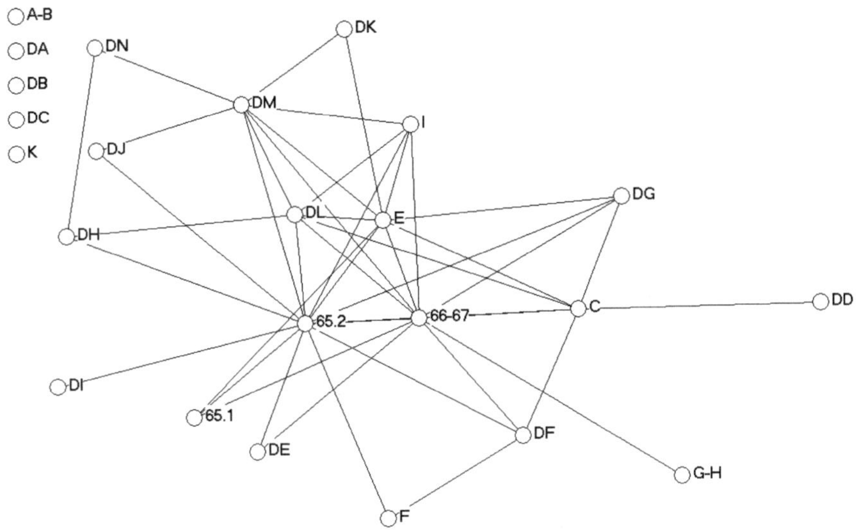

Fig. 6.3.e. Diagram of inter-sectoral relations, 1936

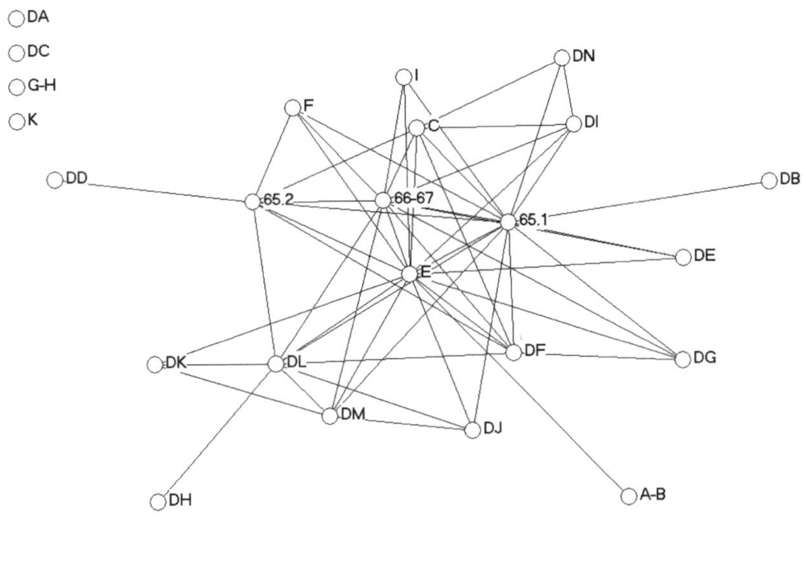

Fig. 6.3.f. Diagram of inter-sectoral relations, 1952

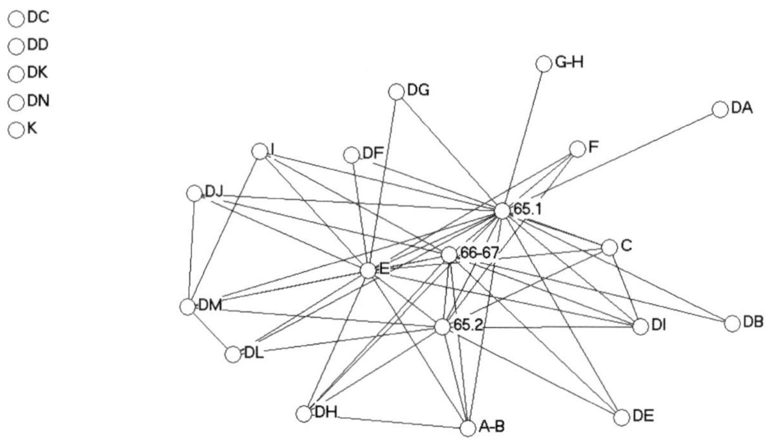

Fig. 6.3.g. Diagram of inter-sectoral relations, 1960

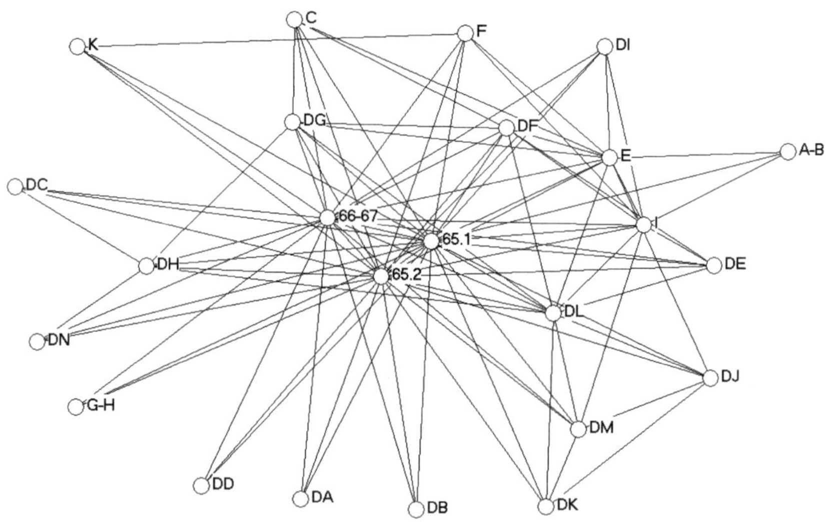

Fig. 6.3.h. Diagram of inter-sectoral relations, 1972

The above diagrams, even though they manage to represent inter-sectoral relations in an effective way, do not give a measure of the relations which exist within each sector. For a more detailed view of the combined dynamics of intra- and inter-sectoral interlocks we calculated the average densities of the main types of interlocks. These measures were subsequently standardized with respect to the average and standard deviation in order to furnish a comparative picture of the different benchmark years (see Table 6.4). In particular we made a distinction between interlocks within the same sector and between similar sectors, on the one hand, and the interlocks centered on the four key sectors identified above - banks (65.1), holding companies (65.2), insurance companies (66-67), utilities (E) - on the other; these typologies were further distinguished on the basis of the *destination* sectors of the interlocks (manufacturing or services).

The data show how the formation of inter- and intra-sectoral interlocks is due to two main types of factors: firstly the need for coordination generated by the aim of exploiting possible economies deriving from productive complementarities; secondly financial motivations appear to be the main engine driving inter-sectoral relations, both those directly linked to financial sectors or to sectors, such as the utilities, characterized by a high availability of capital, which are used to diversify also in sectors far away from their productive core.

Table 6.4. Density by typology of inter-sectoral relations (standardized values with respect to the average), 1911-1972

Types of interlocks	1911	1913	1921	1927	1936	1952	1960	1972
Links due to productive complementarity								
Inter-sectoral links:	0.81	0.91	1.47	1.40	1.61	0.87	1.03	1.10
-in manufacturing	*0.55*	*0.81*	*1.14*	*1.57*	*2.17*	*0.63*	*0.28*	*0.59*
- in services	*1.07*	*1.02*	*1.80*	*1.23*	*1.05*	*1.12*	*1.78*	*1.60*
Inter-sectoral links in DJ-DK-DL-DM sectors	0.73	0.84	0.22	0.18	0.16	0.00	-0.13	-0.11
Links in key sectors								
Inter-sectoral links of banks:	0.54	0.19	0.00	-0.20	-0.05	0.63	0.23	0.63
- with manufacturing	*0.37*	*0.27*	*0.07*	*-0.19*	*-0.05*	*0.02*	*0.04*	*0.18*
- with services (excluding holding and insurance companies)	*0.71*	*0.12*	*-0.06*	*-0.21*	*-0.05*	*1.24*	*0.42*	*1.09*
Inter-sectoral links of holding companies:	-0.06	-0.14	0.61	0.41	0.21	0.14	0.15	0.23
- with manufacturing	*0.10*	*0.18*	*0.64*	*0.55*	*0.26*	*-0.05*	*-0.08*	*0.03*
- with services (excluding banks and insurance companies)	*-0.22*	*-0.45*	*0.59*	*0.27*	*0.16*	*0.34*	*0.38*	*0.44*
Inter-sectoral links of insurance companies:	0.54	0.85	0.22	0.27	0.12	0.53	0.26	0.34
- with manufacturing	*0.89*	*1.12*	*0.23*	*0.37*	*0.11*	*0.00*	*-0.05*	*0.01*
- with services (excluding banks and holding companies)	*0.19*	*0.57*	*0.22*	*0.18*	*0.12*	*1.06*	*0.58*	*0.68*
Inter-sectoral links of utilities:	0.31	0.09	0.35	0.78	0.10	0.22	0.00	-0.17
- with manufacturing	*0.32*	*-0.03*	*0.29*	*0.41*	*0.00*	*0.18*	*0.02*	*-0.18*
- with services (excluding banks, holding and insurance companies)	*0.33*	*-0.15*	*0.23*	*0.04*	*-0.11*	*0.13*	*0.03*	*-0.20*
Links among banks, holding and insurance companies	1.89	2.40	0.57	0.74	1.00	0.71	0.55	1.39
Links between financial sector and utilities	0.60	0.11	1.38	1.13	1.00	0.71	0.56	0.48

There are more intra-sectoral interlocks than the average for the entire period. The relations between different sectors in which productive integration is higher also appear to be relevant, as in the case of the metal products (DJ), machinery (DK), electrical (DL) and transport (DM) equipment, even though the weight of these interlocks progressively declines as the *consolidated* levels of concentration show (see Sect. 3.3).

Finally, it should be noted that the density of intra-sectoral relations is even higher in the services, especially in the financial, real estate and transport sectors. The companies of each of these sectors are in fact connected by numerous reciprocal interlocks with firms operating in the same branch of activity.

The point of maximum cohesion of the industry occurs in 1936 as a result of the constant growth of the previous years, while the years following the Second World War are characterized by a lower and see-sawing density. By contrast, the interlocks within the service sector, after having reached a peak in 1921, remain high also for the period 1952-1972, with a new peak in 1960. This effect is mainly due to the persistence of intra-sectoral interlocks within the financial sectors (65.1, 65.2, 66-67) and, to a much lesser degree, within the transport sector (DM). The dynamics of intra-sectoral relations in the services, therefore, appear to be tightly connected to the role of financial companies, which maintain a high reciprocal cohesion during the entire period. On the other hand, the role of the three components of this sector - banks (65.1), holding companies (65.2) and insurance companies (66-67) - in the relations with the other sectors changes greatly in the course of time. In relations with industry a process of substitution takes place between banks and holdings and insurance companies: if the strength of the relations developed by the latter is greater than that of banks until 1936, the tendency is inverted as from 1952. The explanation for this apparently paradox - already mentioned above and discussed further in Sect. 6.5 - shows how the apparent weakness of banks, especially in 1927 and in 1936, is a consequence of the sector's high concentration during that period. On the other hand, the growth in densities during the post-Second World War period derives from the division of the relations over a greater number of subjects following the structural changes induced by the 1936 banking law and the *IRI-zation* of *mixed banks*.

As a confirmation of the active role of banks also in more recent years, the density of the relations between these and the industrial firms grows significantly from 1952, while that of the insurance companies (66-67) remains substantially stable. Simultaneously, the strength of the utilities (E) declines - especially after nationalization -, while the direct interlocks between industrial firms, as mentioned above, mark time. Furthermore, there is a progressive concentration within the same financial sector, as evidenced by the growth in the density of the relations between banks (65.1), holding companies (65.2) and insurance companies (66-67), which, after 1936, reaches a new peak in 1972; while the interlocks between these firms and the utilities (E) continue to diminish. Overall these tendencies produce the fundamental effect of the centrality of financial sectors, which is a characteristic of the year 1972 (see Fig. 6.3h).

To sum up, the data show the existence of two distinct phases: the first, which lasts until 1936, in which the system is mainly based on the direct relations between industrial firms and on the role of a few banks (the *mixed banks*), assisted by a good number of smaller insurance and financial companies; a second phase (1952-1972) in which the great *mixed banks* leave the scene and a plurality of new subjects enters the system reinforcing the overall weight of the financial sectors. In this setup, the role of the utilities (E) expands especially during the period (1927-1952) astride the two phases, subsequently decreasing to disappear after nationalization. It must however be kept in mind that, even though the system evolves in the manner just described, its structure appears substantially stable - with the exception of the already mentioned effects of nationalization -, and guided by the two main engines of productive integration between similar sectors and by the acquisition of capital, in which certain key sectors operate in a differentiated manner, remaining however always tightly bound one to the other.

To complete the structural picture of the relations, we must now consider the second variable, namely size. Even though the direct proportionality between the size of a firm and its propensity to generate ID has already been observed in the studies on networks of firms [Pennings 1980], the manner in which the relations generated by the main firms are distributed between firms of different sizes is less evident - considering, among other things, that the studies carried out in this field usually use restricted samples of firms which are generally homogenous in terms of size. To this purpose, using a procedure analogous to that adopted for sectoral analysis, we calculated the densities for the four size classes identified on the basis of corporate capital[11] at 1970 constant prices for the 8 benchmark years.

The comparison between the density of the relations of the larger firms (see Table 6.5) and the smaller firms (see Table 6.6) with all the other size classes brings to light a few interesting phenomena. In the first place, the greater tendency of the larger firms to generate interlocks with other firms of the same size is confirmed. The values reported in the last line of Table 6.5 are in fact decidedly higher than the average values for all the years and all the more so with respect to those relating to reciprocal interlocks between smaller firms, which remain modest, even though with a growing trend for the entire period (see Table 6.6, first line). In examining the interlocks with the other classes, it becomes evident that this tendency of the large firms is directly proportional to the size of the *receiving* companies: the density of the interlocks in fact decreases progressively with a decrease in size - except for the year 1911, in which, however, the number of small firms present in the sample is very limited.

It is even more interesting to note how, despite this tendency, the relations generated by the large firms towards the other size classes remain close to the average values. There is, therefore, an extended web of interlocks which, from the top firms, reaches all the other size levels. This result is directly connected to the presence of a large main component in the sample (see Sect. 6.3), which validates the

[11] In this case we did not use assets as a size indicator, even though it has been used in other essays in this book. The availability of this proxy in the Imita.db is limited only to industrial firms (see Appendix), while capital is available also for the companies in the other sectors. The data on assets will be available only as from the second half of the year 2006 when the source will be fully digitalized.

hypothesis formulated above of a strongly pyramidal-type structure, in which there are no counter-weights, but rather a core which is extremely integrated internally around which a great number of firms running the entire size range revolve.

As far as evolution in the course of time is concerned, the density of reciprocal relations between the largest firms shows an almost constant tendency towards growth. The relations with smaller enterprises show an analogous trend, while those with firms in the intermediate classes decrease progressively. This last tendency is probably due to growth in size, which means that in the long term a part of the intermediate size firms - that with the most connections to the top companies - moves into a higher size class, and these firms are in turn substituted by new entries, which are more peripheral with respect to the top of the *pyramid*.

Table 6.5. Density of the relations of the large companies (500 million lire and beyond - 1970 prices), standardized values with respect to the mean

Size classes	1911	1913	1921	1927	1936	1952	1960	1972
0-99 million	-0.37	-0.29	-0.24	-0.25	-0.21	-0.48	-0.25	-0.19
100-249 million	0.86	0.20	-0.02	-0.01	-0.08	-0.08	-0.04	-0.19
250-500 million	0.70	0.64	0.76	0.64	0.42	0.58	0.29	0.26
500 million and over	2.19	2.71	2.70	2.77	2.85	2.79	2.90	2.92

Table 6.6. Density of the relations of the small companies (0-99 million lire - 1970 prices), standardized values with respect to the mean

Size classes	1911	1913	1921	1927	1936	1952	1960	1972
0-99 million	-1.10	-0.67	-0.79	-0.72	-0.64	-0.70	-0.59	-0.52
100-249 million	-1.10	-0.76	-0.72	-0.67	-0.62	-0.65	-0.59	-0.52
250-500 million	-0.34	-0.75	-0.56	-0.55	-0.49	-0.58	-0.50	-0.52
500 million and over	-0.37	-0.29	-0.24	-0.25	-0.21	-0.48	-0.25	-0.19

Basically, the structure of the system of relations among Italian companies, and in particular the presence of an interconnecting network involving the majority of companies (see Sect. 6.3), can be explained through the operation of two distinct, though related, sets of factors. These promote the thickening of the web of relations, which then progressively spread towards the periphery of the system. The first factor is the intermediary role played by certain sectors - banking (65.1), holding companies (65.2), insurance (66-67) and utilities (E) - in the relations between different sectors; the second factor is the presence of a vertex of large companies, which are not only tightly and reciprocally interconnected, but are also capable of extending relations towards firms of every size. In any case, the picture emerges of a network in which the relational fluxes (information, power, etc.) are concentrated in a limited set of privileged points. This result is also due to the type of state intervention, which has made a wide use of the instrument of the state-owned enterprise [Sartori 1957; Saraceno 1975; Barca and Trento 1997]. This solution has favored the institution of numerous inter-enterprise interlocks both within the public sector and towards the private sector (see Sect. 6.3).

6.5. The *central* companies

After having examined the main structural characteristics of the system, and its concentration around a restricted and strongly integrated nucleus of companies with precise sectoral and size characteristics, the attention in this Sect. is focused on the most important part of this nucleus. The analysis is based on the idea of centrality of a company and is measured through the degree namely the number of other companies with which the company studied is directly connected; in particular, here we adopt a normalized measure, proposed for the first time by Freeman (see Sect. 6.2). In order to guarantee comparability between different years, the analysis is restricted to the top 250[12] companies by centrality for each year considered, and the sectoral characteristics of these are studied (see Table 6.7)[13].

From the point of view of centrality the weight of the entire manufacturing sector follows an alternating trend, with a tendency towards progressive resizing (see Table 6.7). This is evident between 1911 and 1936, and in particular, in the central years of the fascist period when the weight of activities in which financial capital plays a predominant role grows - for example the utilities, and real estate activities in 1936. In the post-Second World War period the number of industrial companies again decreases, after a new peak in 1952 - due mainly to the *exit* of several estate agencies -, and thereafter remains substantially stable. During the entire period examined the weight of industry is lower than that of the service sector, the latter showing a linear trend towards growth. The decisive role is played by the financial sectors - to which we will return further on -, even though there are other important sectors, such as transport and real estate, while the more traditional components of the service sector show a declining trend. The role of financial companies, among which there are several holding companies (65.2), is particularly relevant in the substitution process between industrial and service activities. The fall of industrial companies is, therefore, also the effect of the changes in the structure of company ties, with a process of progressive *financialization* of industry.

The data presented in Table 6.7 illustrates the role of each industrial sector. It shows a process of substitution between the traditional sectors and those tied to the Second Industrial Revolution. The textile and food sectors have, in fact, a very significant weight until 1921, but this decreases drastically already as early as

[12] We considered the top 250 companies in line with a comparative study carried out by Stokman, Ziegler and Scott [1985].

[13] In order to enrich the analysis with further qualitative elements, the Annex 6.1 (Tables 6.12.a-h) to this work also supplies a list of the names of the top 20 companies belonging to the industrial and financial sector by centrality; together with the value of the centrality index, the position in the ranking of the top 250 companies by centrality and the sector of activity for each company is shown.

1927. This trend can be ascribed to the delay in the growth of high capital intensity sectors in Italy. The data therefore shows how there is a turning point in the years astride the First World War. While the traditional sectors continue to represent a relevant part of large Italian enterprise also in subsequent years (see Chap. 5), the analysis of centrality shows how these become marginal in the new relations which form the core of Italian capitalism. Evidence for this hypothesis comes from the trend of the textile sector: the number of companies among the top 20 industrial companies is very low - never higher than 2 -, and they are never among the very top companies (see Tables 6.12.a-h in the Annex 6.1). On the other hand, the role of the food sector is tightly connected to that of the sugar industry which is characterized by an oligopolistic structure that forms at the beginning of the century. In the period 1911-1927 this sector is represented by 5-6 companies, among these Distillerie Italiane stands out, being among the top 20 companies for 3 out of 4 years (see Tables 6.12.a-d), and in the fourth absolute position in 1921; the Consorzio Nazionale Produttori di Zucchero becomes prominent in 1936, representing the cartel of national sugar producers [Tonizzi 2001: 96]; subsequently the sector disappears completely from the core of the system, as a consequence of the abovementioned evolution.

Table 6.7. Sectoral distribution of the top 250 companies by centrality

Sector	1911	1913	1921	1927	1936	1952	1960	1972
Agriculture, forestry and fishing (A-B)	2	3	-	5	3	3	4	2
Mining and quarrying (C)	8	7	6	6	6	5	7	2
Food products and tobacco (DA)	24	22	15	13	2	2	3	5
Textiles and textile products (DB)	24	17	20	6	10	5	9	5
Leather and leather products (DC)	2	1	1	-	1	-	1	2
Wood and wood products (DD)	-	-	1	-	-	-	-	1
Paper products, publishing and printing (DE)	3	4	5	3	4	2	6	6
Coke and petroleum products (DF)	-	-	-	1	2	6	2	6
Chemicals and chemical products (DG)	14	16	11	15	11	14	11	23
Rubber and plastic products (DH)	-	-	-	1	1	1	3	-
Other non-metallic products (DI)	4	3	2	1	9	8	14	11
Basic metals and metal products (DJ)	13	13	15	13	9	23	9	8
Machinery and equipment (DK)	7	5	2	2	1	8	3	4
Electrical and optical equipment (DL)	4	6	6	3	8	16	16	14
Transport equipment (DM)	11	12	8	8	6	10	3	3
Manufacturing n.e.c. (DN)	2	3	1	2	1	2	-	1
Total manufacturing (D)	*108*	*102*	*87*	*68*	*65*	*97*	*80*	*89*
Utilities (E)	40	54	57	73	45	43	39	3
Construction (F)	5	2	1	7	3	9	12	4
Trade, hotels and restaurants (G-H)	14	16	17	11	20	10	8	10
Transport, storage and communication (I)	40	30	19	22	13	11	14	30
Banks (65.1)	10	12	17	15	12	17	20	24
Holding companies (65.2)	-	1	8	14	19	29	39	45
Insurance (66-67)	11	11	15	14	14	13	14	19
Total financial sector (J)	*21*	*24*	*40*	*43*	*45*	*59*	*73*	*88*
Real estate, renting, business activities (K)	10	10	20	11	50	10	11	20
Other service activities (L-O)	2	2	3	4	-	3	2	2
Total services (G-O)	*87*	*82*	*99*	*91*	*128*	*93*	*108*	*150*
Total	250	250	250	250	250	250	250	250

In contrast to the fall of the traditional sectors, those linked to the Second Industrial Revolution, such as electrical and optical equipment (DL) or the petrol industry (DF) begin to gain weight as from 1936 (see Table 6.7). As far as the first sector is concerned, the study of the top 20 industrial companies by centrality confirms this trend: from 1911-1921 the sporadic presence of this sector is represented solely by AEG Thomson Houston; from 1927-1936 a small number of companies gains weight (Ing. V. Tedeschi & C., San Giorgio, FATME, Tecnomasio Italiano), subsequently disappearing from the vertex of the industrial firms; as from 1952 the number of companies increases to 5-6 per year, with some becoming stable elements of the vertex, such as F.lli Borletti and Franco Tosi. The latter in particular occupies the absolute centre position, being tenth in 1952, fourth in 1960 and remaining in a practically stable position in 1972. Despite the abovementioned increase, the occurrence of the petrol industry at the apex of the top 20 industrial firms is always rare: there is an exception in 1952, with Condor, the firm in which the interests of the Edison and of the Pesenti group converge, which is first in the industrial sector and eighth in the absolute ranking of companies.

The sectors prevalently centered on traditional activities, such as the manufacture of non-metallic minerals (DI) also grow decisively in the post-Second World War period (see Table 6.7). If we take another look at the group of the top 20 industrial firms, it becomes evident, however, that this growth is linked to activities with strong economies of scale (for example the production of cement) stimulated by the investments following post-Second World War *reconstruction*, as also to the expansion of infrastructures and the boom of housing construction. In particular, the role of Italcementi and Cementerie Siciliane of Pesenti's group becomes noticeable as from 1952, when they become part of the core of the industrial system.

At the same time the other strongly expanding sectors, for instance the transport sector, do not show a corresponding tendency to an increase in their occurrence among the *central* companies. On the contrary, their weight, as from 1960, declines (see Table 6.7). Once again the study of the top 20 industrial firms allows a better understanding of the dynamics of the sector. From 1911-1921 there is a relevant occurrence of shipbuilding (Cantieri Navali Riuniti in 1911, Cantieri Navali and Acciaierie di Venezia in 1921) and railway manufacturing company (Ernesto Breda), besides automobile companies, such as Fabbre & Gagliardi, which subsequently disappear. At the same time, FIAT emerges, being present among the top 20 industrial firms in 1911 and in 1921 - in 27th position in 1913. From 1936 and until 1960 this sector is exclusively represented at the apex by the automobile industry, and in particular FIAT, even though its role - from top position among industrial firms in 1936 - declines progressively. The differentiated trend of the sector is also confirmed by the strong resizing which occurs in the total number of companies as from 1960 - i.e. simultaneously with a strong expansion of the national automobile market (see Table 6.7). This can, in fact, be attributed to the disappearance of companies involved in the production of other types of vehicles, which leave the set of the top 250 companies, while the number of automobile companies remains stable. Finally, 1972 sees a change also in the position of the automobile industry, in that FIAT leaves the group of the top 250 firms.

This can be linked to the complex structure of the group, in which several financial holdings play a decisive role.

The trend of the chemical industry (DG) is decidedly particular. The number of companies in fact, remains relatively stable until 1960. Among these the Società Italiana per la Fabbricazione di Prodotti Azotati is prominent from 1911-1927, which witnesses to the importance of production for the purpose of modernizing national agriculture. In 1936 the role of Montecatini emerges followed, in 1972, by Montedison, together with SNIA Viscosa, acquired in 1972 by Montedison. Finally, in 1972 the number of chemical companies more than doubles as a consequence of the entry of a large number of companies belonging to Nino Rovelli's SIR group among the top 250 companies, due to the formation of the Sardinian chemical pole. These companies, although they are not at the apex of the top 20 industrial companies, are characterized by dense reciprocal interlocks [Zamagni 2003].

The diachronic comparison shows a few tendencies which identify temporal phases with relatively distinct characteristics also for the financial sector. Firstly, the data show a growth in the weight of banks as from 1952 - the year in which they overtake the number of insurance companies for the first time - until 1972, as also the increasing weight of holding companies, while the number of insurance companies remains relatively stable - excepting for a significant increase in 1972. Consequently, if the tendency towards growth in the financial sector is linear and consistent, the internal distribution of firms changes drastically, and three distinct phases can be identified on the basis of the data (see Sect. 6.4): a first phase (1911-1927) in which the weight of banks and insurance companies is similar; a second (1936) in which the weight of insurance companies is greater than that of banks; and a third (1952-1972) in which the banking component seems to become more relevant with respect to the insurance one.

If we observe the core of the Italian financial system - approximated by the top 20 banks and insurance companies by centrality (see Tables 6.12.a-h) -, in even greater detail, the abovementioned temporal trend appears to be the result of extremely complex dynamics. In the period 1911-1913 the first companies of the financial sector by centrality are represented by 4 great banks (Società Bancaria Italiana, Banca Commerciale Italiana, Banca d'Italia and Credito Italiano), and a smaller bank (Banca Bergamasca di Depositi e Conti Correnti). It should be noted that these 5 companies are also among the top 20 *central* companies (see Tables 6.12.a-h). The remaining financial companies, which are predominantly formed by insurance companies (10 out of 15), are instead in a lower position in the overall ranking, and are furthermore much smaller in size than the top 4 banks at the apex.

The predominance of the *mixed banks* is even more evident in 1921, when Banca Commerciale Italiana and Credito Italiano are at the summit both of the financial system and of the set of Italian companies, and Banco di Roma strongly reinforces its role; while Banca Nazionale di Credito, though considerable in size, is in a lower position. It should be noted that, while the number of insurance companies among the top 20 companies decreases (8), 2 insurance companies are at the summit: Società Anonima di Assicurazione contro gli Infortuni and Assicurazioni Generali. The role of the latter is also confirmed, together with the emerging weight of RAS, in 1927 when both are among the top 5 financial companies. Between 1921 and 1927 the process by which these two insurance companies become central to the relations within the Italian financial system, is accompanied by a considerable growth in size - Assicurazioni Generali's capital increases four and a half times, that of RAS four times. Finally, in 1936, these positions are inverted, and these two companies are at the top of the centrality ranking, while the 3 *mixed banks* lose positions also in the general company ranking. This change is the effect of the restructuring processes following the *IRI-zation* of *mixed banks*; nevertheless, as we have seen, the process of growth in the relations and the size of the two insurance companies starts already in 1927.

In 1952 the panorama changes radically: the *ex mixed banks* resize both in terms of capital and in the extension of their relations: only Banca Commerciale Italiana is among the first 5 financial companies, but it is only 43rd in the general ranking. The financial sector is dominated by RAS, together with a few small companies (Credito Commerciale and L'Assicuratrice Italiana), besides the Istituto di Credito per le Imprese di Pubblica Utilità (ICIPU), one of the *Istituti Beneduce*. Overall the system seems to have undergone a substantial decrease in concentration, due to the fact that it is no longer dominated by the great banks, protagonists of the pre-War period; even though the weight of Assicurazioni Generali is now considerable, and exceeds all the other *central* companies in size, becoming the centre of attraction of the system. Finally, we can note the appearance of a new and important *actor* in the financial system, Mediobanca, which is not, however, in the top positions.

In 1960 the summit of the top 5 remains substantially stable (RAS, L'Assicuratrice Italiana, Credito Commerciale), even though there are some new entries (Banca Unione and EFI Banca). Furthermore, there is a consistent increase in polarization in terms of size, with some companies (Assicurazioni Generali, Credito Italiano, Banca Nazionale del Lavoro, Mediobanca, Banco di Roma[14]) leaving the majority of the top 20 far behind, with a growth which is exceptional as compared to 1952. Concentration seems, therefore, once again on the increase, especially if we consider that the main companies just mentioned are reciprocally locked by stockholdings in the IRI group or other state-owned groups.

Finally, in 1972 the role of the insurance component grows even further: 3 of the top 5 *central* companies are insurance companies (RAS, L'Assicuratrice Italiana, Unione Italiana di Riassicurazione), even though the banks are the majority in the top 20 firms. It is interesting to note, however, that two great banks such as Banco di Roma and Banca Nazionale del Lavoro are not at the very top of the ranking of firms by centrality, on the same level as Assicurazioni Generali as far as the insurance sector is concerned. The study of the composition of the top 20 companies by centrality seems at first glance to offer a substantially different perspective as compared to that on the basis of the distribution of the top 250 companies. While in this last case there was a prevalence of banking companies as from 1952, we have just seen that it is exactly in 1952 that the insurance companies be-

[14] We must also add Banca Commerciale Italiana, which is 30th among the most central financial companies.

gin to occupy the top positions in the ranking of the top 20 companies by centrality. By contrast, even though the insurance companies are relevant in number from 1911-1927, the system during that time seems rather to be centered around the banking component, and in particular the great *mixed banks*.

In the first period (1911-1927), therefore, the high concentration of the banking system is accompanied by the existence of a thick network of relations between numerous small insurance companies. The second period (1952-1972), on the other hand, seems to mark a reversal of roles, in that a small number of insurance companies act as the pivot of the system, while the involvement of the banking companies increases, especially in favor of smaller companies. Halfway between the first and the second period there is the banking law of 1936 and the *IRI-zation* of the *mixed banks*, which deprived the predominant great banks of their functions, thus profoundly changing the structure of the system in the long term. However, it should be noted that the role of the banking sector does not disappear, on the contrary, in some ways it is reinforced, changing its structure, through the involvement of new subjects. In support of this hypothesis it is useful to examine the results supplied by a further proxy, known in literature as *betweeness*. This proxy measures the probability that a company can find itself on the geodetic, that is on the shortest path linking two other companies within the network, weighted on [(g-1)*(g-2)]/2, i.e. the number of possible couples between companies excluding the one taken into consideration. In the majority of cases centrality and *betweeness* should give similar values, in that the probability that a firm is on a geodetic between two others is proportional to the number of interlocks that it has with all the rest of the firms. The differences between the two proxies however, can in some cases be significant: while firms at the centre of integrated groups undoubtedly have both a high degree and a high *betweeness*, the bridge-firms between two groups can have a high *betweeness* even though they have a limited number of direct interlocks with other compnaies, and thus a low degree.

In this sense, the data presented in Table 6.8 relative to the financial sector is very indicative: the number of banks among the top 250 companies by *betweeness* is always distinctly higher than the number of banks among the top 250 companies by centrality (see Table 6.7). The same relationship holds true, even though in lesser measure, for the insurance companies, while the holding companies can be found in higher numbers among the top 250 by centrality. Banks and insurance companies therefore, even though in different measures, play a significant role as intermediaries among different groups of firms, in accordance with the characteristics of their activities. By contrast, the role of the financial sector is more centered on the development of relations within groups, also owing to the existence of a considerable number of holding companies classified within this sector. Some financial companies which carry out a role of bridge-firms between different groups are an exception to this tendency [Rinaldi and Vasta 2005], examples are EFI Banca, CONIEL and above all Bastogi, which as from 1921 is always among the top 20 firms by *betweeness*[15].

[15] On the role of Bastogi as an integrator between the public and the private sector in Italian capitalism, see Piluso [1992].

Table 6.8. Number of companies among the top 250 by *betweeness* - financial sector

Sector	1911	1913	1921	1927	1936	1952	1960	1972
Banks (65.1)	12	15	35	27	25	35	34	41
Holding companies (65.2)	0	1	5	11	18	22	36	37
Insurance (66-67)	9	9	18	20	22	21	23	20

Over and beyond these observations, it is important to note how, on the basis of this proxy, the weight of banks increases as from 1952, abundantly overtaking that of insurance companies, whose number remains close to that of 1936. We can, therefore, confirm that, even after the passing of the banking law, banks maintain, and even reinforce, their *hinge* role in the system, even though they exercise this role in different forms and through slightly different *actors* than before.

6.6. The industrial groups

The results of the analysis of the components presented above confirm the existence of high levels of collusion in the network of Italian companies, and show that the motivations underlying the ID phenomenon are complex and not exclusively attributable to the logic of the direct control of companies. The very extension of the relations excludes this explanation, underlining the need to find other reasons. On the other hand, it can be hypothesized that the introduction of restrictions on the nature of the interlocks to be considered could limit the extension of the ID phenomenon, allowing for the identification of relation schemes closer to the logic of company control.

In this Sect. we attempt to verify the validity of this hypothesis. To this end the analysis of the components and bi-components for each benchmark year was carried out on the basis of the distinction between three main types of interlocks:

(i) *in-in* interlocks, namely the ID generated by directors in the position of president, vice-president, sole director or managing director towards analogous positions;

(ii) *in-out* interlocks, namely the ID generated by directors in the position of president, vice-president, sole director or managing director towards analogous positions and towards other positions (board member or board secretary); these correspond to the primary interlocks defined by Scott [1985];

(iii) *out-out* interlocks, namely the ID generated by board members or board secretaries towards analogous positions.

In the sample the *in-in* interlocks represent the minority of overall interlocks for all the benchmark years, even though during the course of time there are relevant variations in the distribution among types of interlocks (see Table 6.9). Between 1911 and 1927 *in-in* interlocks amount to between 14 per cent and 17 per cent while the other types show similar percentages fluctuating between 40 per cent (*in-out* interlocks) and 45 per cent (*out-out* interlocks). In 1936 the quota of *in-in* interlocks exceeds 20 per cent especially at the expense of the *out-out* type, which drops to 37 per cent. In 1952 the percentages realign with the 1927 values, while 1960 is a strongly inconsistent year as compared to the previous ones, with *in-in* interlocks weighing 38 per cent of the total, at the expense of *out-out* interlocks. Finally in 1972, the percentages tend to realign with those of preceding years, even though the weight of *in-in* interlocks remains considerable (28 per cent). Putting forward an interpretative hypothesis for the 1960 values is not a simple matter. However, as we shall see further on (see Tables 6.10-6.11) this year is also characterized by a greater concentration of interlocks. The two phenomena can therefore be explained on the basis of the same factors - linked to the behavior of the electro-commercial firms during that period -, which will be more extensively dealt with in the rest of the Sect.

Table 6.9. Distribution of interlocks between companies by type, 1911-1972

Year		*in-in*	*in-out*	*out-out*	Total
1911	no.	922	2,638	3,090	6,650
	%	13.9	39.7	46.5	100.0
1913	no.	1,453	3,900	4,136	9,489
	%	15.3	41.1	43.6	100.0
1921	no.	4,501	11,957	12,479	28,937
	%	15.6	41.3	43.1	100.0
1927	no.	8,056	19,042	19,456	46,554
	%	17.3	40.9	41.8	100.0
1936	no.	6,535	11,850	10,873	29,258
	%	22.3	40.5	37.2	100.0
1952	no.	5,623	12,320	13,557	31,500
	%	17.9	39.1	43.0	100.0
1960	no.	13,285	14,540	6,959	34,784
	%	38.2	41.8	20.0	100.0
1972	no.	12,401	17,616	14,345	44,362
	%	28.0	39.7	32.3	100.0

The distinction between types was carried out to try to discriminate as much as possible between the relations formed by ID on the basis of their nature and their possible causes. Excluding *out-out* interlocks from the calculation of the components would in fact mean the almost total exclusion of the interlocks generated by the so-called network specialists, i.e. those figures, with no particular affiliation to any firm, which operate in the network as connectors between firms, on the basis of their technical competence or their own personal relations (see Chap. 9). Despite the fact that the role of the network specialist is particularly important for the circulation of information in the system, concentrating only on *in-out* interlocks, or going even further and considering only *in-in* type interlocks, the field of observation could be reduced only to those interlocks determined by the need for decisional coordination and company control, which should, according to the hypothesis, be more in keeping with ownership interlocks between companies. This however calls for a clarification on the nature of the subdivisions which it is possible to generate through the use of this methodology. The limits of the source do not permit a precise distinction between intra-group and inter-group interlocks, because there is no information on the ownership structure of companies which can be compared to the interlocks generated by the ID. The introduction of criteria based on different types of positions, such as those illustrated above, therefore, represents the best approximation available in the source, even though the correspondence between the network of these interlocks and that of ownership quotas, according to the few available studies, is not perfect [Bianco and Pagnoni 1997; Lomi, Corrado and Sandri 1997].

In fact, even if we consider the more restrictive type of interlock (*in-in*), the results confirm the caution expressed above. The extension of the main component of the network, even though strongly diminished in comparison to the data presented in Table 6.2, remains in fact, considerable, varying however between approximately 12 per cent and 40 per cent in the different years considered (see Table 6.10). A relevant part of the firms is, therefore, reciprocally interconnected through positions which are heavily involved in management, making it possible to hypothesize the presence of complex mechanisms of decisional interdependence.

Table 6.10. Components of the network of Italian companies, *in-in* interlocks only, 1911-1972

Year		In the main component	In medium components*	In small components**	Isolated	Total
1911	no.	289	58	75	366	788
	%	36.7	7.4	9.5	46.4	100.0
1913	no.	413	112	160	557	1,242
	%	33.3	9.0	12.9	44.8	100.0
1921	no.	1,085	389	425	1,180	3,079
	%	35.2	12.6	13.8	38.3	100.0
1927	no.	1,559	480,0	605	1,831	4,475
	%	34.8	10.7	13.5	40.9	100.0
1936	no.	1,142	448,0	772	1,879	4,241
	%	26.9	10.6	18.2	44.3	100.0
1952	no.	779	1,046	1,162	3,178	6,165
	%	12.6	17.0	18.8	51.5	100.0
1960	no.	2,689	456	790	2,432	6,367
	%	42.2	7.2	12.4	38.2	100.0
1972	no.	1,722	1,859	2,285	5,934	11,800
	%	14.6	15.8	19.4	50.3	100.0

Legend: * Components (excluding the main component) with 4 or more elements; ** Components with 2 or 3 elements.

Considering the number of companies included in the main component, it seems impossible to attribute this type of interlock to a system formed by a plurality of independent, competing industrial groups; and, consequently, the hypothesis of a high level of collusion in the Italian system is further reinforced. On the other hand, the introduction of more restrictive criteria reveals the presence of intermediate components, with a weight which varies in time from 7 per cent to 17 per cent, besides an increase in the weight of small components. The extension of the *pyramidal* structure highlighted in the preceding Sects. is reduced, while the existence of external poles emerges, even though they are extremely limited in size.

The evolution in time of the size of the main component is even more interesting (see Fig. 6.4): while previously there was a progressive decrease (see Fig. 6.2), here instead we find a fluctuating trend. Until 1927 the extension of the main component varies between 33 per cent and 37 per cent; subsequently a significant resizing takes place: in 1936 it decreases to 26.9 per cent, and in 1952 it reaches an all time low of 12.6 per cent. It should be noted that in the first year the increase is compensated by the growth of isolated firms as well as that of firms in small components; while in the second year it is mainly the firms in medium components which increase in weight. The structure of the network changes radically again in 1960: the weight of the main component increases more than threefold (42.2 per cent), while that of the firms in medium components reaches its minimum level (7.2 per cent), and that of firms in small components is also reduced. Finally, in 1972 the distribution is once again very similar to that of 1952.

It is not easy to identify the factors which contribute to the anomalous trend of 1960, which has already been mentioned in connection with the weight of *in-in* interlocks. We can, however, suggest an explanation based on two types of reasons: firstly, in 1960 there is a strong expansion of the national economy, consequently firms could have increased their level of participation in other firms by using part of the liquidity deriving from the increase in profits; secondly, this year coincides with a crucial period for the electrical industry, which exercises a role in reinforcing the cohesion of the system. These data, in effect, reflect the effort made by the great electrical groups, as from midway through the 1950s, to widen their network of alliances in order to prevent nationalization. During this period, in fact, the number of *central* firms exclusively connected to the electrical sector decreases, while the weight of the financial companies, with which the electrical groups *cohabited* together with the representatives of other industrial sectors, increases [Rinaldi and Vasta 2005].

In any case, the extension of the main component shows that the sole selection of the type of interlock does not give an acceptable approximation of the extension of ID in comparison to the structure of groups of firms. To find a greater correspondence between the two phenomena, a final restriction was introduced, limiting the analysis of the components to the industrial sector.

The intention was to evaluate the tendency of industrial firms to form relations independently without the mediation of non-industrial sectors and, in particular, of the key sectors (banks, holding companies, insurance companies, utilities) identified above. We thus examined only the *in-in* interlocks regarding the firms in the manufacturing sector[16].

[16] This method is used in Chap. 3 (see particularly Sect. 3.3) to evaluate the *consolidated* concentration, that considers the group form, which is widespread in Italian capitalism.

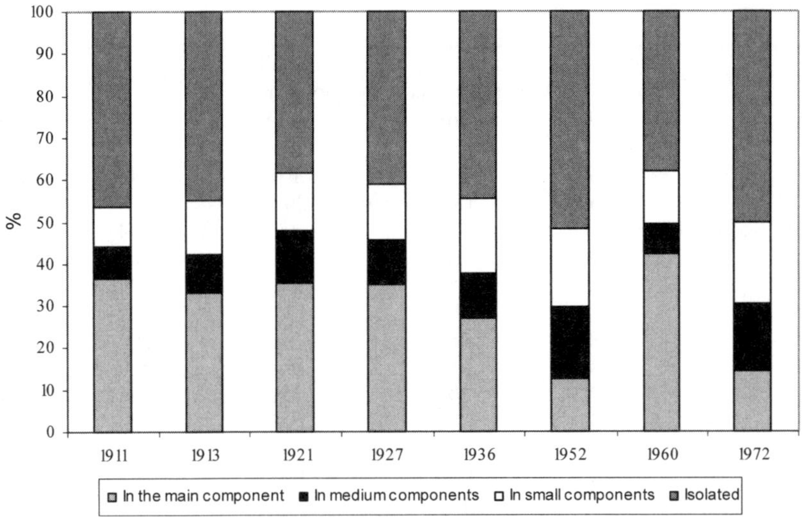

Fig. 6.4. Percentage distribution of companies in components, *in-in* interlocks only (1911-1972)

The data in Table 6.11 show that industrial firms exhibit a strong tendency to form relations with other firms in all the benchmark years, even though there are relevant variations from a maximum of about 50 per cent in 1921 to a minimum of 36 per cent in 1952. The financial sector's mediatory role within the industrial sector does not, therefore, seem exclusive: the industrial companies form relations between each other directly primarily due to integration strategies linked to the complementarity of productive processes (see Sect. 6.3). The exclusion of the interlocks generated by the financial sector, however, produces a fundamental change in the distribution of firms: the weight of the main component once again decreases significantly, and that of firms in small and medium components is finally predominant. What emerges, therefore, is the existence of a network formed by numerous groups, whose function can be mainly ascribed to productive integration causes. An exception to this occurs in 1960, when the firms included in the main component represent 19.4 per cent of the total. This result seems to lead to a reappraisal of the hypothesis proposed above on the role of the electrical companies in the explanation of this year's trend, because the interlocks of industrial firms are in fact largely independent from the mediation of the electrical sector. However, the interlocks generated by this sector can nevertheless entail indirect effects, for example when the same individual is the director of an electrical company and simultaneously of two different industrial companies, and this could increase the cohesion of the industrial sector even though the electrical companies are not directly included. These data, therefore, reflect the abovementioned strategy of the great electro-commercial groups, which in that period aimed at diversifying into the manufacturing industry.

Table 6.11. Components of the network of industrial companies, *in-in* interlocks only, 1911-1972

Year		In the main component	In medium components*	In small components**	Isolated	Total
1911	no.	29	68	79	257	433
	%	6.7	15.7	18.2	59.4	100.0
1913	no.	35	118	131	345	629
	%	5.6	18.8	20.8	54.8	100.0
1921	no.	111	304	287	704	1,406
	%	7.9	21.6	20.4	50.1	100.0
1927	no.	131	486	339	992	1,948
	%	6.7	24.9	17.4	50.9	100.0
1936	no.	58	354	351	1,002	1,765
	%	3.3	20.1	19.9	56.8	100.0
1952	no.	107	397	582	1,933	3,019
	%	3.5	13.2	19.3	64.0	100.0
1960	no.	614	381	521	1,649	3,165
	%	19.4	12.0	16.5	52.1	100.0
1972	no.	71	1,107	1,187	3,766	6,131
	%	1.2	18.1	19.4	61.4	100.0

Legend: * Components (excluding the main component) with 4 or more elements; ** Components with 2 or 3 elements.

6.7. Conclusions

This study confirms the existence in the long term of a high level of collusion in the Italian capitalist system. In particular, only a minority of firms is isolated from the network while the majority is part of a completely *interconnected* group - known as the main component. This result is even more significant because the data refer to a broad section of the population of Italian firms in the years studied. A disaggregated analysis by size and sector reveals that the structure of the network is divided into three types interlocks which, in order of importance act as centralizers of relations: (i) the inter-sectoral relations mediated by a few reciprocally interconnected key sectors (banks, holding companies, insurance companies and utilities), motivated mainly by the intent to facilitate the acquisition of capital for investments and/or to maintain company control; (ii) the reciprocal relations between the larger firms, together with the relations between these and the smaller firms, which form elements of *hierarchization* of the network; (iii) the relations within the single sectors or among similar sectors, probably motivated by the search for productive complementarities.

While the above are the main structural elements which remain stable during the period examined, the diachronic analysis shows the existence of two distinct phases. In the first, which ends with the introduction of the banking law in 1936, the system is based on direct relations between industrial firms and the role of a few banks (the *mixed banks*) assisted by a large number of insurance and holding companies[17]. In the second, (1952-1972) the role of the *mixed banks* disappears and a multitude of new subjects, both public and private, appears. This, in general, reinforces the role of the financial sector. The relations are distributed in a uniform manner between different banking companies, and the role of the smaller banks emerges, while a few insurance companies remain at the summit of the system. In this framework, the function of the utilities expands especially during the period (1927-1960) spanning the two phases, it then subsequently resizes and disappears after the nationalization of the electrical industry, and this leads to the dissolution of the old centre of the system.

The empirical evidence shows how the role of the banking and financial system, as already suggested by other studies [Ferri and Trento 1997; Rinaldi and Vasta 2003, 2005], remains relevant throughout the period. This leads to an at least partial reconsideration of the thesis according to which in the post-Second World War period the banks "were absent from the table of great industrial capitalism" [Chiesi 1985; Amatori and Brioschi 1997]. After the nationalization of the electrical industry the banks, in fact, return to the centre of the system, side by side with the insurance companies, regaining, at least in part, the position held in the 1920s [Vasta and Baccini 1997].

As far as the industrial sector is concerned there are different phases, linked to technological evolution and the level of development of the national economy, in which different sectors predominate. A few qualitative observations were made on these aspects, which nonetheless offer interesting points of discussion. Thus a number of traditional sectors, such as the textile and the food sectors, with particular reference to the production of sugar and distillates, are more central in the first years (1911-1927), losing importance in the subsequent period. At the same time, in the post-Second World War period, other sectors emerge which are more connected both to the *technological regimes* of the Second Industrial Revolution and to the expansion of post-War investments and new models of consumption. Among these, in particular, the role of firms producing electrical equipment, transport equipment - especially the automobile - and cement factories.

The introduction of restrictive criteria in the identification of interlocks (consideration only of *in-in* interlocks, the exclusion of non-manufacturing sectors) allows a further verification with a better approximation of the existence of real groups of firms in the industrial sector. The analysis reveals the existence of a large number of small and medium-sized groups with respect to the number of companies involved, even though the correspondence between ID and company participation remains imperfect. Despite the financial sector's role of *mediator*, it seems, therefore, that industrial firms also tend to form relations directly, probably in search of the market or productive complementarities mentioned above.

Finally, the irregularity of the control mechanisms of Italian capitalism seems connected to the search for *alternative* organizational formulas to permit a latecomer country to *grab* the different opportunities which appear with the succes-

[17] From this point of view, 1936 is undoubtedly a year *astride* the two periods, exhibiting the first signs of the resizing of the *mixed banks* and the increased importance of two insurance companies such as Assicurazioni Generali and RAS.

sion of the different *technological regimes*. In the period examined, in particular, the development of the typical sectors of the Second Industrial Revolution avails itself of the constitution of groups of firms, producing a high level of *consolidated* concentration of the industry (see Chap. 3). This solution can be interpreted as the system's specific answer to a technological path-way that favors large firms, finalized towards a greater vertical integration of production.

Annex 6.1. The *central* companies

Table 6.12.a. The top 20 companies by degree of centrality in banks and industry, 1911

Companies	Degree of centrality	Position in the top 250 by centrality	Sector
Manufacturing			
ILVA	10.419	2	DJ
AEG Thomson Houston	8.895	6	DL
Distillerie Italiane	7.497	14	DA
Società Italiana Fabbricazione Prodotti Azotati	6.607	20	DG
Società Valsacco per la Fabbricazione dello Zucchero	6.607	21	DA
Zuccherera Nazionale	6.480	23	DA
Società degli Altiforni Fonderie ed Acciaierie di Terni	6.226	25	DJ
Società Italiana per l'Industria dello Zucchero Indigeno	6.226	26	DA
Italiana dei Forni Elettrici	6.099	27	DK
Società Ligure Lombarda per la Raffinazione degli Zuccheri	6.099	30	DA
Cantieri Navali Riuniti	5.972	31	DM
Zuccherificio e Distilleria Alcool Sgulinelli	5.845	36	DA
Filatura Vogherese Carminati	5.464	39	DB
Elettrica ed Elettrochimica del Caffaro	5.337	40	DG
FIAT	5.337	41	DM
Cristallerie e Vetrerie Riunite	5.210	42	DI
Fabbre & Gagliardi	5.210	43	DM
Manifattura di Valle Camonica	5.210	44	DB
Società Magazzini Refrigeranti e Ghiaccio Artificiale Gondrand Mangili	5.083	49	DA
Società Italiana per il Carburo di Calcio	5.083	50	DG
Financial sector			
Società Bancaria Italiana	13.088	1	65.1
Banca Commerciale Italiana	10.292	3	65.1
Banca Bergamasca di Depositi e Conti Correnti	8.386	9	65.1
Banca d'Italia	7.497	12	65.1
Credito Italiano	7.497	13	65.1
La Fondiaria Vita	5.845	32	66-67
Società Anonima Italiana di Assicurazione contro gli Infortuni	4.828	60	66-67
Italia	4.701	65	66-67
Savoia	4.574	71	66-67
Unione Continentale	4.574	75	66-67
Banca Lombarda di Depositi e Conti Correnti	4.066	94	65.1
Società Anonima di Assicurazioni contro la Grandine	3.939	106	66-67
La Fondiaria Incendi	3.431	134	66-67
Società Anonima l'Assicuratrice Italiana	3.304	149	66-67
Reale	3.177	157	66-67
Liguria	3.050	166	66-67
Banco Ambrosiano	2.922	169	65.1
Compagnia Anonima d'Assicurazione	2.795	179	66-67
Credito Varesino	2.668	191	65.1
Società Finanziaria e Industriale Torinese	2.668	196	65.1

Table 6.12.b. The top 20 companies by degree of centrality in banks and industry, 1913

Companies	Degree of centrality	Position in the top 250 by centrality	Sector
Manufacturing			
ILVA	7.66	3	DJ
AEG Thomson Houston	6.53	7	DL
Italiana dei Forni Elettrici	4.84	21	DG
Fabbrica Italiana di Carburi e Derivati	4.67	24	DG
Società Italiana Fabbricazione di Prodotti Azotati	4.59	27	DG
Lanificio Carminati	4.51	28	DB
Società Valsacco per la Fabbricazione dello Zucchero	4.51	30	DA
Altiforni Fonderia Acciaieria e Ferriera Gio. Andrea Gregorini	4.43	31	DJ
Società degli Altiforni Fonderie ed Acciaierie di Terni	4.19	38	DJ
Società Italiana per l'Industria dello Zucchero Indigeno	4.11	43	DA
Società Magazzini Refrigeranti e Ghiaccio Artificiale Gondrand Mangili	3.87	50	DA
Fabbre & Gagliardi	3.79	51	DM
Zuccichereria Nazionale	3.79	55	DA
Generale Italiana Accumulatori Elettrici	3.63	59	DL
Unione Italiana Consumatori e Fabbricanti di Concimi e Prodotti Chimici	3.63	61	DG
Elettrica ed Elettrochimica del Caffaro	3.55	63	DG
La Stampa Commerciale	3.55	65	DE
Zuccherificio e Distilleria Alcool Sgulinelli	3.55	66	DA
Cotonificio Cova	3.47	67	DB
Distillerie Italiane	3.47	68	DA
Financial sector			
Società Bancaria Italiana	9.67	1	65.1
Banca Commerciale Italiana	6.77	6	65.1
Banca Bergamasca di Depositi e Conti Correnti	5.08	15	65.1
Credito Italiano	5.08	16	65.1
Banca d'Italia	4.84	20	65.1
La Fondiaria Vita	4.11	42	66-67
Società Anonima Italiana di Assicurazione contro gli Infortuni	3.71	56	66-67
Savoia	2.90	102	66-67
Italia	2.74	112	66-67
Società Anonima l'Assicuratrice Italiana	2.74	117	66-67
Banca Lombarda di Depositi e Conti Correnti	2.66	122	65.1
Società Anonima di Assicurazioni a Premio Fisso contro la Grandine	2.66	126	66-67
Banco Ambrosiano	2.50	134	65.1
Unione Continentale	2.50	144	66-67
Società Italiana di Credito Provinciale	2.26	174	65.1
Società Finanziaria e Industriale Torinese	2.18	179	65.1
La Fondiaria Incendi	2.02	200	66-67
Reale	2.02	203	66-67
Banca Veneta di Depositi e Conti Correnti	1.93	208	65.1
Compagnia Anonima d'Assicurazione	1.93	210	66-67

Table 6.12.c. The top 20 companies by degree of centrality in banks and industry, 1921

Companies	Degree of centrality	Position in the top 250 by centrality	Sector
Manufacturing			
Distillerie Italiane	4.97	4	DA
Società Italiana Tubi Togni	3.83	15	DJ
Società Italiana Prodotti Azotati	3.57	21	DG
Florio & C.	3.54	22	DA
Terni Società per l'Industria e l'Elettricità	3.51	24	DJ
Cantieri Navali e Acciaierie di Venezia	3.44	25	DM
Zuccherificio e Distilleria Alcool Sgulinelli	3.15	32	DA
Fonderia Milanese di Acciaio	2.99	34	DJ
Italiana Ernesto Breda per Costruzioni Meccaniche	2.96	37	DM
Società Ligure Lombarda per la Raffinazione degli Zuccheri	2.96	38	DA
Fabbriche Italiane Materie Coloranti Monelli	2.83	43	DG
Linificio e Canapificio Nazionale	2.73	46	DB
Zuccherificio e Distilleria di Polesella	2.73	47	DA
Franco Tosi	2.57	49	DJ
Costruzioni Meccaniche Riva	2.53	52	DK
Società Commercio Coloniali Droghe & Medicinali Paganini Villani	2.53	53	DG
FIAT	2.47	59	DM
Cotonificio di Solbiate	2.44	60	DB
Saccarifera Lombarda	2.40	66	DA
Società Italiana per la Fabbricazione dell'Alluminio	2.34	70	DJ
Financial sector			
Banca Commerciale Italiana	8.74	1	65.1
Credito Italiano	5.07	3	65.1
Assicurazioni Generali	4.32	12	66-67
Società Anonima Italiana di Assicurazione contro gli Infortuni	3.70	18	66-67
Banco di Roma	3.51	23	65.1
Banca Belinzaghi	2.99	33	65.1
La Pace	2.92	39	66-67
Credito Industriale di Venezia	2.83	42	65.1
Credito Nazionale	2.76	45	65.1
Istituto Italiano di Credito Marittimo	2.57	50	65.1
Società Anonima Italiana di Assicurazioni contro la Grandine	2.50	56	66-67
Banca Bergamasca di Depositi e Conti Correnti	2.40	64	65.1
Banca Unione	2.21	80	65.1
La Riassicuratrice	2.21	83	66-67
Banca Commerciale Triestina	2.18	89	65.1
La Previdente	2.18	90	66-67
Credito Veneto	2.05	109	65.1
Banca Nazionale di Credito	2.01	117	65.1
Riunione Adriatica di Sicurtà	2.01	121	66-67
L'Assicuratrice Italiana	1.95	133	66-67

Table 6.12.d. The top 20 companies by degree of centrality in banks and industry, 1927

Companies	Degree of centrality	Position in the top 250 by centrality	Sector
Manufacturing			
Ansaldo	5.27	6	DJ
ACNA	4.05	14	DG
Distillerie Italiane	3.82	20	DA
Costruzioni Meccaniche Riva	3.22	33	DK
Società Italiana Tubi Togni	3.15	35	DJ
Società Italiana Prodotti Azotati	3.08	40	DG
ILVA Altiforni e Acciaierie d'Italia	3.02	43	DJ
Società Ligure Lombarda per la Raffinazione degli Zuccheri	2.93	45	DA
Società Metallurgica Italiana	2.86	48	DJ
Altiforni e Acciaierie della Venezia Giulia	2.77	49	DJ
Cotonificio Veneziano	2.59	60	DB
Altiforni e Acciaierie della Venezia Giulia Società di esercizio	2.55	64	DJ
Ing. V. Tedeschi & C.	2.55	67	DL
Tecnomasio Italiano Brown Boveri	2.55	68	DL
Zuccherificio Jolanda della Bonifica Ferrarese	2.55	70	DA
L'Appula	2.50	71	DG
Saccarifera Lombarda	2.46	76	DA
Zuccherificio e Distilleria di Polesella	2.35	86	DA
Fabbrica Chimica Arenella	2.32	87	DG
Cotonificio di Solbiate	2.24	95	DB
Financial sector			
Banca Commerciale Italiana	8.29	1	65.1
Credito Italiano	5.52	4	65.1
Banca Nazionale di Credito	4.45	8	65.1
Assicurazioni Generali	3.13	36	66-67
Riunione Adriatica di Sicurtà	2.91	47	66-67
Banco di Roma	2.73	52	65.1
L'anonima Infortuni	2.70	57	66-67
Società Assicuratrice Industriale	2.66	59	66-67
Banca Commerciale Triestina	2.48	73	65.1
L'Assicuratrice Italiana	2.35	83	66-67
Banca Belinzaghi	2.12	111	65.1
Istituto Italiano di Credito Marittimo	2.12	112	65.1
Credito Industriale di Venezia	2.10	115	65.1
Credito Commerciale	2.01	127	65.1
Banca Bergamasca di Depositi e Conti Correnti	1.92	140	65.1
Società Anonima Italiana di Assicurazione contro la Grandine	1.88	147	66-67
Banca d'Italia	1.86	149	65.1
Banca Unione	1.81	157	65.1
Società Italiana di Assicurazione Credito	1.81	160	66-67
Banca Industriale di Busto Arsizio	1.70	175	65.1

Table 6.12.e. The top 20 companies by degree of centrality in banks and industry, 1936

Companies	Degree of centrality	Position in the top 250 by centrality	Sector
Manufacturing			
FIAT	2.31	21	DM
Vetrocoke	2.19	24	DI
Acciaierie e Ferriere Nazionali	2.05	29	DJ
Montecatini	2.05	32	DG
Ing. V. Tedeschi & C.	2.00	34	DL
Linificio e Canapificio Nazionale	1.96	37	DB
Consorzio Nazionale Produttori Zucchero	1.65	55	DA
Franco Tosi	1.65	56	DJ
San Giorgio Società Anonima Industriale	1.63	59	DL
Film Fabbriche Riunite Prodotti Fotografici Cappelli e Ferrania	1.58	64	DG
Alogeno	1.56	66	DG
G.B. Borsalino fu Lazzaro & C.	1.53	70	DB
Centrale Cementerie Italiane SACCI	1.49	77	DI
Società Italiana del Piombo e dello Zinco	1.46	88	DJ
Società Metallurgica Italiana	1.46	89	DJ
SNIA Viscosa Società Nazionale Industrie Applicazioni Viscosa	1.44	94	DG
Unione Cementi Marchino & C.	1.41	100	DI
Cotonificio di Solbiate	1.39	103	DB
Cartiere Pietro Miliani	1.37	108	DE
FATME Fabbrica Apparecchi Telefonici e Materiale Elettrico	1.37	109	DL
Financial sector			
Assicurazioni Generali	4.22	1	66-67
Riunione Adriatica di Sicurtà	3.98	2	66-67
Banca Commerciale Italiana	3.04	8	65.1
Assicuratrice Industriale SAI	2.92	11	66-67
Credito Italiano	2.41	18	65.1
Banco di Roma	2.33	20	65.1
Credito Commerciale	1.79	44	65.1
L'anonima Infortuni	1.72	51	66-67
Unione Italiana di Riassicurazione	1.70	54	66-67
Italiana di Assicurazione Credito	1.65	57	66-67
Credito Industriale di Venezia	1.53	68	65.1
Praevidentia	1.53	71	66-67
Banca Belinzaghi	1.39	101	65.1
Istituto Commerciale Laniero Italiano	1.37	110	65.1
L'anonima Grandine	1.25	133	66-67
Banca Popolare Cooperativa Anonima di Novara	1.23	137	65.1
Società Italiana di Riassicurazione Consorziale	1.23	142	66-67
Banca Nazionale del Lavoro	1.20	143	65.1
La Reale	1.18	155	66-67
Fondiaria Vita	1.13	206	66-67

Table 6.12.f. The top 20 companies by degree of centrality in banks and industry, 1952

Companies	Degree of centrality	Position in the top 250 by centrality	Sector
Manufacturing			
Condor Società per l'Industria Petrolifera e Chimica	1.796	8	DF
Franco Tosi	1.618	10	DL
OSRAM Società Riunite Osra Medison Clerici	1.602	12	DL
FIAT	1.505	20	DM
Cartiere Burgo	1.376	29	DE
FINSIDER Società Finanziaria Siderurgica	1.343	32	DJ
Italcementi Fabbriche Riunite Cemento	1.327	35	DI
Vetrocoke	1.311	38	DI
Industriale San Marco	1.295	40	DG
Montecatini Società Generale per l'Industria Mineraria e Chimica	1.295	41	DG
Terni Società per l'Industria e l'Elettricità	1.279	45	DJ
CGE Compagnia Generale di Elettricità	1.198	55	DL
Pirelli	1.181	58	DH
SISMA Società Industrie Siderurgiche Meccaniche ed Affini	1.181	60	DJ
F.lli Borletti	1.149	64	DL
RIV Officine di Villar Perosa	1.149	67	DJ
Compagnia Generale Contatori CO.GE.CO.	1.133	68	DL
Cokapuania	1.117	73	DF
ACSA Applicazioni Chimiche	1.101	75	DG
Compagnia Generale Elettronica	1.101	76	DL
Financial sector			
RAS Riunione Adriatica di Sicurtà	2.573	4	66-67
Credito Commerciale	1.618	9	65.1
Istituto di Credito per le Imprese di Pubblica Utilità	1.521	19	65.1
L'Assicuratrice Italiana	1.327	36	66-67
Banca Commerciale Italiana	1.279	43	65.1
Unione Italiana di Riassicurazione	1.279	46	66-67
Assicurazioni Generali	1.262	47	66-67
Assicuratrice Industriale	1.246	50	66-67
Compagnia di Roma Riassicurazioni e Partecipazioni Assicurative	1.214	53	66-67
Banca Provinciale di Depositi e Sconti	1.117	72	65.1
Fiumeter Assicurazioni e Riassicurazioni	1.117	74	66-67
Consorzio Nazionale per il Credito Agrario di Miglioramento	1.052	84	65.1
Mediobanca Banca di Credito Finanziario	1.036	90	65.1
Credito Italiano	1.003	96	65.1
Italia Assicurazioni	0.939	110	66-67
La Fondiaria Vita	0.922	116	66-67
Banca d'America e d'Italia	0.906	121	65.1
Consorzio di Credito per le Opere Pubbliche	0.874	131	65.1
Istituto Commerciale Laniero Italiano	0.874	134	65.1
Banca Milanese di Credito	0.858	138	65.1

Table 6.12.g. The top 20 companies by degree of centrality in banks and industry, 1960

Companies	Degree of centrality	Position in the top 250 by centrality	Sector
Manufacturing			
Franco Tosi	2.104	4	DL
Montecatini Società Generale per l'Industria Mineraria e Chimica	1.962	8	DG
Pirelli	1.758	13	DH
Italcementi Fabbriche Riunite Cemento	1.711	15	DI
Cartiere Burgo	1.633	17	DE
F.lli Borletti	1.586	20	DL
Centro Elettrotecnico Sperimentale Italiano Giacinto Motta	1.460	31	DL
SNIA Viscosa Società Nazionale Industrie Applicazioni Viscosa	1.397	38	DG
Metallurgica Italiana	1.381	42	DJ
Terni Società per l'Industria e l'Elettricità	1.287	51	DJ
CGE Compagnia Generale di Elettricità	1.240	55	DL
Cementir Cementerie del Tirreno	1.224	57	DI
Chatillon	1.209	58	DG
Linificio e Canapificio Nazionale	1.209	62	DB
De Angeli Frua Società per l'Industria dei Tessuti Stampati	1.193	64	DB
SIRMA Società Italiana Refrattari Marghera Azionaria	1.162	68	DI
Cementerie Siciliane	1.146	70	DI
FIAT	1.068	85	DM
Istrumenti di Misura CGS	1.052	87	DL
Lancia & C. Fabbrica Automobili Torino	1.052	88	DM
Financial sector			
RAS Riunione Adriatica di Sicurtà	2.920	2	66-67
L'Assicuratrice Italiana	2.088	5	66-67
Credito Commerciale	1.947	9	65.1
Banca Unione	1.554	22	65.1
EFI Banca - Ente Finanziario Interbancario	1.507	26	65.1
Società Assicuratrice Industriale	1.507	27	66-67
Assicurazioni Generali	1.476	28	66-67
Banca Provinciale Lombarda	1.460	30	65.1
Credito Italiano	1.366	43	65.1
Banca d'America e d'Italia	1.272	52	65.1
Consorzio Nazionale per il Credito Agrario di Miglioramento	1.272	53	65.1
La Fondiaria Vita	1.177	66	66-67
Banca Nazionale del Lavoro	1.146	69	65.1
Credito Lombardo	1.146	71	65.1
Mediobanca Banca di Credito Finanziario	1.115	78	65.1
Unione Italiana di Riassicurazione	1.115	80	66-67
La Fondiaria Infortuni	0.001	101	66-67
La Fondiaria Incendio	0.001	109	66-67
Banco di Roma	0.001	143	65.1
Banco Lariano	0.001	153	65.1

Table 6.12.h. The top 20 companies by degree of centrality in banks and industry, 1972

Companies	Degree of centrality	Position in the top 250 by centrality	Sector
Manufacturing			
Franco Tosi	1.025	5	DL
SNIA Viscosa Società Nazionale Industrie Applicazioni Viscosa	0.941	9	DG
Italcementi Fabbriche Riunite Cemento	0.805	20	DI
Cementerie Siciliane	0.797	21	DI
Siemens Elettra	0.754	30	DL
Italsider	0.720	35	DJ
Cotonificio Olcese Veneziano	0.695	40	DB
Montedison	0.669	44	DG
Manifattura Ceramica Pozzi	0.644	46	DI
Acciaierie e Ferriere Lombarde Falck	0.627	47	DJ
Valdadige	0.627	50	DI
Ing. C. Olivetti & C.	0.593	55	DL
Pozzi Ferrandina	0.585	59	DG
Pacchetti S.p.A.	0.576	63	DC
F.lli Borletti	0.559	66	DL
Linificio e Canapificio Nazionale	0.559	68	DB
Tecnomasio Italiano Brown Boveri	0.559	70	DL
Nebiolo	0.542	75	DK
IVISU Industria Vernici e Affini	0.534	78	DG
Montedison Fibre	0.534	80	DG
Financial sector			
RAS Riunione Adriatica di Sicurtà	1.644	1	66-67
L'Assicuratrice Italiana	1.271	3	66-67
Unione Italiana di Riassicurazione	1.051	4	66-67
EFI Banca - Ente Finanziario Interbancario	1.017	6	65.1
Credito Commerciale	0.983	7	65.1
Banca d'America e d'Italia	0.958	8	65.1
Banca Provinciale Lombarda	0.890	11	65.1
Istituto Bancario Italiano	0.830	15	65.1
Unione Subalpina di Assicurazioni	0.813	18	66-67
Istituto Centrale di Banche e Banchieri	0.797	22	65.1
Toro Assicurazioni Compagnia Anonima d'Assicurazioni di Torino	0.797	23	66-67
Banco di Roma	0.788	24	65.1
SIAT Società Italiana Assicurazioni Trasporti	0.729	33	66-67
Banca Cattolica del Veneto	0.669	42	65.1
Credito Legnanese	0.669	43	65.1
Società Italiana di Assicurazione per i Danni di Incendio e per i Rischi	0.593	56	66-67
Società Italiana per l'Assicurazione sulla Vita	0.593	57	66-67
Lavoro e Sicurtà	0.585	58	66-67
Banca Nazionale del Lavoro	0.576	60	65.1
Banca Unione	0.568	64	65.1

Legend: see Fig. 6.3.a.

7. Firm performance (1900–1971)

Michelangelo Vasta

7.1. Introduction

The study of firm profitability has not, until recently, received much attention by economic historians, due both to the lack of availability of systematic data and to the tendency to consider firm balance sheets unreliable. During the last few years, however, have appeared a number of studies which make use of firm balance sheets in order to reconstruct the performance of firms for the different national contexts [Cassis 1997; Tafunell 1998, 2000; Arnold 1999; Capie and Billings 2001]. Studies which reconstruct firm performance in historical perspective are quite rare also in the case of Italy. Duccio Bigazzi's [1990] exhortations towards historians to increase studies on corporate finance over ten years ago did almost nothing to improve the situation. There are, nonetheless, a few studies, which having adopted a long-term perspective, have highlighted the heuristic capacity of balance sheet analysis, these however are limited to a single firm [Toninelli 1990] or a single industrial sector [Rondi Ferla 1993].

This study, though using the same methodology as the above, extends the analysis from the case of a single firm, in which balance sheet analysis can be integrated and substantially improved by the use of other sources (ledgers, minutes of board of directors' meetings, company reports, etc.), to a micro-aggregated perspective in which single balances are used without the possibility of verifying their coherence in detail. The aim is to reconstruct, through the analysis of a broad sample of corporate balances, a representation of the dynamics of profitability and the forms of funding of Italian firms during the period from 1900 to 1971. The text is organized as follows: in Sect. 7.2 we illustrate the regulatory framework discussing the effects of the latter on the quality of the sources used; Sect. 7.3 describes the source used and discusses the methods applied in the analysis; in Sect. 7.4 we furnish an overall picture of the long-term profitability of Italian firms, while Sects. 7.5-7.7 reconstruct the *aggregate* dynamics of manufacturing firms which are subdivided according to different characteristics (sector, technological intensity, size). In Sect. 7.8 we propose an econometric model, estimated on the basis of the profit performance of the single firm, which permits the identification, for different periods, of a relationship between the individual characteristics of a firm and its profitability. Finally, Sect. 7.9 presents a few concluding remarks.

7.2. The regulatory framework

Corporate balance sheets reflect the regulatory framework of a country, which in turn also conditions usability in terms of historical-economical analysis. Italian corporate legislation did not undergo radical changes during the period examined. It was founded on the 1882 mercantile laws, with the addition, in the first half of the century, of a series of supplementary norms contained in the penal legislation for commercial companies, which was introduced by Rocco in 1931, and in the civil code of 1942 [Galgano 1974, 1993]. As legal literature has underlined, this regulatory framework has largely contributed to the great inefficiency of the Italian financial market, with heavy repercussions also regarding the lack of transparency in corporate accounts [Teti 1999]. The period analyzed was, in fact, characterized by grave deficiencies, which were particularly serious until 1942, in the transparency of working balances for the compilation of which there were no precise regulations [Toninelli 1990]. It was only with the 1974 reform, which made provision for, among other things, the institution of a board of control over joint-stock companies (the CONSOB), that there was a break with the past through the introduction, for example, of the new regulation for working balances [Marchetti 1997].

The existence for such a long period of a regulatory framework with such little regard for transparency has surely contributed to greatly delaying the spread of the Anglo-Saxon style practice of accountancy and evaluation [Toninelli 1999a]. Even though it appears difficult to determine the direction of causality between the regulatory framework and the lack of an accountancy culture in Italy, the literature has nevertheless often underlined the recurrent manipulation of the balances of Italian companies [Zanetti and Filippi 1965; Toninelli 1990], a phenomenon which is, moreover, widespread also in the main industrialized countries [Edwards 1989; Parker 1991]. As the Enron and Worldcom cases show, even in this latter age and in the presence of highly evolved systems of protection, which make provision for certification on behalf of the appropriate auditing companies, we cannot exclude the existence of practices to systematically alter corporate balances [Healy and Palepu 2003; Lev 2003]. Some studies which adopt a historical perspective [Spoerer 1998; Capie and Billings 2001] have nevertheless shown how manipulatory practices do not act in a single direction. In general in fact they tend to underestimate the entity of profits during upward trends in the economy and, in contrast, to overestimate them in periods of recession. This phenomenon should, therefore, have a leveling effect on the cyclic trend rather than altering it permanently. When all is said and done, therefore, the data obtainable from company balance sheets seem to be less distorted than is generally thought. Hence, notwithstanding a few difficulties, which suggest much caution in their interpretation, the analysis of balance sheet data, already used in Italy for the study of the more recent periods [Onado 1986; Zanetti 1996], can furnish an important contribution, even in a historical perspective, to the measurement of the performance of firms and to the understanding of the structural framework of the economic system.

7.3. Methodological note

The dataset used in this analysis includes 142,042 balance sheets from firms belonging to sections C (mining sector), D (manufacturing sector) and E (production and distribution of electricity, gas and water - the *utilities* -) of the ATECO-ISTAT 1991 classification. The balance sheets studied are those of all the joint-stock companies included in the different editions of the *Notizie statistiche* and belonging to the three sections mentioned above. The continuity of the occurrence of a firm for all the span of its activity, however, is not guaranteed. In fact, those companies which did not reach the set capital threshold for some of the years in which the source was published were excluded from the source and therefore from the dataset (see Appendix). It is therefore possible that a firm, whose share capital was close to the set threshold, could have a non-continuous series of balances. The sample used is nevertheless very broad, covering, on average from 80 to 90 per cent of the total share capital of Italian firms in the analyzed macro-sectors (see Appendix, Table A1). It is not, however, fully representative of the small enterprises, which were excluded for the years in which they did not reach the set size threshold. The decision not to select a homogenous panel of firms for the entire time span, or even for longer than a sub-period, was taken because this method would have introduced a greatly distorsive survivorship bias. The *worst* companies would in fact have been excluded, which would have led to an overestimation of the calculated proxies. This risk, even though diminished, has not however, been completely excluded, because the existence of a size threshold leads to the fact that firms in the smaller size classes, which have not had particularly positive performances are excluded from the subsequent survey.

The total series of balances covers a time span of seven decades (from 1900 to 1971), with an interruption for the Second World War period (1940-1945) for which there are no available balances. The historical series is therefore divided into two parts: the first covering the interval from 1900-1939 even though, for the first years, at least until 1904, the sample is not sufficiently representative (see Appendix, Table A4); the second part covers the period 1946-1971.

The lack of transparency in Italian commercial law, as mentioned above, means that the information obtainable from balances was meager, even though sufficient to represent the dynamics taking place. Furthermore, the balances were extremely heterogeneous due to the different types of firms and the different periods in which they were compiled. This led to a reclassification of the different balance sheet items into the more simplified scheme shown in Table 7.1, which allowed us to obtain homogenous information even in the presence of different compilation criteria.

The abovementioned difficulties hinder, as we shall see in detail, the calculation of the battery of indices commonly used in modern analyses on accountancy and corporate finance [Onado 1979; Brealey and Myers 2000]. The quality of the company information available permits the calculation of only a few balance sheet ratios, and these must be integrated with other relatively approximate proxies, capable, however, of furnishing a significant picture of company trends.

Table 7.1. Scheme for a standardized balance sheet in the Imita.db archive

Share capital
Physical assets
Inventory
Securities and investments
Cash and credits
Bonds
Various types of debts
Sinking funds
Provisions
Profits (losses)
Total dividends
Allocations
Monetary equalization fund

As far as the indexes relative to financial structure and situation are concerned, the impossibility of distinguishing between short-term and long-term debts excludes the prospect of calculating the usual current ratio and quick - or acid test - ratio. The lack of this distinction does not, however, prevent the calculation of the relationship between the indebtedness (leverage ratio) of a firm, which can be obtained from the relationship between the total invested capital (total gross assets) over shareholders' equity[1]. We therefore made use of the following proxy:

Invested capital (physical assets + inventory + securities and investments + cash and credits) / shareholders' equity (share capital + provisions + profits or losses)[2].

This ratio shows the dependence of a firm on indebtedness. An increase in the value of the index underlines a lesser financial independence of the firm. This proxy is somewhat problematical because at least until the 1920s, the provisions item often includes the sinking fund. An alternative measure of the level of indebtedness of a firm can also be obtained through the following proxy:

total debts (bonds + various types of debts) / invested capital

In this case too, the increase in the value of the index indicates a lesser financial independence of the firm. There are also several difficulties as far as the profitability proxies are concerned, especially with those that link profit to the capital with which the profit is made: (i) the source does not always indicate, at least until the post-Second World War period, the capital actually paid in by the company's shareholders; (ii) it is impossible to distinguish the capital actually used (or the

[1] Usually the modern techniques of balance sheet analysis calculate the leverage ratio by considering only the liabilities deriving from long-term debts.

[2] The indebtedness reflects the greater recourse to borrowed capital, and its range spans from 1 to infinity. If the average indebtedness of the period is used this can also be lesser than 1 when net capital losses occur.

profit produced capital) in the *operative management*; (iii) there is a lack of detailed information on the flow of provisions and on the existence of other allocation funds; (iv) it is also impossible to calculate the profitability indexes from the operating result or better still from the Earnings before interest, taxes, depreciation and amortization (EBITDA) due to the absence of adjusted profits for extraordinary and anomalous items.

The resulting effect of all these elements is that it is impossible to calculate the profitability index of invested capital, Return On Investment (ROI) correctly. Though it is not feasible to calculate the profitability of the *operative management*, we can nevertheless estimate, even with the preceding *caveats*, an index of total profitability for the firm: the relationship between net profits and owners equity, the Return On Equity (ROE).

This is usually calculated as: profits/shareholders equity (share capital + provisions + profits), but in the case of a great number of balance sheets this can lead to problems, which, however, have been solved by normalizing the value of the ROE between a minimum value of -100 per cent and a maximum of +100 per cent[3].

A number of other proxies can be used in aggregate analysis, which may be relatively coarse but are, however sufficiently indicative of the trend of a sample of firms. As far as the financial structure is concerned, we can calculate the percentage quota of the firms that exceed a certain threshold (arbitrarily chosen, but constant in time) of indebtedness. This allows us to have a measure of the overall degree of financial independence of the system. As far as profitability is concerned, the following three proxies can be used [Rondi Ferla 1993]: (i) the percentage quota of the companies with profits over the total number of companies; (ii) total profits/total losses; (iii) dividends/profits.

The first two furnish an overall view of the *state of health* of an aggregation of firms, respectively showing how many of them produced profits and the relationship between the overall profits produced and the losses accumulated. The third proxy also gives an indication, though indirect, of the company trend, measuring the propensity to distribute the wealth produced to shareholders.

---

[3] The calculation of the ROE, as that of other indexes, is usually carried out using the average shareholders equity for the period as a denominator $(SE_t + SE_{t-1})/2$. Given that it is a long run analysis subject to high rates of firm mortality, to simplify the calculation, and to enable us to calculate the ROE for the first year in which the companies enter the dataset, we used only the value referring to the closing of the corporate year. Furthermore, the function of the ROE on profits shows an anomalous trend: for the profit-making companies it is between 0 and 1 (between 0 per cent and 100 per cent), but for companies with losses the situation is more complex: it is negative for losses lesser than the sum of the share capital and provisions (the value of -100 per cent is reached for losses equal to half the sum of share capital and provisions), but tends to infinity; however, it becomes positive, introducing a strong element of distortion, for losses greater than the sum of the share capital and provisions. For example, for a company that has a share capital of 2,000 euros, 400 euros of provisions and losses for -2,401 euros, the ROE becomes -2,401/(2,000+400-2,401)*100, i.e. (-2,401/-1)*100 = 240,100 per cent. In order to eliminate this problem the possibility of oscillation of the ROE was reduced to between -100 per cent and +100 per cent thus preventing the proxy from taking on positive values in the abovementioned case.

7.4. An overall view

The study of the financial structure and the long-term profitability of industrial enterprises allow us to significantly distinguish the different phases of the Italian economy, while at the same time compiling a useful reference framework for the following pages in which attention will be concentrated on the performance of the different types of firms. The analysis is focused on the three great industrial macro-sectors: the mining industry (C), the manufacturing industry (D) and the utilities (E), within which, until nationalization in 1962, the electricity companies prevail. As far as the manufacturing industries are concerned, the ROE is shown both in the *aggregate* form, calculated as the relationship between the sum of the profits and the sum of the net capital of all the firms, and in the *average* form, calculated as the average of the ROEs of all the firms present in the sample. In the first case, profitability is influenced by the size of the firms, while in the second all the firms have the same weight.

In the first phase of the Giolittian era, until 1908, the Italian manufacturing firms show an excellent profitability trend, with *aggregate* values of the ROE fluctuating between 5 and 10 per cent, as can be seen from Fig. 7.1. About 90 per cent of the manufacturing firms close their annual accounts in profit, distributing over 80 per cent of profits in the form of dividends. Analogous results can be observed for the ROE and the distribution of profits and also for the mining industries and the utilities, although both show a less widespread positive trend, with a smaller percentage quota of companies showing a profit as compared to the manufacturing sector. In the second phase of the Giolittian era, in line with the different estimates on the trends of industrial production [Carreras 1999: 190-194], there is a decrease both in *aggregate* and in *average* profitability for the manufacturing macro-sector, with values remaining stable at around 5 per cent until 1914 (see Fig. 7.2). Higher levels of profitability are attained by the mining sector, while the utilities, which are weighed down by the tariff freeze, show a greater homogeneity in profitability from the beginning of the century, with ROE values solidly stable around 6 per cent.

The whole Giolittian era is characterized by an increase in indebtedness (measured on the basis of the relationship between invested capital and owners equity) for the manufacturing enterprises, which moves from values of around 1.4 in the first years of the century to 1.8 in the years preceding the First World War (see Fig. 7.3). In contrast to the growth in indebtedness, which entails a lesser financial independence for firms, the composition of assets changes only slightly, the weight of the fixed assets rising from 36 per cent in 1905 to an average value of around 40 per cent in the years preceding the First World War. The level of indebtedness of the utilities is characterized by a greater stability, and remains, for the entire Giolittian era, in a stable relationship of 1.5 between invested capital and owners equity.

The years of the First World War show, in line with what historiography has often observed [Caracciolo 1978; Zamagni 1990a], the highest values for the entire period, with the *aggregate* ROE peaking, in 1917, at around 15 per cent for the manufacturing industry and even higher, at 20 per cent, for the mining industry. The industrial mobilization programs, aimed at endorsing strategic industries, promoted the realization of exceptional profits, also thanks to the active role played by personalities close to the interests of private industries within government committees [Caracciolo 1978]. The utilities, on the other hand, retreat slightly in comparison with previous years, being unable to directly benefit from state production orders oriented towards the War effort, and also due to the considerable increase in the cost of raw materials.

The years immediately after the First World War show a decrease in profitability levels which nevertheless realign with those registered in the first phase of the Giolittian era. The effects of the *biennio rosso* are clearly discernible only for the year 1921 when there is a sharp fall of the *aggregate* ROE, which shows a negative value of -5 per cent for the entire manufacturing industry and of -10 per cent for the mining industry (see Fig. 7.1). The profitability of the utilities is not affected by the harsh social conflicts taking place in the country and remains substantially in line with the values of the preceding years. Already as from 1922, the ROE reverts to positive values of around 4 per cent for the manufacturing and mining industry, while the utilities show, as from 1923, a significant increase in levels of profitability which remain constant during the 1920s. Considering the *average* value of the ROE, we can observe that the 1921 fall is less sharp than that of the *aggregate* value (see Fig. 7.2). At the same time, however, the delay in the subsequent recovery is also evident.

The advent of Fascism brings with it a strong recovery in the profitability of capital and also a significant change in the financial structure of firms. The manufacturing and mining industries for the duration of the 1920s, with the sole exception of the year 1927 - which is affected by the deflationist effects of *Quota Novanta* and the beginning of a declining trend in exports -, show levels of *aggregate* profitability in line with those registered in the earliest years of the century. The level of indebtedness of the manufacturing firms which had grown significantly during the War years, reaching the value of 2.5 for the relationship between assets and net capital in 1917, decreases considerably, settling at around 2 in the central years of the decade. The recovery is essentially founded on a great increase in exports in the early post-First World War years, due to the *temporary supply void* created by the countries most damaged by the War, such as Austria and Germany [Tattara and Toniolo 1976].

The 1929 crisis marks an abrupt break with the preceding years, with a sharp and generalized fall in the *aggregate* profitability of the manufacturing industry, which remains close to zero for the period 1930-1932, with a slow process of recovery starting only in 1933. These data are, moreover, perfectly in line with the cycle [Delli Gatti, Gallegati and Gallegati 2003]. The analysis of the levels of *average* profitability of the manufacturing firms (see Fig. 7.2) presents a considerably different picture. As from 1927, in fact, these levels are constantly negative, with values reaching -7 per cent in 1927. In this sense we have a first indication of the weight of large firms in positively influencing levels of *aggregate* profitability.

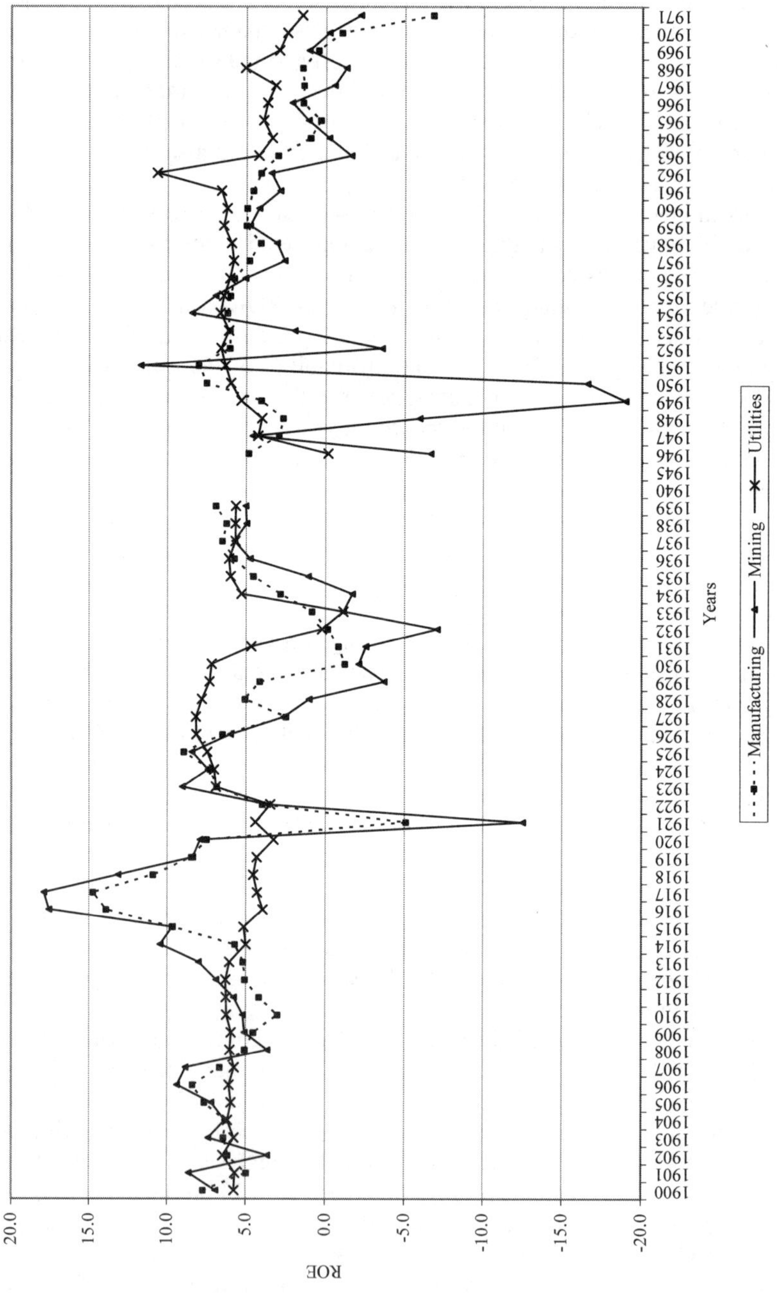

Fig. 7.1. *Aggregate* ROE trend by ISTAT macro-sectors (1900-1971)

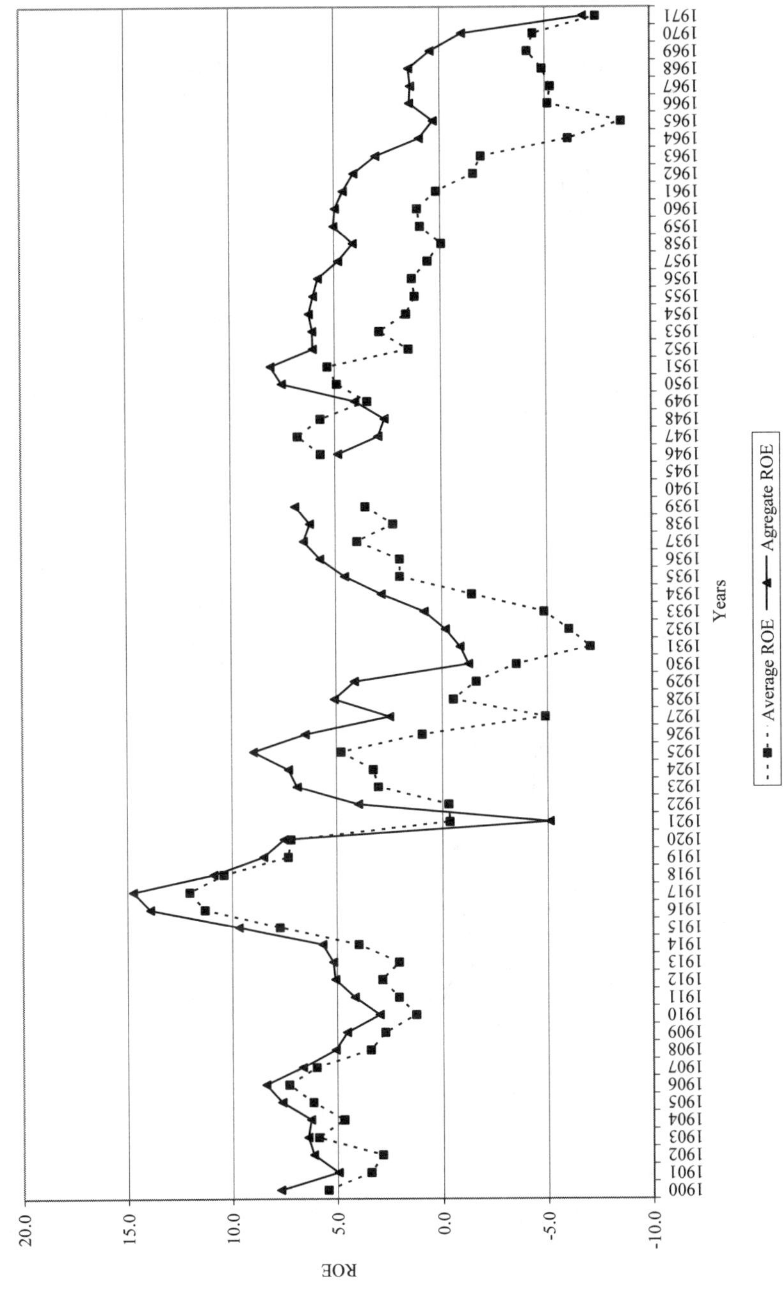

Fig. 7.2. Comparison between *aggregate* and *average* ROE for the manufacturing sector (1900-1971)

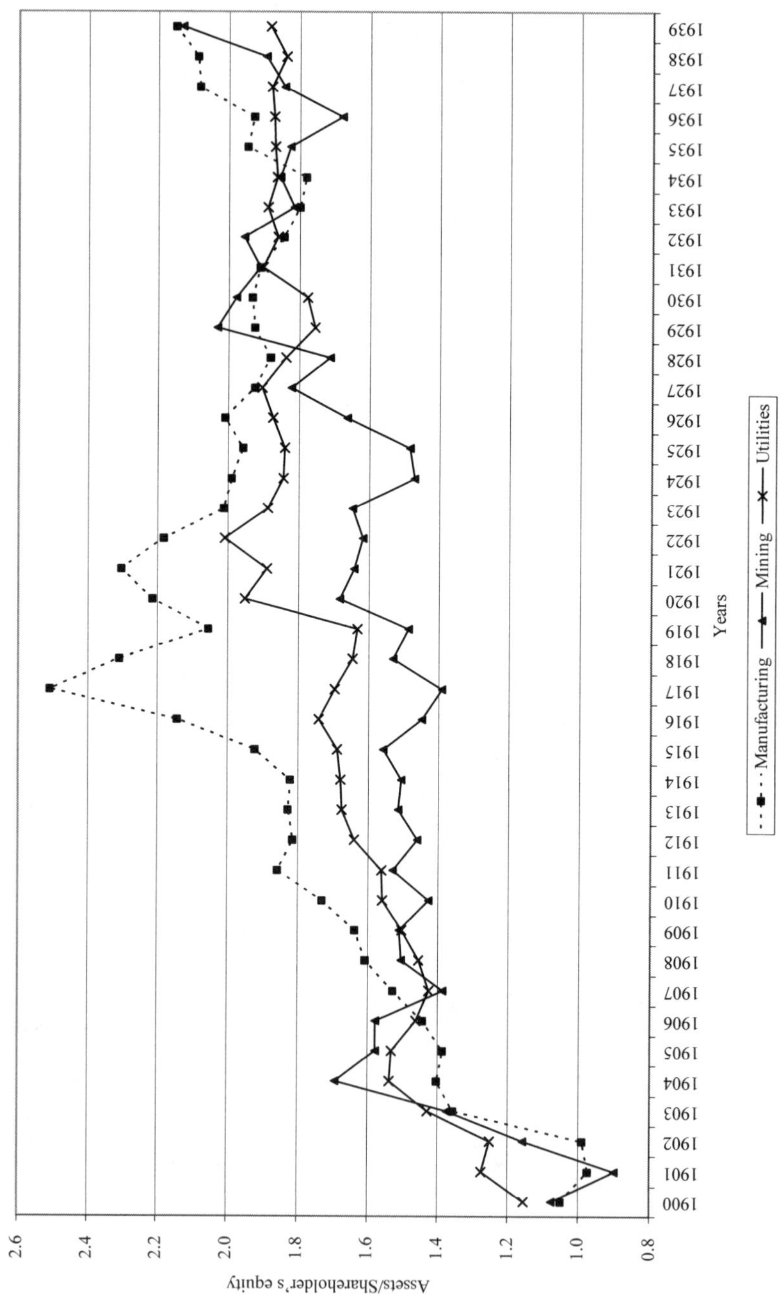

Fig. 7.3. Trend in the relationship between invested capital and owners equity by ISTAT macro-sectors (1900-1939)

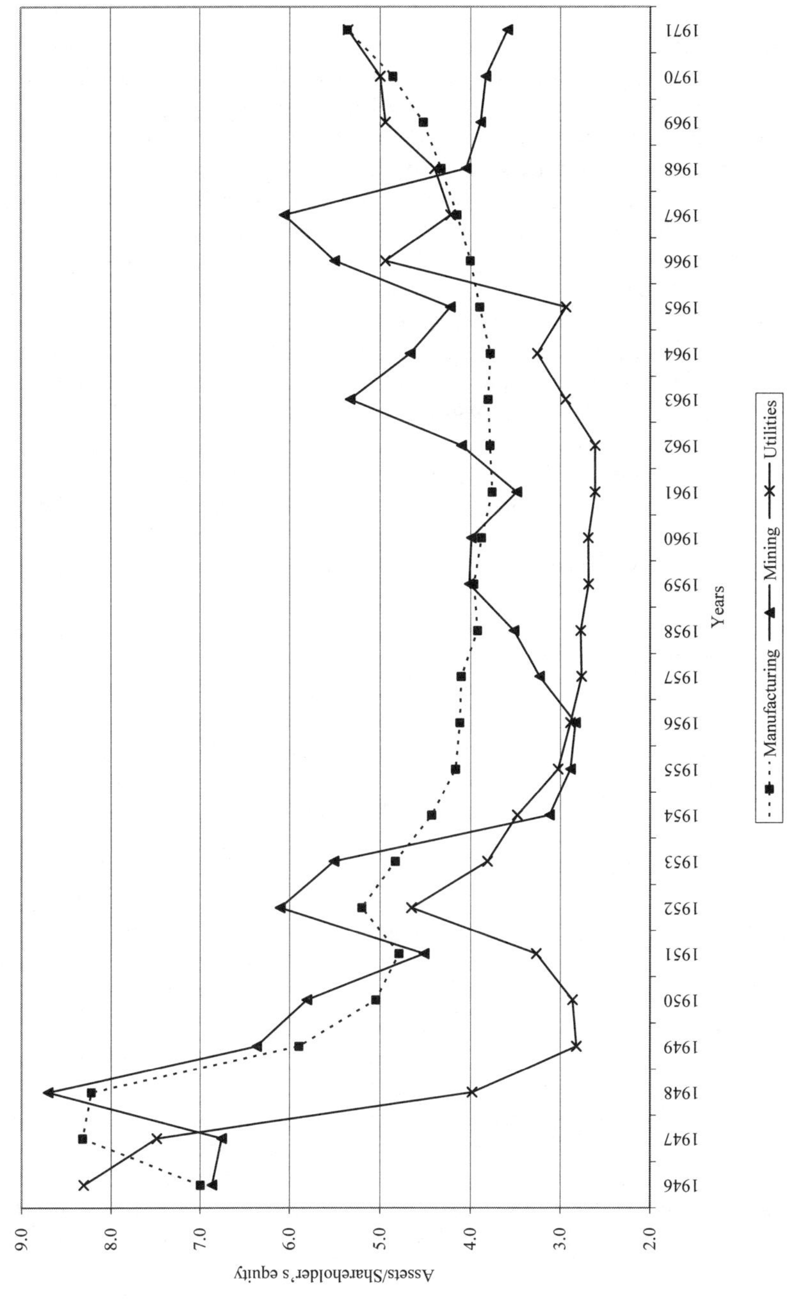

Fig. 7.4. Trend in the relationship between invested capital and owners equity by ISTAT macro-sectors (1946-1971)

The mining industry is heavily affected by the crisis, whose effects persist until halfway through the decade. The utility firms also suffer from the general economic trend, even though the repercussions of the crisis last less as compared to the other industrial macro-sectors, due to the lesser elasticity of electrical consumption to the general economic trend. The 1929 crisis seems, therefore, to have very severe effects on Italian industry, not only due to the sharp although temporary break in profitability, but above all because the high performances reached during the 1920s, chiefly by the utilities, but also by many manufacturing sectors, will never be reached again. The microeconomic data therefore, confirm the most negative interpretations on the entity of the crisis, underscoring the severe repercussions that the latter had on the subsequent capacity for growth of the entire industrial system [Toniolo 1980; Carreras 1999].

Only in the second half of the 1930s, after the great process of reorganization under the aegis of state intervention, does a new phase of expansion begin, with a constant rise in profitability until 1939, the last pre-War year for which balance sheet data are available. The manufacturing firms show good growth dynamics with levels of *aggregate* profitability which exceed 5 per cent per annum as from 1936. The *average* levels of profitability show a slower growth trend, even though values become positive as from the second half of the 1930s (see Fig. 7.2). As far as the utilities are concerned the structure of invested capital changes radically. The weight of the item securities and investments increases considerably; its quota over the total gross assets, which remains stable around 3 per cent during the Giolittian era, tops 20 per cent during the 1920s and early 1930s. The electrical companies exploit the monopolistic revenues deriving from the sector's strong concentration, also partly due to the integration with regional networks, to become the financial centre of the Italian industrial system and set up a group of interwoven holdings acquiring control of firms belonging to other industrial and financial sectors [Giannetti 1985; Baccini and Vasta 1995]. The manufacturing sector also shows a significant increase in investments, even though to a lesser degree, with a marked enlarge in its weight within the balance assets.

The post-Second World War period opens with both *aggregate* and *average* ROE values close to 5 per cent for the manufacturing industry, while both the utilities and the mining sector show negative values for profitability. The first years of the *reconstruction* period are characterized by a relatively speedy recovery, notwithstanding the re-organization of the productive structure, added to the considerable infrastructure problems [Zamagni 1993]. The War produces severe effects on the mining sector, whose levels of profitability are highly volatile during the post-First World War years with strong negative peaks. The utilities, on the other hand, return to pre-War levels of profitability reasonably fast. This occurs due to the strong increase in levels of indebtedness caused by the necessity to rebuild and expand production facilities. Company resources are directed towards plants and machinery, which increases the weight of the latter on the total invested capital.

The *economic miracle* years show levels of *aggregate* profitability stable at around 5 per cent with more positive dynamics in the first half of the 1950s as compared to the subsequent period when, even though there are good levels of profitability, the ROE experiences a declining trend. The comparison between *aggregate* ROE and *average* ROE (see Table 7.2) shows that the largest firms have the best performance. In fact, the *average* ROE falls as from the beginning of the 1950s, reaching values slightly higher than zero as from 1957 and remaining stable.

As compared to the period preceding the Second World War, the weight of the level of indebtedness of manufacturing firms changes considerably: the value of the relationship between assets and shareholders equity rises to about 4 to 1 (see Fig. 7.4). The utilities macro-sector, on the other hand, shows a stably positive trend for the entire period, with a capital profitability which remains constant at around 6 per cent and a peak in 1962 (+10 per cent), concurrently with the nationalization of the electrical industry. Even with excellent levels of profitability, the peak in 1962 is essentially due to the attempt, on behalf of electrical firms, to obtain higher levels of profitability so as to obtain better acquisition conditions from ENEL [Zanetti 1989]. The level of indebtedness of the macro-sector remains below that registered for the manufacturing enterprises for the entire period; however, it reaches considerably higher values than those of the period preceding the Second World War.

The ROE *aggregate* values for 1964 reflect the abrupt deceleration of the Italian economy, characterized by the unfavorable economic situation and the 1963 credit squeeze. In line with the information supplied by the macroeconomic proxies, the data at firm level also confirm 1963 as the watershed year for the dynamics of the Italian economy [Graziani 1998]. There is, in fact, a generalized fall in *aggregate* profitability, which remains low for the rest of the 1960s. *Average* profitability, on the other hand, is strongly negative, with values around -5 per cent as from 1964. The pervasiveness of the crisis is also evident in the percentage quota of firms capable of generating profits over the total number of firms. This quota reaches its lowest value for the entire period considered in 1965, when only 44 per cent of the Italian manufacturing firms show a credit balance. In the second half of the 1970s, the profit-making firms fluctuate between 50 per cent and 60 per cent, with a dive of over 20 points as compared to the 1950s. The levels of indebtedness are also in constant increase and, near the end of the 1970s they reach the same levels as those of the early 1950s. After the nationalization of electricity, the utilities lose relevance in the national economic system, even though maintaining higher levels of profitability than those registered for the manufacturing firms. Simultaneously, however, their indebtedness rises and reaches the same levels as that of the manufacturing companies. The 1970s begin with negative *aggregate* values of the ROE (-1 per cent in 1970), while the following year shows an abrupt and ruinous fall, with significant losses (-6.8 per cent) for the entire manufacturing industry. This is the consequence of the great social conflicts, with wage claims on behalf of the workers, a prelude to the severe crisis of the 1970s, which is accompanied by great changes in the structure of Italian industry [Graziani 1998].

7.5. The profitability of the manufacturing sectors

After having analyzed the performance of Italian firms belonging to the three great industrial macro-sectors in diachronic perspective, in this Sect. attention is focused on the manufacturing sectors, with the analysis limited to *aggregate* data. A first impression on the sectoral long-term trend of the performance of the Italian manufacturing firms can be obtained by subdividing the single firms, on the basis of capital intensity and the prevalent market for their products, into two large categories: *light* and *heavy* sectors[4]. From a first glance at Table 7.2, which illustrates the profitability of firms, divided into the two categories for the sub-periods, two relevant elements emerge. In the first place there is, in general, a greater profitability of the *light* sectors in the period preceding the Second World War and in the *reconstruction* years, while in the *economic miracle* phase during the post-Second World War period, the *heavy* sectors show a constantly higher trend, as can also be seen in Fig. 7.5. In the second place the *heavy* sectors are much more affected by crises. The sharp fall in profitability in 1921 involves almost exclusively the *heavy* sectors, while the ROE values of the *light* sectors, though in decline, remain positive at around 5 per cent. The crisis of the early 1930s, on the other hand, invests the entire Italian manufacturing sector, affecting the *light* and *heavy* sectors to the same extent, even though the latter are more rapidly affected.

In the post-Second World War period we observe the same trend: in the *reconstruction* phase there is a considerable discrepancy in profitability, the *light* sectors reaching high peak values already in 1946, while the *heavy* sectors confirm a slower ability to recover. The same phenomenon takes place in 1971 when the sudden fall in profitability is more evident for the *heavy* sectors. If the remaining few profitability proxies available show a trend in line with that observed for the ROE, the quota of dividends distributed over profits shows a slightly different trend. For the entire period, in fact, we register a greater propensity for the distribution of profits to shareholders among the *heavy* sectors. It seems remarkable, moreover, that this phenomenon should also occur in the *reconstruction* years, when profitability has a markedly unequal trend, with the *light* sectors decidedly more brilliant than the *heavy* sectors which are penalized by infrastructure and energy problems.

The result described above is amply in line with the *ex ante* hypotheses. The crisis periods, in fact, affect high capital intensity firms much more heavily than the less structured firms which can exploit their greater flexibility. Furthermore, the firms belonging to the *light* sectors, usually smaller in size, are generally characterized by a higher rate of natality/mortality, which determines the selection of the *best* firms in a shorter time span than occurs for the firms in the *heavy* sectors. Seen from another point of view, however, the comparison between levels of profitability in the various phases between the two sub-components of the industrial system is quite surprising.

[4] For the sectoral disaggregation of the two categories, see Table 2.1.

Table 7.2. ROE trend by period and sector (1900-1971)

Period	*Light*	*Heavy*	Total	Percentage deviation from average *light*	Percentage deviation from average *heavy*
1900-1921	7.4	6.1	6.7	11.4	-8.1
1922-1939	4.5	3.9	4.3	7.0	-7.6
1946-1949	13.6	0.7	3.6	273.4	-79.9
1950-1963	4.5	5.7	5.4	-17.7	4.7
1964-1971	-1.4	0.0	-0.2	-492.9	89.5
1900-1971	5.3	4.4	4.7	12.6	-7.7

The first half of the 1920s, for example, is characterized by a very well defined gap in profitability in favor of the *light* sectors, which persists, even though to a lesser extent, also in the second half of the decade. Even though the two categories identified are very heterogeneous, it seems reasonable to maintain that historiography, influenced by the economic policies adopted, has overestimated the effects of these in determining the performance of the *heavy* sectors, which in reality is less brilliant than commonly supposed. Moreover, it is precisely the traditional sectors of *light* industry, and in the first place the textiles sector, which have benefited the most from the favorable trend in exports [Tattara and Toniolo 1976]. In the 1930s, on the other hand, there is a gap in profitability in favor of the *heavy* sectors: the average values of the decade for the two sub-groups are respectively 3.3 per cent for the *heavy* sectors and 2.8 per cent for the *light* sectors. In this case it is probable that the *light* sectors, by reducing their employment levels, have managed to maintain a profitability performance not too distant from those sectors receiving the greater part of state subsidies [Federico and Giannetti 1999].

The comparison between the profitability of the two sectoral categories for the *economic miracle* period also produces interesting results. The considerable increase in private consumption, in fact, does not allow the *light* sectors to overtake the *heavy* sectors in profitability. The *heavy* sectors, in effect, benefit from the phase of development of the *technological regime* of the Second Industrial Revolution, which sees the apogee of the Fordist firm.

The disaggregated analysis at the sectoral level allows for a greater specification of the profitability trend of the Italian manufacturing industry, underlining its extreme heterogeneity. An analysis of Table 7.3 and 7.4, in fact, shows that four sectors - food (DA), rubber and plastic (DH), non-metallic minerals (DI) and manufacturing n.e.c. (DN) - have a superior performance for the entire period in comparison with the overall trend. These are sectors with radically different characteristics: the first, the food sector (DA), is distinguished by a modest technological intensity and, in general, by low levels of concentration. Its productive activities, linked to the transformation of the many typical agricultural products, give it the characteristics of a *natural industry*. The ROE values show an increase in profitability performance during the *reconstruction* period and in the period from 1964 to 1971.

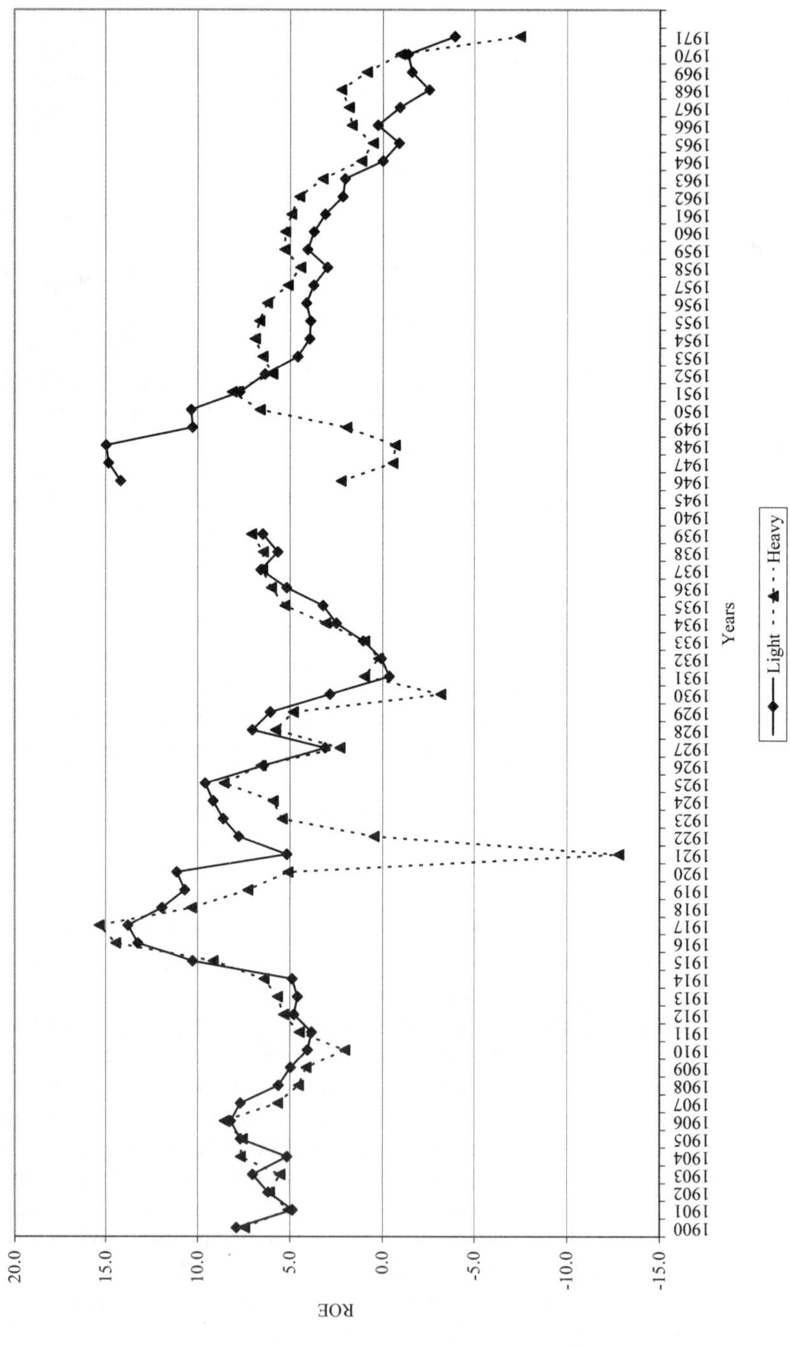

Fig. 7.5. ROE trend by sectoral category (1900-1971)

The second sector, that of rubber and plastic (DH), follows the technological course of the Second Industrial Revolution and is thus characterized, during the period considered, by a significant technological dynamism. Table 7.3 displays the levels of profitability for this sector as from the 1920s onwards because before this period the number of firms in the sector is not sufficiently significant. This sector, while remaining the most concentrated in Italian industry (see Chap. 3), has two great phases of expansion: the first in the 1920s with the development of the production of rubber; the second in the 1950s with the boom of the oil industry, which led to an enormous growth in the production of plastic materials [Zamagni 1990b; Giannetti 1996]. It is exactly in these two periods that we register the greatest levels of profitability.

Another sector with good profitability dynamics in the long run is the production of non-metallic minerals (DI) - glass, cement, ceramics, etc. - whose levels of profitability are higher than the overall values in all the sub-periods. Its dynamics are clearly linked to the construction cycle, with much better than average performances during the *reconstruction* period. This is a rather heterogeneous sector which shares some characteristics with the food sector; it includes the great cement plants, characterized by economies of scale, and smaller firms operating in productive niches. In short, the sector centers its competitive capacity on traditional production, but it is not distinguished by the use of particularly innovative technologies.

Table 7.5, which illustrates the weight of sectors in terms of assets and profits generated[5], permits a better understanding of the effective relevance of the four sectors with the best performances in terms of profitability. The food sector (DA), though it loses positions in the course of time, continues to remain, even in the 1960s, one of the most important sectors in the Italian industrial structure. The rubber and plastic sector (DH), on the other hand, increases its consistency significantly in time but in the 1960s its overall total, both in terms of assets and in terms of profits, is barely above 3 per cent. Moreover, the non-metallic mineral production sector (DI), though not marginal in weight, is not one of the core sectors in the Italian industrial structure. Finally, the manufacturing n.e.c. sector (DN) shows an overall *weight* of assets around 1 per cent. It is, therefore, quite evident that the sectors with the greatest profitability do not, in short, form the core of Italian industry, which, pursuing the technological dynamics, shifts during the period studied, from the sectors of the First Industrial Revolution to those of the Second industrial Revolution.

[5] The weight of profits produced is calculated gross of losses; therefore the only companies considered are those which closed the balance on a profit.

Table 7.3. Trend of the *aggregate* ROE by period and sectors (1900-1971)

	DA	DB	DC	DD	DE	DF	DG	DH	DI	DJ	DK	DL	DM	DN	Total
ROE															
1900-1921	8.5	7.0	4.8	2.4	7.7	-	6.9	-	7.4	5.8	4.0	5.2	5.8	8.1	6.7
1922-1939	5.1	4.6	1.9	1.4	3.3	4.2	3.6	7.2	4.7	4.6	-0.4	1.8	3.5	4.5	4.3
1946-1949	12.7	15.8	6.8	6.7	13.2	5.9	11.9	6.0	10.0	-4.4	2.1	-0.3	-77.5	11.3	3.6
1950-1963	6.0	3.1	1.6	5.3	7.5	2.3	6.8	6.8	9.1	4.7	3.6	5.1	5.4	9.5	5.4
1964-1971	0.6	-4.0	-3.0	-2.0	-4.9	-3.9	1.6	1.0	0.3	-1.4	-3.1	2.7	-0.1	2.0	-0.2
1900-1971	6.3	4.7	2.5	2.5	5.3	6.7	5.6	5.5	6.3	3.8	1.7	3.6	-0.7	6.9	4.7
Percentage deviation from average															
1900-1921	27.1	4.7	-28.4	-63.6	15.1	-	2.7	-	10.7	-13.7	-40.6	-22.1	-13.1	22.0	
1922-1939	20.8	9.0	-55.8	-67.8	-21.5	-0.3	-14.2	69.1	9.9	9.3	-110.3	-57.3	-17.9	6.0	
1946-1949	250.3	335.5	85.8	84.6	262.0	62.2	226.4	65.5	175.6	-221.4	-43.2	-108.2	-2,233.8	210.3	
1950-1963	10.4	-43.1	-70.0	-2.4	38.3	-57.8	25.9	24.1	68.0	-12.8	-34.1	-6.2	-1.3	73.8	
1964-1971	350.0	-1,622.9	-1,173.3	-779.5	-2,032.9	-1,586.6	777.7	534.1	210.4	-497.1	-1,227.9	1,262.6	60.3	969.6	
1900-1971	34.1	-0.1	-47.1	-47.7	11.3	41.2	19.3	16.0	33.5	-20.6	-63.8	-23.5	-114.5	45.4	

Legend: Food products and tobacco (DA); Textiles and textile products (DB); Leather and leather products (DC); Wood and wood products (DD); Paper products, publishing and printing (DE); Coke and petroleum products (DF); Chemicals and chemical products (DG); Rubber and plastic products (DH); Other non-metallic products (DI); Basic metals and metal products (DJ); Machinery and equipment (DK); Electrical and optical equipment (DL); Transport equipment (DM); Manufacturing n.e.c. (DN).

Table 7.4. *Aggregate* ROE trend by year and sectors (1900-1971)

Year	DA	DB	DC	DD	DE	DF	DG	DH	DI	DJ	DK	DL	DM	DN
1900	8.0	8.1	-15.9	-	0.0	-	10.0	-	6.4	8.9	8.0	7.1	5.5	0.1
1901	6.3	3.9	1.7	-	2.6	-	3.5	-	6.4	5.2	6.3	7.0	5.9	1.3
1902	4.4	7.4	0.0	-	1.0	-	4.7	-	6.4	7.9	6.3	-13.0	6.6	-3.4
1903	6.7	7.2	2.7	-	12.9	31.3	6.6	-	10.1	2.6	4.8	2.5	6.5	10.2
1904	5.5	4.8	4.0	-	11.8	37.9	8.5	-	8.4	7.1	6.2	5.0	6.4	12.9
1905	8.3	7.1	8.4	-	11.0	39.6	7.9	-	8.1	8.0	6.4	4.8	5.7	13.9
1906	9.7	7.2	7.8	-	10.5	43.5	8.4	-	9.3	7.6	7.0	6.7	9.7	10.7
1907	7.8	7.6	7.0	6.9	10.0	41.7	8.4	-	6.1	7.1	7.8	4.9	-1.1	8.6
1908	7.8	5.1	-7.7	-9.7	6.2	14.4	5.7	-	5.5	3.7	3.5	5.6	2.7	6.3
1909	8.2	3.8	-12.5	6.7	6.3	12.9	3.3	-	3.4	5.5	5.0	2.7	2.5	1.1
1910	8.5	1.2	7.9	-8.9	5.4	11.5	-8.8	-	3.6	3.9	5.3	4.3	5.0	7.6
1911	9.0	-0.1	7.5	5.8	7.1	8.9	4.4	-	3.4	4.1	4.7	1.6	5.6	7.5
1912	9.2	1.6	8.0	3.2	6.8	0.0	5.9	-2.0	5.4	5.0	5.4	7.1	3.8	7.0
1913	8.6	2.2	7.7	-16.4	3.9	0.0	5.8	3.8	4.2	5.2	4.9	6.0	7.2	7.5
1914	7.0	3.2	7.7	2.3	5.6	4.4	7.4	-	4.4	6.0	4.1	6.8	8.1	7.1
1915	10.3	10.7	13.9	5.7	5.0	13.4	10.1	-	3.9	10.7	5.1	4.8	11.7	9.1
1916	11.4	14.3	25.2	8.4	9.7	21.7	15.2	-	5.9	18.5	9.1	12.0	14.8	13.4
1917	11.6	15.7	12.9	8.3	11.6	12.6	15.5	-	11.3	19.7	13.1	15.9	10.5	15.8
1918	10.4	13.4	7.8	10.4	12.6	10.4	11.2	-	14.8	10.7	9.4	12.1	8.2	18.4
1919	9.1	12.3	10.2	7.3	10.1	12.2	7.1	0.0	13.2	7.3	5.8	7.5	6.3	12.0
1920	10.9	12.3	9.7	6.3	10.4	6.9	6.9	-	14.5	4.2	-1.4	5.0	4.6	8.0
1921	7.8	4.9	-8.9	0.2	8.1	-3.2	3.1	-	7.8	-32.5	-39.8	-2.0	-8.8	3.8
1922	6.5	10.3	-2.0	-6.8	6.4	2.0	-4.3	0.0	7.6	1.8	-0.2	-3.3	0.5	4.7
1923	8.2	10.4	0.5	-4.1	4.3	3.4	6.6	4.4	8.2	5.3	4.2	-0.7	4.5	2.3
1924	7.8	10.9	5.3	5.0	4.8	4.5	6.2	4.5	7.6	7.2	4.0	-0.6	5.1	5.2
1925	7.1	11.9	7.2	5.4	7.4	7.7	9.8	10.2	11.8	7.7	4.0	3.5	6.8	7.7

Table 7.4. (cont.)

Year	DA	DB	DC	DD	DE	DF	DG	DH	DI	DJ	DK	DL	DM	DN
1926	4.6	8.5	4.6	-8.4	7.1	7.7	6.5	9.2	10.0	5.8	3.3	3.7	5.7	3.4
1927	3.2	3.0	2.9	-4.8	4.4	5.1	3.2	5.4	3.5	2.0	-0.6	1.8	-2.0	0.5
1928	6.5	4.7	5.7	1.7	4.5	2.3	5.4	10.6	3.5	5.9	-0.1	4.1	5.2	3.9
1929	5.9	5.1	2.0	3.9	0.8	3.6	4.8	10.4	3.2	4.1	2.1	0.6	0.7	5.1
1930	4.3	-0.3	-0.4	2.2	3.7	3.5	-15.2	7.6	4.0	2.3	1.6	0.7	3.6	4.8
1931	-0.2	-5.2	-23.6	-3.3	-2.2	-0.5	2.6	6.9	-2.1	2.4	-3.2	-3.8	-3.1	1.7
1932	2.7	-3.3	-3.4	-2.6	-0.9	1.4	-0.8	7.1	-3.0	1.5	-4.8	-0.7	1.3	-0.7
1933	3.0	-0.6	0.6	0.9	-6.0	7.8	4.1	7.4	0.2	2.0	-30.5	0.2	-5.4	3.8
1934	4.0	1.5	1.1	5.2	0.5	2.3	3.3	7.4	1.4	4.9	-2.2	-0.9	3.7	4.4
1935	5.8	1.0	5.5	6.6	3.5	2.0	6.6	7.8	4.7	5.8	-0.6	3.6	5.4	6.0
1936	5.3	5.2	5.9	7.0	3.3	4.7	6.3	7.4	4.2	6.4	2.6	5.1	7.9	6.4
1937	5.8	7.3	9.3	7.2	6.8	6.6	6.3	7.1	6.1	6.3	3.6	5.7	7.6	7.3
1938	5.6	6.0	5.5	4.6	6.2	5.1	6.8	7.3	6.4	6.1	3.3	6.6	7.3	7.3
1939	6.4	6.9	7.0	5.0	5.3	7.1	7.4	8.7	6.8	6.1	5.6	7.1	8.0	7.5
1946	12.4	16.6	10.1	8.9	16.3	2.7	12.7	-2.6	12.1	2.6	1.1	4.4	-101.9	12.2
1947	15.6	17.0	9.8	5.3	15.4	5.7	13.4	9.8	11.9	-3.5	4.8	4.6	-126.8	10.4
1948	14.7	17.4	3.0	6.1	10.6	10.0	11.6	8.1	8.8	-12.6	-2.3	-2.8	-53.1	10.5
1949	8.1	12.3	4.2	6.5	10.3	5.2	9.8	8.8	7.3	-4.2	4.7	-7.4	-28.3	12.0
1950	7.6	12.4	2.2	8.2	10.6	5.2	11.4	10.2	13.3	4.1	-7.0	3.4	0.5	14.9
1951	7.5	8.1	-5.7	6.0	14.3	9.6	11.5	9.6	11.0	4.5	7.4	8.4	-0.3	14.2
1952	9.7	4.7	-1.7	7.8	9.8	4.5	7.3	6.8	10.5	5.4	1.0	4.9	2.6	11.9
1953	8.2	1.8	3.9	7.2	8.1	3.3	6.6	7.8	11.5	4.3	6.7	6.3	8.7	10.9
1954	7.7	0.9	4.4	6.6	8.5	5.9	7.0	7.7	10.0	5.6	4.3	6.4	8.1	9.2
1955	8.6	0.5	-0.4	5.8	6.8	4.7	6.9	7.0	10.7	5.5	4.4	5.6	8.6	8.8
1956	7.1	1.8	1.2	3.8	7.7	3.5	7.3	7.1	10.2	5.6	2.5	5.9	7.1	8.6

Table 7.4. (cont.)

Year	DA	DB	DC	DD	DE	DF	DG	DH	DI	DJ	DK	DL	DM	DN
1957	5.3	2.1	1.6	3.5	7.7	2.1	6.6	7.2	7.9	4.2	5.2	3.0	5.5	8.7
1958	5.3	0.3	1.7	4.8	6.7	-0.7	6.6	6.3	6.1	3.5	3.6	3.9	4.6	7.1
1959	5.1	2.6	5.3	5.4	5.6	0.8	7.2	6.3	7.4	3.1	3.4	4.9	7.1	8.6
1960	2.8	3.7	4.1	5.9	5.8	-3.5	5.7	6.0	7.9	4.9	6.7	6.1	6.9	8.2
1961	3.0	2.1	6.6	4.2	6.4	-3.0	4.0	6.5	8.6	6.3	5.3	6.0	6.8	8.0
1962	3.1	1.3	1.5	2.9	4.1	0.8	4.7	3.2	7.2	5.5	3.7	3.7	5.1	6.9
1963	3.1	0.9	-1.9	2.1	3.2	-1.0	3.2	2.8	5.6	4.1	2.9	3.0	4.0	6.3
1964	1.7	-2.0	-3.5	-0.7	-2.4	-3.0	3.6	-0.3	2.7	0.7	-3.3	2.2	0.2	5.0
1965	2.4	-4.1	-5.1	-3.2	-4.5	-3.5	3.5	1.7	-1.9	-1.1	-5.9	1.1	2.2	2.8
1966	1.2	-0.7	-4.6	-1.1	-1.7	-2.1	4.2	3.9	-2.3	-1.0	-1.3	4.4	2.1	3.1
1967	0.1	-2.2	-1.9	-3.5	-1.4	-2.1	3.7	3.6	0.6	-1.0	-1.1	4.5	2.4	2.3
1968	-1.0	-5.2	0.7	-1.9	-6.4	-3.5	3.9	4.1	2.2	0.3	0.1	4.0	5.0	2.8
1969	-0.4	-3.1	-3.5	-3.4	-5.8	-7.6	4.1	0.6	2.0	1.1	-1.3	2.8	-3.9	1.9
1970	0.9	-4.9	-2.0	-0.4	-5.4	-4.3	0.9	2.0	1.6	-1.6	-4.0	2.8	-4.5	0.7
1971	-0.2	-9.9	-3.7	-2.1	-12.0	-5.3	-11.3	-7.5	-2.9	-8.4	-8.0	-0.2	-4.2	-2.5

Legend: see Table 7.3.

Table 7.5. Weight (%) per period and sectors of assets and profits (1900-1971)

	DA	DB	DC	DD	DE	DF	DG	DH	DI	DJ	DK	DL	DM	DN
Assets														
1900-1921	14.8	28.3	0.9	0.3	2.5	0.2	8.6	0.0	3.7	18.6	5.3	3.0	12.6	1.2
1922-1939	13.1	18.6	0.9	0.5	3.4	3.8	17.4	2.2	4.5	13.1	3.4	4.0	14.0	1.2
1946-1949	9.7	10.6	0.8	0.4	2.6	5.9	16.3	2.5	3.0	19.2	2.4	5.9	20.1	0.6
1950-1963	8.1	10.3	0.6	0.4	3.1	9.4	17.6	3.1	4.4	18.1	3.5	6.6	14.3	0.5
1964-1971	7.1	6.3	0.4	0.5	4.1	8.3	21.9	2.9	5.2	16.0	6.3	8.0	12.5	0.6
Profits														
1900-1921	20.2	26.8	1.0	0.2	3.1	0.5	9.7	0.0	4.6	17.1	3.1	2.6	9.5	1.5
1922-1939	15.4	20.7	0.8	0.4	2.9	3.7	21.2	3.1	5.4	11.2	1.3	2.8	9.4	1.6
1946-1949	9.0	19.2	0.7	0.3	4.5	3.3	31.1	3.8	5.0	12.9	1.7	3.4	4.1	1.0
1950-1963	8.7	8.5	0.4	0.5	4.4	5.4	22.2	3.9	7.3	14.5	3.6	6.8	12.7	1.2
1964-1971	9.5	4.2	0.5	0.4	3.0	2.8	31.1	2.9	6.2	9.7	5.8	12.1	10.7	1.0

Legend: see Table 7.3.

Table 7.3 yields further interesting aspects relating to the sectors whose profitability performance shows a much less positive trend than previously observed. The machinery and equipment sector (DK), for example, has a constantly lower performance than the average of the entire manufacturing industry in all the different sub-periods. The profitability performances of the electrical (DL) and transport (DM) equipment sectors are also particularly negative, except in the period 1964-1971, when they show above average values. The latter sectors are consequently characterized by modest profitability in an absolute sense, which appears even more critical when compared to the general trend. Table 7.5 illustrates the relevance of these three sectors in the Italian industrial structure: their overall weight in terms of assets increases in the course of time, reaching a third of the total of the entire manufacturing industry during the 1960s. The weight of the three sectors is also relevant in terms of profits, especially that of the transport sector (DM) and the electrical equipment sector (DL), even though profitability performance is below the average value.

The iron and steel sector (DJ), whose weight in the Italian industrial structure remains constant around 15-16 per cent of the assets value, shows a particularly unsatisfactory profitability performance. The chemical sector (DG), on the other hand, is characterized by a rather interesting trend: until the eve of the Second World War, in fact, it shows a slightly less than average ability to produce profits, after which its profitability performance becomes excellent, with values significantly above the general level. From the post-Second World War period this sector becomes the top sector as far as percentage quota over total profits of the Italian manufacturing industry is concerned. The trends of these last two sectors, which exemplify the Italian industry's attempts, in the post-Second World War period, to follow the course of Fordist large scale economy, are strongly divergent. While the iron and steel sector (DJ) seems incapable of obtaining brilliant results, the chemical industry (DG), even though it has a strong occurrence of foreign firms, which concentrate their activities in heavy technological intensity production [Zamagni 2003], seems able to take advantage of the passage from the carbon-chemical to the petrochemical.

Finally, it is interesting to observe the performance of the textiles sector (DB), which in terms of assets, as can be seen from Table 7.5, remains the most important sector in Italian industry until the 1920s. The ROE shows a rather irregular trend: performance is, in fact, slightly above average in the first two sub-periods of the century. The result of the second period, that from 1922 to 1939, is due to two divergent trends (see Table 7.4): the capacity to generate profits is very high (+72.5 per cent as compared to the average value) during the whole of the 1920s, while it decidedly lower during the 1930s (-40.7 per cent). As from the 1950s the weight of this sector in the Italian industrial structure decreases, and at the same time its capacity to generate profits drops sharply, to values considerably lower than those of the entire manufacturing macro-sector.

The disaggregation of profitability performance at the sectoral level underscores a general tendency, which evidences the pre-eminence of a few oligopolistic sectors in generating profits. Both the food sector (DA) and the non-metallic sector (DI) are in fact characterized by the existence of large oligopolistic enterprises operating at the national level: the sugar firms in the former case and the cement firms in the latter case. Both these sectors, furthermore, are characterized by the existence of oligopolistic firms, in some cases also monopolistic firms, operating at the local level. As an example: the firms involved in the production of milk, fruit, vegetables and oil for the food sector (DA) or the brick-works for the non-metallic mineral sector (DI). The other sectors which also perform well, such as the rubber sector (DH) for the entire period, or the chemical sector (DG) in the post-Second World War period, are also characterized by high levels of concentration. By contrast, the most competitive sectors, such as the textiles sector (DB), the leather (DC) and the machinery equipment (DK) sectors show less positive levels of profitability. It must however be noted that these sectors, especially the first two, are underrepresented in the sample because the size threshold set by the source does not allow for the study of the performance of the small enterprise, which has an extremely relevant weight in these sectors.

7.6. Technological intensity and profitability

The disaggregation by technological level of firms of the levels of profitability allows us to obtain further indications on the characteristics of Italian industry. In order to try to overcome a number of interpretative difficulties, the analysis was carried out using two different taxonomies: the first, proposed by Pavitt [1984], subdivides firms into four distinct types on the basis of their technological characteristics; the second, introduced by the OECD [Hatzichronoglou 1997], classifies industrial sectors on the basis of technological intensity - both direct (production of technology) and indirect (use of technology) - and the expense for R&D. Notwithstanding the length of the time span studied we decided, in both cases, to use the same disaggregation for the entire period since it is not characterized by radical technological discontinuities[6]. The organizational and technological innovations, in fact, continue to follow the *technological regime* of the Second Industrial Revolution which, in the case of a latecomer country, is delayed with respect to the leading countries. The results of the profitability performance obtained using the two classifications are presented in Tables 7.6 and 7.7.

The disaggregation carried out on the basis of the Pavitt classification (Table 7.6) allows an in-depth look at a few aspects which have emerged so far. The profitability performance of the traditional sectors, for example, is particularly positive in the first three sub-periods, while, as from the 1950s, it is very much lower than average values. The traditional sectors seem, therefore, to diminish their performance just as the *science based* sectors become capable of generating, especially during the period 1964-1971, an exceptional profitability. On the one hand, therefore, there is the opening of new technological opportunities, which favor the

[6] In the case of the OECD classification we decided to unite the high technology class and the medium-high class. Had the original classification been maintained we would not, in fact, have obtained a significant number of firms for the highest technological intensity segment.

more innovative firms and, on the other hand, it must be remembered once again that the traditional firms are often small in size and are therefore underrepresented in the sample used. The *specialized suppliers*' category, mostly made up of mechanical firms, has inferior dynamics to the average value for the entire period studied, a confirmation of the profitability difficulties of mechanical firms. The firms based on *economies of scale*, on the other hand, display values not too distant from those observed for the entire manufacturing macro-sector. In this case, this effect is due to the sectoral mix, which includes a multiplicity of firms belonging to different sectors.

The disaggregated analysis according to the technological classification proposed by the OECD, illustrated in Table 7.7, allows a further verification of the hypothesis of the technological discontinuity occurring after the Second World War. In fact, the low technology sectors show a higher than average profitability until the post-War *reconstruction* period. In the period from 1950-1963 their profitability is slightly lower than the average values (-13.7 per cent), but it falls sharply in the subsequent period (1964-1971) when it shows strongly negative values. The dynamics of the high technology sectors show exactly the opposite pattern, as from the 1950s there is a strong growth in profitability with values which during the period 1964-1971, are seven times higher than the average values.

Table 7.6. *Aggregate* ROE trend by period according to the Pavitt classification (1900-1971)

	Economies of scale	*Specialized suppliers*	*Science based*	*Traditional*	Total
ROE					
1900-1921	6.3	5.1	8.6	7.5	6.7
1922-1939	4.0	2.6	4.7	4.7	4.3
1946-1949	4.0	-3.4	-10.7	5.8	3.6
1950-1963	6.2	3.6	5.3	3.9	5.4
1964-1971	-0.4	-2.1	5.6	-1.6	-0.2
1900-1971	4.7	2.7	5.0	4.8	4.7
Percentage deviation from average					
1900-1921	-5.0	-23.8	28.3	12.6	
1922-1939	-6.6	-40.0	11.2	10.2	
1946-1949	10.5	-192.6	-395.6	58.5	
1950-1963	13.1	-33.8	-2.2	-28.4	
1964-1971	-58.8	-788.0	2526.1	-582.6	
1900-1971	-0.6	-42.9	6.5	0.8	

Table 7.7. *Aggregate* ROE trend by period and technological intensity (1900-1971)

	Low	Medium-low	Medium-high	Total
ROE				
1900-1921	7.5	6.2	5.8	6.7
1922-1939	4.6	4.4	3.5	4.3
1946-1949	14.1	-2.0	2.2	3.6
1950-1963	4.7	4.7	6.5	5.4
1964-1971	-2.3	-1.8	1.4	-0.2
1900-1971	5.3	3.9	4.6	4.7
Percentage deviation from average				
1900-1921	12.4	-6.4	-12.8	
1922-1939	8.2	4.0	-18.6	
1946-1949	287.1	-155.9	-40.2	
1950-1963	-13.7	-13.3	18.7	
1964-1971	-908.6	-672.0	724.4	
1900-1971	12.4	-16.6	-3.6	

The Second World War, therefore, seems to represent a watershed in determining considerable changes in the profitability structure of Italian firms. The Italian Golden age appears, in effect, to be founded on the medium-high technology sectors. This phase, thus, seems to bring with it a series of technological opportunities and to allow a latecomer country, which was backwards with respect to the most advanced countries, to change its industrial structure aligning it to that of leading countries.

7.7. Firm size and profitability

The disaggregation of firm size allows us to verify, in the first place, whether there is a relationship between profitability and size. This, in truth, is a very complex question, also because of the difficulty in the choice of the method of disaggregation of the firms by classes of size (see Chap. 4). The peculiarity of the distribution does not allow us to carry out a simple subdivision into quintiles: the majority of the firms would in fact be placed in the first quintile, which of small size, leaving all the others heavily underrepresented. In order to obtain a more homogeneous distribution, capable of offering an explanation for the link between performance and size, we chose size thresholds in order to yield representative samples in all the five classes adopted. The firms were classified on the basis of their gross assets and, to obtain a homogenous subdivision for the whole period, the values were deflated to 1970 lire. We furthermore decided to unite firms in classes on the basis of its size for each year, thus allowing a firm the maximum mobility to change class size during the course of time.

Table 7.8. *Aggregate* ROE by decade and class of size (1900-1971)

	(1)	(2)	(3)	(4)	(5)	Total
ROE						
1900-1921	5.7	6.3	6.4	7.4	6.4	6.7
1922-1939	0.3	2.7	4.3	5.6	4.6	4.3
1946-1949	7.5	9.5	7.1	5.4	-0.9	3.6
1950-1963	2.1	3.1	3.9	4.8	6.1	5.4
1964-1971	-4.8	-3.9	-3.0	-1.5	0.5	-0.2
1900-1971	2.3	3.6	4.2	5.2	4.7	4.7
Percentage deviation from average						
1900-1921	-15.0	-6.1	-4.0	11.1	-3.4	
1922-1939	-93.6	-37.2	0.7	32.7	8.7	
1946-1949	105.7	161.4	96.4	49.3	-123.5	
1950-1963	-62.2	-42.2	-27.9	-11.9	12.2	
1964-1971	-1,981.9	-1,568.5	-1,185.4	-561.9	310.2	
1900-1971	-52.1	-24.1	-11.1	9.3	-0.4	

Legend: (1) 0-499 million lire; (2) 500-999 million lire; (3) 1,000-2,499 million lire; (4) 2,500-9,999 million lire; (5) 10,000 million lire and over.

The results obtained, notwithstanding the *caveat* imposed by the abovementioned choices, seem to prove the existence of a positive relationship between the level of profitability and the size of the firm. From Table 7.8, we can in fact see how, excepting for the *reconstruction* phase following the post-Second World War period, the two largest size classes always show the highest profitability. In the course of the 1920s and the 1930s, for example, the results of the largest classes are considerably superior to those of the two smallest classes. During the *reconstruction* years, as was amply predictable, the relationship between size and profitability is inverted: it is in fact the smaller size firms which have the more positive performance, while the larger firms are heavily penalized by the destruction of plants and by the scant efficiency of the infrastructures which were heavily hit during the War.

As from 1950, the positive relationship between firm size and profitability, already present before the Second World War, becomes even more convincing, with a monotonic increase in performance accompanying the increase in size for both the sub-periods. This phenomenon is observable both in the first period (1950-1963), characterized by a generally high level of profitability, and in the second (1964-1971), when only the highest size class (10,000 million and over) shows slightly positive levels of profitability. The other size classes, on the contrary, show a negative trend which increases in a regular way as the size of the firm decreases.

Significant information, underlining the relationship between size and profitability, can also be gained by the comparison between *average* and *aggregate* ROE, illustrated in Fig. 7.2. The difference between the two series, therefore, reflects the distance between the profitability of large enterprises and the smaller ones. This difference is almost always in favor of the *aggregate* ROE, as further proof of the existence of a positive relationship between size and profitability.

7.8. The determinants of firm performance

The use of *aggregate* data has allowed us to obtain interesting information on the performance of Italian manufacturing firms, but further elements can be obtained by using firm data, as we have already seen in the analysis of the *average* ROE (see Sect. 7.4). Table 7.9.a-d presents the descriptive statistics for the *average* profitability of the single industrial sectors in the different phases. Obviously the results differ from those obtained through the *aggregate* analysis of the data (see Table 7.4). As previously argued (see Sect. 7.4), in fact, the *average* values include all the firms without any distinction with regard to size, while in the *aggregate* computation the sectoral ROE is the sum of all the values of the firms[7].

In the first period analyzed (1900-1921), in which the petrol and coke (DF) and the rubber and plastics (DH) sectors are excluded because they do not reach a sufficient representation for all the years, the sectors showing the greatest profitability are, in line with the results observed for the *aggregate* data, the food sector (DA) and the manufacturing n.e.c. industries (DN). The performance of the non-metallic minerals sector (DI) is less brilliant than previously observed, due to the fact that its positive trend was in large part determined by the profits of the large cement firms.

During the 1920s and the 1930s the *average* levels of profitability, as can be seen in Fig. 7.2, are considerably inferior to the *aggregate* levels. The only sectors which show a positive trend are the chemical sector (DG), the rubber and plastic (DH) and the iron and steel (DJ) sectors.

During the *economic miracle* phase the two sectors with the highest profitability are, in line with the *aggregate* data, those of the non-metallic minerals (DI) and manufacturing industries n.e.c. (DN). The differences lie in the levels of profitability of the food sector (DA), which in contrast to the *aggregate* data, shows negative values, and in the levels of profitability of the machinery equipment (DK) and the electrical equipment (DL) sector, which in contrast show positive values above the average trend. In the first case there is the positive weight of the large firms, while in the second the larger firms have a negative effect.

In the last period studied (1964-1971), the *average* performance shows extremely negative trends and no sector manages to show any profits. In line with the *aggregate* trend it is the chemical sector (DG) which has the least negative performance (-2.3), while the transport sector (DM) still shows extremely negative results (-8.8).

---

[7] It must, however, be remembered that ROE values have been *normalized* (see note 3) so that the particularly negative performance of a few firms does not influence the general trend.

The multivariate analysis which follows aims at estimating how belonging to homogeneous groups of firms (by sector, size, age, etc.) can determine different levels of profitability. The analysis is based on a multiple regression model and was carried out separately for the four sub-periods (1900-1921, 1922-1939, 1950-1963, 1964-1971) so as to reduce the heterogeneity of the data. The specified model relates the normalized profit rate (see note 3) for each manufacturing firm, represented by the ROE, to a series of regressors: (i) the sector of the firm belongs to, specified on the basis of the ATECO-ISTAT classification (*Sector*); (ii) the size of the firm by class of assets at constant 1970 prices (*Size_c*). The classes are thus subdivided: 0-499 million lire (class 1), 500-999 (2), 1,000-2,499 (3), 2,500-9,999 (4), and 10,000 million and over (5); (iii) the age of the firm (*Age_c*). The classes are thus subdivided: 0-5 years (class 1), 6-10 (2), 11-20 (3), 21-40 (4), over 40 years (5); (iv) the level of indebtedness of the firm (*Indeb*).

Table 7.9. *Average* ROE by sector

(*a*) 1900-1921

Sector	Observations	Mean	Standard deviation
Food products and tobacco (DA)	1,937	6.8	12.6
Textile and textile products (DB)	2,628	5.4	15.3
Leather and leather products (DC)	229	5.5	20.6
Wood and wood products (DD)	156	2.8	17.4
Paper products, publishing and printing (DE)	673	3.9	17.1
Chemicals and chemical products (DG)	1,370	6.8	15.8
Other non-metallic products (DI)	1,065	4.6	12.4
Basic metals and metal products (DJ)	1,239	5.0	15.7
Machinery and equipment (DK)	337	3.9	17.5
Electrical and optical equipment (DL)	389	2.7	19.0
Transport equipment (DM)	900	4.1	17.4
Manufacturing n.e.c. (DN)	240	6.0	12.3

(*b*) 1922-1939

Sector	Observations	Mean	Standard deviation
Food products and tobacco (DA)	5,072	-0.2	18.4
Textile and textile products (DB)	6,882	-0.3	18.0
Leather and leather products (DC)	675	-0.6	16.8
Wood and wood products (DD)	512	-3.4	20.5
Paper products, publishing and printing (DE)	2,157	-0.3	16.9
Coke and petroleum products (DF)	488	-0.1	18.7
Chemicals and chemical products (DG)	4,064	1.0	18.0
Rubber and plastic products (DH)	156	1.4	20.4
Other non-metallic products (DI)	2,963	-0.7	18.1
Basic metals and metal products (DJ)	2,913	0.8	16.6
Machinery and equipment (DK)	1,207	-2.5	20.8
Electrical and optical equipment (DL)	1,618	-2.2	20.6
Transport equipment (DM)	1,517	-1.7	21.0
Manufacturing n.e.c. (DN)	749	-4.3	21.0

Table 7.9 (cont.)

(*c*) 1950-1963

Sector	Observations	Mean	Standard deviation
Food products and tobacco (DA)	6,101	-0.8	23.4
Textile and textile products (DB)	6,491	-0.7	20.9
Leather and leather products (DC)	723	0.3	22.3
Wood and wood products (DD)	827	3.1	15.1
Paper products, publishing and printing (DE)	2,892	1.8	21.9
Coke and petroleum products (DF)	1,170	-0.2	19.5
Chemicals and chemical products (DG)	5,051	2.4	20.0
Rubber and plastic products (DH)	803	1.5	19.9
Other non-metallic products (DI)	3,099	3.7	19.6
Basic metals and metal products (DJ)	4,501	1.7	20.8
Machinery and equipment (DK)	3,270	2.4	22.7
Electrical and optical equipment (DL)	2,926	2.8	20.4
Transport equipment (DM)	1,480	-4.9	28.3
Manufacturing n.e.c. (DN)	590	4.6	16.8

(*d*) 1964-1971

Sector	Observations	Mean	Standard deviation
Food products and tobacco (DA)	4,991	-6.0	23.7
Textile and textile products (DB)	5,053	-8.0	24.0
Leather and leather products (DC)	521	-8.9	26.2
Wood and wood products (DD)	775	-5.3	18.6
Paper products, publishing and printing (DE)	2,754	-8.7	26.7
Coke and petroleum products (DF)	810	-5.5	19.0
Chemicals and chemical products (DG)	4,571	-2.3	21.6
Rubber and plastic products (DH)	1,318	-4.5	21.2
Other non-metallic products (DI)	3,880	-5.1	21.1
Basic metals and metal products (DJ)	4,796	-5.1	22.5
Machinery and equipment (DK)	4,167	-5.4	24.4
Electrical and optical equipment (DL)	2,681	-4.4	23.6
Transport equipment (DM)	1,413	-8.8	27.5
Manufacturing n.e.c. (DN)	909	-6.4	24.1

In order to adjust the relationships examined for a time interval higher than one year, a variable indicating the year of observation was also included in the regression model. Schematically, the model states that the expected value of the ROE can be obtained by using the following equation:

$$E(roe) = c + \beta \times Indeb + \gamma_{Sector} + \gamma_{Size\_c} + \gamma_{Age\_c} + Year$$

where c is the constant, β is the coefficient of regression of the continuous variable *Indeb* which represents the level of indebtedness of a firm, γ_{Sector}, γ_{Size_c}, γ_{Age_c} respectively represent the coefficients of the dummy variable for sector, class of size and class of age. *Year* is the proxy for the calendar year.

In order to account for the panel structure of the data, the model was estimated using the Generalized Estimation Equations (GEE) method, specifying a first order autoregressive correlation structure for each firm [Liang and Zeger 1986][8]. The standard errors and therefore the confidence intervals of the coefficients reported here have however been obtained by using the robust error estimate method in the specification of the correlation structure within each firm. The GEE method, as implemented in the STATA function *xtgee*, can also be applied in the case of non-balanced panel data (in this case variable length historical series)[9] but, when an autoregressive structure is specified, the interval between observations must be constant. In other words there must be an observation for each year. For this reason, when the historical series of a single firm presented missing values in the data for some years, they were *forced* to be equispaced. This has introduced a possible element of distortion in the model, which, however, can be considered negligible because the series do not contain long periods for which there is an absence of information. In order to verify the effectiveness of the model, and the appropriateness of the hypothesis on which it is based, a diagnostic analysis of the residues (not reported here) was carried out with particular reference to the specification of the first order type autoregressive correlation structure.

Table 7.10 lists for each coefficient: the punctual estimate, the standard error, the p-value and the 95 per cent confidence interval and, in the last column, the Wald test for significance for each variable included in the multiple regression model (with the exception of the *Year* variable). This econometric exercise to a large extent confirms the results obtained in the first part of the study, and adds further interpretative cues. As far as the first period (1900-1921) is concerned, the interpretation must be cautious due to a certain heteroschedasticity which is not accounted for in this type of model. The effect of the *sector* variable is not statistically significant; however, a few considerations can be made as to the sign of the single coefficients. In general, the textile sector (DB), taken as a reference point, presents a higher level of profitability than almost all the other sectors, with the exception of the food (DA), the chemical (DG) and the manufacturing industries n.e.c. (DN) sectors. Even adopting all the necessary caution, we can observe a prevalence of the traditional sectors linked to the First Industrial Revolution in generating profits, while the trend of all the new sectors is generally more negative. The Italian industrial structure changes slowly and the Second Industrial Revolution sectors, notwithstanding the support provided by state intervention and the favorable dynamics of the First World War, experience difficulties in generating profits. In the second period analyzed (1922-1939), the situation changes, with an increase in the sectors with a higher profitability than the reference sector ($x^2(13)$ =38.81, $p<0.001$). The sectors with the highest profits are the chemical (DG) and the iron and steel (DJ) sectors, proof that the new Second Industrial Revolution sectors begin to take on a central role in the Italian industrial system.

[8] The elaborations were carried out using STATA/SE 7 [Stata Corporation 2002].

[9] It should be noted that the variability in the length of the series of each single firm is determined by the possibility of the *death* of the firm or the possibility that it could fall below the set capital threshold for inclusion in the source used.

Table 7.10. The determinants of profitability

(*a*) 1900-1921

Variable	Coefficient	Standard error	P>|z|	Confidence interval (95%)		Wald test
DA	0.375	0.592	0.527	-0.786	1.536	χ^2 (11) = 15.89
DC	-0.016	1.938	0.994	-3.813	3.782	p = 0.145
DD	-1.427	1.876	0.447	-5.105	2.251	
DE	-0.851	1.163	0.464	-3.130	1.428	
DG	0.594	0.812	0.464	-0.997	2.185	
DI	-1.749	0.682	0.010	-3.085	-0.413	
DJ	-0.435	0.755	0.565	-1.915	1.045	
DK	-0.964	1.380	0.485	-3.669	1.741	
DL	-2.274	1.461	0.120	-5.138	0.590	
DM	-0.957	0.837	0.253	-2.597	0.684	
DN	0.718	1.357	0.597	-1.942	3.378	
Size_c 2	1.498	0.492	0.002	0.534	2.463	χ^2 (4) = 17.00
Size_c 3	1.779	0.607	0.003	0.590	2.968	p = 0.002
Size_c 4	2.859	0.741	0.000	1.406	4.312	
Size_c 5	2.825	1.215	0.020	0.444	5.206	
Age_c 2	1.468	0.475	0.002	0.537	2.399	χ^2 (4) = 120.72
Age_c 3	5.124	0.527	0.000	4.090	6.158	p < 0.001
Age_c 4	5.686	0.686	0.000	4.341	7.031	
Age_c 5	6.760	1.547	0.000	3.728	9.793	
Indeb	-15.166	1.712	0.000	-18.522	-11.809	

Reference: Sector: DB (Textiles and textile products); Size: class 1; Age: class 1.

(*b*) 1922-1939

Variable	Coefficient	Standard error	P>|z|	Confidence interval (95%)		Wald test
DA	0.140	0.600	0.816	-1.037	1.316	χ^2 (13) = 38.81
DC	0.017	1.201	0.989	-2.338	2.371	p < 0.001
DD	-0.905	1.446	0.531	-3.739	1.929	
DE	0.676	0.755	0.371	-0.804	2.155	
DF	0.419	1.505	0.781	-2.530	3.368	
DG	1.788	0.643	0.005	0.528	3.049	
DH	0.861	3.210	0.788	-5.430	7.153	
DI	-0.040	0.631	0.949	-1.277	1.197	
DJ	1.007	0.610	0.099	-0.188	2.202	
DK	-1.709	1.118	0.127	-3.901	0.483	
DL	-1.539	1.026	0.134	-3.550	0.473	
DM	-2.760	0.940	0.003	-4.603	-0.917	
DN	-3.083	1.220	0.011	-5.473	-0.692	
Size_c 2	2.002	0.387	0.000	1.244	2.759	χ^2 (4) = 76.22
Size_c 3	3.070	0.481	0.000	2.127	4.013	p < 0.001
Size_c 4	4.344	0.572	0.000	3.222	5.465	
Size_c 5	3.145	1.193	0.008	0.806	5.483	

Table 7.10 (cont.)

(*b*) 1922-1939

Variable	Coefficient	Standard error	P>|z|	Confidence interval (95%)		Wald test
Age_c 2	1.478	0.371	0.000	0.751	2.205	χ^2 (4) = 138.86 p < 0.001
Age_c 3	3.717	0.412	0.000	2.910	4.525	
Age_c 4	5.393	0.514	0.000	4.385	6.400	
Age_c 5	7.009	0.924	0.000	5.198	8.820	
Indeb	-0.032	0.026	0.223	-0.082	0.019	

Reference: Sector: DB (Textiles and textile products); Size: class 1; Age: class 1.

(*c*) 1950-1963

Variable	Coefficient	Standard error	P>|z|	Confidence interval (95%)		Wald test
DA	0.048	0.692	0.945	-1.309	1.405	χ^2 (13) = 124.11 p < 0.001
DC	1.255	1.387	0.365	-1.463	3.974	
DD	4.952	1.014	0.000	2.964	6.939	
DE	2.955	0.844	0.000	1.300	4.610	
DF	1.298	1.087	0.233	-0.833	3.429	
DG	3.453	0.687	0.000	2.107	4.800	
DH	3.641	1.171	0.002	1.345	5.937	
DI	4.770	0.764	0.000	3.273	6.268	
DJ	2.943	0.743	0.000	1.486	4.400	
DK	3.918	0.853	0.000	2.245	5.590	
DL	3.998	0.801	0.000	2.429	5.567	
DM	-4.232	1.490	0.005	-7.153	-1.310	
DN	6.357	1.279	0.000	3.851	8.863	
Size_c 2	0.493	0.374	0.188	-0.241	1.227	χ^2 (4) = 16.02 p = 0.003
Size_c 3	1.353	0.430	0.002	0.510	2.196	
Size_c 4	1.668	0.524	0.001	0.642	2.695	
Size_c 5	2.335	0.746	0.002	0.872	3.797	
Age_c 2	2.344	0.430	0.000	1.502	3.186	χ^2 (4) = 76.41 p < 0.001
Age_c 3	3.463	0.475	0.000	2.532	4.393	
Age_c 4	3.419	0.472	0.000	2.494	4.345	
Age_c 5	4.031	0.630	0.000	2.796	5.266	
Indeb	-0.252	0.212	0.234	-0.668	0.163	

Reference: Sector: DB (Textiles and textile products); Size: class 1; Age: class 1.

Table 7.10 (cont.)

(*d*) 1964-1971

Variable	Coefficient	Standard error	P>|z|	Confidence interval (95%)		Wald test
DA	2.772	0.814	0.001	1.177	4.367	χ^2 (13) = 90.48 p < 0.001
DC	-0.556	2.107	0.792	-4.685	3.573	
DD	3.703	1.214	0.002	1.323	6.082	
DE	-0.724	1.119	0.517	-2.919	1.470	
DF	3.062	1.340	0.022	0.436	5.688	
DG	5.863	0.774	0.000	4.346	7.381	
DH	4.302	1.111	0.000	2.124	6.479	
DI	3.816	0.783	0.000	2.282	5.351	
DJ	3.237	0.774	0.000	1.721	4.753	
DK	2.907	0.836	0.001	1.269	4.546	
DL	3.351	0.934	0.000	1.520	5.182	
DM	-1.145	1.408	0.416	-3.905	1.614	
DN	2.749	1.464	0.060	-0.121	5.619	
Size_c 2	2.134	0.457	0.000	1.239	3.030	χ^2 (4) = 37.92 p < 0.001
Size_c 3	2.711	0.502	0.000	1.727	3.695	
Size_c 4	3.110	0.585	0.000	1.964	4.257	
Size_c 5	3.452	0.839	0.000	1.807	5.097	
Age_c 2	1.189	0.420	0.005	0.365	2.012	χ^2 (4) = 18.20 p = 0.001
Age_c 3	1.486	0.504	0.003	0.498	2.474	
Age_c 4	1.932	0.576	0.001	0.804	3.060	
Age_c 5	2.384	0.677	0.000	1.057	3.710	
Indeb	-0.001	0.000	0.003	-0.002	0.000	

Reference: Sector: DB (Textiles and textile products); Size: class 1; Age: class 1.

The situation changes radically in the first phase of the post-Second World War period (1950-1963), when the majority of the coefficients are significant. The results for all the sectors, except the transport sector (DM), show higher levels of profitability than the textiles sector (DB). The performances of the manufacturing industries n.e.c. sector (DN), the wood sector (DD) and the non-metallic minerals sector (DI), respectively 6.3 per cent, 4.9 per cent and 4.8 per cent, are particularly significant. The mechanical sectors (DK, DL) also show a 4 per cent higher performance than the reference sector.

The subsequent period (1964-1971), though displaying negative levels of profitability, as mentioned above, shows results substantially in line with the preceding period. In general, performances are higher in comparison to the textiles sector (DB), and particularly positive for the chemical sector (DG) and the rubber and plastic sector (DH), respectively +5.9 per cent and +4.3 per cent. The machinery equipment (DK) and electrical equipment (DL) sectors also show high levels of profitability, while the transport sector (DM) confirms its negative trend.

The model also covers the effects of a further two variables (size and age) which show clearer results than those obtained previously and are always significant. In general, there is an evident trend towards an increase in profitability with the increase in the size of the firms (see Table 7.10). This phenomenon is confirmed for all the sub-periods analyzed. The larger size firms show higher levels of profitability than those in the lower size class, taken as a reference point, with values fluctuating from a minimum of 2.3 per cent in the period from 1950-1963 to a maximum of 3.4 per cent in the period 1964-1971.

As far as age is concerned the results are even clearer and, in this case too, amply significant. As the firm increases in age there is a considerable increase in the level of profitability. This is more evident in the first two periods when the older firms show 6-7 per cent higher levels of profitability than the young firms. In the two phases during the second post-War period, on the other hand, the gap narrows, with a 4 per cent increase in the 1950-1963 period and a 2.3 per cent increase in the 1964-1971 period. This difference is probably due to the greater turnover in the Italian industrial structure during the post-Second World War period with the opening of opportunities in the new sectors.

Finally, through the use of a model similar to the one used previously we estimated how the technology variable, represented by the four categories of the Pavitt taxonomy, determines the level of profitability of firms. Schematically the model specifies that the expected value of the ROE can be obtained through the following equation:

$$E(roe) = c + \beta \times Indeb + \gamma_{Pavitt} + \gamma_{Size\_c} + \gamma_{Age\_c} + Year$$

where c is the constant, β is the regression coefficient of the continuous variable *Indeb* which represents the level of indebtedness of a firm, γ_{Pavitt}, γ_{Size_c}, γ_{Age_c} represent, respectively the coefficients of the dummy variables of the Pavitt classification, of the size class and the age class. *Year* is the proxy for the calendar year. Table 7.11 shows the coefficients, the standard error and the Wald test of the single Pavitt variable.

Table 7.11. The weight of technology in determining levels of profitability

	1900-1921	1922-1939	1950-1963	1964-1971
Economies of scale	-1.227 (0.437)	0.266 (0.381)	0.716 (0.421)	0.038 (0.462)
Specialized suppliers	-1.051 (0.785)	-1.208 (0.759)	2.376 (0.622)	0.807 (0.611)
Science based	1.652 (1.790)	0.797 (1.118)	1.028 (0.844)	2.656 (0.873)
Wald test	$\chi^2(3) = 9.85$ $p = 0.019$	$\chi^2(3) = 4.23$ $p = 0.237$	$\chi^2(3) = 15.06$ $p = 0.002$	$\chi^2(3) = 10.89$ $p = 0.012$

Reference: Pavitt: *traditional* sectors.

The results presented show that the *science based* firms, generally, have higher levels of profitability than firms in the *traditional* sectors, chosen as a reference point. The levels of profitability are higher for all the sub-periods analyzed and, are 2.7 per cent higher than those in the *traditional* sectors in the last period analyzed (1964-1971). Technological potential seems, therefore, to be one of the key factors in the success of a firm. This is also observable in the case of Italy even though the number of firms belonging to these sectors is always relatively small. The firms belonging to the *specialized suppliers*' category, on the other hand, show a strongly unequal trend: their level of profitability is lower to that of the traditional sectors in the first two sub-periods, while in the second post-War period their performance is particularly positive. This could be due to the difficulties they encounter in specializing, especially in the case of the mechanical firms, because of the *narrowness* of the market which characterizes the period preceding the Second World War. As from the post-Second World War period on the other hand, a greater commercial opening and the increase in sectoral integration could have given rise to a greater specialization of firms, thus completing the productive matrix and, consequently increasing the performance of the *specialized suppliers* firms. In this case the results obtained in the model, which uses data at the single firm level, are decidedly different from those obtained from the *aggregate* data (see Table 7.6) which show only a modest performance for the *specialized suppliers* sectors. This is due to the size effect, in other words, within this set of firms it is the smaller firms which obtain the best performances.

7.9. Conclusions

The analysis carried out represents a first step in the study of the profitability dynamics of Italian firms, and the examination of balance sheet data is, notwithstanding the problems highlighted, an essential instrument in the comprehension of the above dynamics. A long run representation of the dynamics of profitability in the Italian economy thus emerges. This representation shows the existence of high levels of profitability in concomitance with the First World War, of less positive dynamics between the 1920s and the 1930s and a recovery, led by the large firms, in the second half of the 1930s. As far as the *reconstruction* period is concerned the levels of profitability are in line with those of the pre-War years. The 1950s are characterized by good levels of profitability, especially for the large firms, while as from 1964, there is a strong contraction in profits in conformity to the historiographical account.

During the entire period, there is a positive relationship between the size of the firm and profitability: the largest enterprises remain stable at ROE levels 2-3 per cent higher than those of the smaller firms. Age also has a positive influence, particularly evident in the period preceding the Second World War, on the ability to generate profits: the older firms reach higher profitability levels compared to the young firms for all the sub-periods studied. The analysis of the technological characteristics of firms confirms that the higher technological intensity sectors are those with the greatest profitability. Technical potential can therefore be identified as one of the main determinants of the capacity to generate profits. It must, however, be noted that the *science based* sectors remain constantly and heavily under-represented in the Italian industrial structure.

As far as the sectoral trend is concerned, results are less clear than those associated with the previous variables, but in this case too, interesting indications emerge. Firstly, at least until the end of the 1920s, it is the traditional *light* industry sectors which show the highest levels of profitability, while the *heavy* sectors, especially the chemical sector (DG), show a higher capacity for profitability as from the second half of the 1930s. It is often the less relevant sectors in the Italian industrial structure, such as the manufacturing industries n.e.c. (DN) or the non-metallic minerals (DI), which show the most positive dynamics. The performance of the chemical sector (DG), which in the post-Second World War period exhibits the best performance, also stands out. The machinery (DK) and electrical (DL) equipment sectors, on the other hand, are characterized by a peculiar trend: they show decidedly negative levels if the *aggregate* data are taken into account, while the data at the single firm level show one of the highest levels of profitability especially in the post-Second World War period. This is probably due to the size effect, which in this case, plays a negative role. Finally, the negative performance of the transport sector (DM), which remains constant for the entire period, is worthy of note.

8. Business strategies from Unification up to the 1970s

Giovanni Federico and Pier Angelo Toninelli

8.1. Introduction

The previous Chaps. shed light on features of the market structure of Italian industry that serve in some way to describe mechanisms acting systematically throughout the industry, such as concentration, scale economies and business size distribution. Yet it is well known that, as well as being determining elements, such mechanisms are also the result of more or less rational strategies by firms (and other economic operators). The material forms taken by the mechanisms in different situations are thus heavily dependent on the influence exerted by the history of the firms themselves and on the context they find themselves working in. This Chap. therefore represents the other pole of the *generalization-event* pairing in modern industrial economics [Sutton 1998], where the focus is on historical exceptions rather than statistic regularities.

The present contribution includes a series of case studies, re-read to find criteria useful for identifying the strategies. We thus attempted to supply answers to questions such as: did Italian firms aim at diversification or at concentrating around a core business? Did they adopt modern, Chandler style organizational models? Did they invest in R&D and human capital? Where did they sell their products? To what extent were they state-aided? How were they financed? In other words, on the basis of the answers to these and other questions, we aimed to supply a preliminary map of the micro-economic behavior of business concerns with regard to a ready-made set of variables.

Such an experiment would have been almost impossible to carry out thirty years ago. At that time little was known about Italian business strategies and the little that was - as recalled in a famous article by Giorgio Mori [1959, see also Mori 1959-60] - came from jubilee publications by firms, a source by its very nature partial to say the least. Today the situation is greatly improved. Starting with the pioneering work of Franco Bonelli [1975] on Terni, business historians have published an impressive amount of studies[1]. It is difficult to use this literature,

---

Although the present work was set up and closely monitored by both authors, only Sects. 8.1 and 8.12 were actually co-written. Sections 8.3-8.6 must be attributed to Giovanni Federico and Sects. 8.7-8.11 to Pier Angelo Toninelli. The authors wish to thank Carlo A. Brambilla, Gianpiero Fumi and Paolo Raspadori for their precious assistance in compiling the questionnaires.

[1] For a review see Bigazzi [1990]; Bigatti [1994, 1999].

however, owing to its highly diversified nature. In fact, together with the triumphalistic publications already mentioned (in their most recent versions often written by eminent historians), it includes biographies of individual entrepreneurs and traditional histories of enterprise, works on single aspects of the evolution of a business (for example on the technological or financial strategies), studies on single sectors, and so on. Some great companies, such as Ansaldo (that makes available to scholars what is probably the most complete historical archive in Italy), are the object of a large number of studies approached from different angles[2]. In other cases there are only brief essays to go by. Castronovo's book [1985] on Gilardini, for example, contains information about several firms taken over by Gilardini. Some studies concentrate on individual phases in the history of a business, others go through every episode from its foundation or start of its industrial activity, or maybe from its transformation into a limited company or some other, similar change in its legal status. Some of the firms selected for the sample, such as the Conte wool company (founded in 1757) or Nardini (founded in 1778), have very long traditions, but most of the *great* Italian firms (important enough to be the subject of history studies) were founded later, in the second half of the 19th century or first half of the 20th.

On the whole, the bibliographical sources consulted (see Annex 8.1) contain an enormous amount of information potentially useful but in need of standardizing. For this purpose, following the methodology already used in a previous work [Giannetti, Federico and Toninelli 1994], a type-file was compiled for each firm. This is illustrated in Sect. 8.2, while Sect. 8.3 deals with the sample of firms taken into consideration (142) and analyses their representativeness. The following eight Sects., from 8.4 to 8.11, present the main results of the research. The examination concerns, in order, ownership (Sect. 8.4), market (Sect. 8.5), diversification (Sect. 8.6), commercial strategies (Sect. 8.7), organizational changes (Sect. 8.8), innovation (Sect. 8.9), human capital (Sect. 8.10), and financing (Sect. 8.11). The last Sect. discusses the implications of the results in the light of some recent general works on the history of Italian industry.

8.2. How the survey works

As the literature consulted contains a mixed bag of information on the individual firms, based largely on the authors' interests and sources used, it was decided to compile the loosest type of file possible (see Annex 8.2), preferably leaving a question unanswered rather than risk missing some information. The file therefore includes eight main fields, containing various questions concerning: (i) sector of activity and any possible changes undergone in it, with reasons for any sector and/or production diversifications; (ii) type of market (supply and demand) it operates in, selling and marketing policies; (iii) ownership structure and any possible

[2] Ranging from Doria's classic [1989] to the *official* nine-volume history [Castronovo, Hertner and Mori 1994-2002].

changes; (iv) company structure; (v) technological traits and innovative policies practiced; (vi) organizational structure and its evolution; (vii) financial strategies and investment policies; (viii) training of the human capital[3].

To take into account the passing of time, eight periods are considered separately (before 1876, 1876-1894, 1895-1914, 1915-1921, 1922-1929, 1930-1938, 1939-1947, 1948-1973)[4]. Each question contains an *information lacking* area, which unfortunately turns out to be the most frequent answer. Though the structure of the file was undoubtedly made for empirical purposes, it also permits a reading based on some theoretical categories. It should also be made clear at once that where business theory is concerned, no single and/or standard approach was favored, but in line with some recent ideas [Sutton 1998], an eclectic approach was chosen.

The starting point was provided by the traditional paradigm *structure-behavior -performance*, which assumes that the results of industry - that is its performance (in a wide sense, including objectives such as productive efficiency, full employment or equitable income distribution[5]) - depend on its behavior, that is how well it adapts to the market structure. The latter includes characteristics such as the number and territorial extension of buyers and sellers, to what extent the product differs from its competitors, the ability to differentiate products within the individual firm, together with the presence or absence of barriers to new enterprises and degree of vertical integration in the firms [Porter 1980; Scherer 1980]. Many of these aspects are examined in more depth at points 1.1, 1.2, 2, 3.1, 3.2, 3.3 and 3.4 of the questionnaire.

The performance of an industry or industrial sector depends on the behavior of those operating in it (producers, sellers, buyers) in fields like pricing policies, open or tacit collaboration among firms, advertising strategies, choice of product lines, commitment to R&D, investment in factories, exclusive contracts, and so on. These aspects were the object of specific inquiry in the questionnaire and the relative questions can be found at points 3.5, 4.4 and 4.5 of the file.

Up to this point, therefore, the questionnaire file conforms to the indications given by the mainstream of industrial economics and school of business strategy revolving around Harvard Business School. In that line of study, however, a business enterprise is mostly seen as a "unit of economic decision that adapts, albeit in the best possible way, to a 'given' and unmodifiable environment" [Ricciardi 1985: 211]. In such a state of affairs a business would be cramped and above all have little chance to act as a stimulus to its environment. How restrictive this approach could be becomes even more conditioning in a survey proposing strong diachronic valences, as is the case here. No study of business history can therefore

---

[3] The file, set out in Annex 8.2, includes information about the main sector the firm belongs to, any changes in the company name, the period of reference, and ends with a section providing any quantitative information about accounting, staff number, working premises, social capital, etc.

[4] Attribution to a period is inevitably approximative. In fact, the reference period in the works consulted hardly ever coincides with the dates in the file.

[5] The basic reference is Scherer [1980].

fail to take into account what modern industrial economy has to say when it stresses the active role of an enterprise and its *equipe* in helping to shape the economic reality around it, through feedback between the two parts[6]: in this sense the entire line of study stretching from Schumpeter to the modern theory of business development [Nelson and Winter 1982] and the strategic foundations of the theory of interplay applied to business dynamics [Kreps and Wallis 1995].

The question of the quality of human capital - labor and management - and thus of its - more or less formal - training and impact on the modernization process in general and industrial growth in particular, is today more than ever the centre of debate among economic and social historians and economists[7]. This is only one strand of the wider theme of training/development which since the pioneering works of Schultz [1960, 1962] and Anderson and Bowman [1965] has revolved around the connection between the two terms. Though further proof of the connection might be required, there now seems to be solid convergence towards the idea that adequate training is one of the crucial qualities needed if countries lagging behind are to catch up, that is one of the most important factors in modern economic development [Easterlin 1981; Abramovitz 1986, 1994; Baumol, Batey Blackman and Wolff 1989; Romer 1994].

With regard to industrialization, however, what may interest us more among the various channels through which training influences the transformation of modern economies is its impact on technological know-how and the ability to streamline production processes by applying innovations in technology. It is also opportune to remember that the connection runs in the opposite direction too, as suggested by the complementary nature of high tech and human capital, namely that new technology influences the employment structure of companies as they try to adapt their work forces to make their production processes more efficient [Griliches 1969; Goldin and Katz 1998]. The importance of training human capital has thus grown with the march of high tech and its ever closer link with scientific research. These traits of factory production, coming above all with the second wave of industrialization, are typical of *new* sectors and require increasingly specialized training of the human capital. The most mature sectors, that is those typical of the First Industrial Revolution, textiles in particular, did not require specific skills, and learning through experience in the field often proved the key to improvement-making. This has been taken into account in the questionnaire at points 4.1, 4.2, 4.3, 8.1 and 8.2.

Diversification strategies too - and the still lively debate about the past role and future destinies of diversification in sectors far from the historical boundaries of business enterprise (the conglomerate model) - should make a significant contribution (point 1.4). Limited diversification can be considered a sign of backwardness and/or meager growth in an enterprise. At the same time it is well known that diversification is not necessarily synonymous with winning strategies and thus with gratifying business performance. Theory supplies various arguments advising caution with respect to big, (over) diversified enterprises - or, to put it better, diversified in sectors too far from the core business or too weakly linked to it - not to

[6] For a concise presentation of these themes, see Toninelli [1999b].

[7] For a summary of the debate see Giannetti [1998] and Vasta [1999: Chap. 5].

mention conglomerate enterprises [Rumelt 1986; Dosi, Teece and Winter 1992; Teece et al. 1994]. For example, many of the giant American corporations have been accused since the 1960s of being particularly slow in noticing changes in demand and eliminating inefficient activities, with the resulting misallocation if not waste of resources, so that they have gone on producing in unprofitable areas, covering their losses with profits from other more successful ones. More generally speaking they have seemed sluggish and shown an increasing inability to introduce the most efficient methods or get rid of superfluous staff [Scherer 1980]. However, the debate over the last few decades and empirical researches brought to support or criticize the viability of diversified or conglomerate enterprise have not produced any single, clear response [Kay 1997, 2002; Whittington, Mayer and Curto 1999; Whittington and Mayer 2000, 2002].

Last, but by no means least, is the contribution of conceptual elaboration (with its possible generalizations) coming from the realms of economic and business history, areas of study that are dynamic by their very nature. Essential ideas have been supplied by the seminal works - in terms of business management, ownership and control - of Sombart [1927], Berle and Means [1932] and more recently Williamson [1986] and Lazonick [1991], as well as by the now classic studies on the relationship between strategy and structure/organization by Alfred Chandler [1962, 1977]. The questions proposed by fields 5 and 6 of the file were therefore framed to gather information about the relative originality (but also the tardiness) of Italy's industrial capitalism concerning permanent ownerships, corporate governance and management transparency. Finally, what could not help but provide obvious material for inspiration - for the formulation of the questions on finance and investment (field 7) - were the studies by Gerschenkron [1962] and Sylla and Toniolo [1991] on the problem of the relative backwardness of latecomers, in their application to the Italian case, with strong emphasis on the universal role of banks - to the brink of over-exposure - [Confalonieri 1974] - in the industrialization process of a country traditionally classified in literature as bank-oriented [Rybczinski 1974, 1984; Zamagni 1992].

8.3. The sample and its representativeness

It was possible to compile 142 standard files for the same number of firms, even if they do not all provide information for the whole period. Predictably, they are mostly from the North (104, corresponding to 73.3 per cent of the whole). Of these the North-West, including the *Industrial Triangle* has the lion's share, with 74, against 30 in the North-East. The companies belonging to the central regions number 33 (or 22.3 per cent) while only 6 (thus 4.2 per cent) belong to the South.

Table 7.1 divides the companies considered by sector and period, according to a shortened version of the ATECO-ISTAT 1991 classification. For each company the dominant sector is shown, according to the indication of Imita.db, integrated for individual firms and if necessary corrected with information from business history sources.

The time span concentrates on the *classic* period of Italian industrialization - from the Giolittian boom years to the Second World War. Beforehand there were few companies big enough to leave documented trace, while the post-Second World War period is still too recent to consider: not only are there fewer cases (partly because of the disappearance of electricity companies after nationalization), but also because they are less documented owing to the reluctance of many firms to open their archives to outside scholars.

Table 8.1. Distribution of firms

Sector	before 1876	1876-1894	1895-1914	1915-1921	1922-1929	1930-1938	1939-1947	1948-1973	Total
Mining	0	0	2	2	2	2	2	1	3
Food and tobacco	8	8	15	14	17	17	14	13	20
Textile, wearing and leather	15	19	19	16	18	16	11	10	22
Paper and publishing	2	3	6	5	5	4	4	4	8
Chemicals	2	2	5	5	7	8	6	6	12
Non metallic minerals	4	4	5	4	3	2	2	2	5
Iron, steel and engineering	14	23	35	36	38	41	38	34	53
Utilities	0	5	12	11	16	13	11	11	17
Other services	0	0	0	2	2	2	2	2	2
Total	45	64	99	95	108	105	90	83	142

Legend: ATECO-ISTAT 1991 classification: Mining 13-14; Food and tobacco 15-16; Textiles, wearing and leather 17-19; Paper and publishing 21-22; Chemicals 23-25; Non metallic minerals 26; Iron, steel and engineering 27-35 and 37; Furniture and other manufactures 20 and 36; Utilities (electricity, gas, water e telephones) 40, 41 and 64; Other services (shipping and retailing) 52 and 61.

As can be seen from Table 8.1, the number of cases for each box is rather limited, especially if compared to the whole universe of companies. The Imita.db used in other contributions to this volume includes a number of companies increasing from 869 in 1913 to over 6,500 in 1973. The 142 cases selected may thus seem very few, but probably refer to the largest or most successful companies. The documentary archives of such firms are more likely to survive and thus become the subject of history studies. Anyway, in theory even a small sample can be enough for a statistical analysis (think of opinion polls taken on a sample of a few hundred people). It must, however, be representative, that is it must satisfy two precise conditions: (i) its distribution according to relevant parameters (in this case the related sector) must faithfully reflect the whole universe of cases; (ii) each case (company) must be a good representative of its category.

The degree of representativeness in the first meaning can be verified with a χ-square test. In the absence of data on the total number of companies per sector, the population used is the number of workers given by the censuses[8]. We must obviously dismiss the idea that the same distribution exists for all the years[9]. In particular, the sample over-represents heavy industry (especially steel and engineering) and under-represents some light industry sectors. Case studies on woodworking industries, for example, are completely lacking, even though these accounted for about 10 per cent of industrial workers.

It is harder to verify the second condition. One possibility is to compare the position of the 124 companies in the sample that appear from 1913 onwards in the universe of shareholder companies. The other 18 cases include companies only taken into account for the preceding period (such as the Milani paper mill), firms with staff and shareholders with capital below the minimum required to be included in ASIPA publications. Several of these make no appearance in all seven benchmark years (1913, 1921, 1927, 1936, 1952, 1960 and 1972), so the comparison is largely based on 434 cases. For each it is possible to calculate the ranking (based on capital) from their position in the ATECO-ISTAT classification[10]. From these cases it is possible to make some simple calculations which are presented for benchmark year (Table 8.2) and sector (Table 8.3).

Table 8.2. The representativity of the sample: a comparison with the Imita.db by year

Year	(*a*)	(*b*)	(*c*)	(*d*)	(*e*)
1913	51	5.9	13.7	39.2	84.3
1921	62	3.5	17.7	48.4	77.4
1927	72	3.0	15.3	45.8	77.8
1936	69	3.2	15.9	40.6	88.4
1952	59	1.7	15.3	49.2	88.1
1960	63	1.7	17.5	46.0	87.3
1972	58	0.9	13.8	60.3	94.8

Legend: (*a*) number of firms; (*b*) percentage of the firms in the sample on the total number of firms in the Imita.db; (*c*) share of cases when the sample include the largest company in its sector; (*d*) share of firms in the sample belonging to the first decile of the Imita.db; (*e*) share of firms in the sample belonging to the first five deciles of the Imita.db.

As can be seen, the survey is heavily tilted in favor of *big* companies according to the division they belong to. A representative sample should in fact include about a tenth of firms belonging to the first decile and about half the firms belonging to the first five deciles - while the percentages of the survey are much higher - see Table 8.2 and 8.3, columns (*d*) and (*e*).

---

[8] Such procedure involves the added supposition that the number of employees in the firms surveyed was equal to the sector average.

[9] The coefficients are 53.6 in 1911, 43.9 in 1927, 28.2 in 1937, 31.6 in 1951, 35.0 in 1961 and 34.1 in 1971, against a test-statistics of 16.92 at 5 per cent and 21.67 at 1 per cent.

[10] Each firm appears only once in each year, but the sector may change from one year to another. Pirelli, for example, appears among electric-material producers in 1913 and 1921, and among the chemical industries from 1927 onwards.

Table 8.3. The representativity of the sample: a comparison with the Imita.db by sector

Sector	(*a*)	(*c*)	(*d*)	(*e*)
Mining	10	30.0	50.0	100.0
Food and tobacco	60	8.3	63.3	83.3
Textile, wearing and leather	66	12.1	27.3	90.9
Paper and publishing	17	23.5	41.2	64.7
Chemicals	24	16.7	33.3	95.8
Non metallic minerals	15	40.0	60.0	86.7
Iron, steel and engineering	165	14.5	51.5	85.5
Furniture and other manufactures	68	11.8	48.5	91.2
Utilities	9	66.7	22.2	33.3
Other services	434	15.7	46.8	85.3

Legend: see Table 8.2.

Table 8.2 suggests a slight increase in the imbalance over time - probably due to the smaller size of the new firms, which on account of their recent founding have little chance of being the subject of business history. Table 8.3 in fact shows that the imbalance is present in all sectors - without much distinction between heavy and light industry. It must therefore be concluded that it reflects more the nature of the source (business histories) than the sector. It is likely, however, that people firms or companies (omitted from Imita.db and consequently also from the comparison of Table 8.2 and 8.3) were more common in the *light* sectors than in the *heavy* ones. In that case the sample would be more unbalanced in the former than in the latter. As already mentioned, the sample includes some firms with a legal form different from capital companies, but such firms are definitely under-represented in comparison with the world of industrial enterprises in Italy. This represents a further limitation in the sample, with the (perfectly feasible) idea that people firms were smaller and behaved differently from shareholding companies.

On the whole, therefore, the sample cannot be defined as representative in the technical sense of the term, but a qualitative approach still seems useful, with the aim of indicating specific strategies or behaviors and presenting some significant examples of the way Italian industry took one direction rather than another.

8.4. Who owned Italian industry?

Among other things, modern Italy can be distinguished by its small number of public companies along Anglo-Saxon lines. Not surprisingly, this characteristic can also be found in the sample companies. The most important exceptions from a historical perspective are Montecatini, Edison and Eridania, and the last two cases are to some extent *spurious*. A large slice of Edison still belonged to the banks during the first thirty years of its existence. Eridania, controlled from its foundation by a hard core of shareholders, long remained a wide-based shareholding company even after merging with Ligure Lombarda, until it was scaled down by Attilio Monti in the mid-1960s. Big multi-nationals like FIAT or Pirelli, though quoted on the stock exchange, are still controlled and managed by one or more families, perhaps with reduced capital quotas.

The vast majority of firms in the sample maintained a family character, that is a business structure where short and long-term decisions came from inside the family, which either owned the entire business or held the great majority of shares. All the firms in the traditional *light* sectors, such as the food industry, were of a family nature - apart from the sugar, textile and publishing sectors [Tonizzi 2001], irrespective of the legal form or stock-market quotation. At most, and only in a couple of cases, ownership and control, instead of belonging to a single family, was subdivided among a group of big shareholders (or business families). For example, in the case of the Brescia Manifattura di Pontoglio (formerly Sacconaghi) front line cotton manufacturers such as Mylius, Cantoni, Frua and De Angeli entered into the capital right from the start, alongside the management - and therefore before it was transformed into a joint-stock company and then taken over by SNIA BPD in the 1960s. The Ferrarelle company, which was licensed to exploit and bottle the mineral water from the Riardo spring near Caserta, was bought in 1924 by the Sangemini mineral water company, in its turn controlled by a group of notable Umbrian families. In the sugar sector, large companies created through the participation of a large number of partners, sooner or later fell under the control of one main shareholder. Ligure Lombarda, founded by 28 partners from Genoa and Milan was scaled down in 1926 by Emilio Raggio, while another Genoese shipbuilder, Erasmo Piaggio, had taken over Italiana Zuccheri at the end of the 19th century. Family ownership was very frequent, if not actually dominant, in modern sectors, too. Some steel companies such as Magona, Lucchini and Riva Siderurgica are still family owned and managed. Even in sectors like chemicals and engineering, family control has been the rule not the exception for both small and medium-sized companies, especially before the Second World War. There have been a few cases of foreign ownership, especially in the early stages of a company's life, such as Tubi Mannesmann (later Dalmine) and Costruzioni Meccaniche di Saronno, both founded by German firms and expropriated when the First World War broke out.

Before the Great Crash, the real alternative to family control was bank ownership, especially in the case of heavy industry, which required a huge amount of capital with deferred (if not non-existent) profits. In some cases, Terni and Edison for example, the companies were largely bank-owned from the start. In many others, the founding families were unable to finance acquisitions or product investments (particularly onerous during the First World War) and ended up losing control. This happened to the Franchi-Griffin steel company. In the War years, taking advantage of the favorable combination of huge war commissions and the elimination of much-feared German competition in the production of tempered steel, cast iron, and steel wheels and cylinders for rolling mills, the company embarked on a massive, if short-lived expansion program of production and acquisition, taking control of S.A. Gregorini, Metallurgica Bresciana (formerly Tempini) and Tubi Mannesmann among others. The number of staff increased 35 times. At the end of the War, demobilization and post-War re-conversion drastically reduced the productive prospects and many of the debts the firm claimed from the State proved irrecoverable. In the end COMIT, which had financed the expansion, transformed the credit into shares, ousting the founder and managing director Attilio Franchi. Other steel and engineering companies went the same way, especially in the Triest area [Grifone 1945; Confalonieri 1997; Mellinato 2001: Chaps. 2 and 3]. As we know, by the end of the 1920s *mixed banks* were in possession of a considerable part of Italian industry - especially in sectors such as steel, telephones, building, heavy engineering, and so on. Then, as a result of the 1930s' depression, the part they played was taken over by the State. The banking law of 1936 actually made it illegal for banks to own industrial firms, and state-ownership of industry was to become an Italian characteristic right up to the wave of privatizations in the 1990s [Amatori 2000].

The debate on the peculiarities of this original road to capitalism in Italy has hotted up over the last few years but, where arguments for and against state intervention in productive activities are concerned, to all appearances some solid certainties have been reached[11]. On the contrary, the debate concerning the virtues of family capitalism, especially where small to medium-sized firms are concerned, is far from over. Some stress the advantages of continuity, a solid corporate governance and the greater ease of re-investing all profits back into the firm [Saba 1995; Bonomi 1997; Colli 2002a, 2003]. Others maintain that family control reduces the amount of resources available for long-term growth, the capacity for innovation and potential to compete on the international market [Barca et al. 1994a; Amatori 1997; Amatori and Brioschi 1997; de Cecco 2000, 2001a]. Such sweeping generalizations are hard to prove, even on the basis of a sample of companies. Cases can be found to support either argument, none of them conclusive and for obvious reasons. Success or failure depends on a host of factors and a different ownership structure would not necessarily have brought about a different result. An interesting example is afforded by the Marzotto wool company. This started as a family firm in the 19th century and was run most successfully by Gaetano Marzotto Sr. until his death in 1910. There then began a heated dispute on how to manage the inheritance between his son Vittorio Emanuele, long-term manager of the firm and real soul of the business, and the *young Marzottians* - grandchildren of the favorite son, Luigi, who had died prematurely. The industrial patrimony was subdivided into S.A. Lanificio Vittorio E. Marzotto (VEM) and S.A. Filatura di lana a pettine Gaetano Marzotto & Figli (GMF), thus interrupting the cycle of production and causing onerous settlement processes in the subdivided factories in order to try and restore *correct economic functioning* [Roverato 1986: 86]. The two firms were to have different destinies - the one dynamic and innovative, the other technologically obsolete and abysmally managed. When, over twenty years later (1938) the GMF found itself on the verge of bankruptcy, it was the VEM that saved it, re-

[11] For further development of these points see Toninelli [2000, 2003]. In particular, state intervention seems to have been a determining factor in a certain stage of the country's growth in terms of replacing - and saving - inadequate private initiatives in strategic activities such as energy, steel, public services, etc.

incorporating it into the production lines, though the family feud was to go on for decades. The case is interesting for another reason as well: in 1919, V.E. Marzotto chose to return to the legal form of individual firm rather than continue as a limited company. The former in fact made it easier to simplify and control management, while fiscal laws imposed fewer budget restrictions. The case did not remain an isolated one; despite an acceleration in the transformation process to limited companies in the early 20th century, because of these kinds of advantages quite a few firms in the sample preferred different forms to capital companies.

8.5. Between State and market

However uneven, information on supply and demand is present in all the files and makes it possible to highlight some common traits as well as important differences between sectors. In the first place it shows quite predictably that much of Italian industrial output was for the domestic market. Before the Second World War it was mainly in light industry that exports represented a significant outlet. Many textile and food companies had already started exporting before the First World War, as part of a growth process that began with the conquest and saturation of the local market and went on to expand nationally and then internationally, usually over the course of a few decades. Such behavior cannot, however, be taken as a model for all companies in the sector. A centuries-old firm like Nardini was to complete the process only in the 1970s whereas STAR, created after the Second World War, was able to break into the international market in little more than a decade. Instead, for the engineering sector, exporting gathered momentum especially after the Second World War, even if exceptions are not lacking - such as Riva, Franco Tosi and, in general, companies in the automobile sector, all present on the international scene since the beginning of the century. A prominent case was Ansaldo, already exporting warships to Spain, South America and the Far East by the end of the 19th century; it even set up a production unit in Constantinople in 1902, though with most disappointing results. On the whole, however, only about ten companies in our sample set up branches abroad, and only half of those pre-date the Second World War. The best known case is probably Pirelli, but among Italian multinationals some food firms are also worthy of note (Bertolli, Perugina, Buitoni, Campari) [Colli 2002b].

Business sources are unable to solve the vexed question of the role played by customs protection for Italian industry [Federico and Tena 1998, 1999; Federico and O'Rourke 2000]. The file does include a question on protectionism, but defining the latter varies too much for the answers to be really useful. It does however confirm the high protection given to sugar and, to a lesser extent, steel. On the contrary, the files provide plenty of information on the nature of the domestic market. Differences between sectors emerge quite clearly in the type of demand (public or private), its level of concentration and the degree of regulation present. In many cases - textiles, food, printing and publishing, and in the areas of light engineering, pharmaceutics and fine chemicals - the market was prevalently competitive, public demand of relatively little importance and regulation non-existent, or almost. Naturally, like all rules, this also has its exceptions. Some firms achieved a dominant position, in tanning (Gilardini), ceramics (Ginori), textiles/clothing (Borsalino), food (Birra Peroni and in the inter-War period UNICA for plain chocolate and its low quality derivatives for mass consumption), in light engineering (RIV for ball bearings and BOA for flexible metal tubes). Magneti Marelli specialized in the production of small electric engines, exploiting a niche of the market that enabled it to gain a dominant place in Italy and to compete internationally even before the First World War.

Supplying the military represented an important source of demand for some textile firms, especially wool manufacturers like Rossi, Pontoglio and Bonucci, as well as food producers such as UNICA and Peroni, and not only during the two World Wars and dictatorship years. Public commissions are cited by four fifths of the files for mechanical engineering firms, including some from light engineering such as Officine Bosco, DB, and De Pretto-Escher. Unfortunately none of the works examined contain precise data on the quota of public demand (or exports).

Lastly, some attempts at creating cartel agreements are noted. Already in 1904 the leading sugar companies, headed by Eridania and Ligure Lombarda, joined together to form the Unione Zuccheri, with the aim of setting and maintaining prices at the maximum level for production throughout the country. Renewed several times under different guises, the cartel agreements lasted till the 1960s, even though the Unione Zuccheri attempted to break them up between 1955 and 1957, causing a short-lived lowering of prices. In fact the proposals made by Giovanni Buitoni, director of Perugina, to set up a consortium for the supply of cocoa fell on deaf ears, as did the attempt later to rationalize production and distribution, which was supported by Riccardo Gualino with the creation of UNICA, the National Union of chocolate and its derivatives industry. Despite his success in managing various firms in Turin and Milan for several years, he first came up against determined resistance from Perugina and then left the scene completely, having fallen foul of the regime.

Understandably, the situation was different in the steel and building industries, chemicals, rubber, cement and the car industry too (not to mention public services such as energy and telephone companies, which were local scale monopolies almost by definition, right up to the 1990s). Before the Second World War the car market had been dominated by FIAT, despite the presence of companies like Alfa and Lancia, which stood out above all in specialized lines. Firms like Breda, Pirelli, Montecatini, Magona, the Cantieri Riuniti dell'Adriatico and, after the War, the Nuovo Pignone all enjoyed monopoly or oligopoly status in their sectors. They were thus in a powerful position with respect to their potential suppliers, such as RIV (ball bearings), BOA (flexible tubes) and Walser-Cromadora (non-ferrous alloy products) and Valentinigomma (car mats and other rubber products). The heavy sectors were characterized by a particularly high quota of public demand (the case of Ansaldo springs to mind) in an industrial policy climate that gave the creation of a strong military and industrial complex a decisive role in modernizing the economy [Federico and Giannetti 1999].

To conclude, the many (more or less successful) attempts to create voluntary consortia should be remembered - particularly between the two World Wars - from the steel producers' famed attempt in 1911, to the lesser known one by the Vetrerie e Cristallerie Riunite - including the Vetrerie Bormioli at the turn of the century - or the cartel of flexible metal tube producers formed in 1935 on the initiative of Rodolfo De Benedetti. As we know, consortia became obligatory from 1936 onwards. The level of inside competition certainly increased in the postwar period, due partly to the freeing of international trade (think of the automobile case) and partly to entry into the market of inside competitors.

8.6. Diversification or core business?

The type-file only distinguishes production diversification from real sectoral diversification and the information gathered on this aspect is the most complete and comprehensive of all. In fact almost all the works consulted describe, sometimes in fine detail, the growth strategies and above all financial operations (mergers, takeovers, etc.) of the businesses. The latter are well documented on the basis of archive sources. On the other hand, it is not easy to interpret the distinction in concrete cases. The concept of industrial sector is by nature ambiguous and hard to define [Sutton 1998]. Besides, in the long-term sectoral boundaries have been modified not only for changes in the goods component but, above all, for the evolution of technology peculiar to the individual sector (that is its degree of technological similarity or replaceability). It is no coincidence that international classifications of economic activity have been altered again and again over the last few decades.

Despite the abovementioned limitations, the information received makes it possible to draw some fairly neat conclusions. Very few firms are defined as single-product makers. These can be found more in services - the telephone rather than the electricity sector - and to a lesser degree in light industry. Among single-product firms we can point out three particularly successful cases, still in operation today: Frette (linen), Cucirini Cantoni Coats, and in the steel sector Magona d'Italia (cladded sheet metal). The overwhelming majority of manufacturing firms produced goods that varied from one another too much to be classified as multi-products. It may have been a way of keeping factories busy and exploiting any possibilities for expansion. In a large number of factories in the Lecco area Giuseppe Redaelli & Fratello produced both steel - specializing in high carbon content after the War - and second-stage metallurgical products, special cables (for elevators, cable cars, etc.), springs, thin wire cables, wheel spokes, and in the Dervio factory wire-drawing and carding machines, and various other machines. These products imply sectoral diversification according to two-digit ATECO-ISTAT classification.

The case of Redaelli - also a medium-sized company but one that would burgeon to a work force of several thousands after the Second World War - is quite typical of the behavior of steel and engineering firms (the latter especially after the

First World War). In fact such enterprises diversified either towards machine products, like Redaelli, or towards steel-producing. This strategy was adopted by about half the steel companies and by a consistent minority (from a third to a quarter) of engineering (before 1940), chemical and energy-producing companies[12].

The most spectacular success is that of FIAT. From the very beginning it diversified both by taking over various companies (from foundries to machine tool producers) and by involving itself in direct distribution. From 1906 it began to expand its output towards other engineering sectors such as shipbuilding and submarine production (FIAT San Giorgio, Cantieri di Muggiano), and the construction of aircraft engines (SIA, from 1907), in order to exploit technological sphere economies. Then, in the 1920s, with the setting up of SAVA to finance sales and the acquisition of La Stampa newspaper, the lines of inter-sectoral diversification by the great Turin-based group were largely drawn up.

A similar strategy was pursued by Ansaldo, but far more aggressively and over a shorter time frame. Starting life as a shipyard, Ansaldo went on to diversify towards other products of heavy industry in one direction, and in the other towards steel-production, mining and electricity interests, as well as marine transport. As we know, the results were disastrous and the dream of creating a kind of Italian *zaibatsu* led to the group's demise [Pavese 2003].

Sectoral diversification seems to have been negligible in the traditional sectors of the food, textile and paper/printing industries, though in the latter, the publishing houses in the sample, as well as book-printing, had distribution (Laterza, Olschki) or paper-making (Mondadori) interests. An exception to the rule is the aggressive diversification strategy of Motta after the Second World War. Beginning in the late 1940s, the strategy was purposefully pursued in the 1960s with the launching under license of Schweppes and Heineken drinks, the opening of carton-making factories, five poultry farms for the supply of fresh eggs, various commercial enterprises (including the famous service area of Cantagallo on the Bologna-Florence motorway), and the management of self-service restaurants and hotels. Debts piled up and the market results were modest, partly due to increased competition from abroad following the removal of protective barriers. In spite of an attempt to re-structure the company in the latter 1960s, Motta was finally taken over by SME, the state-owned group.

On the whole, therefore, sectoral diversifications prove to have been fairly widespread among the companies in the sample, but as a minor interest. It is important to stress that, exceptions apart, diversifying seems to have been a fairly natural consequence of business growth. Sorties into apparently distant sectors can almost always be explained by the envisaged need to guarantee the supply of raw materials, widen the scope for one's own products or reduce transaction costs by internalizing them, and so on. Steel firms bought mines, Ansaldo bought navigation lines, engineering firms (like FIAT) or food-producers (like Motta) expanded towards widespread distribution, while other food firms (like Buitoni and Perugina, or Motta again) bought carton-making firms to package their own prod-

[12] These figures exclude investments of a purely financial nature without any management responsibilities.

ucts. Lastly, at least two (Gaetano Marzotto and Montecatini) built private railroads to link their factories to the main lines. The most frequent objective for this kind of diversification in (only apparently) unrelated sectors was, however, the production of electric energy.

Many companies built electric power stations to meet the needs of their factories, selling on the market any excess kilowatts (as in the case of Moto Guzzi, the Venetian metallurgical company Beltrame or the Cazzola wool company). Franco Tosi built and for a decade personally managed the thermo-electric plant of Rome's municipal company. It was no accident, therefore, that diversification almost always took place through the development of new production lines inside the firm, on the German model [Kocka and Dornseifer 1993], rather than through mergers and takeovers on the Anglo-Saxon model. The most important exceptions lie in the sugar industry and, above all, Montecatini, which started off as a mining industry and went on to become the most important chemical concern in the country, taking over other, long-established firms.

Finally, there are some diametrically opposed cases to consider, either concentrating on the core business or making a clean break from it. For example, after the First World War the Vicenza firm, Beltrame, changed from a machine-making plant with annexed foundry to a steel and iron works with annexed workshop. In the early 20th century the Orobia company (which ever since its foundation had gravitated in the Edison orbit), as well as producing and distributing electric energy, was responsible not only for the Lecco city gas service and drinking water plant for the town of Montavecchia, but also for a lime kiln and zinc mine in Val Brembana. In 1913, these last two activities were ceded to the Austro-Belgian Company, and as a result of re-structuring in 1925 the gas and drinking water activities were also ceded, while Orobia devoted itself exclusively (with the help of control companies) to the production and distribution of electricity, mainly in the provinces of Bergamo and Lecco. Better known, perhaps, but certainly more complicated was the case of SNIA from Gualino that in the course of a few years abandoned its original navigation and trans-oceanic transport sector to concentrate on the production of artificial fibers, only to make another great change of direction in the early 1950s.

8.7. Market and commercial policies

A comprehensive evaluation of business strategies is no easy task, partly because this theme has attracted less attention among historians than other subjects treated so far. It is clear that the strategy depended on the market structure. In sectors with a mainly public demand lobbying was essential, as Vincenzo Stefano Breda proved with pioneering skill when he won state commissions at the time Terni was founded, or the Cosulich family's professional style during Fascism, with the transfer of a young Cosulich, the lawyer Antonio Nicolò, to Rome with the express aim of establishing privileged relations with the regime.

The most interesting business strategies can be found in the production of consumer goods. Many food-producing firms began their expansion into foreign markets by supplying the colonies of Italian emigrants. This was the case, for example, with Bertolli, that exported olive oil and pecorino cheese, Buitoni (pasta), Gancia (sparkling wine), Costante Villani (ham and salame), Peroni (beer), Campari (spirits), Perugina (confectionery), Ferrarelle (mineral water) and Galbani (cheese), though the last four soon started to reach a wider public than the one represented by emigrants alone. More generally speaking, a basic discrimination is the distinction between firms aiming at quality and those opting for quantity. In the food sector, for instance, the firms in the sample were divided equally for having adopted one policy rather than the other, at least during the launching and early growth period. It was above all in quality-choosing firms that aggressive sales strategies were put into action in order to win lucrative niches in the market. For example, to stay with the food sector, the launching of *Luisa* bitter chocolate bars in 1919 and *Bacio* in 1922, with increasingly recognizable branding techniques by Perugina; and participation in Exhibitions both at home and abroad in the launching stage of a product by firms dating back to the 19th century, such as Buitoni and the Fratelli Gancia. The latter, who had also long enjoyed the prestige of acting "by appointment to the Royal House", in 1932 promoted the Asti Spumante Protection Consortium to prove their consolidated high-quality policy, at competitive prices compared with French champagne, but more expensive than the rest of Italian producers. The firm was also quick to avail itself of a well organized sales network: traveling salesmen, exclusive agents and retailer contacts. Campari's success can also be said to have had a lot to do with its skill in building up an efficient sales network, especially abroad. Aggressive advertising policies were also the key to growth after the Second World War by such firms as STAR, Birra Peroni and Motta. For example, Motta, which even before the War had entrusted its image to the care of Dino Villani, a highly valued advertising expert and designer, by the mid-1950s was contributing to over 7 per cent of the total amount of advertising expenses incurred in Italy. But the most sensational case was that of the prize picture-card collection with Perugina and Buitoni products, "the greatest advertising success in the history of Italian industry" [Gallo 1990: 26], though in the end the Finance Ministry, afraid of an unjustified increase in consumer spending out of line with national objectives, suspended the competition (obliging the firm to pay out over 6 million prizes).

In the textile sector, too, we can find a mix between firms which, at least to begin with, aimed at quantity, launching on the market medium or low-quality products for mass consumption (Rossi, Gaetano Marzotto, F.lli Mazzonis, Conte, Cazzola, Ferrarin, and even Loro Piana) and firms that opted for pure quality, like V.E. Marzotto, Visconti di Modrone and Frette, or which reverted to it after the Second World War (G. Marzotto, Loro Piana), when quality seems to have been the only winning strategy for growth in an increasingly competitive market. A telling example was that of Frette, the Monza firm of household linen and cotton goods which, in keeping with its French origins, concentrated its business strategy on high-quality niche markets right from the start. As well as supplying luxury hotels at most advantageous prices (with the aim of attracting their upper class patrons), it organized distribution through its own shops and elegant postal sales catalogues. A different ploy obviously worked for S.A. Ferrarin, an average-sized wool producer, which took advantage of the aviation exploits of a family member - as well as president of the firm - before his premature death during a test flight: Arturo Ferrarin, pioneer and acrobat of Italian aeronautics, performer of the famous Rome-Tokyo raid (1920) and later world record holder for flight time and distance. As well as the reflected image and advertising opportunities his fame procured for the company, Arturo Ferrarin also attempted to take advantage of his exploits in the Far East to open up the promising Japanese market for his firm (and Italian textiles in general).

Sports competitions were quite naturally an important means of advertising for car manufacturers, especially for those aiming at up-market sales. After FIAT, Isotta Fraschini also became so involved with racing that in 1906 it began building a special sports car for professional drivers. It also started sending its cars to major automobile shows abroad, procured agents in Germany, Holland, Belgium, France, Great Britain and Portugal, and set up activities with a large number of other companies with the aim of enlarging its clientele. Alfa Romeo, too, obtained remarkable prestige from sports competitions, especially after its return to racing in 1919, which required big investments in planning and manufacturing specially high-powered cars. In the case of Lancia, on the contrary, involvement in the sector only goes back to 1951 and notwithstanding initial successes it very soon came to an end on account of technical and financial difficulties.

Lastly, in the chemical sector a couple of examples of commercial strategies bear mention, relating to two firms at opposite ends of the production scale. The first refers to Montecatini in the 1920s and 1930s, and in particular to its commercial policy in the fertilizer sector. Guido Donegani set himself the ambitions aim of tripling the consumption of super-phosphates (without lowering prices) and to this end he organized a vast advertising campaign which included using the new means of communication: cinema. Fratelli Maimeri, a small Milanese firm producing art colors, managed to make a name for itself on a market dominated by German companies, co-opting as partner a Florentine trader who was already representing its products in Florence, the city whose unique role as capital of art made it one of the major consumers of art colors. Then, after the Second World War the Fratelli Maimeri attempted to expand into the mass market but without much success, so they reverted to the specialist art colors sector, targeting amateurs more than professionals, and from the 1970s also started exporting.

8.8. Internal organization

According to Chandler [1962, 1977], the adoption of organizational innovations such as the *U-form* (multifunctional, centralized form) or the *M-form* (multidivisional, decentralized form) has been an almost indispensable factor in the success of the great American corporations. Outside the United States such innovations came relatively late and were far more limited, but nowhere has tardiness in introducing them been more obvious than in Italy [Pavan 1976; Hannah 1976, 1991; Nye 1987; Chandler 1990; Kocka and Dornseifer 1993; Cassis 1997]. In the vast majority of firms in the sample the organizational structure remained minimal and mono-functional at least up to the Second World War. Firms were on the whole managed by a single entrepreneur, sometimes assisted by one or two managers (often members of his own family) together with some office staff (accountants in particular). This was the case in all the traditional sectors - textile, food, publishing - but also in many family-run businesses in new areas such as mechanical engineering, chemicals and pharmaceutics.

The files only provide information on organizational structures for roughly a third of the firms, but the gaps almost all concern small businesses, where it seems highly unlikely that complex structures could have been adopted. To a large extent these were long the prerogative of a few big firms in advanced sectors like electronics, mechanical engineering and steel. Edison was probably the first to adopt the *U-form* in Italy, back in 1899, and during the First World War it was already being used in firms like FIAT and Lancia in the automobile industry, Ansaldo in mechanical engineering, ILVA, Terni and Magona in steel and Montecatini and Pirelli in chemicals. In the inter-war period the *U-form* became further entrenched and was also adopted by firms in the chemical/pharmaceutical sector (Monte Amiata, Bracco and Recordati), large scale distribution (Rinascente), food (Peroni), textiles (G. Marzotto & Figli, but with poor results), and again in the mechanical engineering sector (De Pretto-Escher, A. Pellizzari). Finally, after the Second World War it seems to have spread to most of the firms that gave relevant information (for example, Loro Piana in textiles; Ceccato, Nuovo Pignone, Franco Tosi and Breda in mechanical engineering; STAR, Buitoni and Perugina in the food sector).

It took much longer to adopt the multi-divisional form, which the literature considers more useful to the growth of big business. Martinoli [1971] and Pavan [1976] authoritatively claim that it was not introduced before the 1960s and then only by a few large firms. In actual fact, there were some pioneers in the 1920s among the telephone companies. From 1926, the year after it was founded, STIPEL had its own network, soon to number over a hundred thousand subscribers in eleven locations. Nine of these, the smallest ones, were functionally dependent on the headquarters in Turin, but the branches in Turin and Milan with the highest number of subscribers were organized separately and allowed a great deal of autonomy. In the 1930s STIPEL was followed by two other telephone companies operating in the IRI ambit (TELVE and TIMO) and by TETI (Società Telefonica Tirrena)[13]. On the initiative of Pietro Sette, the multi-divisional structure was adopted by Terni, in 1958. The firm was divided into nine autonomous sections

[13] See for the structure of the single concessionaires - STIPEL, TELVE and TIMO - "it was close to being a multi-sector holding, with the sectors replaced by the concession areas ... it was an expansion of the service ... that justified a functional organization - also at the level of the divisional structures - by geographical area corresponding to the three concessions" [Bottiglieri 1990: 241-242].

but the results could not be fully evaluated[14]. Sette's directorship only lasted three years and the ensuing nationalization of the electricity sector rapidly changed the frame of reference to be used for tackling company problems. In the next two decades, however, many other firms, such as Mondadori, Buitoni-Perugina, SNIA Viscosa, Recordati, Welser-Cromadora, FIAT, Nuovo Pignone and Rinascente, imitated these pioneers, adopting a multi-divisional form of organization.

As in the case of ownership already discussed, likewise in their internal organization, Italian firms (like others in Europe) have experimented with alternative forms of co-ordination, such as the group or the *industrial district*. The group choice is typical of many big business enterprises, which have allowed the firms under their control a certain autonomy, in some cases taking on the connotation of a financial holding. As far back as 1890, Edison started to participate in other, smaller electric companies for which it had built plants, and by the turn of the century it had created an impressive network of strategic presences in the Società Monzese di Elettricità, in the Società per Imprese Elettriche Conti, in the Società per le Forze Idrauliche Benigno Crespi and in the Società per la Distribuzione di Energia Elettrica Ing. Banfi, as well as other minor ones. Such acquisitions entered into a strategy of indirect expansion that would lead Edison, right up to the eve of the First World War, to concentrate more on distribution than production monopolies, making sure that the Milanese market enjoyed a ready supply of energy produced by the companies it was involved in. Between the Wars Edison was to assume the role of a financial holding with respect to "its planetary system of connected companies" [Pavese 1986: 166].

From the 1910s, as amply documented elsewhere in this volume, strategies like purchasing quotas in other companies, inter-connecting, and creating satellite companies became quite common practice among Italian companies, especially in utilities. In the inter-War period practically all the electric and telephone companies in the sample belonged to a group, while the percentage falls to about a third for the other, heavy sectors (mechanical engineering, steel, chemicals) and becomes insignificant in the traditional sectors, where firms tended to be smaller and have less market power (exceptions include Perugina, Buitoni and Bertolli in the food sector, and Marzotto in textiles). The groups were composed of an extremely varied number of firms. The biggest ones, created around the First World War (for

[14] "The sections were to be likened to single production organisms, all to be measured for profits and losses, as well as for the comparative costs of goods and services exchanged between them. Each section was expected to produce a proper annual balance sheet, and Terni's took on the appearance of a consolidated one for the single sections. The greatest merit of this attempt at reform lay in an admirable effort to use more clarity in ascertaining the economic results of the various sectors and establishments. The aim of the experiment was to apply the methodology necessary to show what was implied in the transfer of turnover from the electric branch to the other branches of activity ... it also demonstrated that the '1920s style' organization of a company had lost credibility. The reform involved moving personnel, applying new administrative procedures, re-organizing the service and introducing a whole new methodology in accounting, evaluating economic results and defining the amortization quota" [Bonelli 1975: 282-283].

example Ansaldo, Montecatini, FIAT, Italcementi and Edison) included dozens of companies, sometimes involved in such diversified activities that they look like conglomerate enterprises. On the other side, many groups were formed by a mere handful of companies. In 1923 Mazzucchelli, a chemical concern, founded the celluloid company and in the 1930s Caolino Panciera & C. was joined by Valdol, a company authorized to extract bentonite in the Valle dell'Agno. In a fair number of cases formally autonomous enterprises acted as divisions of the group leader, often specialized by geographical area (as happened with the electric industries) or by kind of activity. For example - and again with reference to Edison - when in 1919 Giacinto Motta embarked on a radical restructuring of the firm's organization and management, he separated the tramline side of activities and sold it to a specially formed company, obviously controlled by the group leader, the Società Trazione Elettrica Lombarda.

The literature we used is of little help, however in analyzing the other potential *alternative* form of organization, the *industrial district*. The typical firm in a *district* is in fact too small and too young to be the object of a business history, especially of the celebratory kind. But there are a few exceptions, especially among small textile firms, wool manufacturers in particular, with the Schio-Valdagno-Thiene area in Venetia and Valsesia in Piedmont, and light engineering in the lower Vicenza-Padua valley, as well as areas around Reggio-Emilia and Lecco.

8.9. Innovative activities

The information gathered on the behavior of the firms analyzed where innovative and research capacities are concerned is also incomplete and often inconsistent. Although only seven cases in the sample gave no information at all, even the information given by the others does not always allow an adequate reconstruction of the innovative dynamics of the individual firms. What does seem to be largely confirmed, however, is the now consolidated image of an Italian industry seldom at the cutting edge of technology and heavily dependent on technology imported from abroad, yet able in case of need to adapt innovations to the requirements of a particular market like ours[15].

On the other hand, several of the works consulted report significant innovative activities - often with autonomous structures - in the mechanical engineering and chemical sectors in particular. The most important case is Montecatini. Stimulated by the purchase of the Fauser patent for the production of ammonia, in 1934 Montecatini set up an organic chemistry research laboratory at Cesano Maderno. In 1936 it helped to found Istituto per lo Studio dei Metalli Leggeri (ISML), and between 1939 and 1941 it devoted most of its R&D activity to the new Istituto Scientifico per Ricerche e Sperimentazioni Chimiche (later Istituto Donegani). These institutes enjoyed considerable exemption from the short-term needs of produc-

[15] For further development of these themes see in particular Giannetti [1998, 1999] and Vasta [1999a, 1999b].

tion, and from this point of view Montecatini represents an exception in the pre-war period. In the majority of cases, in fact, before the Second World War most R&D had been carried out in laboratories and variously named technical departments, consisting largely of assorted teams of technicians and planning engineers. For example at Alfa Romeo a planning office had come into being in 1910, directed by Giuseppe Merisi, while at FIAT the planning function (known as studies and tests) had been separated from real production since 1905, but kept subservient to it. This state of affairs was to remain practically unchanged till after the Second World War, when all study, research and testing activities were placed under the control of the Study and Reseach Committee. In the case of Riva-Calzoni, the separate turbine and pump planning sections were joined together in a technical department in 1935. Again during the inter-War period, S.A. Pignone, equipped itself with a study and planning department specializing above all in the design and manufacture of armaments, but it was only after two changes of ownership and transfer to ENI that it succeeded in developing its own research laboratories, formally independent of the other company structures and directly responsible to the company president. In the late 1940s Moto Guzzi concentrated all its planning activities on an autonomous Study Centre at Mandello Lario and, in 1950, provided itself among other things with a wind tunnel for high speed aerodynamic tests, until that time the reserve of an elite group of automobile companies. Wide scope for innovation was also given in the organizational restructuring started in the 1920s by the Cosulich in the Monfalcone shipbuilding yard at Triest, especially when some highly qualified, dynamic young engineers were put in charge of the technical department. Despite the lack of a section devoted specifically to R&D, the leap in quality was beyond doubt: innovations in procedure and production came in swift succession.

On the whole, the same can be said where chemicals were concerned (with the abovementioned exception of Montecatini). A particularly meaningful case was that of Bracco. Like many firms it started by importing technology from more developed countries, by means of concessions and patent purchases. Founded in 1927 as the Società Italiana Prodotti Merck, its aim was the manufacture, packaging and sale of chemical and similar products belonging to the German firm. In 1936 the company changed its name to S.A. Bracco and in 1939 produced its first original product, *Novotrans*, an anti-coagulant for transfusions. In the post-Second World War period there were notable investments in research, including the foundation of the Institute for Research and Testing (with headquarters at Schaffausen in Switzerland). Concentrating mainly on production, Bracco swiftly made its mark on the Latin-American market too, developing on its own or in collaboration with Merck and Cilag a vast range of new medicines.

In the mechanical engineering sector a similar story is that of Franco Tosi. It had started out with various kinds of activities ranging from repair and construction of machine frames to the sale of English farm machines and steam engines. Around 1890 it specialized in the production of boilers and steam engines, importing machinery not only from Europe but also from the United States (a choice clearly inspired by a standardization strategy, quite new for the time). In more or less the same period, it began to design and produce machinery and engines for the electric industry. In the early years of the 20th century Tosi was among the first in Europe to develop steam turbines to generate electricity as well as diesel engines for marine propulsion. Even more significant, perhaps, was the case of the Pisan CMASA (Costruzioni Meccaniche Aeronautiche S.A.). The initial technology came largely from the German designer Claude Dornier, owner and director from 1914 of Dornier Metallbauten of Manzell which produced airplanes and hydro-planes. After the Treaty of Versailles Dornier sought opportunities to pursue the firm's activities abroad, contributing studies, plans and patents to the new Italian company created in 1921; and from Germany, too, came materials and machinery, some proto-types, together with many managers, technicians and skilled workers. In the 1920s and 1930s the factory at Pisa functioned as an experimental centre for engines, hulls, etc., also for the German company. In the early 1930s a new kind of hydro-plane (mod. F4), fitted with FIAT engines and responding to the particular requirements of the Marine Industry, was studied independently as well as another, commercially unsuccessful one, intended for civilian uses (mod. F5). From 1934 onwards the FIAT connection became so close that the following year CMASA's Technical Department moved permanently to Turin to enhance co-ordination between chassis and engine design. In the post-war period, having become by now the Marina di Pisa Workshop Section of the Turin-based company, it embarked on a remarkable expansion of output devoted above all to sheet-steel working for the large-scale construction of automobile accessories, characterized by an ever-increasing degree of mechanization.

Finally, it should be noticed that several important examples of original technologies are to be found among the cases analyzed in the questionnaire, both for product and process, even in the more traditional food industry. Campari's success both at home and abroad was due first of all to its creation of an innovative product with an alluring taste: *Bitter Campari*. The Fratelli Gancia also broke free of the restricted local market when they succeeded (through a continuous process of learning by doing) in developing an original method of preparing Italian *Spumante* and, successively, brought notable improvements to the production process of *Vermouth*, too. Nardini managed to impose on the domestic market a drink as humble as grappa when it successfully experimented with aging the product in durmast oak barrels. Finally, Buitoni's success can be largely attributed to the launch of gluten *pastina*, Galbani's to *Robbiola* (1881), and *Bel Paese* (1906), and Motta's to a series of oven-baked products (from *Panettone* to *Buondì*), to *Mottarello*, but also to various foods produced on an American license. In the chemical field a small but solid Friuli firm, Amideria L. Chiozza, was created in 1865 and thrived as a result of a technological innovation - the extraction of starch from maize - the product of research and experimentation by a chemist friend and pupil of Pasteur, Luigi Chiozza[16], whose patent brought its inventor international fame and also contributed greatly to the industrial processing of maize in the United States. In the following decades the initial invention underwent continual improvements, particularly when rice replaced maize as the raw material to extract the starch

[16] Also teacher of industrial chemistry at the Scuola d'Incoraggiamento d'Arte e Mestieri in Milan, which he directed after the death of Alessandro Kramer.

from; then, early in the 20th century, the technology became fixed and the firm from Perteole went on producing starch with techniques that remained virtually unchanged.

There are a variety of examples to be found in mechanical engineering, too, and taken as a whole this sector of production is definitely the most dynamic in the entire national system. For example, a medium-sized firm like Savara of Turin, created in 1924 as an accessory-selling company, almost immediately started producing its own patents for the manufacturing of accessories and spare parts. After a new type of friction-regulated shock absorbers and a new type of pantographic car jack in 1934 it added a third innovation, a self-cleaning blade filter, and in 1937 a diaphragm type petrol pump (commissioned by FIAT). Innovations continued after the War with the creation of new products: regulating valves in heating circuits, industrial filters for marine engines and above all, from the 1960s onwards, dilating thermostats of waxy pastes continually being improved and ordered in great series by FIAT. The Italian flexible-tube company (BOA-Flexider), created in the 1920s to exploit German patents for the production of flexible tubes, already by 1930 was able to produce an independent patent that represented a real novelty in petrol conduction: a flexible metal tube formed by a small-pitch spiral, which included a ducted fan made of a cellulose derivative, impervious to petrol or other liquids, crossed by transverse channels that made it extendable, as well as a superimposed rubber covering. Flexible tubes like this resolved once and for all the problem of channeling oil, petrol and water and the related patent was quickly extended to most countries in Europe, opening the way to a joint venture with American partners for production in the United States. Other important innovations followed in the 1950s and 1960s, including the revolutionary one of substituting vulcanized rubber in the tubes with a new material heat-resistant even to temperatures beyond 200 degrees, teflon, for the production of which Flexider obtained an exclusive license for Italy. Finally, a dynamic company like Campagnolo of Vicenza was able to develop from an ironmonger's workshop to an avant-garde bicycle manufacturer thanks to the intuition and perseverance of Tullio Campagnolo, an ex-racer who for twenty years experimented with components capable of improving the performance and agility of bicycles. Through a series of improvements, in 1946 he produced the prototype of the famous parallelogram speed gear bicycle which immediately revealed itself a winning weapon in bicycle races and sanctioned the Campagnolo company's definite affirmation on the market at home and abroad. In the meanwhile, the Vicenza firm's range increased to other products and components (wheel hubs, light alloy wheels, brakes) which now interested the motor-cycle and automobile industry: Lamborghini, Maserati, Harley Davidson and other prestigious makes thus became Campagnolo company customers, and the firm was able to put out a long series of patents (over 200) in the course of a few decades.

Notice how the examples presented so far refer to a wide variety of sectors, but not to textiles or steel. In these cases business growth passed essentially through the importing and imitation of processes and machinery technologies from abroad. The expansion of productive capacity, in fact, came about primarily through the purchase of new machinery or production lines, often not in substitution but simply in addition to the pre-existing structures[17].

8.10. Labor and human capital

The replies to the questions on this specific point are incomplete and poor in detail[18], but they do reveal a great deal about the Italian situation. Once again the general picture differs little from the one already afforded by economic and social historiography, and it also follows the canons of development in other latecomer countries. Even up to the 1950s almost the entire labor force in the traditional sectors - textile, food, glass, cement, metallurgy - was unqualified and the situation was not much different in newer sectors (chemicals, rubber, heavy engineering). In these cases tradition required meeting the needs for qualified workers through the employment of foreign technicians, whose duties also included instructing the locals. This practice, widely used in Lombard textiles from the mid-19th century was taken up in the closing decades by Pirelli, for example, and in the inter-war years by CMASA, when a few dozen technicians and office staff were taken on from the Dornier Metallbauten before a homegrown training school was inaugurated just before the Second World War.

The presence of a qualified labor force was instead conspicuous in the car industry (FIAT in the lead, at least until the adoption of assembly lines), as well as in the electric and electro-mechanical, telephone and engineering sectors. Often such labor was, at least partly, trained within the firm itself. At Franco Tosi there had been an in-plant school for apprentices with evening and holiday courses as far back as the 1880s, though with no particular professional direction until, in 1939, it was transformed into a course for skilled workers. At FIAT, in the early years of the 20th century the division of work was minimal, so that one of the basic problems in the firm's early life had been to form a squad of skilled workers with the technical know-how to intervene and to solve problems in the various phases of a hitherto un-standardized working process and in whichever areas they occurred. From these specialized workers - the original nucleus in FIAT having been created by mechanics in the late 19th century ex-government workshops - came the middle-ranking staff, workshop foremen responsible not only for overseeing but also for organizing the work inside the department, and thus becoming key figures in the production process. As we will see further on, from the early 1920s, with the changes in the terms of production, the task of training these workers would be performed by FIAT's own training school. At Magneti Marelli professional training courses were in place from 1924 and later became a fully fledged business school. However, from the 1950s, with the unstoppable spread of

[17] The only exception worth noting is the raw silk industry, where Italy was an absolute leader technologically from the mid-19th century to the Second World War [Federico 1994a], though no firm from the sector is represented in the sample.

[18] No less than 38 files contain no information at all relating to this field.

mechanization and adoption of automation processes, in certain lines of production labor became prevalently female and unqualified. After the Second World War, on the contrary, the setting up of business schools became quite a common feature in the engineering industry and involved, as well as the cases already recorded, large numbers of machine manufacturers: Tecnomasio, Nuovo Pignone, Riva-Calzoni, Guzzi, RIV, Motofides and Zanussi.

In other cases training was entrusted to outside institutes, sometimes financed by the firms themselves. Since 1888 De Pretto, a Venetian machine making firm, had promoted and financed the creation of an evening school for geometric design applied to machines. Half a century later, a similar initiative was started at Montecchio Maggiore by Ceccato, and Laverda and Pellizzari were important supporters of the Rossi technical institute in Vicenza and the technical school annexed to it, where the qualified work force employed there was trained. In the post-Second World War period Laverda founded the Giulio Laverda training school at Breganze. Initiatives like these produced spillover effects of expertise in the area, typical of country districts. As regards the telephone sector, however, the need to find qualified staff existed from the 1930s, for example in the STET group, which was already involved in activities to ensure there would be an adequate supply of specialized technicians, who represented a vital force for the development of the service. From 1937 training and specialization courses multiplied, usually run by STIPEL. The specialist staff needed in the three companies - STIPEL, TELVE and TIMO - were then selected from among the pupils at these courses. In 1940 STET asked the Istituto Tecnico Industriale of Turin to set up a specialist course in telephony, with the assistance of STIPEL technicians and practical experience in the workshop.

The picture is more uniform if we go on to consider the training of upper management and entrepreneurial forces. A good level of formal or applied training seems to have been an indispensable ingredient in the foundation and even more in the consolidation of successful enterprises. Many of the initiators of productive activities in new sectors, such as chemicals, electricity and the automobile were highly valued engineers or scientists (think of Giuseppe Colombo, Giacinto Motta or Ettore Conti in the electric industry, of Luigi Chiozza, Giovanni Battista Pirelli and Giuseppe Recordati in chemicals, of Nicola Romeo, Alberto Riva, Silvio De Pretto and Rodolfo De Benedetti in mechanics, of Ernesto Breda in the steel industry).

The founders of firms in the traditional sectors, such as textiles, were often without any qualifications, but they saw to it that their successors were provided with an adequate preparation, through degrees and diplomas, or at least with a long period of experience abroad. The latter appears to have been the way preferred by the Venetian textile industry. In the footsteps of Alessandro Rossi, many second generation representatives of Vicenza's middle-ranking entrepreneurs went for study tours and work experience abroad: Giuseppe Roi, Luigi Cazzola, Angelo Ferrrarin, Alvise Conti, Vittorio Emanuele Marzotto. In firms expanding from artisan status to a medium size, second generation managers or entrepreneurs received a technical education, often including an engineering degree. At Saccardo, on the founder's death in 1926, his son Girolamo, graduate in industrial engineering at the Zurich Polytechnic, took over the management. Bruno and Angelo Beltrame, the two sons of Antonio, founder of the Vicenza Steel and Ironworks, were engineers and industrial experts. Silvio Mazzucchelli, the managing director of the Società Italiana della Celluloide, was a graduate too, but the technical direction was entrusted to engineers. Giacomo Pellizzari - son of Antonio, founder of the Pellizzari engineering company - was a graduate at the abovementioned Rossi Institute and a highly valued technician. Antonio Laverda's sons were graduates, and an Agordo engineer was entrusted with the technical management of Caolino Panciera from 1908.

Obviously, the space reserved for staff with formal preparation and higher education generally increased with the size of the firm, the complexity of its organizational structure and need to keep up with technology. In the Study Departments of many big companies by the 1950s and 1960s there were already tens if not hundreds of technicians, specialists and graduates. And in general, though somewhat tardily, there was also a great enlargement in some firms' management hierarchies as well as close contact with Higher Education, universities and polytechnics. Montecatini, Pirelli, Edison, FIAT, Italcementi and STET are good examples of this trend, which was already in full operation between the two World Wars. FIAT is a perfect case, where the creation of the new factory at Lingotto - and above all the organization of production according to Taylorist criteria - brought about some important changes. It became necessary, in fact, to form a class of low and middle management, that is, people in charge of departments and offices for the technical and administrative working of the various business departments and sectors. From the last years of the First World War, FIAT took in a large number of engineers from the Politecnico of Turin. These were than given an apprenticeship period when they were expected to acquire the necessary technical and practical know-how and to become familiar with factory life. At the end of this time there was a strict selection for final admission to the firm. From 1922 onwards a growing role in this middle-management training was played by the FIAT Training School, structured as it was to provide specialized workers, experts and engineers by means of annual and two-year courses. The serialization of the car industry after the Second World War, with the setting up of the Mirafiori plant, was to lead to an explosion of managerial hierarchies in the 1950s and 1960s and the employment of thousands of middle to high ranking, highly trained staff in all the technical, legal and administrative sides of the business.

8.11. Business financing

Information on business strategy and financial sources obtained through the questionnaires is somewhat incomplete, but the theme has been amply discussed by economic historians, starting with the seminal work by Gerschenkron [1962]. They have concluded that the financial market did not represent an autonomous source of capital, even for businesses quoted on the stock exchange, except in exceptional cases, and this supposition is amply confirmed in the cases we examined. Very often increases in capital were attained in order to create security for bank loans, forming a kind of camouflaged bank financing, or were agreed on by shareholders to confirm or change the ownership. At Magneti Marelli for example, all increases in capital in the late 1940s were reserved for old share-holders (E. Marelli and FIAT in particular). At Isotta Fraschini, instead, as the result of a crisis the previous year, in 1909 the company's capital was first devalued and then revalued, and that occasion witnessed the substitution of the reference capitalists that is the French Lorraine-Dietrich, by a group of Milanese industrialists (Visconti di Modrone, Scheibler, Crespi, Gadda, etc.). The financial market has only become a real financing alternative for Italian firms in the last few decades, and always within obvious limits. Many firms, especially middle-sized and/or small operators in the traditional sectors, have financed investments with their profits, making use of bank credit only to finance current activities. This practice can be found for example in the history of the Cotonificio Caprotti up to 1914, in Cucirini Cantoni Coats, S.A. Benigno Crespi, Visconti di Modrone and Frette. Self-financing also proved decisive throughout the existence of the Mazzotto firm (first G. Marzotto & Figli, then V.E. Marzotto), up to its transformation/takeover in 1952 by the joint-stock G. Marzotto company.

In the food sector most businesses financed their own industrial *take-off*, relying above all on inner resources, as in the case of Gancia, Nardini, Peroni, Novi and Perugina. Here again the contribution made by bank credit to finance current activity became increasingly important as the businesses grew. Becoming limited companies then made it easier, of course, to approach the financial market, as happened with Perugina and Buitoni. Self-financing was widespread throughout Italian industry, however, even though it was not always as transparent as it could have been. For example, in the case of a middle-sized firm in the engineering sector, such as the abovementioned Isotta Fraschini, the remarkable expansion - in plants and market participation - in the years following the First World War was mainly financed through (war) profits[19]. Then, in its first ten years, Franco Tosi's self-financing of investments was made by re-investing profit well beyond the statutory limits, as well as through loans from family and friends in case of need. A big steel firm like Falck behaved in a similar manner, at least until the 1930s. In fact firms' financial policies "hinged on some fixed imperatives: resort to short-term profit, re-invest to finance real estate and avoid bank debts ..." [Pozzobon 1982: 192]. Even Edison, the most important firm in the electricity sector, at least up to the 1920s, partly financed expansion by re-investing its profits, drawn from hidden reserves created by shrewd accounting and made possible by the loopholes present in a permissive legislation where balance sheets were concerned [Toninelli 1990]. The Welser-Cromadora company, which ever since the 1930s had relied on bank credit to finance ongoing activities, still supported its own expansion financially throughout the 1950s. Not until the early 1960s, when it needed investment to restructure plants and rationalize its production cycle, did it turn to banks for medium and long-term loans. In many cases, however, above all in the heavy

[19] According to Confalonieri [1997: vol. 1, 12 and ff.] in 1918 an invoice for 32.7 million gave an official profit of 2.1 million and an unofficial profit of 7.8 million.

and/or so-called new sectors, self-financing was unable to provide sufficient resources. Businesses then resorted to bank loans to finance both production investments and possible acquisitions. Up to the 1920s, financing was done in current accounts, which were continually renewed and covered by shareholder drafts guaranteed by the bank or credit banks [Confalonieri 1976; Warglien 1987; Pavese and Toninelli 1988]. So, for example, the pool of banks headed by COMIT financed Edison's first important expansion at the turn of the century: the construction of the first hydro-electric plant to enter into operation in 1899 at Paderno d'Adda, and entry into the capital of newly formed electric companies operating in the Lombard area. Alfa Romeo - which up to the First World War had to rely mainly on its own resources or on borrowed capital, and which during the War was able to finance expansion thanks to large advances from the State - in the following years was able to rely increasingly on short-term debts, especially in current accounts - granted by Banca Italiana di Sconto. In 1921 Redaelli was among the biggest debtors of Credito Italiano for debts in current accounts, I.O.U.'s, drafts and guarantees. Until becoming a joint-stock company, Franch-Griffin (later Franchi Gregorini) relied on bank credit to expand, and even in the period of high profit excess in the War, self-financing remained a limited resource, a connotation that it shared with many of the steel and building industries in Italy.

Several firms also took advantage of state aid, by means of grants, subsidies, agreements and advances on commissions. This aid, becoming glaringly obvious in the latter 1920s with the creation of the Istituto di Liquidazione, later IMI and IRI, had in fact already taken on the appearance of a permanent structure in Italian industry, especially as regards the steel and building sectors, where ever since the 1880s their affirmation, considered crucial to the economic growth and security of the country, was able to count on state support, both directly and indirectly. During the First World War, however, public subsidies came to interest almost every sector of Italian industry, from food (Bertolli, Peroni) to textiles (Lanificio Conte, Fratelli Mazzonis, Crespi etc.), to engineering (Alfa Romeo, Laverda, FIAT, etc.), to electricity (Edison, SME, Bresciana, etc.), to chemicals (Montecatini, Pirelli, Mazzucchelli, etc.) and mining (Monte Amiata).

Bringing up the rear, foreign investment seems to have been less important in the first half of the 20th century, although it had made no small contribution previously to the creation of companies destined for lasting success, like Ansaldo, Magona and Edison. In fact firms that benefited from direct foreign investment were mainly ones that had in their corporate assets controlled quotas of foreign investors like Legler, Cucirini Cantoni Coats, Tubi Mannesmann, SME, Lips Vago and De Pretto-Escher Weiss. Instead, indirect portfolio investments only gathered momentum in the 1920s and tended to benefit larger firms such as SIP, FIAT, Edison and Montecatini. The latter, for example, in 1927 took out a bonded loan for 10 million dollars at 7 per cent with two big New York banks, Marshall Field Glore Ward and Guaranty Trust, and again with the help of the same banks increased its capital by 100 million. Simultaneously it was able to have itself placed on the Paris Stock Exchange. Of course the financing obtained at the turn of the 1950s through the European Recovery Program plan by various Italian firms, those especially benefiting, as we know, being firms in the steel and mechanical engineering sector, such as FIAT, Magneti Marelli and Breda.

8.12. Conclusions

The sample of firms considered in this Chap. confirms that in the Italian case there was an original way of forming business strategies where the stages traditionally considered by historiography are concerned: ownership, size and form of the market; opening to the international market, production and innovation strategies; internal organizational formulas; financing.

Italy stands out for the small number of public companies in comparison with the Anglo-Saxon model, a characteristic found in the firms taken into consideration. The most important exceptions from a historical perspective are Montecatini, Edison and Eridania, even if the last two, as more fully argued in the text, are to some extent *spurious* cases. Giant multinationals like FIAT or Pirelli, though quoted on the stock exchange, are still controlled or managed by one or more families, often with reduced capital quotas. The overwhelming majority of firms in the sample are family businesses, that is a firm where short and long-term decisions are made by the family, which owns the business entirely, or with a huge quota. All the firms in the traditional light sectors such as food (except sugar), textiles and publishing are of a family nature, irrespective of the legal form and stock exchange quotation.

Before the Great Crash of 1929-1933, the real alternative to family control was bank ownership, especially in heavy industry which called for an enormous amount of capital and deferred profit-making. In some cases, Terni and Edison for example, the firms were substantially bank owned right from the start. By the end of the 1920s, *mixed banks* found themselves owning a large chunk of Italian industry - especially in sectors such as steel, telephones, building. heavy engineering, and so on.

Business histories are of no help in answering the question of whether family businesses were more rationalized and efficient than corporate forms of business organization. In fact, historians sometimes stress the advantages of continuity, a solid corporate governance and greater facility in re-investing all a firm's profits; while in other cases they maintain that family control reduces the amount of resources available for long-term growth, capacity for innovation and potential to compete on the international market. Size and competitiveness in the Italian market are a crucial theme for Italian industry historians, as we can see in more detail in the Chap. devoted to them. The sample of firms highlights some interesting traits. In many cases - textiles, food, printing/publishing and sections of light engineering, pharmaceuticals and fine chemicals - the market seems mainly competitive, public demand of relatively little importance and regulations almost or entirely non-existent (though with some important exceptions, as we have seen). Lastly, some attempts to form cartel agreements have been noted. Predictably, the situation is different in the steel industry and building trade, in chemicals, rubber and cement, as well as in the automobile industry (not to mention public utilities like electric energy and telephone companies, which were monopolies till the 1990s). Up to the Second World War the automobile market was dominated by FIAT, despite the presence of firms like Alfa and Lancia, which distinguished themselves above all in the niche market. Firms like Breda, Pirelli, Montecatini, Magona, Cantieri Riuniti dell'Adriatico and after the War, Nuovo Pignone, enjoyed a status of monopoly or oligopoly in their sectors, while mention should also be made of the numerous (more or less successful) attempts to create voluntary consortia, especially in the inter-war period.

Sectoral diversification strategies are generally linked with forward or backward integration of production linked to the cycle of the main product. These strategies developed between the 1920s and the 1960s and affected the heavy industry sectors of shipbuilding (Ansaldo), steel (Ansaldo e Finsider), chemicals (Montecatini) and means of transport production (FIAT), being much the same as those observed in other countries. More interesting are the conclusions to be drawn from an observation of production strategies and related forms of innovation used in consumer goods production. Two characteristics emerge here, typical of Italian firms operating in these sectors: the ability to occupy market niches and successfully hold on to them by means of innovations in the product.

The comparatively smaller size of the domestic market and business enterprises is an obstacle to the adoption of efficient, well-structured organizations in many European countries, but perhaps in no other industrialized country is tardiness in organizational innovation so evident as it is in Italy. Multi-divisional organization only made an appearance in the late 1960s, when problems associated with it emerged even in the leader country, the United States. As regards internal organization, as in ownership, Italian (like other European) firms have experimented with alternative forms of coordination, such as groups or *industrial districts*. Starting with the first decade of the 20th century, as recorded elsewhere in this volume, quota purchases in other companies, interconnections and the creation of satellite companies are common expansion strategies in the Italian business world.

Backwardness and a simple lack of diffusion of modern organizational formulas are also reflected in the way Italian firms organize R&D activities and train management. In most cases, up to the end of the Second World War, R&D in firms took place mostly in laboratories and technical departments, which consisted substantially of technicians and planning engineers. The most important innovations, as for example, those of Fauser, of Giustiniani and Natta for Montecatini, are actually relatively isolated episodes of scientist inventors rather than the result of strategic initiatives taken by their employers. As far as management is concerned, a good level of education, both formal and applied, seems to have been indispensable for the founding or at least the consolidation of successful enterprises like Edison, Esterle, Motta and Pirelli, and many others when Italian industry was taking off in the age of Giolitti. On the contrary, a worsening in the preparation of managers is considered one of the causes of the decline of public and private enterprise in the 1970s and 1980s. The founders of firms in the traditional sectors, like textile, were often without any qualifications, but they saw to it that their successors received training through diploma courses or at least experience abroad.

Information on financial strategies and financial sources of firms gleaned from the questionnaires is patchy, but consistent with historians' observations, starting with Gerschenkron's seminal work. It emerges that the financial market does not represent an autonomous source of capital, even for the firms quoted on the stock exchange, except in exceptional cases. Very often increases in capital are produced to create security for bank loans, making a camouflaged type of bank financing, or they are agreed on among the shareholders to confirm or change the ownership.

The financial market has only become a real alternative for financing Italian firms over the last few decades and even then within obvious limits. Many firms, especially middle to small ones and/or operating in the traditional sectors, finance investments with their profits, resorting to bank credit only to finance current activities. Self-financing is, however, widespread throughout Italian industry, though not always in the most transparent of ways. In many cases, especially in the heavy and/or new sectors, self-financing is unable to provide adequate resources. In this case firms resort to bank credit to finance both production investments and any possible acquisitions. For example, up to the 1920s, current account financing was used, continually renewed and covered by share issues as security for the bank or credit banks. A fair number of firms have taken advantage of state aid, through grants, subsidies, agreements and advances on commissions.

To conclude, less importance seems to have been given in the first half of the 20th century to foreign investment, whereas in the 19th century it had made no small contribution to the creation of firms destined for lasting success like Ansaldo, Magona and Edison. Be that as it may, foreign investment seems to have made a strong come-back at the close of the last century with numerous take-over of middle-sized firms by giant multinationals and international investment funds.

Annex 8.1. Sources: jubilee publication and business histories

1800-1950 - 150 anni di lavoro. Lips Vago S.A. Italiana, [n.d. (c. 1951)], Milan.
1834-1984 - Centocinquant'anni di vita della Calzoni, [1986], Milan, Riva Calzoni SpA.
1916-1966. Cinquantenario delle industrie A. Zanussi SpA, [1966], Milan, Zanussi SpA.
1930-1980. Cinquant'anni di industrie Merloni, [1982], Milan, Merloni SpA.
A.F. Formiggini editore (1878-1938). Mostra documentaria, [1980], Modena, Stem.
Amatori, F. [1996], *Impresa e mercato. Lancia 1906-1969*, Bologna, Il Mulino.
Amatori, F. [1989], *Proprietà e direzione. La rinascente 1917-1969*, Milan, Franco Angeli.
Amatori, F., Bezza, B. (eds), [1990], *Montecatini 1888-1966. Capitoli di storia di una grande impresa*, Bologna, Il Mulino.
Annibaldi, C., Berta, G. (eds), [1999], *Grande impresa e sviluppo italiano. Studi per i cento anni della Fiat*, Bologna, Il Mulino.
Anselmi, A.T. [1977], *Isotta Fraschini*, Milan, Edizioni Dilani.
Anselmi, A.T. [1985], *Alfa: immagini e percorsi 1910-1985. Tecnologia, design, creatività di una casa automobilistica*, Milan, Electa.
Aquila S.p.A. Trieste, 1935-1955, [n.d.], Triest.
Armanni, V. [1996], *Ettore Conti tra industria elettrica e banca mista (1895-1933)*, in D. Bigazzi (ed.), *Storie di imprenditori*, Bologna, Il Mulino: 329-356.
Azzarà, F. [1996-97], *L'industria laniera nel vercellese: l'azienda Loro Piana (1924-1975)*, Milan, Università Cattolica del Sacro Cuore, B.A. thesis, Faculty of Economics.
Bairati, P. [1986], *Sul filo di lana. Cinque generazioni di imprenditori: i Marzotto*, Bologna, Il Mulino.
Balconi, M. [1991], *La siderurgia italiana (1945-1990). Tra controllo pubblico e incentivi di mercato*, Bologna, Il Mulino.
Balsamo, L., Cremante R. [1981], *A.F. Formiggini, un editore del Novecento*, Bologna, Il Mulino.
Barberis, C. [1987], *Aristide Merloni. Storia di un uomo e di un'industria in montagna*, Bologna, Il Mulino.
Barberis, G. [1989], *Omaggio al cappello. La Borsalino di Teresio Usuelli*, Milan, Schweiller.
Barberis, G., Subbrero, G. [1986], *Produzione e commercializzazione dell'industria del cappello alessandrino: la Borsalino (fine '800-1939)*, in VV.AA., *Mercati e consumi: organizzazione e qualificazione del commercio in Italia dal XII al XX secolo*, Bologna, Ifoa: 195-232.
Battilani, P., Bigatti, G. [2002], *Oro bianco. Il settore lattiero-caseario in Val Padana tra Ottocento e Novecento*, Lodi, Giona.
Bedosti, M. [1984], *Landini. Cento anni (1884-1984)*, Fabbrico, M.F. Landini.
Berta, G. [1998], *Mirafiori*, Bologna, Il Mulino.

Bezza, B. [1987], "L'attività multinazionale della Pirelli (1883-1914)", *Società e Storia*, 10: 53-80.

Bianco, F. (ed.), [1986], *L'attività imprenditoriale di Luigi Chiozza. Dalla tenuta modello all'edificio macchina (l'Amideria di Perteole)*, Udine, Istituto per l'Enciclopedia del Friuli Venezia Giulia.

Bigatti, G. [1988], "Commercianti e imprenditori nella Milano post-unitaria: le origini della Riva (1861-1896)", *Società e storia*, 11: 53-99.

Bigazzi, D. [1981], "La Pirelli e la Fiat nel mercato mondiale", *Storia della società italiana. L'Italia di Giolitti*, Milan, Teti, 20: 126-143.

Bigazzi, D. [1986], "Un'impresa italiana sul mercato mondiale: l'attività multinazionale della Fiat fino al 1940", *Annali di storia dell'impresa*, 2: 209-263.

Bigazzi, D. [1988], *Il Portello. Operai, tecnici e imprenditori all'Alfa Romeo (1906-1926)*, Milan, Franco Angeli.

Bigazzi, D. (ed.), [1996], *Storia di imprenditori*, Bologna, Il Mulino.

Bonelli, F. [1975], *Lo sviluppo di una grande impresa in Italia. La Terni dal 1884 al 1962*, Turin, Einaudi.

Bonelli, F. (ed.), [1982], *Acciaio per l'industrializzazione*, Turin, Einaudi.

Borruso, E. [1996], *Studi di storia dell'industria milanese*, Milan, Guerini e associati.

Borruso, E. [1996], *Una ditta francese di tele sul mercato italiano: la Frette (1838-1879)*, in ibid.: 59-80.

Borruso, E. [1996], *L'arte dell'industria: la F.lli Maimeri & C. (1923-1983)*, in ibid.: 209-244.

Borruso, E., Bossaglia, R. [1989], *E. Frette & C. Una casa monzese tra Ottocento e Novecento*, Milan, Franco Maria Ricci.

Bottiglieri, B. [1987], *Stet. Strategia e struttura delle telecomunicazioni*, Milan, Franco Angeli-Ciriec.

Bottiglieri, B. [1993], *Sip. Impresa, tecnologia e stato nelle telecomunicazioni italiane*, Milan, Franco Angeli-Ciriec.

Bova, F. [1987], "La Cucirini Cantoni Coats e il settore dei cucirini in Italia", *Storia in Lombardia*, 2: 49-97.

Bova, F. [1987], "L'evoluzione di una grande azienda cotoniera: la Cucirini Cantoni Coats dal 1912 al 1939", *Annali di storia dell'impresa*, 3: 323-368.

Bovini, G. [1984/85], "La società industriale elettrica della Valnerina (1886-1911)", *Annali della Facoltà di Lettere dell'Università degli studi di Perugia*, 8: 99-123.

Bovini, G. [1991], *Per una storia dell'Elettrocarbonium: la vicenda della Società italiana dei forni elettrici (1897-1917)*, in G. Bovini, R. Covino, *I grandi passi. Narni, la città "antica" e la fabbrica*, Perugia, Editoriale umbra: 83-130.

Bracco 1927-1967, [1967], Milan, Amilcare Pizzi.

Brignone, D. [1995], *Birra Peroni 1846-1996. Centocinquant'anni di birra nella vita italiana*, Milan, Electa.

Brignone, D. [2001], *Ferrarelle. Una effervescente storia italiana*, Milan, Silvana editoriale.

Bruno, G. [1987], "Capitale straniero e industria elettrica nell'Italia meridionale", *Studi storici*, 28: 943-984.

Buitoni, B. [1992], *Pasta e cioccolato. Una storia imprenditoriale,* (Interview by Giampaolo Gallo), Perugia, Protagon.
Busino, G. [1977], *Vilfredo Pareto e l'industria del ferro nel Valdarno*, Milan, Banca Commerciale Italiana.
Buti, S. [1990], *La manifattura Ginori. Trasformazioni produttive e condizione operaia (1860-1915)*, Florence, Olschki.
Caiaffa, M. [1989], "Una piccola Fiat a Vicenza? La Alte Ceccato 'azienda dimostrativa della produttività'", *Rivista di storia contemporanea*, 17: 576-604.
Calligaris, G. [1993], *L'industria elettrica in Piemonte dalle origini alla prima guerra mondiale*, Bologna, Il Mulino.
Candela, S. [1986], *I Florio*, Palermo, Sellerio.
Canovi, A., Mietto, M., Ruggerini, M.G. [1988], *Nascita di una città. Il territorio di Santa Croce: la storia, la memoria, le "Reggiane"*, Milan, Franco Angeli.
Carparelli, A. [1978], "La siderurgia italiana nella prima guerra mondiale. Il caso dell'Ilva", *Ricerche storiche*, 8: 143-161.
Carparelli, A. [1982], *I perché di una mezza siderurgia. La società Ilva, l'industria della ghisa e il ciclo integrale negli anni Venti*, in F. Bonelli (ed.), *Acciaio per l'industrializzazione*, Turin, Einaudi: 5-158.
Casali, A., Cattaruzza, M. [1990], *Sotto i mari del mondo. La Whitehead 1875-1990*, Bari, Laterza.
Castagnoli, A. [1976], "La crisi economica degli anni '30 in Italia: il caso della Sip", *Rivista di storia contemporanea*, 5: 321-346.
Castronovo, V. [1985], *Gilardini 1905-1985: storia di un gruppo industriale*, Turin, Ages arti grafiche.
Castronovo, V. [1999], *Fiat 1899-1999. Un secolo di storia d'Italia*, Milan, Rizzoli.
Castronovo, V. et al. [1987], *Dalla luce all'energia. Storia dell'Italgas*, Rome-Bari, Laterza.
Castronovo, V., Hertner, P., Mori, G. [1994-2002], *Storia dell'Ansaldo*, Rome-Bari, Laterza.
Catanelli, L. [1974], *La fabbrica di fiammiferi igienici a Perugia*, Perugia.
Cenato, G. [1960], *Campari 1860-1960. Vicenda di un aperitivo e di un cordial*, Milan, Edizioni Campari.
Cenciarini, R.A., Licini, S. [1996], *Magneti Marelli. La storia e la business transformation*, Milan, Giuffré.
Chiapparino, F. [1989], "Nascita di una grande impresa: la Perugina 1907-1923", *Proposte e ricerche*, 23: 235-250.
Chiapparino, F. [1990], "Il tentativo di concentrazione dell'industria dolciaria italiana negli anni venti: Gualino e l'Unica (1924-1934)", *Annali di storia dell'impresa*, 5/6: 323-373.
Chiapparino, F. [1996], *Nota per una biografia imprenditoriale di Riccardo Gualino*, in D. Bigazzi (ed.), *Storie di imprenditori*, Bologna, Il Mulino: 357-381.
Chiapparino, F. [1997], *L'industria del cioccolato in Italia, Germania e Svizzera. Consumi, mercati e imprese tra '800 e prima guerra mondiale*, Bologna, Il Mulino.

Cimorelli, D. (ed.), [1994], *Tutto il sapore di casa mia. Star 1848-1995*, Cinisello Balsamo, Amilcare Pizzi.

Cirio, P. [1990], *Carlo e Camillo Gancia. Strategie industriali, 1850-1953*, Cavallermaggiore, Gribaudo.

Cirio, P., Rapetti, V. [1986], *Alle origini dello spumante italiano: l'industria enologica di Canelli (fine '800-1939)*, in VV.AA., *Mercati e consumi: organizzazione e qualificazione del commercio in Italia dal XII al XX secolo*, Bologna, Ifoa: 261-294.

Colli, A. [1999], *Legami di ferro. Storia del distretto metallurgico e meccanico lecchese tra Otto e Novecento*, Rome, Donzelli.

Colli, A. [2000], "La Motta: da bottega artigiana a impresa di stato", *Annali di storia dell'impresa*, 11: 571-629.

Confalonieri, A. [1975-76], *Banca e industria in Italia, 1894-1906*, Milan, Banca Commerciale Italiana, 3 vols.

Confalonieri, A. [1982], *Banca e industria in Italia, 1907-1914*, Milan, Banca Commerciale italiana, 2 vols.

Confalonieri, A. [1997], *Banche miste e grande industria in Italia, 1914-1933*, Milan, Banca Commerciale Italiana, 2 vols.

Conti, E. [1946], *Dal taccuino di un borghese*, Milan, Garzanti.

Coriasco, G. [1986], *Storia operaia della RIV*, Milan, Franco Angeli.

Cortella, G. [1988], *I Badoni e l'industria del ferro nell'Ottocento lecchese*, Milan, Franco Angeli.

Covino, R., Cesarani, G. [1997], *Perugina. Una storia d'azienda, ingegno e passione*, Cinisello Balsamo, Amilcare Pizzi.

Crepas, N. [1992], "Sistema di famiglia, efficienza e rischi di impresa; i primi quarant'anni di attività della Legler a Ponte S. Pietro", *Annali di storia dell'impresa*, 8: 451-536.

Crimeni, F. [1997], "I Donegani. Una famiglia del primo capitalismo italiano", *Studi Storici*, 38: 383-428.

D'Angelo, M. [1980], "The origins of the Florio, a leading family of Italian entrepreneurs in the XIXth and XXth centuries", *Journal of European Economic History*, 9: 169-183.

De Benedetti, A. [1990], "L'equilibrio difficile. Politica industriale e sviluppo dell'impresa elettrica nell'Italia meridionale: la Sme", *Rivista di storia economica*, 7 (2-3): 163-222.

De Benedetti, R. [1989], *Nato ad Asti. Vita di un imprenditore*, Genoa, Marietti.

Doria, M. [1989], *L'Ansaldo. L'impresa e lo stato*, Milan, Franco Angeli-Ciriec.

Esticino Milano. Cinquantenario 1905-1955, [1955], Milan.

Farina Cini, N. [1947], *La famiglia Cini e la cartiera della Lima, 1807-1943*, Florence, Le Monnier.

Farina Cini, N. [1960], *Centocinquanta anni di un'industria famigliare toscana*, Florence, Le Monnier.

Ferri, P. [1985], *Grande industria e banca d'affari: l'emblematica vicenda del gruppo Franchi-Gregorini*, in AA.VV., *Maestri e Imprenditori. Un secolo di trasformazioni nell'industria bresciana*, Brescia, CAB-Grafo: 97-127.

Ferriera 1897-1997, [1997], Triest.

Fontana, G.L. (ed.), [1985-6], *Schio e Alessandro Rossi. Imprenditorialità, politica, cultura e paesaggi sociali del secondo Ottocento*, Rome, Edizioni di storia e letteratura, 2 vols.
Fontana, G.L. [1993], *Mercanti, pionieri e capitani d'industria. Imprenditori e imprese nel Vicentino tra '700 e '900*, Vicenza, Neri Pozza.
Fontana, G.L. [1993], *I Cazzola e la media impresa laniera*, in ibid.: 155-184.
Fontana, G.L. [1993], *Da 'fittanzieri' a lanaioli: i Ferrarin di Thiene*, in ibid.: 185-214.
Fontana, G.L. [1993], *Industriali, possidenti, notabili. Il caso Roi e il canapificio nazionale*, in ibid.: 215-242.
Fontana, G.L. [1993], *Aristocrazie laniere. Famiglia e impresa nella G.B. Conte*, in ibid.: 111-154.
Fontana, G.L. [1993], *Spole e navette. I Saccardo tra commercio, banca e industria*, in ibid.: 283-298.
Fontana, G.L. [1993], *Impresa, scienza e attività pubblica. I De Pretto e le origini dell'industria meccanica*, in ibid.: 299-322.
Fontana, G.L. [1993], *I Panciera e la "terra bianca del Tretto"*, in ibid.: 323-344.
Fontana, G.L. [1993], *Un'azienda a propria immagine: Giacomo Pellizzari e l'elettromeccanica*, in ibid.: 318-410.
Fontana, G.L. [1993], *I Laverda e la meccanizzazione agricola*, in ibid.: 411-440.
Fontana, G.L. [1993], *Antonio Beltrame e le acciaierie ferriere vicentine*, in ibid.: 441-452.
Fontana, G.L. [1993], *Pietro Ceccato e la comunità-fabbrica di Alte*, in ibid.: 453-476.
Fontana, G.L. [1993], *Tullio Campagnolo self made man del ciclo*, in ibid.: 477-488.
Fontana, G.L. [1993], *Terre, culture, prodotti: i Nardini e la grappa*, in ibid.: 499-508.
Fragiacomo, P. [1985], *Una periferia industriale. Alle origini del decollo economico di Monfalcone (1850-1918)*, Ronchi dei Legionari, Centro Culturale polivalente.
Fragiacomo, P. [1997], *La grande fabbrica, la piccola città. Monfalcone e il cantiere navale: la nascita di una company town 1869-1940*, Milan, Franco Angeli.
Franco Tosi. Società per azioni (1876-1956), [1956], Milan, Unione tipografica.
Frumento, A. [1952-1962], *Imprese lombarde nella storia della siderurgia. Il contributo dei Falck*, Milan, Afl Falck, 2 vols.
Fumagalli, C. [1964], *La Italcementi. Origini e vicende storiche*, Milan, Italcementi.
Fumi, G. [1990], *La Recordati nella storia dell'industria farmaceutica italiana*, Milan, Università Cattolica del Sacro Cuore.
Gallo, G. [1997], *Dai Bonucci ai Ginocchietti. Il Lanificio di Ponte Felcino*, in id., *La storia e i suoi strumenti*, Foligno, Editoriale Umbra: 309-319.
Gallo, G. (ed.), [1990], *"Sulla bocca di tutti"*, Perugia, Electa Editori Umbri.
Gasparinetti, A.F. [1963], *Pietro Milani fabbricante di carta*, Fabriano.

Giuntini, A. [1989], *Dalla Lyonnaise alla Fiorentinagas 1839-1989*, Rome-Bari, Laterza.

Giuseppe e fratello Redaelli, 1870-1970, [1970], Milan.

Hertner, P. [1978], "La società "Tubi Mannesmann" a Dalmine. Un esempio di investimento internazionale (1906-1917)", *Ricerche storiche*, 8: 105-123.

Hertner, P. [1982], "Capitale tedesco e industria meccanica in Italia: la Esslingen di Saronno, 1887-1918", *Società e storia*, 17: 583-621.

Hertner, P. [1984], *Il capitale tedesco in Italia dall'Unità alla prima guerra mondiale. Banche miste e sviluppo economico italiano*, Bologna, Il Mulino.

I cinquant'anni di vita della "DB" 1921-1971, [1971], Milan.

I cinquant'anni della "RIV", 1906-1956. Storia di una valle, di un uomo, di un'industria, [1956], Milan.

Il Lloyd triestino 1836-1986, [1986], Triest, Lloyd Triestino di Navigazione.

Ilva altiforni e acciaierie d'Italia 1897-1947, [1948], Bergamo.

La Breda. Dalla società italiana Ernesto Breda alla Finanziaria Ernesto Breda 1886-1986, [1986], Milan, Amilcare Pizzi.

La S.p.A. Vizzola, 1897-1947, [1947], Turin.

Le officine Bosco di Terni, [1987], Perugia, Electa-Editori umbri associati.

Le vetrerie Bormioli 1825-1967, [1967], Milan.

Lentini, R. [1981], "Vicende economiche e finanziarie di casa Florio (1842-1902)", *Nuovi quaderni meridionali*, 19: 34-72.

Levi, F. [1984], *L'idea del buon padre. Il lento declino di un'industria famigliare*, Turin, Rosenberg & Sellier.

Licini, S. [1990], "Ercole Marelli e Tecnomasio italiano dalle origini agli anni Trenta: un tentativo di comparazione", *Annali di storia d'impresa*, 5/6: 299-321.

Licini, S. [1982], "Dall'Elvetica alla Breda. Alle origini di una grande impresa milanese (1846-1918)", *Società e storia*, 17: 79-123.

Locatelli, A. [1991-92], *Un'azienda nel suo ambiente: il caso Mazzucchelli a Castiglione Olona dal 1849 al 1940*, Milan, Università Cattolica del Sacro Cuore, B.A. thesis, Faculty of Economics.

Loggioni, A. [1996-97], *L'evoluzione dell'industria motociclistica in Italia. La Moto Guzzi (1921-1965)*, Milan, Università Cattolica del Sacro Cuore, B.A. thesis, Faculty of Economics.

Luchetti, R., Poli, G. [1982], *La magona di Piombino (1944-1970)*, Florence, La Nuova Italia.

Lungonelli, M. [1976], "Alle origini della grande industria siderurgica in Italia: la società Elba di miniere e altiforni", *Ricerche storiche*, 8: 71-94.

Lungonelli, M. [1991], *La Magona d'Italia. Impresa, lavoro e tecnologie in un secolo di siderurgia toscana (1865-1975)*, Bologna, Il Mulino.

Lungonelli, M. [1997], *Un passato industriale. Miniere e siderurgia d'Elba fra Otto e Novecento*, Turin, Edizioni della Fondazione Giovanni Agnelli.

Macchione, P. [1985], *L'aeronautica Macchi. Dalla leggenda alla storia*, Milan, Franco Angeli.

Macchione, P. [1987], *L'oro e il ferro. Storia della Franco Tosi*, Milan, Franco Angeli.

Mandressi, F. [1999], "La nascita del caseificio industriale in Lombardia", *Annali di storia dell'impresa*, 10: 565-592.

Mantegazza, A. [1986], "La formazione del gruppo Caproni", *Storia in Lombardia*, 5: 139-155.

Mantegazza, A. [1986], "La formazione del settore aeronautico italiano", *Annali di storia dell'impresa*, 2: 361-413.

Mantegazza, A. [1994], "Caproni e l'industria aeronautica italiana (1910-1952)", *Archivi e imprese*, 9: 3-45.

Maranesi, P. [1996], "Le officine "Cecchetti", 1892-1994: un secolo di storia", *Proposte e ricerche*, 3: 216-252.

Mellinato, G. [2001], *Crescita senza sviluppo. L'economia marittima della Venezia Giulia tra Impero asburgico ed autarchia (1914-1936)*, Monfalcone, Consorzio culturale del monfalconese.

Mezzo secolo di Snia Viscosa, [1970], Milan, Amilcare Pizzi.

Mori, G., De Rosa, L., Galasso, G., Castronovo, V. Zanetti, G. (eds), [1992-94], *Storia dell'industria elettrica in Italia*, Rome-Bari, Laterza, 5 vols.

Nel cinquantenario della fondazione della Società Elettrica Bresciana. L'energia elettrica nello sviluppo economico della Lombardia Orientale, [1955], Milan.

Nava, P. [1988], *Il paese dei salami. L'industria Villani e Castelnuovo Rangone 1911-1940*, Turin, Rosenberg & Sellier.

Nones, M. [1990], *Dalla San Giorgio alla Elsag. Da grande gruppo meccanico ad industria elettronica avanzata (1905-1969)*, Milan, Franco Angeli.

Novi cioccolato caramelle e affini. Mezzo secolo di cooperazione produttiva, [1953], Milan, Giuntoli Arte Grafica.

Olmo, C. (ed.), [1994], *Il Lingotto 1915-1939. L'architettura, l'immagine, il lavoro*, Turin, Allemandi.

Olmo, C. (ed.), [1997], *Mirafiori, 1936-1962*, Turin, Allemandi.

Orsi, M. [1999], "L'evoluzione della Snia Viscosa tra gli anni Venti e Trenta", *Imprese e storia*, 19: 7-45.

Ottanelli, A. [1987], *Auto, treni, aerei. Le officine meccaniche San Giorgio di Pistoia. Un'industria genovese in Toscana tra Giolitti e la resistenza (1905-1949)*, Pistoia, Edizione del Comune di Pistoia.

Patat, L. [1991], *L'industria tessile goriziana: dalla seconda metà dell'Ottocento alla crisi degli anni '30*, Udine, Istituto friulano per la storia del movimento di liberazione.

Patat, L. [1996], *Il cotonificio triestino: gli stabilimenti di Gorizia e Ronchi dalla seconda guerra mondiale alla crisi degli anni Ottanta (1945-1983)*, Udine, Istituto friulano per la storia del movimento di liberazione.

Patuzzi, C. [1978], *Mondatori*, Naples, Liguori editore.

Patuzzi, C. [1982], *Laterza*, Naples, Liguori editore.

Pavese, C. [1986], *Le origini della società Edison e il suo sviluppo fino alla costituzione del gruppo*, in B. Bezza (ed.), *Energia e sviluppo*, Turin, Einaudi: 23-169.

Penchini, M. [1977], *Nascita e sviluppo del servizio di elettricità a Perugia. La società anonima Elettricità Umbra (1899-1929)*, in R. Covino, A. Grohman, L. Tosi (eds), *Uomini, economie, culture. Saggi in memoria di Giampaolo Gallo*, Naples, Esi.

Piluso, G. [1999], "Impresa, mercato, consumi: la Star di Danilo Fossati tra autonomia e alleanze (1948-99)", *Annali di storia dell'impresa*, 10: 565-592.

Pirelli, A. [1946], *La Pirelli. Vita di un'azienda industriale*, Milan.

Pirelli & C. nel suo cinquantenario, [1922], Milan.

Pirelli 1914-1980. Strategia aziendale e relazioni industriali nella storia di una multinazionale. Tomo primo. Dalla prima guerra mondiale all'autunno caldo, [1985], Milan, Franco Angeli.

Pozzobon, M. [1982], *L'industria padana dell'acciaio nel primo trentennio del Novecento*, in F. Bonelli, (ed.), *Acciaio per l'industrializzazione*, Turin, Einaudi: 161-214.

Puppini, M. [1992], *La terra e la fabbrica*, Udine, Istituto friulano per la storia del movimento di liberazione.

Riva, D. [1990], *I velluti dell'Adda. Un caso di pionierismo manifatturiero in Lombardia: il cotonificio di Vaprio d'Adda*, Milan, Edizioni dell'Economia.

Romano, R. [1975], "Il cotonificio Cantoni dalle origini al 1900", *Studi storici*, 16 (2): 461-494.

Romano, R. [1985], *I Crespi*, Milan, Franco Angeli.

Romano, R. [1990], *I Caprotti. L'avventura economica e umana di una dinastia industriale della Brianza*, Milan, Franco Angeli.

Roverato, G. [1986], *Una casa industriale. I Marzotto*, Milan, Franco Angeli.

Roverato, G. [1991], *Nuovo Pignone*, Bologna, Il Mulino.

Row, T. [1997], *Il nazionalismo economico dell'Italia liberale. L'Ansaldo*, Bologna, Il Mulino.

Schiannini, G., Zane, M. [1997], *La manifattura di Pontoglio*, Brescia, Grafo.

Segreto, L. [1997], *Monte Amiata. Il mercurio italiano. Strategie internazionali e vincoli extraeconomici*, Milan, Franco Angeli-Ciriec.

Segreto, L., *Giovanni Buitoni*, in *Dizionario biografico degli italiani*, vol. 34, *ad vocem*.

Segreto, L., *Francesco Bertolli*, in *Dizionario biografico degli italiani*, vol. 34, *ad vocem*.

Sicca, L. [1987], *Strategia d'impresa. La formazione di un gruppo italiano: la Sme*, Milan, Etas Libri.

Sicola, C. [1998], *125 anni per l'energia*, Milan.

Sironi, V.A. [1992], *Le officine della salute. Storia del farmaco e della sua industria in Italia*, Rome-Bari, Laterza.

Sironi, V.A. [1995], *Da speziali a imprenditori. Storia dei Recordati*, Rome-Bari, Laterza.

S.A. Novi 1903-1953. Mezzo secolo di cooperazione produttiva, [1953], Milan.

Snia Viscosa, 1917-1957, [1958], Milan.

Società anonima Orobia, 1906-1956, [1956], Milan.

Sperandio, S. [2000], *Le sorgenti minerali Sangemini e Amerino nella storia del territorio*, Terni, Thyrus.

Spreafico, S. [1968], *Un'industria, una città. Cinquant'anni alle Officine "Reggiane"*, Bologna, Il Mulino.

Staccioli, V. (ed.), [1988], *In cantiere. Tecnica, arte e lavoro. Ottant'anni di attività dello stabilimento di Monfalcone*, Monfalcone, Edizioni della laguna.

Stefani, G., Astori, B. [1938], *Il Lloyd triestino, contributi alla storia italiana della navigazione marittima*, Milan, Mondadori.

Subbrero, G. [1977], *La grande avventura del cemento*, in V. Zamagni, S. Zaninelli (eds), *Storia economica e sociale di Bergamo. Fra Ottocento e Novecento*, t. II, Bergamo: 215-269.

Subbrero, G. [1999], "L'industria dolciaria novarese (1860-1995)", *Annali di storia dell'impresa*, 10: 625-640.

Taddei, F. [1980], *Il Pignone di Firenze, 1944-1954*, Florence, La Nuova Italia.

Tagliaferri, C., De Rosa, S. [1986], *Olschki. Un secolo di editoria*, Florence, Olschki, 2 vols.

Tecnomasio. Vicenda di un'impresa elettromeccanica, [1988], Milan, Amilcare Pizzi.

Terni 1884-1984. Dalla storia al museo della città, [1985], Terni, Cestres.

Toninelli, P.A. [1990], *La Edison. Contabilità e bilanci in una grande impresa elettrica, 1884-1913*, Bologna, Il Mulino.

Tonizzi, M.E. [1988], "L'industria dello zucchero in Italia dal blocco continentale alla vigilia della grande guerra (1807-1914)", *Annali di storia dell'impresa*, 4: 211-278.

Tonizzi, M.E. [2001], *L'industria dello zucchero. La produzione saccarifera in Italia e in Europa 1800-2000*, Milan, Franco Angeli.

Ucelli, G. [1952], *La Riva 1861-1951*, Milan.

Ucelli, G. [1961], *La Riva in cento anni di lavoro*, Milan, Alfieri e Lacroix.

Villaggi operai in Italia. La Val padana e Crespi d'Adda, [1981], Turin, Einaudi.

VV.AA. [1986], *Mercati e consumi: organizzazione e qualificazione del commercio in Italia dal XII al XX secolo*, Bologna, Ifoa.

Zaccaria, G. [1980], "Il lanificio Rossi dal dopoguerra all'autarchia", *Impresa e manodopera nell'industria tessile*, *Annali dell'Istituto veneto per la storia della Resistenza*, 1: 1-76.

Zerbini, M. [1986], "Arnoldo Mondadori tra impresa e organizzazione della cultura", *Storia in Lombardia*, 1: 127-138.

Zamagni, V. (ed.), [1991], *Dall'ammoniaca ai nuovi materiali. Storia dell'Istituto di ricerche chimiche Guido Donegani*, Bologna, Il Mulino.

Annex 8.2. The questionnaire

File no........... Researcher...
FIRM..foundation year...........................
Firm's following changes (names and years) ....
....
Final year...............................1991 Classification. ATECO-ISTAT (first two digits)............
Bibliographic sources..
Time period..

1. SECTOR

1.1. Mono-sector	0 1 2 3 4 5 6 7	**1.2. Multi-sector**	0 1 2 3 4 5 6 7
* no information	0 1 2 3 4 5 6 7	* no information	0 1 2 3 4 5 6 7
		1.2.1. from the beginning	0 1 2 3 4 5 6 7
		1.2.2. later	0 1 2 3 4 5 6 7

1.3. Diversified		**1.4. Multi-national**	
* no information	0 1 2 3 4 5 6 7	* no information	0 1 2 3 4 5 6 7
		1.4.1. West Europe	0 1 2 3 4 5 6 7
1.3.1. into related sectors		1.4.2. East Europe	0 1 2 3 4 5 6 7
- horizontally	0 1 2 3 4 5 6 7	1.4.3. North America	0 1 2 3 4 5 6 7
- vertically	0 1 2 3 4 5 6 7	1.4.4. South America	0 1 2 3 4 5 6 7
- backward	0 1 2 3 4 5 6 7	1.4.5. Africa	0 1 2 3 4 5 6 7
- forward	0 1 2 3 4 5 6 7	1.4.6. Asia or Oceania	0 1 2 3 4 5 6 7

1.3.1.1. with regard to	
- technical economy of scope	0 1 2 3 4 5 6 7
- product. economy of scope	0 1 2 3 4 5 6 7
- financial economy of scope	0 1 2 3 4 5 6 7
- market economy of scope	0 1 2 3 4 5 6 7
1.3.2. into not related sectors	0 1 2 3 4 5 6 7
* no information	0 1 2 3 4 5 6 7
1.3.3. into service activities to the firm	0 1 2 3 4 5 6 7
* no information	0 1 2 3 4 5 6 7
1.3.3. abandonment of the initial sector	0 1 2 3 4 5 6 7
* no information	0 1 2 3 4 5 6 7

2. PRODUCT

2.1. Mono-product	0 1 2 3 4 5 6 7		
2.2. Multi-product			
2.2.1. from the beginning	0 1 2 3 4 5 6 7	2.2.3. with regard to	0 1 2 3 4 5 6 7
* no information	0 1 2 3 4 5 6 7	* no information	0 1 2 3 4 5 6 7
		- technical economy of scope	0 1 2 3 4 5 6 7
2.2.2. since when?	0 1 2 3 4 5 6 7	- product. economy of scope	0 1 2 3 4 5 6 7
* no information	0 1 2 3 4 5 6 7	- financial economy of scope	0 1 2 3 4 5 6 7
		- market economy of scope	0 1 2 3 4 5 6 7

3. MARKET

3.1. Does the firm operate in a protect market?

* no information	0 1 2 3 4 5 6 7
- if yes, when?	0 1 2 3 4 5 6 7

3.2. Does the firm operate in a regulated market?

* no information	0 1 2 3 4 5 6 7
- if yes, when?	0 1 2 3 4 5 6 7

3.3. Supply Structure

* no information	0 1 2 3 4 5 6 7
3.3.1. competitive	0 1 2 3 4 5 6 7
3.3.2. oligopoly	0 1 2 3 4 5 6 7
3.3.2. monopoly	0 1 2 3 4 5 6 7

3.4. Typology of demand

* no information	0 1 2 3 4 5 6 7
3.4.1. public	0 1 2 3 4 5 6 7
* no information	0 1 2 3 4 5 6 7
3.4.2. private	0 1 2 3 4 5 6 7
* no information	0 1 2 3 4 5 6 7
- competitive	0 1 2 3 4 5 6 7
- oligopsony	0 1 2 3 4 5 6 7
- monopsony	0 1 2 3 4 5 6 7

3.5. Market Policy

3.5.1. quality of product	
* no information	0 1 2 3 4 5 6 7
- high	0 1 2 3 4 5 6 7
- medium	0 1 2 3 4 5 6 7
- low	0 1 2 3 4 5 6 7
3.5.2. size of the market	
* no information	0 1 2 3 4 5 6 7
- local or regional	0 1 2 3 4 5 6 7
- national	0 1 2 3 4 5 6 7
- international	0 1 2 3 4 5 6 7
3.5.3. distribution	
* no information	0 1 2 3 4 5 6 7
- direct	0 1 2 3 4 5 6 7
through branches	0 1 2 3 4 5 6 7
through agents	0 1 2 3 4 5 6 7
- indirect	0 1 2 3 4 5 6 7
exclusive contracts	0 1 2 3 4 5 6 7
3.5.4. marketing	
* no information	0 1 2 3 4 5 6 7
- pricing policies	0 1 2 3 4 5 6 7
- advertising	0 1 2 3 4 5 6 7

4. TECHNOLOGY AND RESEARCH

4.1. Innovative

* no information	0 1 2 3 4 5 6 7
4.1.1. product	0 1 2 3 4 5 6 7
4.1.2. process	0 1 2 3 4 5 6 7

4.2. Imitative

* no information	0 1 2 3 4 5 6 7
4.2.1. Italy	0 1 2 3 4 5 6 7
4.2.2. abroad	0 1 2 3 4 5 6 7
- Europe	0 1 2 3 4 5 6 7
- America	0 1 2 3 4 5 6 7
- Japan	0 1 2 3 4 5 6 7
- other	0 1 2 3 4 5 6 7

4.3. Diffusive

* no information	0 1 2 3 4 5 6 7
4.3.1. learning by doing	0 1 2 3 4 5 6 7
4.3.2. learning by using	0 1 2 3 4 5 6 7

4.4. R&D

* no information	0 1 2 3 4 5 6 7
4.4.2. decentralized	0 1 2 3 4 5 6 7
4.4.3. within the firm	0 1 2 3 4 5 6 7

4.5. Investment

* no information	0 1 2 3 4 5 6 7
4.5.1. in technology	0 1 2 3 4 5 6 7
4.5.2. to enlarge	0 1 2 3 4 5 6 7
4.5.3. mixed	0 1 2 3 4 5 6 7

5. OWNWERSHIP STRUCTURE

5.1. Family control 0 1 2 3 4 5 6 7
* no information 0 1 2 3 4 5 6 7

5.2. External control 0 1 2 3 4 5 6 7
* no information 0 1 2 3 4 5 6 7
5.2.1. banks 0 1 2 3 4 5 6 7
5.2.2. market 0 1 2 3 4 5 6 7
5.2.3. groups 0 1 2 3 4 5 6 7
5.2.4. State 0 1 2 3 4 5 6 7
5.2.5. foreign 0 1 2 3 4 5 6 7
- U.S. 0 1 2 3 4 5 6 7
- G.B. 0 1 2 3 4 5 6 7
- France/Belgium 0 1 2 3 4 5 6 7
- Germany/Austria 0 1 2 3 4 5 6 7
- Switzerland 0 1 2 3 4 5 6 7

5.3. Juridical form
* no information 0 1 2 3 4 5 6 7
5.3.1. personal firm 0 1 2 3 4 5 6 7
5.3.2. unlimited respons. 0 1 2 3 4 5 6 7
5.3.3. corporation 0 1 2 3 4 5 6 7

6. ORGANIZATIONAL STRUCTURE
* no information 0 1 2 3 4 5 6 7

6.1. Monofunctional 0 1 2 3 4 5 6 7
* no information 0 1 2 3 4 5 6 7

6.2. Multifunctional 0 1 2 3 4 5 6 7
* no information 0 1 2 3 4 5 6 7

6.3 Multidivisional
* no information 0 1 2 3 4 5 6 7

6.4. Conglomerate
* no information 0 1 2 3 4 5 6 7

6.5. It belongs to a group 0 1 2 3 4 5 6 7
* no information 0 1 2 3 4 5 6 7
6.5.1. core business 0 1 2 3 4 5 6 7
6.5.2. diversification 0 1 2 3 4 5 6 7

6.6. It belongs to a *district* 0 1 2 3 4 5 6 7
* no information 0 1 2 3 4 5 6 7

7. FINANCE

7.1. Long-term financing
* no information 0 1 2 3 4 5 6 7
7.1.1. self-financing 0 1 2 3 4 5 6 7
7.1.2. external financing 0 1 2 3 4 5 6 7
7.1.2.1. banks
- short-term
- medium/long-term

7.1.2.2. market
- bonds 0 1 2 3 4 5 6 7
- securities 0 1 2 3 4 5 6 7

7.1.2.3. foreign 0 1 2 3 4 5 6 7

7.2. Short-term financing
* no information 0 1 2 3 4 5 6 7
7.2.1. banks 0 1 2 3 4 5 6 7
7.2.2. self-financing 0 1 2 3 4 5 6 7

8. HUMAN CAPITAL

8.1. Labour force
* no information 0 1 2 3 4 5 6 7
8.1.1. unskilled 0 1 2 3 4 5 6 7
8.1.2. skilled
- training on the job 0 1 2 3 4 5 6 7
- formal training 0 1 2 3 4 5 6 7

8.2. Management
* no information 0 1 2 3 4 5 6 7
8.2.1. no formal education 0 1 2 3 4 5 6 7
8.2.2. techn./scient. education 0 1 2 3 4 5 6 7
8.2.3. business school 0 1 2 3 4 5 6 7
8.2.4. law education 0 1 2 3 4 5 6 7
8.2.5. other 0 1 2 3 4 5 6 7

9. QUANTITATIVE DATA

9.1. No. of employees

* no information 0 1 2 3 4 5 6 7
- < 50 0 1 2 3 4 5 6 7
- 50 - 99 0 1 2 3 4 5 6 7
- 100 - 249 0 1 2 3 4 5 6 7
- 250 - 999 0 1 2 3 4 5 6 7
- 1000 - 5000 0 1 2 3 4 5 6 7
- > 5000 0 1 2 3 4 5 6 7

9.2. Turn over

* no information............................1 2 3 4 5 6 7
0 from.............................to.......................
1 ....
2 ....
3 ....
4 ....
5 ....
6 ....
7 ....

9.3. Share capital

* no information 0 1 2 3 4 5 6 7
0 from........................ to.................
1 from........................ to.................
2 from........................ to.................
3 from........................ to.................
4 from........................ to.................
5 from........................ to.................
6 from........................ to.................
7 from........................ to.................

9.4. Profits

* no information 0 1 2 3 4 5 6 7
0 from........................... to.................
1 from........................... to.................
2 from........................... to.................
3 from........................... to.................
4 from........................... to.................
5 from........................... to.................
6 from........................... to.................
7 from........................... to.................

9.5. Investments

* no information 0 1 2 3 4 5 6 7
0 from........................ to.................
1 from........................ to.................
2 from........................ to.................
3 from........................ to.................
4 from........................ to.................
5 from........................ to.................
6 from........................ to.................
7 from........................ to.................

9.6. Self-financing

* no information 0 1 2 3 4 5 6 7
0 from........................... to.................
1 from........................... to.................
2 from........................... to.................
3 from........................... to.................
4 from........................... to.................
5 from........................... to.................
6 from........................... to.................
7 from........................... to.................

9.7. No. Horse Power (HP)

* no information 0 1 2 3 4 5 6 7
0 from........................ to.................
1 from........................ to.................
2 from........................ to.................
3 from........................ to.................
4 from........................ to.................
5 from........................ to.................
6 from........................ to.................
7 from........................ to.................

9.8. Spindles

* no information 0 1 2 3 4 5 6 7
0 from........................... to.................
1 from........................... to.................
2 from........................... to.................
3 from........................... to.................
4 from........................... to.................
5 from........................... to.................
6 from........................... to.................
7 from........................... to.................

9.9. No. of establishments and their localization

* no information 0 1 2 3 4 5 6 7
0 ....
1 ....
2 ....
3 ....
4 ....
5 ....
6 ....
7 ....

PERIODS LEGEND

0 = < 1876
1 = 1876-1894
2 = 1895-1914
3 = 1915-1921
4 = 1922-1929
5 = 1930-1938
6 = 1939-1947
7 = 1948-1973

Annex 8.3. Compiled files

Sector/company	Localization	Area	Period
Textile, wearing and leather			
Lanificio Conte	Schio	NE	1757-1950
Cucirini Cantoni Coats	Busto	NW	1890-1939
Cotonificio Cantoni	Legnano	NW	1820-1900
Lanificio Rossi	Schio	NE	1872-1940
Fratelli Mazzonis	Turin	NW	1858-1939
V.E. Marzotto	Valdagno	NE	1800-1952
G. Marzotto e Figli	Valdagno	NE	1920-1970
Borsalino	Alessandria	NW	1880-1940
Cotonificio Crespi	Trezzo	NW	1805-1930
Caprotti	Ponte Albiate	NW	1830-1914
Frette	Milan	NW	1860-1940
Canapificio Nazionale Roi	Vicenza	NE	1857-1915
Lanificio P. Cazzola	Schio	NE	1835-1955
Lanificio A. Ferrarin	Thiene	NE	1850-1958
Cotonificio Brunner	Triest	NE	1918-1928
Loro Piana	Quarona Sesia	NW	1924-1970
Visconti di Modrone	Vario	NW	1839-1970
Pontoglio Spa	Legnano	NW	1882-1970
Lanificio Bonucci	Ponte Felcino	C	1858-1970
Legler	Ponte San Pietro	NW	1874-1914
Iron, steel and shipping building			
Beltrame	Vicenza	NE	1895-1945
Falck	Sesto S.G.	NW	1906-1929
Cantiere Navale Triestino	Triest	NE	1918-1970
Lloyd Triestino	Triest	NE	1918-1970
ILVA	Piombino	C	1897-1961
Terni	Terni	C	1884-1962
Magona	Piombino	C	1891-1970
Ferriere Altiforni di Servola	Triest	NE	1897-1924
Elba	Piombino	C	1899-1911
Giuseppe Badoni & C.	Lecco	NW	1829-1900
Carlo e Antonio F.lli Badoni	Lecco	NW	1878-1900
Franchi Gregorini	Brescia	NW	1886-1930
Tubi Mannesmann	Dalmime	NW	1906-1917
Construction			
S.A. Cementi Salerno	Salerno	S	1909-1927
S.A. Fabbrica Calce e Cemento	Casale M.	NW	1870-1917
Cementi Calci Idrauliche F.lli Pesenti	Bergamo	NW	1878-1906
Italcementi	Bergamo	NW	1864-1964
Mechanical and motor vehicle			
Lancia	Turin	NW	1906-1969
Alfa Romeo	Arese	NW	1906-1970

Sector/company	Localization	Area	Period
Tecnomasio	Milan	NW	1863-1970
Industrie Saccardo	Schio	NE	1885-1970
Laverda	Breganze	NE	1873-1970
Ceccato	Montecchio	NE	1934-1956
De Pretto-Escher Wyss	Schio	NE	1884-1920
A. Pellizzari	Milan	NW	1901-1958
Campagnolo	Vicenza	NE	1930-1960
Flexider	Turin	NW	1921-1970
Pignone	Florence	C	1922-1970
Whitehead	Fiume	NE	1918-1934
Whitehead - Motofides	Livorno	C	1934-1970
Savara	Turin	NW	1924-1972
CMASA	Pisa	C	1921-1970
Franco Tosi	Legnano	NW	1874-1956
Officine Meccaniche San Giorgio	Genoa	NW	1905-1949
Ansaldo	Genoa	NW	1852-1970
Caproni	Varese	NW	1911-1920
F.lli Macchi	Varese	NW	1905-1913
Niuport - Macchi	Varese	NW	1913-1940
Ausa	Foligno	C	1934-1940
Riva	Milan	NW	1889-1970
Breda	Sesto S.G.	NW	1886-1970
Officine Meccaniche Reggiane	Reggio-Emilia	NE	1904-1951
RIV	Villar Perosa	NW	1906-1970
Guzzi	Lecco	NW	1921-1965
FIAT	Turin	NW	1899-1970
Industrie Zanussi Spa	Udine	NE	1916-1966
Lips Vago S.A. Italiana	Milan	NW	1800-1951
Isotta Fraschini	Milan	NW	1900-1953
A. Cecchetti	Rome - Civitanova	C	1892-1957
Officine Bosco	Terni	C	1890-1960
Costruzioni Meccaniche di Saronno	Saronno	NW	1887-1918
Giovanni Landini e figli	Reggio-Emilia	NE	1884-1984
Merloni	Fabriano	C	1897-1970
Redaelli Giuseppe e fratello	Lecco	NW	1870-1970
Società Industria del ferro	Arezzo	C	1870-1894
Magneti Marelli	Sesto SG	NW	1919-1970
DB Spa	Milan	NW	1921-1970
Food and beverages			
Salumificio Villani	Modena	NE	1913-1946
Fratelli Gancia	Turin	NW	1850-1940
Campari	Milan	NW	1860-1960
Buitoni	Perugia	C	1827-1970
Bertolli	Rome	C	1928-1940
Perugina	Perugia	C	1903-1970
UNICA	Turin	NW	1924-1934
Florio	Marsala	S	1833-1906
STAR	Monza	NW	1948-1970

Sector/company	Localization	Area	Period
Peroni	Rome	C	1903-1970
Novi S.A.	Novi L.	NW	1903-1970
A.M. Sangemini	Rome - Sangemini	C	1837-1999
Cardini	Bassano	NE	1778-1970
Ferrarelle	Rome	C	1894-2000
Motta	Milan	NW	1923-1968
Galbani	Melzo	NW	1882-1940
Eridania	Genoa	NW	1899-1970
Ligure Lombarda	Genoa	NW	1873-1935
Italiana Zuccheri	Rome - Genoa	NC	1898-1970
Paper and publishing			
Formiggini editore	Modena - Rome	C	1908-1938
Giuseppe Laterza	Bari	S	1901-1970
Mondadori	Verona, Milan	NW	1907-1970
Olschki	Florence	C	1886-1970
Cartiera Pietro Milani	Fabriano	C	1780-1817
Società Cartaria Cini	Florence	C	1807-1930
Chemicals, mining and rubber			
Valentinigomme	Turin	NW	1937-1970
Welser & C. - Cromadora	Turin	NW	1928-1970
Ricordati	Milan	NW	1926-1970
Caolino Panciera	Vicenza	NE	1908-1950
Agricola Industriale Cellulosa Italiana	Torviscosa	NE	1937-1970
Montecatini	Milan	NW	1888-1940
Pirelli	Milan	NW	1872-1922
Società Italiana della Celluloide	Castiglione Olona	NW	1923-1940
Mazzucchelli	Castiglione Olona	NW	1849-1940
Monte Amiata	Abbadia San Salvatore	C	1917-1970
Bracco	Milan	NW	1927-1967
SNIA Viscosa	Turin	NW	1917-1970
Vetrerie Bormioli	Parma	NE	1825-1967
Umbra Fabbrica Fiammiferi	Perugia	C	1899-1905
Luigi Chiazza	Cervignano	NE	1860-1918
F.lli Maimeri	Milan	NW	1923-1970
Utilities			
SIP	Turin	NW	1899-1964
SME	Naples	S	1899-1925
Edison	Milan	NW	1884-1962
Bresciana di Elettricità	Milan	NW	1905-1940
Conti Imprese Elettriche	Milan	NW	1901-1926
Italgas	Turin	NW	1838-1968
Fiorentina Gas	Florence	C	1839-1970
STIPEL	Turin	NW	1924-1964
TETI	Florence	C	1924-1964
SET	Naples	S	1924-1964
TELVE	Venice	NE	1923-1964
TIMO	Bologna	NE	1923-1964

Sector/company	Localization	Area	Period
Esticino Spa	Milan	NW	1905-1955
Vizzola	Milan	NW	1897-1962
Orobica S.A.	Lecco	NW	1906-1956
Società Elettrocarbonium	Rome - Narni	C	1900-1917
Società Italiana dei Forni Elettrici	Narni	C	1897-1917
Elettrica della Valnerina	Terni	C	1886-1911
Elettricità Umbra	Perugia	C	1899-1929
Aquila Spa	Triest	NE	1935-1955
Other			
Gilardini (leather)	Turin	NW	1865-1970
Castagnetti	Turin	NW	1924-1970
Manifattura Ginori	Florence	C	1860-1915
La Rinascente	Milan	NW	1917-1970

Legend: *C* Centre, *NC* North-Centre, *NE* North-East, *NW* North-West, *S* South.

9. Entrepreneurs and managers (1913–1972)

Alberto Rinaldi

9.1. Introduction

Until the 1970s historians almost completely neglected the role played by entrepreneurs in the industrialization of Italy whereas they emphasized the function of such factors as state policies, *mixed banks*, raw material and natural endowments. However, the successes that enabled Italy to catch up with more industrialized nations have more recently induced some scholars to reconsider the whole growth process of the country and, in this context, the contribution given to it by entrepreneurs [Cafagna 1999; Toninelli 2001; Castagnoli and Scarpellini 2003].

These authors have argued that the long prevailing thesis that Italian capitalism was seriously lacking of *true* entrepreneurs, was vitiated by a fundamental prejudice, that is the dominance of vertically integrated managerial big business is the one best way all countries have to adhere to in their development process [Chandler 1990].

In the case of Italy, Schumpeterian entrepreneurs who carried out path-breaking innovations that radically changed production, products and markets [Schumpeter 1939] were much more uncommon than elsewhere in the Western world, while a central role was played by entrepreneurs who carried out small, incremental, adaptive and cumulative innovations, often clustered in the country's *industrial districts* [Rosenberg 1976; Amatori and Toninelli 2003].

This essay presents the results of an analysis of the individuals who held the largest number of board positions in Italian joint-stock companies and commonly referred to as *big linkers* (BL). In capitalist countries, the BL perform an extremely important function in ensuring the cohesion of the economic system, for they are usually the business community's opinion leaders, the vehicle through which information is collected and spread, as well as the principle channel connecting the business world and the political domain [Scott 1985].

The study of these figures can thus shed light upon some aspects of the structures of control of an economic system. It is not aimed at judging the control models or the mechanisms used to exercise that control, but rather, at examining how these mechanisms have evolved over time in response to changing needs.

I would like to thank the editors of this volume for their useful comments on a previous version of this paper. I also wish to thank Marco Doria and Maria Elisabetta Tonizzi of the University of Genoa, Alberto Gottarelli of the Historical Archives of the Banca Commerciale Italiana and Stefania Dal Rio of the Monrif Group for the help provided during the research work carried out. This, however, does not imply any responsibility on their part as regards the content of this essay, which is entirely the author's.

In particular, the study of the BL can be very insightful for four topics that have received special attention by historians concerning Italian firms and their structures of control: (i) the evolution of such structures, (ii) the interdependence existing between banks, other financial intermediaries and industry, (iii) inter-sectoral relations, (iv) the relations between private and state-owned enterprises [Grifone 1945; Bonelli 1978; Chiesi 1982, 1985; Legnani 1987; Amatori 1995; Amatori and Brioschi 1997; Barca 1997; Ferri and Trento 1997; Vasta and Baccini 1997; Rinaldi and Vasta 2003, 2005].

This study considered a sample that was selected from the Imita.db database and consisted of the top 20 BL for each one of six benchmark years (i.e. 1913, 1927, 1936, 1952, 1960 and 1972). The essay is structured as follows. Section 9.2 describes the characteristics of the sample. The individuals included in the sample are analyzed with reference to several variables, the definition of which was possible in at least 70 per cent of the cases. These variables are commonly adopted in prosopographical analyses of business elites: age and place of birth (Sect. 9.3), education and training (Sect. 9.4), parliamentary seats obtained by appointment or election (Sect. 9.5), and titles of nobility (Sect. 9.6)[1]. Section 9.7 outlines the distribution of the board seats held by the BL according to the prevalent sector of business activity. Section 9.8 analyses the interlocking directorates generated by the BL, while Sect. 9.9 attempts to define a typology of BL. Lastly, Sect. 9.10 contains some concluding comments.

9.2. Characteristics of the sample

The list of BL, for each benchmark year, appears in Table 9.1.a-f, complete with the personal data and attributes indicated above and the number of offices held. First of all, note that some individuals appear more than once. Six persons reappeared in three separate benchmark years, and another 21 reappeared twice. The 135 positions available overall were thus covered by 102 persons, 27 of whom appeared more than once[2]. Continuity proved to be especially strong between 1952 and 1960. In fact, of the 21 BL in 1960, 13 (61.9 per cent) also appeared in 1952. These findings are not at all surprising, given that it was the shortest time interval considered, but also the only interval in which the Italian economy did not experience major shocks. Conversely, the most marked discontinuity is observable in the interval between 1936 and 1952, with just 3 figures present in both survey periods, and not by chance, for this was the longest time interval considered, including the years of Second World War and the period of transition from fascism to the Republic.

[1] Owing to the lack of reliable data for some benchmark years, the positions held in Confindustria or other business associations have not been included.

[2] The actual number of seats identified was 135, rather than the 120 speculated, as several individuals proved to be matched up in twentieth place with the same number of seats, in four of the six benchmark years.

Table 9.1.a. *Big linkers* in 1913

Surname and name	Age	Region of birth	Education	Member of Parliament	Titles of Nobility	Career sector	Seats
1. Esterle Carlo	60	Trentino-A.A.	BA: Engineering	Yes	No	Electrical power	33
2. Mazzoni Cesare	-	-	BA: Law	No	No	Finance	25
3. Mazzotti Biancinelli Lodovico	43	Lombardy	BA: Law	No	Yes	Finance	21
4. Belloni Gaetano	-	Lombardy	Not indicated	No	No	Banking	18
4. Mangili Cesare	63	Lombardy	SSD: Commerce	Yes	No	Banking	18
6. Barberis Giovanni	-	-	BA: Engineering	No	No	Finance	17
6. Conti Ettore	42	Lombardy	BA: Engineering	No	No	Electrical power	17
8. Della Torre Luigi	52	Piedmont	BA: Economics & Bus. Adm.	Yes	No	Banking	16
8. Baragiola Pietro	59	Lombardy	BA: Agriculture	Yes	No	Banking	15
8. Capuano Maurizio	48	Campania	BA: Law	No	Yes	Electrical power	15
8. Cutolo Teodoro	51	Campania	Not indicated	No	No	Finance	15
8. Da Zara Giuseppe	58	Veneto	Not indicated	No	Yes	Finance	15
13. Bruzzone Emilio	52	Liguria	Not indicated	No	No	Sugar	14
13. Carminati Angelo	57	Lombardy	BA: Economics & Bus. Adm.	No	No	Finance	14
13. Dell'Acqua Carlo	65	Lombardy	Primary school	Yes	No	Textiles	14
16. Falcone Giacomo	-	-	BA: Law	No	No	Finance	13
16. Gualco Angelo	-	-	SSD: Accountancy	No	No	Sugar	13
16. Pollone Eugenio	64	Piedmont	Not indicated	No	No	Banking	13
16. Sacchi Guido	46	Lombardy	SSD: Accountancy	No	No	Finance	13
16. Stoffel Giuseppe	-	-	Not indicated	Yes	No	Textiles	13

Legend: *BA* Bachelor of Arts, *Bus. Adm.* Business Administration, *SSD* Secondary School Diploma.

Table 9.1.b. *Big linkers* in 1927

Surname and name	Age	Region of birth	Education	Member of Parliament	Titles of Nobility	Career sector	Seats
1. Mazzotti Biancinelli Lodovico	57	Lombardy	BA: Law	No	Yes	Finance	55
2. Gaggia Achille	54	Veneto	BA: Engineering	No	No	Electrical power	54
3. Garbagni Mario	49	Lombardy	BA: Engineering	No	No	Finance	42
4. Lodolo Alberto	54	Piedmont	BA: Engineering	No	No	Electrical power	41
5. Conti Ettore	56	Lombardy	BA: Engineering	Yes	No	Electrical power	40
6. Feltrinelli Carlo	46	Lombardy	SSD: Classical school	No	No	Finance	38
7. Panzarasa Rinaldo	-	Piedmont	BA: Law	No	No	Finance	37
8. Bolchini Ferruccio	-	-	BA: Law	No	No	Finance	36
9. Sacchi Guido	60	Lombardy	SSD: Accountancy	No	No	Finance	35
10. Borletti Senatore	47	Lombardy	SSD: Accountancy	No	No	Finance	32
11. Della Torre Luigi	66	Piedmont	BA: Economics & Bus. Adm.	Yes	No	Banking	30
12. Toeplitz Giuseppe	61	Poland (overseas)	SSD: Classical school	No	No	Banking	29
13. Carminati Angelo	71	Lombardy	BA: Economics & Bus. Adm.	No	No	Finance	28
14. Pogliani Angelo	56	Lombardy	SSD: Accountancy	No	No	Banking	26
14. Ponti Gian Giacomo	49	Lombardy	BA: Engineering	Yes	No	Electrical power	26
14. Rossello Mario	50	-	SSD: Accountancy	No	No	Banking	26
17 Pesenti Antonio	47	Lombardy	SSD: Classical school	No	No	Cement	24
18. Bocciardo Arturo	51	Liguria	BA: Engineering	No	No	Steel	23
18. Cini Vittorio	42	Emilia-Romagna	BA: Economics & Bus. Adm.	No	No	Shipping	23
18. Morpurgo Edgardo	61	Friuli-V.G.	SSD: Classical school	No	Yes	Insurance	23
18. Motta Giacinto	57	Lombardy	BA: Engineering	Yes	No	Electrical power	23

Legend: *BA* Bachelor of Arts, *Bus. Adm.* Business Administration, *SSD* Secondary School Diploma.

Table 9.1.c. *Big linkers* in 1936

Surname and name	Age	Region of birth	Education	Member of Parliament	Titles of Nobility	Career sector	Seats
1. Ciatto Attilio	-	-	Not indicated	No	No	Real estate	50
2. Sacchi Guido	69	Lombardy	SSD: Accountancy	No	Yes	Finance	34
3. Agnelli Giovanni	70	Piedmont	SSD: Classical school	Yes	No	Motor-vehicles	32
4. Bruno Luigi	40	Campania	BA: Law	No	No	Electrical power	29
5. Parisi Enrico	60	Sicily	Not indicated	No	Yes	Banking	28
6. Cenzato Giuseppe	54	Veneto	BA: Engineering	No	No	Electrical power	27
6. Donegani Guido	59	Tuscany	BA: Engineering	Yes	No	Chemistry	27
8. Pesenti Antonio	56	Lombardy	SSD: Classical school	Yes	No	Cement	26
9. Morpurgo Edgardo	70	Friuli-V.G.	SSD: Classical school	No	Yes	Insurance	25
10. Borletti Senatore	56	Lombardy	SSD: Accountancy	Yes	No	Finance	24
10. Cartesegna Francesco	54	Emilia-Romagna	BA: Engineering	No	No	Finance	24
12. Motta Giacinto	66	Lombardy	BA: Engineering	Yes	No	Electrical power	23
13. Gaggia Achille	63	Veneto	BA: Engineering	No	No	Electrical power	22
14. Liguori Pirro	57	Umbria	BA: Engineering	No	No	Electrical power	21
15. Balsamo Natale	59	Lombardy	BA: Engineering	No	No	Electrical power	20
15. Bevione Giuseppe	57	Piedmont	BA: Law	Yes	No	Finance	20
15. Chiesa Pietro	63	Lombardy	BA: Engineering	No	No	Finance	20
18. Galletti Guglielmo	62	Tuscany	SSD: Accountancy	No	No	Chemistry	19
18. Garbaccio Lionello	51	Piedmont	Not indicated	Yes	No	Textiles	19
18. Pesenti Mario	-	Lombardy	BA: Engineering	No	No	Cement	19

Legend: *BA* Bachelor of Arts, *Bus. Adm.* Business Administration, *SSD* Secondary School Diploma.

Table 9.1.d. *Big linkers* in 1952

Surname and name	Age	Region of birth	Education	Member of Parliament	Titles of Nobility	Career sector	Seats
1. Valerio Giorgio	48	Lombardy	BA: Engineering	No	No	Electrical power	44
2. De Biasi Vittorio	57	Lombardy	BA: Engineering	No	No	Electrical power	42
3. Bruno Luigi	56	Campania	BA: Law	No	No	Electrical power	33
4. Ottolenghi Enrico	64	Umbria	BA: Engineering	No	No	Electrical power	31
5. Pesenti Carlo	45	Lombardy	BA: Engineering	No	No	Cement	28
6. Cartesegna Francesco	70	Emilia-Romagna	BA: Engineering	No	No	Finance	27
7. Spada Massimo	47	Latium	BA: Law	No	No	Finance	25
8. Bonadè Bottino Vittorio	63	Piedmont	BA: Engineering	No	No	Constructions	22
9. Beria Biagio	63	Piedmont	BA: Engineering	No	No	Motor-vehicles	21
9. Corridori Giuseppe	64	Lombardy	BA: Economics & Bus. Adm.	No	No	Banking	21
11. Bozzola Carlo	-	-	SSD: Accountancy	No	No	Finance	20
11. Malnati Carlo	43	Lombardy	SSD: Accountancy	No	No	Textiles	20
11. Nogara Bernardino	82	Lombardy	BA: Engineering	No	Yes	Finance	20
11. Samaritani Aldo	48	Latium	BA: Economics & Bus. Adm.	No	No	Constructions	20
15. Boeri Giovanni Battista	69	Liguria	BA: Law	Yes	No	Finance	19
15. Parodi Giacomo	-	Liguria	BA: Engineering	No	No	Sugar	19
15. Vola Annibale	-	-	SSD: Accountancy	No	No	Finance	19
18. Bobbio Carlo	66	Lombardy	BA: Law	No	No	Electrical power	18
18. Camerana Giancarlo	43	Latium	BA: Agriculture	No	Yes	Finance	18
18. Luraghi Giuseppe	47	Lombardy	BA: Economics & Bus. Adm.	No	No	Metal-engineering	18
18. Mizzi Leonida	48	Emilia-Romagna	SSD: Accountancy	No	No	Agro-food	18
18. Prinetti Castelletti Ignazio	-	Lombardy	BA: Engineering	No	Yes	Electrical power	18
18. Rossello Mario	75	-	SSD: Accountancy	No	No	Finance	18
18. Valletta Vittorio	69	Liguria	BA: Economics & Bus. Adm.	No	No	Motor-vehicles	18

Legend: *BA* Bachelor of Arts, *Bus. Adm.* Business Administration, *SSD* Secondary School Diploma.

Table 9.1.e *Big linkers* in 1960

Surname and name	Age	Region of birth	Education	Member of Parliament	Titles of Nobility	Career sector	Seats
1. Pesenti Carlo	53	Lombardy	BA: Engineering	No	No	Cement	38
1. Spada Massimo	55	Latium	BA: Law	No	No	Finance	38
3. Bruno Luigi	64	Campania	BA: Law	No	No	Electrical power	37
4. Bozzola Carlo	-	-	SSD: Accountancy	No	No	Finance	35
4. De Biasi Vittorio	65	Lombardy	BA: Engineering	No	No	Electrical power	35
6. Rossello Mario	83	-	SSD: Accountancy	No	No	Finance	26
7. Samaritani Aldo	56	Latium	BA: Economics & Bus. Adm.	No	No	Real estate	25
7. Valerio Giorgio	56	Lombardy	BA: Engineering	No	No	Electrical power	25
9. Bonadè Bottino Vittorio	71	Piedmont	BA: Engineering	No	No	Constructions	22
9. Lodolo D'Oria Alessandro	-	-	BA: Engineering	No	No	Electrical power	22
9. Mizzi Leonida	56	Emilia-Romagna	SSD: Accountancy	No	No	Agro-food	22
9. Torchiani Tullio	59	Sardinia	BA: Law	No	No	Finance	22
13. Beria Biagio	71	Piedmont	BA: Engineering	No	No	Motor-vehicles	21
13. Marchesano Enrico	66	Sicily	BA: Law	No	No	Finance	21
13. Prinetti Castelletti Ignazio	-	Lombardy	BA: Engineering	No	Yes	Electrical power	21
16. Bobbio Carlo	74	Lombardy	BA: Law	No	No	Electrical power	19
16. Radice Fossati Eugenio	50	Lombardy	BA: Engineering	No	Yes	Finance	19
16. Rossi Guido	29	Tuscany	BA: Law	No	No	Finance	19
19. Faina Carlo	66	Umbria	BA: Law, Economics & Bus. Adm.	No	Yes	Chemistry	18
19. Lazzati Gaetano	-	Lombardy	BA: Economics & Bus. Adm.	No	No	Real estate	18
19. Zanon di Valgiurata Lucio	57	Piedmont	BA: Law	No	Yes	Finance	18

Legend: *BA* Bachelor of Arts, *Bus. Adm.* Business Administration, *SSD* Secondary School Diploma.

Table 9.1.f *Big linkers* in 1972

Surname and name	Age	Region of birth	Education	Member of Parliament	Titles of Nobility	Career sector	Seats
1. Spada Massimo	67	Latium	BA: Law	No	No	Finance	42
2. Pesenti Carlo	65	Lombardy	BA: Engineering	No	No	Cement	33
2. Zuccolotto Oscar	-	-	Not indicated	No	No	Chemistry	33
4. Quaratino Licio	-	-	BA: Engineering	No	No	Finance	26
4. Radice Fossati Eugenio	62	Lombardy	BA: Engineering	No	Yes	Finance	26
4. Riffeser Bruno	46	Trentino-A.A.	BA: Economics & Bus. Adm.	No	No	Petroleum	26
4. Rovelli Nino	55	Lombardy	BA: Engineering	No	No	Chemistry	26
8. Zurzolo Antonio	49	Umbria	BA: Economics & Bus. Adm.	No	No	Finance	25
9. Monti Attilio	66	Emilia-Romagna	Not indicated	No	No	Petroleum	24
10. Dosi Mario	69	Apulia	BA: Law	Yes	No	Finance	23
10. Ferrari Alberto	58	Emilia-Romagna	BA: Law	No	No	Banking	23
10. Galeati Giambattista	72	Emilia-Romagna	SSD: Accountancy	No	No	Petroleum	23
13. Bassetti Giovanni	79	Lombardy	SSD: Technical school	No	Yes	Real estate	22
14. Martelli Giuseppe	65	Sardinia	BA: Law	No	No	Finance	21
15. Baldini Riccardo	62	Tuscany	BA: Engineering	No	No	Metal-engineering	20
15. Costa Angelo	71	Liguria	BA: Economics & Bus. Adm.	No	No	Shipping	20
15. Mizzi Leonida	68	Emilia-Romagna	SSD: Accountancy	No	No	Agro-food	20
15. Torchiani Tullio	71	Sardinia	BA: Law	No	No	Finance	20
19. Villa Alessandro	-	-	BA: Economics & Bus. Adm.	No	No	Agro-food	19
20. Bassetti Giansandro	49	Lombardy	BA: Economics & Bus. Adm.	No	Yes	Textiles	18
20. Bernero Virginio	-	Piedmont	BA: Economics & Bus. Adm.	No	No	Textiles	18
20. Bucarelli Domenico	-	-	BA: Engineering	No	No	Chemistry	18
20. Capanna Alberto	62	Abruzzo	BA: Economics & Bus. Adm.	No	No	Steel	18
20. Corsi Giorgio	49	-	BA: Law	No	No	Finance	18
20. Jacoboni Attilio	67	Latium	BA: Chemistry	No	No	Finance	18
20. Lazzati Gaetano	-	Lombardy	BA: Economics & Bus. Adm.	No	No	Real estate	18
20. Lolli Ettore	64	Emilia-Romagna	BA: Engineering	No	No	Finance	18
20. Maccaferri Guglielmo	60	Emilia-Romagna	BA: Economics & Bus. Adm.	No	No	Metal-engineering	18
20. Valeri Manera Mario	51	Liguria	BA: Law	No	No	Finance	18

Legend: *BA* Bachelor of Arts, *Bus. Adm.* Business Administration, *SSD* Secondary School Diploma.

Although the biographical data collected are partial, their quantity and quality do permit the definition of some typological characteristics for the sample. This does not mean that they have led to an exhaustive and systematic processing of the individual biographical profiles, and thus to the formulation of true career models for these persons. To be specific, the information gathered permitted a reconstruction of the family background of only a relatively limited number of cases of BL. As a result, it was not possible to examine the correlation between social extraction and occupational mobility.

9.3. Origins of the BL: age and place (region) of birth

Table 9.2 reports information regarding the age of the BL in the various benchmark years. In 1913, the average age of these individuals was 54 years; in 1927 it remained the same and then in 1936, it increased to 59 years. The years that followed did not register any other substantial variations such as those, although there was a constant increase between 1952 and 1972, from 58 to 62 years of age. The pattern resulting for the median age did not differ substantially. After an almost imperceptible decrease (from 54.5 to 54 years) between 1913 and 1927, the median age increased to 59 in 1936 and then to up to 60 years in 1952. There was an additional drop down to 59 years in 1960 and then another increase to 62 years of age in 1972.

Table 9.2. *Big linkers* by age

Age	1913	1927	1936	1952	1960	1972
Minimum	42	42	40	43	29	46
Average	54	54	59	58	61	62
Median	54.5	54	59	60	59	62
Maximum	65	71	70	82	83	79
Variance (s^2)	59	51	52	130	134	73

Over time, the age of the BL gradually increased, particularly between 1927 and 1936, precisely at the time when the collapse of the *mixed banks* - which had occupied a central position for four decades within Italian capitalism - and the advent of the banking and entrepreneurial State, could have left room for a rejuvenated business class. Though less accentuated, similar evidence exists for the 1960-1972 interval, documenting the situation that was created as a result of the nationalization of the electrical power industry. In this case as well, a break-up of the institutional structures of Italian capitalism was followed by the ageing of the BL, rather than a rejuvenation.

This circumstance is not easy to interpret. One could surmise that in the first two decades of the 20th - in a nation only recently industrialized as was Italy at the time - the entrepreneurial class, especially in the newer sectors, was made up mainly of relatively young *new men*. Subsequently, owing also to the increased complexity of corporate organization, it is possible that business careers became longer and slower, and that a greater number of years were required to reach the top positions. And, above all, once those positions were reached, they were held for long periods of time, often until retirement or even beyond. However, there is no factual evidence to support this hypothesis, which under the current circumstances, can only be proposed as a cautious conjecture.

Some interesting indications also emerge from Table 9.3, which reports the distribution, for each benchmark year, of the BL by year of birth. In 1913, one-half of the persons included in the sample were born before the Unification of Italy in 1861 and only one person, after 1870. In 1927, there were virtually no individuals born prior to Unification, whereas the prevailing generation consisted of individuals born in the first two decades after Unification. The situation registered in 1936 is basically similar, confirming the fact that the reorganization at the top levels of the Italian economy brought about by the crash of the *mixed banks*, does not seem to have been followed by generational mobility into the nation's business elite. Such a change was to come only in 1952, when the individuals born before 1880 disappeared almost completely. The new entrants were concentrated in the birth years of 1881-1890 and 1901-1910, while the middle birth period (1891-1900) seems to have been *skipped* over, but that is a period in which most of the soldiers who fought in First World War were concentrated. This *polarization* of the sample into two non-contiguous birth periods probably accounts for the sudden surge in the variance (s^2) of the age of the BL registered for 1952 (Table 9.2). The year 1960 saw a prevalence of those born between 1901 and 1910, along with a comeback of those born in the 1891-1900 period and a marked decline in those born in the 1881-1890 period and now nearing their definitive disappearance. Lastly, in 1972, the predominance of the 1901-1910 birth period became even more consolidated, in spite of the institutional breach induced by the nationalization of the electrical power industry. A significant batch of directors born after 1910 appeared thereafter.

Table 9.3. *Big linkers* by year of birth

	1913	1927	1936	1952	1960	1972
Prior to 1861	7	1	-	-	-	-
1861-1870	6	6	4	1	-	-
1871-1880	1	10	10	1	1	-
1881-1890	-	2	3	8	3	-
1891-1900	-	-	1	2	4	2
1901-1910	-	-	-	8	8	13
1911-1920	-	-	-	-	-	3
1921-1930	-	-	-	-	-	5
After 1930	-	-	-	-	1	-

Table 9.4 reports the distribution of the BL according to the region of birth. First of all, it should be noted that 5 regions out of 20 - Valle d'Aosta, Marches, Molise, Basilicata and Calabria - had never supplied a single individual. Lom-

bardy stands out among the regions represented. However, its weight dwindled after 1952, so much so that in 1972, Emilia-Romagna caught up with it. Overall, for a long period of time, from 1913 to 1960, there had been a prevalence of figures born in the regions with the longest history of industrialization - the so-called *Industrial Triangle* made up of the regions of Piedmont, Lombardy and Liguria - which considered together, accounted for more than one-half of the BL in each benchmark year. However, in 1972, the *Industrial Triangle* was the birthplace of just 9 of the 24 figures whose birthplace is known, and was matched by the regions of Central and North-Eastern Italy with a more recent history of industrialization, the so-called *Third Italy* (Trentino-Alto Adige, Emilia-Romagna, Tuscany and Umbria). In the period following Second World War, the BL from Latium, Southern Italy and the Islands also grew in number, mainly in connection with the expansion of the intervention of the *partecipazioni statali*, i.e. state-owned enterprises. They had virtually disappeared in the period between 1913 and 1927, then reappeared in 1936 with the presence of 2 individuals, and increased to 4 in 1952, 5 in 1960 and 6 in 1972.

Table 9.4. *Big linkers* by region of birth

Region	1913	1927	1936	1952	1960	1972
Piedmont	2	3	3	2	3	1
Lombardy	8	11	7	9	7	6
Liguria	1	1	-	3	-	2
Trentino-Alto Adige	1	-	-	-	-	1
Veneto	1	1	2	-	-	-
Friuli-Venezia Giulia	-	1	1	-	-	-
Emilia-Romagna	-	1	1	2	1	6
Tuscany	-	-	2	-	1	1
Umbria	-	-	1	1	1	1
Latium	-	-	-	3	2	2
Abruzzo	-	-	-	-	-	1
Campania	2	-	1	1	1	-
Apulia	-	-	-	-	-	1
Sicily	-	-	1	-	1	-
Sardinia	-	-	-	-	1	2
Overseas	-	1	-	-	-	-
Total	15	19	19	21	18	24
Not available	5	2	1	3	3	5

9.4. Education and training

The analysis of the level of education and the type of university degree obtained (e.g., engineering, economics or law) can serve as a proxy for the personal qualifications of the BL. This type of close examination appears to be very useful, for the literature has indicated the existence of a connection between the latter and the management models of the firms in which these figures served as directors [Ferratini Tosi et al. 1983]. More specifically, though referring to chairmen and general managers, rather than to board members in general, it has been held that there is a correlation between the qualifications and the duties (in production, sales or administration) performed prior to taking on management responsibilities, and the policies of the firms, such as the pursuit of diversification strategies in related or unrelated sectors [Fligstein 1990].

Table 9.5 presents the distribution of the BL by the level of education achieved. In 1913, university graduates made up exactly one-half of the sample, while, along with a small number of accountants (i.e. secondary-school graduates), there was a significant batch of individuals whose level of education (quite likely very low-level education) is not available. The impression is that the national business elite was somehow split in half. On the one hand, there was one part consisting of managers, with a solid university-level backgrounds and on the other hand, the persistence of a group of more traditional entrepreneurs with low-level formal educational training, qualified mainly in terms of their tacit skills and whose training was probably acquired through a long apprenticeship and training period at the helm of family businesses and sometimes also in foreign plants and banks [Chiesi 1981]. However, it cannot be excluded that there may have been individuals with secondary-school diplomas among the persons for whom this information was not available.

Table 9.5. *Big linkers* by level of education

Education	1913	1927	1936	1952	1960	1972
University degree	10	13	11	19	20*	24
- *Engineering*	*3*	*7*	*9*	*10*	*9*	*7*
- *Law*	*4*	*3*	*2*	*4*	*8*	*7*
- *Economics and Business Administration*	*2*	*3*	-	*4*	*3*	*9*
- *Agriculture*	*1*	-	-	*1*	-	-
- *Chemistry*	-	-	-	-	-	*1*
Secondary-school diploma	3	8	6	5	2	3
- *Classical school*	-	*4*	*3*	-	-	-
- *Accountancy (and commerce)*	*3*	*4*	*3*	*5*	*2*	*2*
- *Technical school*	-	-	-	-	-	*1*
Primary school	1	-	-	-	-	-
Not indicated	6	-	3	-	-	2
Total	20	21	20	24	22*	29

Legend: * in 1960 the number of university degrees exceeded the number of university graduates by 1, as one of the BL, Carlo Faina, had two university degrees: one in Law and the other in Economics and Business Administration.

The year 1927 saw a slight increase in the number of university graduates and a more substantial increase in the number of holders of secondary-school diplomas - now equally divided between commercial school and classical school diplomas -

while subjects without educational qualifications disappeared, at least for the time being. The situation did not change much in 1936: university graduates dropped from 62 to 55 per cent of the sample, as did the number of known holders of secondary-school diplomas, from 38 to 30 per cent. However, it is possible that one or two of the three persons whose educational qualifications are unknown may have had classical school diplomas. In the period after Second World War, the average level of education of the BL rose markedly to very high levels. University graduates were just short of 80 per cent of the sample in 1952, exceeded 90 per cent in 1962 and then stabilized at 83 per cent in 1972. Conversely, the number of holders of secondary school diplomas decreased and persons with no educational qualifications vanished almost completely from the scene.

There was a significant development regarding the type of university degree held. Between 1913 and 1936, engineers represented by far the most dynamic component, rising from 30 to over 80 per cent of the university graduates. The situation progressively started to balance out in 1952, in favor of law graduates and graduates in the fields of economics and business administration[3]. The economics and business administration graduates managed to surpass the engineers and the law graduates in 1972. The successful establishment of the law and economics degrees is actually a phenomenon that has characterized all industrial societies during the process of the growth and transformation of their business management systems, even if it became evident in Italy only in the early 1970s [Ferratini Tosi et al. 1983].

Table 9.6 reports some data that permit an evaluation as to the possibility of an interconnection between the year of birth, place of origin and the educational background of the BL[4]. First of all, note that the percentage of university graduates increased over time. In fact, just 7 (39 per cent) of the 18 individuals born before 1871 were university graduates. However, the same item shot up to 71 per cent (12 out of 17) for the persons born between 1871 and 1880, and to 83 per cent (10 out of 12) for those born between 1881 and 1890. In the next age group, that is, those born between 1891 and 1900, the percentage of university graduates dropped to two-thirds (4 out of 6). Then there was a rapid increase to 84 per cent (16 out of 19) for those born between 1901 and 1910, followed by an increase reaching the total number of persons born after that date (8 out of 8).

The *Industrial Triangle* supplied 56 per cent of the individuals making up the sample, the *Third Italy*, 28 per cent, and the remaining regions, 16 per cent. Yet, the latter, consisting of Latium, the South and the Islands, were the regions that placed the highest percentage of university graduates (85 per cent), followed by the *Third Italy* (73 per cent) and the *Industrial Triangle* (68 per cent).

This circumstance seems to depend only partly upon the fact that the *Industrial Triangle* counted a higher proportion of BL from less recent birth periods, in

[3] The term *Economics and Business Administration* is used in this essay to refer to the following Italian university degrees: *Scienze economiche e commerciali*, *Economia e commercio* and *Amministrazione aziendale*.

[4] Of course, this procedure was possible only for those 79 persons (77 per cent of the total) for whom all three items of information were available.

which the weight of university graduates was lower. In fact, for any given birth period, the *Industrial Triangle* never presented a percentage of university graduates higher than either one of the other two regional areas, and it was surpassed by the *Third Italy* in three birth periods (up to 1860, 1871-1880 and 1881-1890) and by Latium, the South and the Islands also in three other birth periods (1861-1870, 1891-1900 and 1901-1910). The fact that the regions comprising the North-West contributed a lower proportion of subjects with upper level educational qualifications to their own business elite is almost inherent in their structural characteristics, probably a consequence of the more precocious economic dynamism of those areas. In the presence of a more developed industrial matrix, the mechanisms of upward mobility at work were probably faster than those leading to the acquisition of a university education.

Table 9.6. *Big linkers* by year and macro-region of birth and by type of university degree

	Prior to 1861	1861-1870	1871-1880	1881-1890	1891-1900	1901-1910	1911-1920	After 1920	Total
Industrial Triangle: Total	5	7	11	8	2	8	1	2	44
- University graduates	2	3	8	6	1	7	1	2	30
- Engineering	-	*1*	*7*	*2*	*1*	*4*	*1*	-	*16*
- Law	-	-	*1*	*2*	-	*1*	-	*1*	*5*
- Economics and Bus. Adm.	*1*	*2*	-	*2*	-	*2*	-	*1*	*8*
- Agriculture	*1*	-	-	-	-	-	-	-	*1*
- Chemistry	-	-	-	-	-	-	-	-	-
Third Italy: Total	2	1	5	4	2	3	2	3	22
- University graduates	1	-	4	4	1	1	2	3	16
- Engineering	*1*	-	*4*	*3*	-	*1*	-	-	*9*
- Law	-	-	-	-	*1*	-	*1*	*1*	*3*
- Economics and Bus. Adm.	-	-	-	*1*	-	-	*1*	*2*	*4*
- Agriculture	-	-	-	-	-	-	-	-	-
- Chemistry	-	-	-	-	-	-	-	-	-
Latium-South-Islands: Total	-	2	1	-	2	8	-	-	13
- University graduates	-	1	-	-	2	8	-	-	11
- Engineering	-	-	-	-	-	-	-	-	-
- Law	-	*1*	-	-	*2*	*4*	-	-	*7*
- Economics and Bus. Adm.	-	-	-	-	-	*2*	-	-	*2*
- Agriculture	-	-	-	-	-	*1*	-	-	*1*
- Chemistry	-	-	-	-	-	*1*	-	-	*1*
Italy as a whole: Total	7	10	17	12	6	19	3	5	79
- University graduates	3	4	12	10	4	16	3	5	57
- Engineering	*1*	*1*	*11*	*5*	*1*	*5*	*1*	-	*25*
- Law	-	*1*	*1*	*2*	*2*	*5*	*1*	*2*	*14*
- Economics and Bus. Adm.	*1*	*2*	-	*3*	*1*	*4*	*1*	*3*	*15*
- Agriculture	*1*	-	-	-	-	*1*	-	-	*2*
- Chemistry	-	-	-	-	-	*1*	-	-	*1*

Legend: *Bus. Adm.* Business Administration.

This, however, is a personal qualification that faded away in the more recent birth periods (for those born after 1910), the members of which, as we have seen, were all university graduates. In short, a sort of convergence seems to have taken place: holding high-level educational qualifications now appears to have become a prerogative of the BL, regardless of the region or economic status of origin.

A good 44 per cent of the university graduates consisted of engineers (25 out of 57), followed by specialists in economics and business administration (26 per cent) and law (25 per cent), with two agronomists and a specialist in chemistry as well. A correlation exists between the year of birth, place of origin and type of university degree. All of the engineers were from the Central and Northern regions of Italy (16 from the *Industrial Triangle* and 9 from the *Third Italy*). None were born after 1921 and just one was born in the period between 1911 and 1920. Conversely, even though they did not contribute any engineers, Latium, the South and the Islands supplied one-half of the university graduates in law (7 out of 14). The geographical distribution of university degrees in economics and business administration appears to have been more uniform, varying from a minimum of 18 per cent in the Central-Southern sector to a maximum of 27 per cent in the *Industrial Triangle*.

Thus, as we have seen, while a university degree seems to have become more and more of a prerogative of the BL as such, it no longer consisted of a degree in engineering, not even for directors born in the Central and Northern regions of Italy. There seems to have been a convergence in this case as well, with a growing tendency of BL to be university graduates in law or in economics and business administration, regardless of the region of birth.

9.5. Parliamentary offices and appointments

Column 4 in Table 9.1.a-f provides information on parliamentary offices and appointments held by the BL. This serves as a proxy for the degree of overlap - and thus also of the cohesion, in a certain sense - between the nation's business elite and political elite. In the first three benchmark years, the number of BL who also sat in Parliament appears to be anything but negligible.

They were 6 in 1913 (30 per cent), 4 in 1927 (19 per cent) and 7 in 1936 (35 per cent). In the new Republic of Italy, however, the corresponding figure dropped drastically. In 1952, there was only one (4 per cent), none in 1960 and again just one in 1972 (3 per cent). In short, it seems to be confirmed that with the fall of fascism and the transition from the monarchy to the republic, a change also took place in the manner in which entrepreneurial interests were represented in the political sphere. In addition, unlike common practice in the previous period, the representation of their interests no longer took place through the direct participation of the leading entrepreneurs in the life of parliamentary institutions. These circumstances are strongly connected with the basic changes that had taken place in the political life of the country, during the transition from the dictatorship to a democratic government. Politics was now dominated by two large parties appealing to the masses - the Christian Democrat party and the Italian Communist party - with ideologies and political leaders alien to those of the industrial elite, albeit for different reasons. With the advent of the broadly based parties, political professionalism also took root. Thus the relationship between the social classes and public institutions became increasingly mediated by party and business association, leaving less room for the direct participation of the entrepreneurs in the nation's political life [Doria 1999].

9.6. Titles of nobility

Column 5 in Table 9.1.a-f furnishes information on any titles of nobility held by the BL. This operation serves as a proxy for the contribution of the aristocracy to the formation of the business elite. In this regard, it can be noted that very few titled individuals figured among the BL in all the benchmark years considered. In fact, they ranged between 2 and 3 for the period between 1913 and 1952, increased to 4 in 1960, and dropped to 3 again in 1972. The noble titles proved to have been passed on by virtue of hereditary privilege only in 2 cases for the monarchical period and in 6 for the period of the Republic. In short, the general impression is that overall, though not completely marginal, the contribution of the old aristocratic ruling class to the formation of the industrial and financial elite was a limited one for the entire period considered. In any case, these results are in keeping with the results of a previous study by Chiesi [1981].

9.7. The BL by career sector

The distribution of the directorships of the BL often proved to span over a very wide range of sectors. However, the reconstruction of their individual biographies made it possible to identify the prevalent career sector for each one of them. The prevalent career sector was defined as the sector in which an individual had dedicated most of his career, and by virtue of the affiliation with which he was able to accumulate a number of board positions sufficient to make him a BL. The results of this procedure are reported in column 6 of Table 9.1.a-f.

Table 9.7 outlines the abovementioned information in a concise form, for each benchmark year. In 1913, finance was the sector most represented, with 8 individuals out of 20, followed by banking with 5 persons, electrical power with 3, and textile and the sugar industry with 2[5]. There were no significant variations in 1927. There were still 8 individuals from the financial sector, electrical power experts jumped to 5 and ranked second, overtaking the bankers who dropped to 4.

[5] The sugar industry was considered separately from the other agro-food sections as it was a new sector, dominated by large-scale companies from the very beginning, unlike the other sections, which were deeply rooted in long-standing artisan traditions and in which small and very small firms prevailed for many years.

Table 9.7. *Big linkers* by career sector

Sector	1913	1927	1936	1952	1960	1972
Agro-food	-	-	-	1	1	2
Sugar	2	-	-	1	-	-
Textiles	2	-	1	1	-	2
Cement	-	1	2	1	1	1
Electrical power	3	5	6	6	6	-
Petroleum-chemistry	-	-	2	-	1	6
Steel	-	1	-	-	-	1
Metal-engineering	-	-	-	1	-	2
Motor-vehicles	-	-	1	2	1	-
Shipping	-	1	-	-	-	1
Banking	5	4	1	1	-	1
Finance	8	8	5	8	8	11
Insurance	-	1	1	-	-	-
Construction	-	-	-	2	1	-
Real estate	-	-	1	-	2	2
Total	20	21	20	24	21	29

In 1936, the crisis of the *mixed banks* almost led to the complete disappearance of the bankers, who dropped from 4 to one, and also to a significant reduction in the number of financiers, with a decrease from 8 to 5. The sector most represented was now the electrical power industry, with 6 individuals out of 20. There was also an increase in the number of subjects occupied in other sectors related to the Second Industrial Revolution - cement, chemicals, iron and steel, and motor vehicles - from 2 to 5. In the post-Second World War period, the bankers did not regain the positions they had lost after the decline of the *mixed banks*, but the financiers managed to recover first place already in 1952, with 8 persons out of 24, preceding the electrical power industry, which had come to a halt at 6. The situation remained basically the same in 1960. The financiers were still leading the ranks with 8 persons, followed by electrical power experts with 6. Another radical change, comparable only to the one that took place in 1936, occurred in 1972. Ten years after the nationalization effort, the electrical power industry was no longer supplying any BL. The financiers remained as the most numerous group, with 11 out of the 29 individuals (amounting to 37.9 per cent, just slightly lower than the 38.1 per cent of 1960), now followed by the chemical and oil executives, with 6.

There is a certain correlation between the career sector and some of the socio-demographic variables examined previously. For example, the electrical power experts - with a total of 17 persons, considering that as noted above, several individuals appeared in more than one benchmark year - were all university graduates, and a good 82 per cent of them consisted of engineers. The percentage of engineers gradually decreased as we move away from the *core* of the Second Industrial Revolution. Thus, the other sectors characterizing the Second Industrial Revolution (other than electrical power) tallied a 36 per cent share of engineers, finance a share of 22 per cent, while no engineers figured among the BL from the banking sector and sectors characterizing the First Industrial Revolution (textile and agro-food). This circumstance could lead one to sustain that the particular complexity of the technology of the Second Industrial Revolution (and particularly the technology adopted for the production and distribution of electrical power) required the high-level technical qualifications that only a graduate in engineering could offer, for many of the executive positions. Conversely, the highest percentage of law graduates - 16 subjects out of 36, amounting to 44 per cent - was found among the financiers, probably indicating that work in this capacity was exonerated from the technical requisites related to the specific characteristics of any individual industrial sectors and took the form of a role that could be assigned to many and highly diversified corporate contexts [Martinelli and Chiesi 1981]. Graduates in the fields of economics and business administration were, however, more numerous among the BL from the First Industrial Revolution sectors, although it should be noted that they included only 3 out of 7 subjects (37.5 per cent). Moreover, they were also the only university graduates existing in those sectors, which probably indicates that an entrepreneurial career in this sphere did not require particularly sophisticated codified technical skills.

BL from the *Industrial Triangle* prevailed in all sectors, although the percentages differ, ranging from a maximum of 83 per cent in sectors characteristic of the First Industrial Revolution to a minimum of 52 per cent in finance. The findings regarding the financiers are of particular interest. The nature of the skills required, which could be acquired mainly by law graduates, put this role within reach of the persons born in Latium, the regions of the South and the Islands, more than others. In fact, the incidence of the latter reached a maximum (30 per cent) precisely among the financiers, while their share decreased to 13 per cent in the electrical power industry, to 10 per cent of bankers and to 5 per cent of experts in other sectors relating to the Second Industrial Revolution. None of them figured among BL affiliated with sectors of the First Industrial Revolution. Lastly, the individuals born in regions of the *Third Italy* fluctuated between a maximum of 42 per cent of BL with careers in sectors of the Second Industrial Revolution other than electrical power, and a minimum of 10 per cent of those with banking careers.

9.8. The interlocking directorates among the BL

Throughout the entire historical period considered, the BL demonstrated a pronounced tendency to generate interlocking directorates (ID) among themselves, thus proving to have been - though with gradations varying between the different benchmark years - a markedly cohesive elite group over time.

Table 9.8 reports some essential data regarding the ID existing between the BL. The first row shows how many subjects were linked by interlocks to at least one other figure, for each benchmark year. In 1913, the number included all of the subjects: 20 out of 20. In the next four time intervals, all subjects but one were included: 20 out of 21 in 1927, 19 out of 20 in 1936, 23 out of 24 in 1952, and once again, 20 out of 21 in 1960. Then in 1972, the number of those with no links to others rose to 3 out of a total of 29, a circumstance in line with the system's reduced cohesion overall, following the nationalization of the electrical power industry [Rinaldi and Vasta 2003, 2005].

Table 9.8. Interlocking directorates (ID) between *Big linkers*

	1913	1927	1936	1952	1960	1972
BL with at least one ID with another BL	20	20	19	23	20	26
Number of total ID between BL	280	794	324	514	460	364
Average number of ID per BL	14.0	37.8	16.2	21.4	21.9	12.6
Total BL	20	21	20	24	21	29

The second row shows the number of total ID between the BL in the six benchmark years selected. In 1913, there were 280. In 1927, the number shot up to 794, reaching the peak value for the entire period considered, and which, probably not by coincidence, was registered precisely at the time of the apogee of the *mixed banks*. In 1936, there was a downturn by about 60 per cent, dropping down to 324. Later, there was another increase, bringing the number to 514 in 1952. In 1960, they dropped to 460, actually only an apparent fall, as the reduction in the total number of individuals considered, from 24 to 21, fully accounts for it. In 1972, there was a further decrease to 364.

Lastly, the third row shows the average number of ID per BL. It rose from 14 in 1913 to 37.8 in 1927, registering in this case as well the peak value for the entire period considered, offering further confirmation of the fact that the elite group reached the point of its greatest cohesion in the golden era of the *mixed banks*. In 1936, it plunged down to 16.2, a value only slightly higher than the average for 1913, and then rose to 21.4 in 1952 and to 21.9 in 1960. In 1972, it plummeted down to the lowest point reached in the entire period examined, 12.6, which underscores the fact that even the business elite became less cohesive, at the time marked by the reduction in the overall cohesion of the system as a result of the nationalization of the electrical power industry.

9.9. Typology of the BL

An attempt to define a typology of BL was made on the basis of the biographical information available and an analysis of the number of seats held by each one of them. Seven types were identified as follows: (i) top managers of large private enterprises; (ii) intra-group fiduciaries; (iii) finance capitalists; (iv) network specialists; (v) owners of smaller private groups; (vi) local integrators; (vii) fiduciaries of state-owned enterprises. At this point, it should be kept in mind that in the course of their careers, various figures presented characteristics that could be classified under more than one type. In such cases, the classification was decided on the basis of the type that seemed to be prevalent upon the entry of their name among the BL.

9.9.1. The top managers of large private enterprises

A first group of BL consists of those persons who, in different periods of time, held top positions in the largest private entrepreneurial groups. There was a total of 22 individuals, 8 of whom appearing in more than one benchmark year; 15 of them were salaried managers and 7 were the principals of the firms that they managed.

All but one of the salaried top managers (93 per cent of the total) were university graduates: 9 in engineering, 4 in law and one in economics and business administration; 8 of them were born in regions of the *Industrial Triangle*, 5 in regions of the *Third Italy* and 2 in the South.

Ten of them - 7 graduates in engineering and 3 law graduates - were directors of large private electrical power companies. In fact, in this sector, an early process of separation between ownership and management was observable as far back as the early pioneer phase. The capital of the first electrical power companies was subscribed by banks, financiers, industrialists and persons of local prominence animated by modernization efforts. Men capable of interweaving local relations, adept at raising funds for financing and with the skills needed to manage advanced technology, were placed at the helm of these firms. At a later stage, starting in the first two decades of the 20th century, when the sector underwent an intense process of concentration, in which a few large regional groups gained a dominant position, the *system builders* emerged, who managed these groups as salaried managers [Segreto 1992; Hertner 1993]. Among them, a pre-eminent position is occupied by the top executives of Edison, the largest company in the sector: Carlo Esterle, managing director of the company from 1896 to 1918, who combined company expansion with the safeguarding of the interests of the principle financing bank, the Banca Commerciale Italiana (COMIT); then his successor, Giacinto Motta, managing director from 1918 to 1942 and chairman from 1935 to 1942, who steered the company away from the COMIT bank orbit and over to the Credito Italiano (CREDIT) bank in the early 1920s, and led the way in 1935 to its denationalization two years after it had fallen under the state-owned IRI holding's control; and Motta's two successors, Giorgio Valerio and Vittorio De Biasi who managed the company from the end of the Second World War to the 1962 nationalization and the merger with Montecatini in 1965 [Pavese 1993; Vitiello 1993].

Among the salaried top managers not operating in the electrical power sector, there were two main executives of what until 1965 was the nation's largest chemical company, Montecatini: Guido Donegani, who was at the head of the company from 1910 to the end of Second World War, and Carlo Faina, who managed the company from 1946 until the 1965 merger with Edison [Amatori 1992, 1994]. Joining them, there was Emilio Bruzzone - the only one of the group who was not a university graduate - general manager from 1896, vice-chairman from 1919 and chairman of Ligure Lombarda (sugar) from 1923, an office he was to hold until his death in 1929; Arturo Bocciardo, from 1921 to 1945 managing director and chairman of a number of steel companies; and Vittorio Valletta, chairman of FIAT between 1946 and 1966 [Bonelli 1969; Bairati 1983; Tonizzi 2001].

Almost all salaried top managers showed a high occupational stability within the same company. Such a circumstance - totally different from what was the case in the US and other Anglophone countries - seems to reflect an insecurity of managerial status in Italy. In fact, according to US experience, top managers in large firms may be considered as professionals in that they have a specialized university background plus a varied working experience. However, as far as Italian top managers are concerned, they did not appear to be as *real* professionals, that is persons who should be identified more with their roles as organizers than with the firms which employed them. Although armed with a university degree, they seemed still uncertain of their professional status as managers, as this status was conferred by the firm that employed them, but not recognized or guaranteed outside of it. Italian top managers could therefore be best compared to Japanese managers, who presented the same immobilized characteristics, since they also spent their whole working life within the firm that first employed them [Derossi 1976].

Lastly, we must observe that salaried top managers figured among the BL in all the benchmark years, except for the last one, 1972, a circumstance that seems to be in keeping with the thesis put forth by Ragozzino [1969]. According to his line of thought, the nationalization of the electrical power industry brought what had thus far been Italy's most significant experience in private managerial capitalism to an end, resulting in the emergence of a new structure of control in which family capitalism resumed a central position.

As for the top owner-managers, only 4 out of 7 (57 per cent of the total) were university graduates: 2 in engineering, one in law and one in economics and business administration. They were joined by 2 managers with classical secondary school diplomas and one with no secondary school education; 5 were from regions in the *Industrial Triangle* and 2 from the *Third Italy*.

In this group, Giovanni Agnelli, the founder of FIAT, and the two members of the Pesenti family - owners of Italcementi, the nation's largest cement company - stand out. Antonio Pesenti was at the head of the company between the two World Wars, whereas his nephew, Carlo, directed the enterprise between 1942 and 1984, the year of his death. Under his management, Italcementi became a large conglomerate with activity extending beyond the cement industry, into banking, insurance, metal and mechanical industries, electrical power production, paper manufacturing, real estate and finance. However, starting in the 1970s, the group was forced to rescale drastically and this process was completed in the mid 1980s by his son Giampiero, with a return to the core business, that is, to the cement industry [Cingolani 1990; Bruno and Segreto 1996].

The ID generated by the top managers of large private enterprises - including both salaried managers and principals - consisted largely of board positions overlapping share control relations. However, as many as 16 top managers out of 22 also held offices in banking and insurance firms. These ID were originally generated mainly by entrepreneurs allied with the *mixed banks*, sometimes just for short periods of time [Cohen 1967]. However, while reflecting a change in the relations between banks and industries after the crisis of the *mixed bank* system, starting in 1936 the persisting continuance of this type of ID, should not generally be seen as the manifestation of a dominance of the industrial enterprises over the banks and insurance companies. Undoubtedly, such cases existed, but they do not seem to have constituted the prevailing condition. Rather, the impression is that they were ID of the type defined as *persuasive* by Pennings [1980]. For a better understanding of the nature of these ID, it should be considered that the banks and insurance companies also have a role in the collection of data on the general business trends and status of the various individual productive sectors, a role which, in a certain sense, resembles that of trade associations. Thus, banks and insurance companies end up becoming depositories of information and the top managers of industrial enterprises may be very interested in gaining access to that information. However, banks and insurance companies may have every reason for opening up their boards of directors to the managers of industrial enterprises that could become excellent clients owing to their size and solidity.

9.9.2. The intra-group fiduciaries

This category consists of 19, not very well known persons, apparently minor executives or consultants for large industrial enterprises, who held offices above all, and sometimes exclusively, in firms within the entrepreneurial group of affiliation.

As a whole, 5 of them were affiliated with the electrical power sector and they were all engineers. Of the remaining fiduciaries, 4 - one engineer, one law graduate, one accountant and one whose educational background was unknown - were in the chemical sector, 3 - a graduate in agriculture and 2 accountants - were in the finance sector, 2 - one graduate in economics and business administration and one accountant - in the oil sector, 2 - one engineer and one accountant - in the sugar industry, whereas the last 3, all of whom were engineers, were distributed amongst the cement industry, construction and the automotive industry. The region of origin was known for just 12 out of the 19 individuals: 7 were from the *Industrial Triangle*, 4 from the *Third Italy* and one from Latium.

9.9.3. The finance capitalists

The finance capitalists consist of individuals whose positions generated ID that can be traced back to Rudolf Hilferding's [1910] theory of finance capital. The underlying idea is that the control of credit flows and more infrequently, of share capital, permits banks to exercise a strong influence over the management of industrial enterprises through the creation of a system of asymmetrical interdependent relations. The latter exercises its control also through the introduction of its own fiduciaries on the boards of directors of the companies with which it has financial relations. The presence of the fiduciaries strengthens the personal relations existing between the group of bank executives and the group of company executives from the company being assisted and allows the banks prompt access to knowledge about thc goings-on and prospects of the various industrial sectors. This guiding knowledge serves the banks to act accordingly in its credit and commercial activities and also in fostering the formation of syndicates and combinations.

It was possible to identify several types of finance capitalists. First of all, there was the set of individuals indicated in Table 9.1.a-f as bankers. They were professional managers of credit institutions, trained and *raised* in the banking sector, within which they passed through all of the most important stages of their careers. All the bankers present among the BL also held a number of seats on the boards of directors of industrial firms. Among the latter, the most numerous proved to be those linked up with the COMIT, the largest *mixed bank* in the country [Conti and La Francesca 2000].

Secondly, the finance capitalists include part of the persons who were classified as financiers in Table 9.1.a-f, that is, individuals who sat on the boards of directors of industrial companies in the capacity of representatives of the lending credit institutions, but who were not professional bankers. For the Società Bancaria Italiana, there were 2 attorneys, upon whom the institution probably relied also for the dispatch of legal matters. For the CREDIT bank, there were an attorney and an entrepreneur, the owner of an allied conglomerate with large shareholdings in the banking sector. Instead, for the COMIT bank there were 2 engineers to whom the bank entrusted the management of the holdings in a sector like the electrical power sector with its particularly complex technology.

In the first two benchmark years, the finance capitalists were particularly numerous: as many as 8 of the 20 BL in 1913 would seem to be referable to this figure. In 1927, they were 7 out of 21. Starting in 1936, the incidence of finance capitalists dropped drastically: only one of those appearing in 1927 figured on the list that year. In truth, this circumstance is not at all surprising, after the 1936 Banking Law had taken measures to separate commercial credit from industrial credit. In the period following Second World War, very few finance capitalists remained, totaling 5 in all.

9.9.4. The network specialists

This type consists of those financiers who held a large number of seats on the boards of firms belonging to several different entrepreneurial groups, but without a *strong* or prevalent affiliation with any of them. In most cases, these figures were relatively unknown, people who functioned as *zipper figures* between the largest state-owned and private groups, in many ways comparable to the network specialists described by Stokman and Wasseur [1985]. In addition to contributing to a more rapid circulation of information, these board members seem to have performed - as Raffaele Mattioli [1962] originally had occasion to observe - an essential function in ensuring a strategic co-ordination and stabilization of the positions of control in the most important private entrepreneurial groups. In some cases, such as that of Lodovico Mazzotti Biancinelli (1927), Mario Rossello (1952 and 1960) and Enrico Marchesano (1960), the network specialists were ex-fiduciaries or ex-executives of the *mixed banks*. Their biographies are extremely interesting. Consider for example the case of Rossello. Born in 1877, Rossello, an accountant, became the CREDIT bank's alternate auditor in 1913 and the following year, the bank's statutory auditor. In 1918 he was hired and nominated central manager by the bank. In 1921 he was appointed managing director and he remained in that office until 1924, when he transferred to the Banca Nazionale di Credito. He was the managing director of the latter institution and became its vice-president in 1927, upon the merger with the CREDIT bank, which he served as a board member until 1945. After Second World War, his role tended to take on more and more of the characteristics of a financier setting himself up as a *trait d'union* between the nation's leading entrepreneurial groups. Thus, in 1952 he was chairman of Franco Tosi, vice-chairman of Italcable and a board member for Edison, Bastogi, Distillerie Italiane (Eridania group), Fratelli Borletti, Rinascente (Borletti group), Rhodiatoce (Montecatini group) and Metallurgica Italiana (GIM group). In 1957, he returned as a board member for the CREDIT bank, a position he left definitively in 1966. In the meantime, he had become chairman of Edison, vice-chairman of Italpi and a member of the board of the Banca Unione, Credito Lombardo, Montecatini, SNIA Viscosa and RAS. He died in 1973 [Conti and La Francesca 2000].

A second group of network specialists was made up of engineers, such as Pietro Chiesa (1936), Francesco Cartesegna (1936 and 1952) and Eugenio Radice Fossati (1960 and 1972). These men began to have this role at a relatively mature age, after long careers spent managing large construction projects or industrial plants. Cartesegna appears to be the most interesting figure among them. He was born in 1882 in the Province of Modena of a family of Piedmontese magistrates. He graduated in engineering from the Politecnico of Turin, and was soon to stand out in the engineering department of one of the city's most well known construction firms, Giannassi & Pollino. He fervidly applied himself to the new technique of reinforced concrete and had Giacomo Mattè Trucco as a master. In 1920, Giovanni Agnelli entrusted him with the management of the construction of the Moncenisio hydroelectric power plant. He later joined Mattè Trucco in directing the construction of the FIAT factory in Lingotto. Between 1923 and 1927 he took part in the creation of the first group of plant facilities built by SME in Sila mountains. Later, Giovanni Agnelli wanted him in again as the planner and road-builder for the Milan-Turin motorway. His activity took a different direction starting in 1932, gradually becoming less occupied with the direction of large-scale construction sites and more involved with consulting work and seats on the boards of directors of joint-stock companies. He was a consultant for the hydroelectric problems with FIAT's automotive production, a board member for La Centrale and also FIAT, consultant and then managing director of Imprese Italiane all'Estero of the FIAT group. He was appointed vice-chairman of Bastogi in 1945. In 1952, he was chairman of CO.GE.CO. (Edison group), Imprese Italiane all'Estero and Autostrada Torino-Milano (both belonging to the FIAT group), vice-chairman of Idroelettrica Medio Adige (a joint-venture between Edison, SADE and La Centrale), La Centrale and Bastogi, as well as a member of the board of directors for CONIEL, FIAT, Idroelettrica Alto Liri (a joint-venture between SME and La Centrale), Immobiliare L'Edificio (La Centrale group), Società Elettrica Ala (a joint-venture between La Centrale and Montecatini) and for Trentina di Elettricità (IRI group). He died in 1955 [Vitiello 1993].

Then there were two figures who could be defined as *professional financiers*: Tullio Torchiani (1960 and 1972) and Giuseppe Martelli (1972). They functioned as network specialists in the capacity of managers and fiduciaries of the nation's largest finance company, Bastogi, which took on a central role in ensuring the stability of the positions of control characterizing Italian capitalism from the mid 1930s on through to the nationalization of the electrical power industry in 1962 [Piluso 1992].

Two more figures, Giuseppe Bevione (1936) and Mario Dosi (1972), functioned as *zippers* between the major entrepreneurial groups - and also between the latter and public institutions - mainly by virtue of their political affiliations, with the National Fascist Party in the case of Bevione and with the Christian Democratic Party in the case of Dosi, parties in whose ranks they were long-standing members of Parliament [Badon 1994-95].

To conclude, Guido Sacchi (1913, 1927 and 1936), with a background in accounting, should be included among the network specialists. Sacchi, an accountant, was born in Milan in 1867, the son of one of Milan's most respected professionals. He started his career in accounting in the offices of one of city's most important accounting firms. He was nominated to sit as a director or as an auditor on the boards of many of the earliest large joint-stock companies established between the close of the 19th century and the early decades of the 20th century, such as Cotonificio di Solbiate, Lanificio di Gavardo, Società Tessuti Stampati De Angeli Frua, S.A. Frette, Manifatture Rossari e Varzi, Linificio e Canapificio Nazionale, and many more. He also held offices in banking firms. In fact, he was a member of the board of the Banca Belinzaghi and also of the COMIT bank, after a period in which he served as an auditor. He decided to leave the profession of accountant in order to oversee the business affairs of the companies he was serving as a board member more closely and to which he had decided to devote himself entirely. He died in Milan in 1937[6].

9.9.5. The owners of smaller private groups

This group consists of 11 persons whose unifying feature is that they were owners of entrepreneurial groups that were smaller than the ones discussed above, though larger than an overwhelming majority of the other remaining enterprises in Italy. Seven of them were university graduates: 4 in economics and business administration, 2 in law and just one in engineering. There is probably some connection between this circumstance and the fact that the groups they owned showed little or

[6] An obituary for Guido Sacchi is contained in the Historical Archives of the Banca Commerciale Italiana, *Amministratori Delegati, Carte di Raffaele Mattioli 1925-1972,* Serie: *Segreteria degli Amministratori Delegati Facconi e Mattioli (AD2) 1927-1972*, Cart. 15-18: *Rapporti con Terzi (persone e società)*, Faldone 16: *Persone P-V e corrispondenza varia (1933-1972)*, Fascicolo 21: *Condoglianze*, Guido Sacchi.

no inclination towards sectors of the Second Industrial Revolution. In fact, in 5 cases, the groups took on the form of conglomerates, in 3 cases the groups were active mainly in the textile industry, and in one case each in the electrical power industry, in the mechanical sector and in the shipping sector. As for their geographic origins, as many as 9 of these individuals were natives of regions in the *Industrial Triangle*, one was a native of the *Third Italy* and one of Southern Italy.

As many as 10 of them also held seats on the boards of directors of banking firms; 7 of them were members of the boards of small banks. This appears to be of great interest and also seems to underscore that alongside the networks that involved the large banks and the largest industrial groups, highly specific networks were developing at the local level, networks in which banks and smaller firms could find a point of coalescence. The presence of the owners of smaller enterprises on the boards of directors of local banks was not usually an expression of the dominance of the owners over the banks, however, it did generate ID of the *persuasive* type. The other 3 were members of the boards of *mixed banks*: one for the COMIT bank, one for the CREDIT bank, and one for a bank controlled by the latter, the Banca Nazionale di Credito.

9.9.6. The local integrators

There were also several figures who were not the principals of any entrepreneurial groups, but seem to have been core figures in networks of firms (both manufacturing and non-manufacturing firms) strongly marked by local connections.

One has the impression that there were two different types of local integrators. On the one hand, one finds a figure like Guido Rossi - future CONSOB (the Italian Security Exchange Commission) chairman, but originally linked up with Pirelli - who in 1960 seemed to function as a vector of hierarchical relations, the expression of the dominance of a large industrial group over an aggregate of smaller firms. In fact, in that year he was the director of Pirelli & C. (the group's holding), 2 banks, 3 finance companies and about 10 small and medium-sized firms operating in Milan in the food, textile and mechanical sectors.

On the other hand, a different type of local integrator seems to come to light. Consider the cases of Giuseppe Stoffel (1913), Carlo Malnati (1952) and Virginio Bernero (1972). None of them had a seat on the boards of directors of large firms. All 3 concentrated their positions in small and medium-sized firms, the first 2 in Milanese firms and Bernero in Piedmont. Malnati and Bernero did not even have any connections with the other BL. It would seem that these figures served a very important function in ensuring the cohesion of the local networks that were the expression of the ability of some of the small and medium-sized firms - especially in the textile and mechanical sectors - to develop interrelations, create alliances and gain access to strategic resources, without this necessarily involving subordinate relations with the banks or larger enterprises.

9.9.7 The fiduciaries of state-owned enterprises

There was a last group of 8 figures whose positions were prevalently (and in one case, exclusively) concentrated in state-owned enterprises. They seem to differ from the managers and fiduciaries of private enterprises more in terms of the region of birth than the university degree obtained. In fact, only one of the 8 board members of state-owned enterprises was from the *Industrial Triangle*, while of the remaining 7, 4 were from regions of the *Third Italy*, one from Latium and 2 from the South. As for their educational background, 7 of them were university graduates - 3 in engineering, one in chemistry and 3 in economics and business administration - and one had a diploma from a secondary school of accounting. None of them sat in Parliament, although almost all were affiliated with, or supporters of, the Christian Democratic Party. Lastly, 3 of them had significant previous professional experience also in the private sector, 4 had spent their entire careers within the state-owned enterprises and public institutions, whereas biographical information was not available for the remaining one.

9.10. Conclusions

At this point, an attempt can be made to provide some concluding considerations.

Firstly, the analysis conducted demonstrated that the existence of persons who held a great number of positions on the boards of directors of joint-stock companies - the BL - remained a significant phenomenon throughout the entire period of time considered. It can thus be considered to be a structural feature of Italian capitalism, a distinguishing characteristic even under conditions of changing institutional arrangements, in spite of the fact that the maximum incidence was reached during the period of the apogee of the *mixed banks*.

The prosopographical investigation highlighted the progressive ageing of the BL over time, probably as a consequence of the augmented complexity of corporate organization, which generally slowed down and lengthened entrepreneurial careers. Such a circumstance also reflected the high degree of occupational stability of top managers of the larger private companies. While there was a longstanding prevalence of figures with origins from the North-Western regions of Italy, this situation underwent readjustment in the period following Second World War, with the Central and North-Eastern regions taking the lead, along with the Southern regions, though to a lesser degree. Already fairly high in 1913 with precisely one-half of the BL being university graduates, the average level of education increased in the years that followed, to the point that all of the BL born after 1911 proved to have university degrees. Significant changes did take place regarding the field of study. In fact, while engineers prevailed in the beginning, generally graduates of the prestigious universities of applied sciences of Milan and Turin, over time there was a gradual turn towards law and the economics and business administration faculties. The subjects holding seats in Parliament, which reached 35 per cent of the total during the monarchy, were virtually non-existent during the period of the Republic, whereas the presence of titled individuals was basically insignificant during the entire time interval considered.

The analysis of the distribution of seats held by sector, the ID and types of BL showed a prevalence of figures affiliated with the *mixed banks* (finance capitalists) for the first two benchmark years (1913 and 1927), replaced by a predominance of the electrical power sector between 1936 and 1960. A new rotation occurred after the nationalization of the electrical power industry, bringing a core group of figures connected with finance and the chemical and oil sectors, to the system's core level in 1972. Two further considerations can be made on the basis of these observations. The first regards the fact that the shift that occurred, starting at a certain point in time, from university degrees in engineering to degrees in law and economics and business administration can only be partially interpreted as a reflection of a trend shared with all industrialized countries, in connection with the transformation of corporate management systems. In this case, in Italy, the consequences of a purely domestic situation, that is, the nationalization of the electrical power industry in 1962, must be considered along with this circumstance. This act not only demolished the primary example of private managerial capitalism existing in Italy, but it also swept away the sector in which, owing to the complexity of the technical and scientific knowledge required, the proportion of top managers with university degrees in engineering was highest.

The second consideration concerns the role of the *mixed banks*. While on the one hand, a position largely consolidated by previous research was confirmed and namely that in the first three decades of the 20th century, the *mixed banks* played a central role in Italian capitalism, this study seems to suggest that in a certain sense, the *mixed banks* continued to serve an extremely important function in ensuring the cohesion of the system, even after their disappearance. This cohesion was brought about by the transformation of several figures who had served as fiduciaries of the *mixed banks*, into network specialists.

One last note concerns the relations between state-owned and private enterprises. The identification of a type of BL consisting of fiduciaries of state-owned enterprises does not mean that the private sector and state-owned sector were not closely interconnected. It suffices to keep in mind that already in 1936, no less than 12 out of 20 BL (60 per cent) simultaneously held offices in state-owned and private enterprises and that through the ID that they generated, the IRI group proved to be linked up with almost all of the largest private financial and industrial groups and with IOR, the Vatican bank. In 1952, the number of BL simultaneously present in state-owned and private enterprises had risen to 16 out of 24 (67 per cent) and through them, IRI companies were interconnected with 15 of the 20 largest private groups. In 1960, the situation was basically unchanged. The number of figures holding offices in state-owned and private enterprises amounted to 13 out of 21 (62 per cent) and their ID linked IRI to 14 of the 20 largest private groups. Lastly, the incidence of the BL present in state-owned and private enterprises continued to be significant in 1972, though it dropped to 16 out of 29 (55 per cent). The IRI group companies were linked up with 7 of the 20 largest private groups, while 2 other important state-owned groups, ENI and EFIM, proved to be interlocked with 5 and 2 large private groups, respectively.

Conclusions

Renato Giannetti and Michelangelo Vasta

As underlined in Chap. 1 of this volume, the historiography of the enterprise followed two different approaches during the 20th century. The first, and oldest, is based on the paradigm structure-behavior-performance and identifies a number of long run regularities in industrial structure. These are represented, firstly, by the correlation between concentration and profitability based on the existence of technical barriers to entry, economies of scale, and economies of the financial type - monopolistic groups - who can influence prices manipulating the level of production. Barriers to entry, in their turn, slow down innovation and market growth, which derives from the introduction of new products and new processes. This, finally, gives rise to a size distribution of firms which is strongly skewed to the right, namely a configuration made up of few large firms and a plethora of small firms with high levels of mortality. This is the basis on which historiography develops, in general it is critical of the Italian experience, of *financial capitalism*, of the *narrowness* of the market, of monopolies and of the size *dualism* of firms.

The second, and more recent approach, is based, more or less consciously, on the paradigm of modern industrial economics. According to the latter, the explanation of industry and firm dynamics depends on the description of the *actor*'s strategy, that is, on the construction of models according to the specificities of each firm and on the detailed description of the institutional contexts in which it operates. Moreover the rationality of firm strategies must be contextualized with respect to the cultures and the mental models of the economic *actors*. Finally, in this perspective, the statistical regularities of size distribution lose their importance, and are substituted by a polymorphism which depends on the history of the single firms *tout court*. In following this approach, historiography's attention is concentrated on niches (textiles, food, and iron and steel) and on the meticulous description of the strategies of dominant firms in these sub-markets. This historiography, moreover, is decidedly less critical of the Italian experience than the other approach and is inclined to enhance the rationality of the strategies used by the economic *actors* to cope with historical exogenous shocks.

The aim of this study is to act as a bridge between the two approaches with the conviction that the search for generalizations - structural bounds and statistical regularities - can avoid the risk of "Explaining everything, explaining nothing", as John Sutton [1990] argued fifteen years ago when dealing with the state of industrial economics. This observation, however, can currently be applied to a considerable part of the historiography of the firm. For this reason, three essays (Chaps. 2-4) describe the industrial structure in search of statistical regularities, and another (Chap. 7) proposes a cross-section approach to the analysis of profits dynamics, typical of the structure-behavior-performance tradition. Following the same perspective, another traditional theme, that of groups and their characteristics, is investigated (Chap. 6) with the aid of network analysis. This study proposes two further *strong* structural dimensions, even though they are new in comparison to the traditional structural approach: *technological regimes* and product life cycle. These are discussed in the analysis of the largest 200 firms (Chap. 5) and in the dynamics of firms aggregated according to historical phases (Chap. 4). In the first case we link the technological dynamics characterizing the world economy with the evolution of the structure of the large Italian firm; in the second, we measure the entry/exit flow of firms, linking them to the different phases of product maturity. These are strong and disputed bounds which, however, have been useful in discovering a number of regularities in the system of enterprises.

The structure of Italian industrial enterprises differs in a few important ways from the stylized pattern of the main industrialized countries. Firstly, even though there is significant structural change, there is a certain delay in the spread of the technologies of the Second Industrial Revolution and consequently the persistence of firms linked to the technologies of the First Industrial Revolution. This aspect is evident both from the analysis of the census data (Chap. 2) and from the dynamics of largest 200 firms (Chap. 5). This delay is also clear in the current structure of Italian industry, which is characterized by a prevalence of traditional sectors and much smaller firms as compared to the leading countries. Large Italian firms are also comparatively smaller in average size, even though there is a tendency to growth as from the beginning of the 1970s. The analysis of their sectoral composition shows, in contrast to industry as a whole, a growing capacity in adapting to new *technological regimes* in the introductory phase, but this is almost always followed by difficulties in consolidating. In the Third Industrial Revolution it is often foreign firms who introduce the new technologies, particularly in the computers and pharmaceutical industries.

In contrast to Chandlerian inspired literature, the large Italian firm is, moreover, characterized by a high level of turbulence, also at the intra-sectoral level. In other words, there seem to be no robust barriers to entry, but on the contrary, there is even a frequent turnover of firms operating within the same sector. The few consolidated firms seem incapable of reinforcing their positions or of diversifying into new sectors. The dynamic distribution of the major firms shows convergence towards the bottom of the size class. In other words these firms grow, but there is only a modest growth in absolute size because the firms which reach the higher levels often recede. The whole universe is also characterized by a large number of *leaping frogs*, i.e. the phenomenon by which firms, in the different phases, leap many positions forward in the size ranking. However, firms also leap backwards, confirming the fact that those with the fastest growth are not able to stabilize.

Survival analysis, carried out for all the historical phases with reference to life cycle and *technological regime* (Chap. 4), presents a few interesting regularities. The first is the higher mortality of the small firms, mainly in mature sectors and in those with a high technological intensity. The larger firms also encounter greater risks in the high technological intensity sectors while their life expectancy is greater in the mature sectors and those with a low technological intensity. A further interesting characteristic is the fact that until 1971 there are no small firms in the mature sectors with a high technological intensity in the Italian system of enterprises, and therefore the niche enterprise discussed in recent literature is missing. This allows us to exclude the possibility of the phenomenon having historical roots, and to attribute it, if necessary, to the *surprises* of the 1970s.

In general, the Italian system of manufacturing firms does not appear to be very concentrated. Sectoral concentration, furthermore, shows a weak tendency towards a decrease especially in the post-Second World War period (Chap. 3). The result, however, is decidedly different if we consider the effects which the spread of the group form had on increasing the market power of a small number of subjects. If we consider *consolidated* concentration, the competitive structure of the industrial sectors changes considerably showing, on the one hand, a strong decrease in the number of *competitive* sectors. On the other, a rise of the *monopolistic* characteristics of the capital goods sector, with a peak in 1960 underlining how even post-War expansion was accomplished through the development of great industrial groups (Chap. 6). Only a minority of firms is isolated from the network, while the majority forms part of a global entirely interconnected network. Empirical evidence also shows that the role of the banking and financial system is relevant at least until the beginning of the 1970s, in contrast to the conventional wisdom hypothesis according to which, the bank is "absent from the table of great industrial capitalism" at least from the 1950s. After the nationalization of the electrical industry the banks, together with the insurance companies, return to the centre of the system, reacquiring, at least in part, the position they had held in the 1920s. Despite the financial sector's role, industrial firms tend to connect to each other directly, probably in search of productive or market complementarities.

Further evidence of the high level of collusion can also be found in the study of the individuals most present on the boards of directors, the *big linkers* (Chap. 9). There is, in fact, evidence for a thick network of company connections centered around a small group of individuals. Finally, another characteristic that emerges is the existence of very close relationships between public and private firms, these relationships also appear decidedly more intense than hitherto assumed by historiography. The IRI group, for example, is connected to almost all the major private industrial and financial groups.

Large enterprise is generally considered more capable of producing profits because of its competitive advantage in terms of innovative capacity and the barriers to entry with which it can exclude new incomers. The analysis of the profitability of firms (Chap. 7) shows how, also in the Italian case - traditionally characterized by smaller size compared to those of the leading countries - there is a positive relationship between size of the firm and profitability. Technological potential is considered one of the key factors in the success of firms, as the general expectation is for new sectors to be the most profitable. This applies also in the case of Italy, even though the number of firms in these sectors is low. Historiography has often commented on the *narrowness* of the market and the incomplete technological matrix which characterizes Italian industry. This evaluation is confirmed as regards the period preceding the Second World War, given the particularly negative performance of the *specialized supplier* firms, which are crucial to the completion of the productive matrix. The *narrowness* of the market, in fact, hinders the specialization of Italian mechanical firms reducing productivity; the lack of specialization, in its turn, creates bottlenecks in product offer, as in the case of machine tools, necessary for the completion of the productive matrix. As from the post-Second World War period, on the other hand, the greater opening to trade and the increase in sectoral integration seems to produce greater levels of firm specialization, thus completing the productive matrix and leading, as a consequence, to the better performance of the *specialized supplier* firms.

Amongst the sectors with the highest profitability in aggregate terms, there are, in fact, the non-metallic mineral and the manufacturing n.e.c. sectors, while the mechanical and the transport equipment sectors show very much more modest performances. The study also shows that in a first phase, at least until the end of the 1920s, the traditional *light* industry sectors have the highest levels of profitability, while the *heavy* sectors, especially the chemical, show a greater capacity to generate profits from the second half of the 1930s and during the Golden age.

The identification of generalizations is useful, but in order to explain the industrial structure and the dynamics of firms a greater attention to the history of the single firms is also necessary. Chapters 8 and 9 open a perspective on the variety of historical experiences linked to the events or single personalities which determine the path of development taken by single firm. From this an extreme variety in the strategies of firms emerges, confirming, however, a few permanencies already amply dealt with in historiography. A few elements of the Italian delay in firm's structure in fact are confirmed, such as the scarceness of public companies, the limited introduction of organizational innovation - as shown by the slow affirmation of the multidivisional form - or the scarcity of investments in R&D. At the same time, there is also a significant and original entrepreneurial liveliness as shown, for example, by the success strategies linked to product innovation and marketing of a few firms in the food sector and, more generally, by the brilliant results of a number of medium-sized family business firms. These, for example Perugina and Campari in the food sector or Campagnolo in the light mechanics sector, were capable of competing on the international market. The prosopographical survey (Chap. 9) shows the existence of a large variety of entrepreneurial and managerial typologies characterized by different training, competencies and strategies. Well-known figures emerge, such as the top managers of the large private firms, for example Motta (Edison) and Valletta (FIAT), but also apparently secondary managers who undertook the role of technical trustees of great industrial groups, for example Zuccolotto for the SIR-Rumianca group or Parodi in the Eridania group. At the same time, side by side with the figures of the great Italian bankers (Toeplitz, Baragiola, etc.) traditionally brought to the fore by historiography, other characters emerge such as the network specialists, Mazzotti Biancinelli or Rossello, who accumulated several positions in the boards of directors of companies belonging to various entrepreneurial groups.

To conclude, this study has tried to explain the historical experience of the Italian industrial firm in the 20th century at the crossroads between the search for generalization and the complexity of historical *accidents* which mark the real course of life of firms. The search for empirical regularities, however, currently seems the most urgent task.

Appendix: the source and the Imita.db dataset

Michelangelo Vasta

The serial source used in the study (henceforth *Notizie statistiche*) is composed of a series of volumes - the complete list can be found below - edited and published by Credito Italiano, from 1906 to 1925, and since 1928, by the Associazione fra le società italiane per azioni (ASIPA).

Credito Italiano (ed.), *Notizie statistiche sulle principali società italiane per azioni quotate nelle borse del Regno 1908*, Milan, 1908.
Credito Italiano (ed.), *Notizie statistiche sulle principali società italiane per azioni 1910*, Milan 1910.
Credito Italiano (ed.), *Notizie statistiche sulle principali società italiane per azioni 1912*, Milan, 1912.
Credito Italiano (ed.), *Notizie statistiche sulle principali società italiane per azioni 1914*, Milan, 1914.
Credito Italiano (ed.), *Notizie statistiche sulle principali società italiane per azioni 1916*, Rome, 1917.
Credito Italiano (ed.), *Notizie statistiche sulle principali società italiane per azioni 1918*, 2 vols., Rome, 1919.
Credito Italiano (ed.), *Società italiane per azioni. Notizie statistiche 1920*, 4 vols., Milan, 1921.
Credito Italiano (ed.), *Società italiane per azioni. Notizie statistiche 1922*, Rome, 1923.
Credito Italiano (ed.), *Società italiane per azioni. Notizie statistiche 1925*, Rome, 1926.
Associazione fra le società italiane per azioni (ed.), *Notizie statistiche sulle società italiane per azioni 1928*, Rome, 1928.
Associazione fra le società italiane per azioni (ed.), *Notizie statistiche sulle società italiane per azioni 1930*, Rome, 1930.
Associazione fra le società italiane per azioni (ed.), *Notizie statistiche sulle società italiane per azioni 1932*, Rome, 1932.
Associazione fra le società italiane per azioni (ed.), *Notizie statistiche sulle società italiane per azioni 1934*, Rome, 1934.
Associazione fra le società italiane per azioni (ed.), *Società italiane per azioni. Notizie statistiche 1937*, Rome, 1937.
Associazione fra le società italiane per azioni (ed.), *Società italiane per azioni. Notizie statistiche 1940*, Rome, 1940.
Associazione fra le società italiane per azioni (ed.), *Società italiane per azioni. Notizie statistiche 1949*, Rome, 1949.
Associazione fra le società italiane per azioni (ed.), *Società italiane per azioni. Notizie statistiche 1953*, Florence, 1954.

Associazione fra le società italiane per azioni (ed.), *Società italiane per azioni. Notizie statistiche 1956*, Rome, 1956.
Associazione fra le società italiane per azioni (ed.), *Società italiane per azioni. Notizie statistiche 1958*, Rome, 1958.
Associazione fra le società italiane per azioni (ed.), *Società italiane per azioni. Notizie statistiche 1961*, Rome, 1962.
Associazione fra le società italiane per azioni (ed.), *Società italiane per azioni. Notizie statistiche 1964*, Rome, 1964.
Associazione fra le società italiane per azioni (ed.), *Repertorio delle società italiane per azioni 1967*, 2 vols., Rome, 1967.
Associazione fra le società italiane per azioni (ed.), *Repertorio delle società italiane per azioni 1970*, 2 vols., Rome, 1970.
Associazione fra le società italiane per azioni (ed.), *Repertorio delle società italiane per azioni 1973*, 3 vols., Rome, 1973.

Notizie statistiche include all the joint-stock companies listed on one of the Italian stock exchanges, together with all those companies located in Italy, whose share capital at the closure of the last balance was higher than a set threshold, this last varying from year to year[1]. As can be seen from Table A.1, the sample shows a good representativity as far as the number of companies in the universe of Italian joint-stock companies is concerned, with quotas varying from 18 per cent in 1960 to about 50 per cent in 1921. Representativity in terms of capital is decidedly higher, with the sample covering well over 90 per cent of the total universe in all the years, with the exception of the first two benchmark years, 1911 and 1913, when the quota is around 75 per cent. This last figure is, however, misleading due to the differences in the data on capital reported in the source. It is in fact not always possible to distinguish between nominal capital and paid-up capital and therefore the data in the sample are underestimated because paid-up capital values are listed for some companies while nominal capital values are listed for others. It is therefore possible to state that also for the first two benchmark years the sample, in any case, covers a total of representative companies in terms of capital similar to the quota registered for the following years. The comparison presented in Table A.1 refers to the entire set of companies, without any distinction on the basis of sector. In fact the data reported in the tables which summarize the single volumes of *Notizie statistiche* often contain gaps and are incomplete, and it is not possible to disaggregate the universe's data into manufacturing companies and other companies. Furthermore, the complete historical series [ASIPA 1977] used as a refer-

[1] The threshold is set at 1 million lire until the 1940 volume, with the sole exception of 1914 when it amounts to 500,000 lire. In 1953 the threshold is raised to 10 million lire, to 25 in 1956, to 50 in 1961 and then from 1964 to 1973 it is set at 100 million lire. Until the 1937 volume a few companies which were members of ASIPA were included even though they did not reach the set threshold, as were the Italian companies with head-office abroad which, however, are excluded from the digital archives. The threshold for the 1912 and the 1914 volumes is defined on the basis of paid-up capital, while for all the other volumes it is based on nominal capital.

ence for the universe, do not contain a sectoral disaggregation. Even adopting the *caveat* mentioned above, the comparison nevertheless represents a good approximation of the significativity of the sample used in the study.

Table A.1. Comparison between the companies included in the sample and those in the universe*

	Sample		Universe		Sample/universe	
Year	no.	Share capital	no.	Share capital	% no.	% Share capital
1911	787	4,039,199	2,836	5,363,459	27.8	75.3
1913	1,241	4,490,169	3,069	5,642,965	40.4	79.6
1921	3,072	19,451,854	6,191	20,350,537	49.6	95.6
1927	4,464	38,487,906	13,201	42,253,478	33.8	91.1
1936	4,227	41,645,840	19,353	44,805,429	21.8	92.9
1952	6,162	1,878,898,878	24,006	1,926,081,969	25.7	97.6
1960	6,352	5,826,246,000	34,199	5,997,365,113	18.6	97.1
1972	11,783	12,402,701,000	45,089	13,398,886,160	26.1	92.6

Legend: share capital values are expressed in thousand of current lira.
* a few companies included in the *Notizie Statistiche* and in the Imita.db, but excluded from the reference data for the universe are excluded from the calculations.
Source: our elaborations on the Imita.db and from ASIPA [1977: 16-19].

The process of digitalization the source, is still in progress, and includes all the volumes listed above ending therefore, with the publication of the 1973 volume. Subsequently ASIPA published two further editions, in 1980 and 1984[2], which will also be computerized, but the data from these could not be included in the study. The relational Imita.db database (IMprese ITAliane Data Base) includes all the data contained in the *Notizie Statistiche* volumes, grouped according to mining sector (section C of the ATECO-ISTAT 1991 classification), manufacturing sector (section D) and public utility sector (section E), and divided into three archival units:

(i) company archive (*Company* dataset) for the benchmark years (1911, 1913, 1921, 1927, 1936, 1952, 1960, 1972)[3], which includes a series of data relative to firms: year of foundation; sector of activity[4], location; share capital and paid-up capital. On the basis of the information gathered from the brief *company profiles*

---

[2] Associazione fra le società italiane per azioni (ed.), *Repertorio delle società italiane per azioni 1980*, 2 vols., Rome, n.d.; Associazione fra le società italiane per azioni (ed.), *Repertorio delle società italiane per azioni 1984*, 2 vols., Rome, 1984.

[3] The reference years are those for which the source contains data and they do not always correspond to the year in which the volume was published or to the year stated in the title.

[4] The sectors of activity were standardised on the basis of the ATECO-ISTAT 1991 classification by section, subsection, division and group. The firms were first classified according to the sectors identified, then further classified on the basis of subdivisions relative to sectoral characteristics of the technology, such as those proposed by Pavitt [1984] and Hatzichronoglou [1997].

found in the source, each company was assigned an identificatory code, allowing us to track company continuity even in cases of changes in company name;

(ii) composition of board of directors and board of auditors (*Director* dataset) for the benchmark years (1911, 1913, 1921, 1927, 1936, 1952, 1960, 1972); this archive contains the name, the qualifications and the position held within the company directorate;

(iii) balances sheet (*Balance sheet* dataset), which cover all the years between 1900 and 1971[5], for all the companies contained in the *Company* archive - together with all the companies present in the benchmark years[6]- the following balance items: share capital; physical assets; inventory; securities and investments; cash and credits; bonds; various types of debts; sinking founds; provisions; profits (losses); total dividends; allocations; monetary equalization fund.

As far as the companies which do not belong to the ISTAT sections C, D and E the dataset is complete as far as the first two archival units are concerned, while the data on balances is still being completed.

The actual consistency of the dataset is illustrated in Tables A.2-A.4. The number of companies surveyed for each benchmark year varies from a minimum of 788 in 1911 to a maximum of 11,802 in 1972; the number of administrators varies from a minimum of 5,904 (1911) to a maximum of 81,419 (1972), and the number of balances from 54 (1900) to 5,789 (1971). On the whole the dataset contains 38,182 companies, 294,335 administrators, 142,042 balances.

Table A.2. Records in the *Company* dataset

Benchmark year	Sector C	Sector D	Sector E	Other sectors	Total companies
1911	26	433	80	249	788
1913	41	629	179	393	1,242
1921	83	1,406	227	1,364	3,080
1927	127	1,948	273	2,128	4,476
1936	94	1,765	224	2,160	4,243
1952	127	3,019	169	2,865	6,180
1960	144	3,165	167	2,895	6,371
1972	163	6,131	76	5,432	11,802
Total	*805*	*18,496*	*1,395*	*17,486*	*38,182*

Legend: sectors by ATECO-ISTAT 1991 classification.

[5] There are only a limited number of balance sheets for the years 1940-1945. For this reason these years were excluded from the analyses. The 1972 balance sheets were also excluded because they were incomplete.

[6] All those companies founded and closed in the period between two benchmark years, which therefore do not appear in the benchmark year volumes.

Table A.3. Records in the *Director* dataset

Benchmark year	no. directors and auditors
1911	5,904
1913	8,423
1921	30,071
1927	40,698
1936	33,728
1952	46,189
1960	47,903
1972	81,419
Total	*294,335*

Table A.4. Records in the *Balance sheet* dataset

Year	no.	Year	no.	Year	no.
1900	54	1922	1,655	1950	2,603
1901	72	1923	1,521	1951	2,757
1902	74	1924	1,703	1952	3,321
1903	136	1925	1,912	1953	2,699
1904	161	1926	2,174	1954	2,898
1905	219	1927	2,351	1955	3,073
1906	339	1928	2,294	1956	2,546
1907	482	1929	2,444	1957	2,988
1908	659	1930	2,201	1958	3,022
1909	721	1931	2,267	1959	3,371
1910	753	1932	2,056	1960	3,613
1911	787	1933	2,105	1961	3,032
1912	835	1934	1,928	1962	3,824
1913	922	1935	2,002	1963	3,879
1914	783	1936	2,108	1964	4,070
1915	833	1937	1,919	1965	4,679
1916	887	1938	2,111	1966	4,463
1917	938	1939	2,058	1967	4,609
1918	884	1946	1,084	1968	5,452
1919	1,037	1947	1,303	1969	5,462
1920	1,243	1948	2,330	1970	5,700
1921	1,462	1949	2,385	1971	5,789
					142,042

References

Abramovitz, M. [1986], "Catching Up, Forging Ahead, and Falling Behind", *Journal of Economic History*, 46: 385-406.

Abramovitz, M. [1994], *Catch-up and Convergence in the Post-War Growth Boom and After*, in W.J. Baumol, R.R. Nelson, E.N. Wolff (eds), *Convergence of Productivity. Cross-National Studies and Historical Evidence*, Oxford, Oxford University Press: 86-125.

Affinito, M., de Cecco, M., Dringoli, A. [2000], *Le privatizzazioni nell'industria manifatturiera italiana*, Rome, Donzelli.

Agarwal, R., Audretsch, D.B. [2001], "Does Entry Size Matter? The Impact of the Life Cycle and Technology on Firm Survival", *Journal of Industrial Economics*, 49: 21-43.

Albert, M. [1991], *Capitalisme contre capitalisme*, Paris, Éditions du Seuil; Eng. trans. as *Capitalism Against Capitalism*, London, Whurr, 1993.

Amatori, F. [1992], *Donegani, Guido*, in *Dizionario biografico degli italiani*, Rome, Istituto della Enciclopedia Italiana, 41: 134-142.

Amatori, F. [1994], *Faina, Carlo*, in *Dizionario biografico degli italiani*, Rome, Istituto della Enciclopedia Italiana, 44: 208-212.

Amatori, F. [1995], *Il tormentato sviluppo della grande impresa industriale fra Stato e famiglie: il caso italiano in prospettiva storica*, in G. Airoldi, F. Amatori, G. Invernizzi (eds), *Proprietà e governo delle aziende italiane*, Milan, Egea: 241-252.

Amatori, F. [1997], *Italy: the Tormented Rise of Organizational Capabilities between Government and Families*, in A.D. Chandler Jr., F. Amatori, T. Hikino (eds), *Big Business and the Wealth of Nations*, Cambridge (Mass.), Cambridge University Press: 246-276.

Amatori, F. [1999], *Gli uomini del Professore. Strategie, organizzazioni, management alla Fiat fra anni Venti e anni Sessanta*, in C. Annibaldi, G. Berta (eds), *Grande impresa e sviluppo italiano. Studi per i cento anni della Fiat*, vol. I, Bologna, Il Mulino: 257-342.

Amatori, F. [2000], *Beyond State and Market: Italy's Futile Search for a Third Way*, in P.A. Toninelli (ed.), *The Rise and Fall of State-Owned Enterprises in the Western World*, Cambridge, Cambridge University Press: 128-156.

Amatori, F., Brioschi, F. [1997], *Le grandi imprese private: famiglie e coalizioni*, in F. Barca (ed.), *Storia del capitalismo italiano dal dopoguerra a oggi*, Rome, Donzelli: 118-153.

Amatori, F., Colli, A. [1999], *Impresa e industria in Italia dall'Unità ad oggi*, Venice, Marsilio.

Amatori, F., Toninelli, P.A. [2003], *Gli imprenditori nello sviluppo economico italiano: un fattore residuo?*, in P. Ciocca, G. Toniolo (eds), *Storia economica d'Italia*, vol. III: *Industrie, mercati, istituzioni*, t. I: *Le strutture dell'economia*, Rome-Bari, Laterza: 427-457.

Anderson, C.A., Bowman, M.J. (eds), [1965], *Education and Economic Development*, Chicago, Aldine Publishing Co.

Aoki, M. [1990], "Toward an Economic Model of the Japanese Firm", *Journal of Economic Literature*, 28: 1-27.

Archibugi, D., Evangelista, R., Nascia, L. [1999], *Il ruolo delle piccole e medie imprese nel sistema innovativo italiano*, in C. Antonelli (ed.), *Conoscenza tecnologica. Nuovi paradigmi dell'innovazione e specificità italiana*, Turin, Edizioni della Fondazione Giovanni Agnelli: 115-165.

Arnold, A.J. [1999], "Profitability and Capital Accumulation in British Industry During the Transwar Period, 1913-1924", *Economic History Review*, 52: 45-68.

Arrighetti, A., Seravalli, G. [1997], *Istituzioni e dualismo dimensionale dell'industria italiana*, in F. Barca (ed.), *Storia del capitalismo italiano dal dopoguerra a oggi*, Rome, Donzelli: 335-388.

Arrighetti, A., Seravalli, G. (eds), [1999], *Istituzioni intermedie e sviluppo locale*, Rome, Donzelli.

ASIPA (Associazione fra le Società Italiane per Azioni) [1977], *Statistiche sulle società italiane per azioni*, 23, Rome.

Audretsch, D.B. [1995], *Innovation and Industry Evolution*, Cambridge (Mass.), The MIT Press.

Audretsch, D.B. [1997], "Technological Regimes, Industrial Demography and the Evolution of Industrial Structures", *Industrial and Corporate Change*, 6: 49-82.

Baccini, A. [2002], *Artigiancassa: da Istituto di credito speciale a banca per le imprese artigiane*, in Atti e Documenti di Artigiancassa S.p.a., *Artigiancassa: da Istituto di credito speciale a banca per le imprese artigiane 1953-2001*, Florence, Giunti: 7-101.

Baccini, A., Vasta, M. [1995], "Una tecnica ritrovata: *interlocking directorates* nei rapporti tra banca e industria in Italia (1911-36)", *Rivista di Storia economica*, 12: 219-251.

Badon, C. [1994-95], *Gli imprenditori italiani nel secondo dopoguerra (1961-1972)*, BA thesis, University of Florence.

Bagnasco, A. [1977], *Tre Italie. La problematica territoriale dello sviluppo italiano*, Bologna, Il Mulino.

Baia Curioni, S. [1995], *Regolazione e competizione. Storia del mercato azionario in Italia (1908-1938)*, Bologna, Il Mulino.

Bain, J.S. [1956], *Barriers to New Competition: Their Character and Consequences in Manufacturing Industries*, Cambridge (Mass.), Harvard University Press.

Bairati, P. [1983], *Vittorio Valletta*, Turin, Utet.

Balconi, M. [1991], *La siderurgia italiana (1945-1990) tra controllo pubblico e incentivi di mercato*, Bologna, Il Mulino.

Balconi, M., Orsenigo, L., Toninelli, P.A. [1995], *Tra gerarchie politiche e mercato. Il caso delle imprese pubbliche in Italia (acciaio e petrolio)*, in M. Magatti (ed.), *Potere, gerarchie, mercati. Storici, economisti e sociologi a confronto*, Bologna, Il Mulino: 299-338.

Balloni, V., Iacobucci, D. [2001], "I 'nuovi protagonisti' dell'industria italiana", *L'industria*, 22: 633-675.

Barca, F. [1996], *Imprese in cerca di padrone. Proprietà e controllo nel capitalismo italiano*, Rome-Bari, Laterza.

Barca, F. [1997], *Compromesso senza riforme nel capitalismo italiano*, in F. Barca (ed.), *Storia del capitalismo italiano dal dopoguerra ad oggi*, Rome, Donzelli: 4-117.

Barca, F. et al. [1994a], *Assetti proprietari e mercato delle imprese*, vol. I: *Proprietà, modelli di controllo e riallocazione nelle imprese industriali*, Bologna, Il Mulino.

Barca, F. et al. [1994b], *Assetti proprietari e mercato delle imprese*, vol. II: *Gruppo, proprietà e controllo nelle imprese italiane medio-grandi*, Bologna, Il Mulino.

Barca, F., Trento, S. [1997], *La parabola delle partecipazioni statali: una missione tradita*, in F. Barca (ed.), *Storia del capitalismo italiano dal dopoguerra ad oggi*, Rome, Donzelli: 186-236.

Battara, P. [1965], *La concentrazione industriale*, in *Atti della Commissione Parlamentare di inchiesta sui limiti posti alla concorrenza nel campo economico*, Rome, Camera dei Deputati, Studi e monografie, 4: 158-363.

Battilossi, S. [1999], *Mercati e concentrazione*, in F. Amatori, D. Bigazzi, R. Giannetti, L. Segreto (eds), *Storia d'Italia. Annali 15, L'industria*, Turin, Einaudi: 275-345.

Baumol, W.J. [1959], *Business Behaviour, Value and Growth*, New York, Harcourt & Brace.

Baumol, W.J., Batey Blackman, S.A., Wolff, E.N. [1989], *Productivity and American Leadership. The Long View*, Cambridge (Mass.), The MIT Press.

Becattini, G. (ed.), [1987], *Mercato e forze locali: il distretto industriale*, Bologna, Il Mulino.

Becattini, G. [1998], *Distretti industriali e made in Italy. Le basi socioculturali del nostro sviluppo economico*, Turin, Bollati Boringhieri.

Becattini, G., Bellandi, M. [2002], "Forti pigmei e deboli vatussi. Considerazioni sull'industria italiana", *Economia italiana*, 3: 587-618.

Becattini, G., Bellandi, M., Dei Ottati, G., Sforzi, F. [2001], *Il caleidoscopio dello sviluppo locale. Trasformazioni economiche nell'Italia contemporanea*, Turin, Rosenberg & Sellier.

Beesley, M.E., Hamilton, R.T. [1984], "Small Firms' Seedbed Role and the Concept of Turbulence", *Journal of Industrial Economics*, 33: 217-232.

Belfanti, C.M., Maccabelli, T. (eds), [1997], *Un paradigma per i distretti industriali. Radici storiche, attualità e sfide future*, Brescia, Grafo edizioni.

Bellandi, M. [1999], *"Terza Italia" e "distretti industriali" dopo la Seconda Guerra mondiale*, in F. Amatori, D. Bigazzi, R. Giannetti, L. Segreto (eds), *Storia d'Italia. Annali 15, L'industria*, Turin, Einaudi: 841-891.

Benedetti, E., Toniolli, M. [1963], "Concentrazione industriale e potere di disposizione", *Rivista internazionale di scienze economiche e commerciali*, 10: 633-652.

Berle, A.A., Means, G.C. [1932], *The Modern Corporation and Private Property*, New York, Macmillan.

Berta, G. [2001], *L'Italia delle fabbriche. Genealogie ed esperienze dell'industrialismo nel Novecento*, Bologna, Il Mulino.

Berta, G. [2004], *Metamorfosi. L'industria italiana fra declino e trasformazione*, Milan, Egea.

Bianchi, P. [2002], *La rincorsa frenata. L'industria italiana dall'unità nazionale all'unificazione europea,* Bologna, Il Mulino.

Bianco, M., Pagnoni, E. [1997], "Interlocking Directorates Across Listed Companies in Italy: the Case of Banks", *BNL Quarterly Review*, 50: 203-227.

Bigatti, G. [1994], *Bibliografia della storia d'impresa in Italia (1946-1990)*, Milan, Camera di Commercio.

Bigatti, G. [1999], "La storia d'impresa in Italia: rassegna degli studi", *Annali di storia dell'impresa*, Bologna, Il Mulino, 10: 317-381.

Bigazzi, D. [1990], *La storia d'impresa in Italia. Saggio bibliografico: 1980-1987*, Milan, Franco Angeli.

Bigazzi, D. (ed.), [1996], *Storie di imprenditori*, Bologna, Il Mulino.

Bolchini, P. [2003], *Piccole e medie industrie, liberismo e protezionismo*, in P. Ciocca, G. Toniolo (eds), *Storia economica d'Italia*, vol. III: *Industrie, mercati, istituzioni*, t. I: *Le strutture dell'economia*, Rome-Bari, Laterza: 347-426.

Bologna, S., Fumagalli, A. (eds), [1997], *Il lavoro autonomo di seconda generazione. Scenari del postfordismo in Italia*, Milan, Feltrinelli.

Bonelli, F. [1969], *Bocciardo, Arturo*, in *Dizionario biografico degli italiani*, Rome, Istituto della Enciclopedia Italiana, 11: 89-93.

Bonelli, F. [1975], *Lo sviluppo di una grande impresa in Italia. La Terni dal 1884 al 1962*, Turin, Einaudi.

Bonelli, F. [1978], *Il capitalismo italiano. Linee generali di interpretazione*, in R. Romano, C. Vivanti (eds), *Storia d'Italia. Annali*, vol. I: *Dal feudalesimo al capitalismo*, Turin, Einaudi: 1195-1255.

Boni, M., Gros Pietro, G. [1967], *La concentrazione industriale in Italia*, Milan, L'impresa edizioni.

Bonomi, A. [1997], *Il capitalismo molecolare. La società al lavoro nel Nord Italia*, Turin, Einaudi.

Borgatti, S.P., Everett, M.G., Freeman, L.C. [2002], *Ucinet for Windows: Software for Social Network Analysis*, Harvard, Analytic Technologies.

Bottiglieri, B. [1984], *La politica economica dell'Italia centrista, 1948-1958*, Milan, Edizioni di Comunità.

Bottiglieri, B. [1990], *SIP. Impresa, tecnologia e Stato nelle telecomunicazioni italiane*, Milan, Franco Angeli-Ciriec.

Bovi, M., Castellucci, L. [2001], "Cosa sappiamo dell'economia sommersa in Italia al di là dei luoghi comuni. Alcune proposizioni empiricamente fondate", *Economia pubblica*, 31: 78-119.

Brealey, R.A., Myers, S.C. [2000[6]], *Principles of Corporate Finance*, Boston-London, McGraw-Hill.

Brioschi, F., Buzzacchi, L., Colombo, M.G. [1990], *Gruppi di imprese e mercato finanziario. La struttura di potere nell'industria italiana*, Rome, La Nuova Italia Scientifica.

Bruno, G., Segreto, L. [1996], *Finanza e industria in Italia (1963-1995)*, in F. Barbagallo (ed.), *Storia dell'Italia repubblicana*, vol. III: *L'Italia nella crisi dell'ultimo ventennio*, t. I: *Economia e società*, Turin, Einaudi: 497-694.

Brusco, S., Paba, S. [1997], *Per una storia dei distretti industriali italiani dal secondo dopoguerra agli anni Novanta*, in F. Barca (ed.), *Storia del capitalismo italiano dal dopoguerra a oggi*, Rome, Donzelli: 265-333.

Cafagna, L. [1989], *Dualismo e sviluppo nella storia d'Italia*, Venice, Marsilio.

Cafagna, L. [1999], *Contro tre pregiudizi sulla storia dello sviluppo economico italiano*, in P. Ciocca, G. Toniolo (eds), *Storia economica d'Italia*, vol. I: *Interpretazioni*, Rome-Bari, Laterza: 297-325.

Cainelli, G., Leoncini, R. [1999], *Il ruolo della manifattura nel cambiamento strutturale e nello sviluppo locale di lungo periodo*, in IDSE-CNR, *Trasformazioni strutturali e competitività dei sistemi locali di produzione. Rapporto sul cambiamento strutturale dell'economia italiana*, Milan, Franco Angeli: 43-87.

Cainelli, G., Stampini, M. [1999a], *Appendice 1. Problemi di standardizzazione a livello provinciale dei consimenti industriali italiani: 1951-1991*, in IDSE-CNR, *Trasformazioni strutturali e competitività dei sistemi locali di produzione. Rapporto sul cambiamento strutturale dell'economia italiana*, Milan, Franco Angeli: 285-297.

Cainelli, G., Stampini, M. [1999b], *Appendice 2. Problemi di standardizzazione a livello regionale dei censimenti industriali italiani:1911-1951*, in IDSE-CNR, *Trasformazioni strutturali e competitività dei sistemi locali di produzione. Rapporto sul cambiamento strutturale dell'economia italiana*, Milan, Franco Angeli: 299-309.

Cainelli, G., Stampini, M. [2002], "I censimenti industriali in Italia (1911-1991). Problemi di raccordo ed alcune evidenze empiriche a livello territoriale", *Rivista di Storia economica*, 18: 217-242.

Capie, F., Bilings, M. [2001], "Profitability in English Banking in the Twentieth Century", *European Review of Economic History*, 5: 367-401.

Capra, L. et al. [1994], *Assetti proprietari e mercato delle imprese*, vol. III: *Gli intermediari della riallocazione proprietaria in Italia*, Bologna, Il Mulino.

Caracciolo, A. [1978^3], *Il processo d'industrializzazione*, in G. Fuà (ed.), *Lo sviluppo economico in Italia*, vol. III: *Studi di settore e documentazione di base*, Milan, Franco Angeli: 104-191.

Carnevali, F., [1998], "A Review of Italian Business History from 1991 to 1997", *Business History*, 40: 80-94.

Carreras, A. [1999], *Un ritratto quantitativo dell'industria italiana*, in F. Amatori, D. Bigazzi, R. Giannetti, L. Segreto (eds), *Storia d'Italia. Annali 15, L'industria*, Turin, Einaudi: 181-272.

Carreras, A., Tafunell, X. [1993], "La gran impresa en España, 1917-1974: una primiera aproximación", *Revista de Historia Industrial*, 3: 127-175.

Cassis, Y. [1997], *Big Business. The European Experience in the Twentieth Century*, Oxford, Oxford University Press.

Castagnoli, A., Scarpellini, E. [2003], *Storia degli imprenditori italiani*, Turin, Einaudi.

Castronovo, V. [1985], *Gilardini 1905-1985. Storia di un gruppo industriale*, Turin, Ages Arti grafiche.

Castronovo, V., Hertner, P., Mori, G. (eds), [1994-2002], *Storia dell'Ansaldo*, Rome-Bari, Laterza, 9 vols.

Caves, R.E. [1998], "Industrial Organization and New Findings on the Turnover and Mobility of Firms", *Journal of Economic Literature*, 36: 1947-1982.

Chandler Jr., A.D. [1962], *Strategy and Structure. Chapters in the History of the American Industrial Enterprise*, Cambridge (Mass.), The MIT Press.

Chandler Jr., A.D. [1977], *The Visible Hand. The Managerial Revolution in American Business,* Cambridge (Mass.), Harvard University Press.

Chandler Jr., A.D. [1982], "The M-Form: Industrial Groups, American Style", *European Economic Review*, 19: 3-23.

Chandler Jr., A.D. [1990], *Scale and Scope. The Dynamics of Industrial Capitalism*, Cambridge (Mass.), Harvard University Press.

Chandler Jr., A.D. [1994], "The Competitive Performance of U.S. Industrial Enterprise Since the Second World War", *Business History Review*, 68: 1-72.

Chenery, H. [1979], *Structural Change and Development Policy*, Oxford, Oxford University Press.

Chiapparino, F. [1997], *L'industria del cioccolato in Italia, Germania, Francia e Svizzera*, Bologna, Il Mulino.

Chiaventi, R. [1987], "I censimenti industriali italiani 1911-1951: procedimenti di standardizzazione", *Rivista di Storia economica*, 4: 119-151.

Chiesi, A.M. [1981], *Le origini della classe dirigente economica*, in A. Martinelli, A.M. Chiesi, N. Dalla Chiesa (eds), *I grandi imprenditori italiani. Profilo sociale della classe dirigente economica*, Milan, Feltrinelli: 23-62.

Chiesi, A.M. [1982], "L'élite finanziaria italiana", *Rassegna italiana di sociologia*, 23: 571-595.

Chiesi, A.M. [1985], *Property, Capital and Network Structure in Italy*, in F.S. Stokman, R. Ziegler, J. Scott (eds), *Networks of Corporate Power. A Comparative Analysis of Ten Countries*, Cambridge, Polity Press: 199-214.

Cingolani, S. [1990], *Le grandi famiglie del capitalismo italiano*, Rome-Bari, Laterza.

Ciocca, P., [2003], *L'economia italiana: un problema di crescita*, paper presented at *44th Annual meeting of the Società italiana degli economisti*, Salerno, October.

Ciocca, P., Filosa, R., Rey G. [1973], "Integrazione e sviluppo economico nell'ultimo ventennio: un riesame critico", *Contributi alla ricerca economica*, 3: 57-135.

Cohen, J. [1967], "Financing Industrialization in Italy, 1894-1914: The Partial Transformation of a Late-Comer", *Journal of Economic History*, 17: 363-382.

Cohen, J., Federico, G. [2001], *The Development of Italian Economy, 1820-1960*, Cambridge, Cambridge University Press.

Cohen, W.M., Klepper, S. [1991], *Firm Size versus Diversity in the Achievement of Technological Advance*, in Z.J. Acs, D.B. Audretsch (eds), *Innovation and Technological Change: An International Comparison*, Ann Arbor, University of Michigan Press: 183-203.

Colli, A. [1997], "Produzione e consumo di birra in Italia dall'Unità alla seconda guerra mondiale", *Rivista di Storia economica*, 13: 283-325.

Colli, A. [2002a], *I volti di Proteo: storia della piccola impresa in Italia nel Novecento*, Turin, Bollati Boringhieri.

Colli, A. [2002b], *Il quarto capitalismo. Un profilo italiano*, Venice, Marsilio.

Colli, A. [2003], *The History of Family Business, 1850-2000*, Cambridge, Cambridge University Press.

Commissione Economica della Costituente [1945-46], *Rapporto della Commissione Economica all'Assemblea Costituente,* II*: Industria,* I*: Relazione*, Rome.

Confalonieri, A. [1974-76], *Banca e industria in Italia, 1894-1906*, Milan, Banca Commerciale Italiana, 3 vols.

Confalonieri, A. [1982], *Banca ed industria in Italia dalla crisi del 1907 all'agosto 1914*, Milan, Banca Commerciale Italiana, 2 vols.

Confalonieri, A. [1992-97], *Banche miste e grande industria in Italia, 1914-1933*, Milan, Banca Commerciale Italiana, 2 vols.

Conti, G. [1999], *Le banche e il finanziamento industriale*, in F. Amatori, D. Bigazzi, R. Giannetti, L. Segreto (eds), *Storia d'Italia. Annali 15, L'industria*, Turin, Einaudi: 441-504.

Conti, G., Ferri, G. [1997], *Banche locali e sviluppo economico decentrato*, in F. Barca (ed.), *Storia del capitalismo italiano dal dopoguerra a oggi*, Rome, Donzelli: 429-465.

Conti, G., La Francesca, S. (eds), [2000], *Banche e reti di banche nell'Italia postunitaria*, Bologna, Il Mulino, 2 vols.

Cowan, R., David, P.A., Foray D. [2000], "The Explicit Economics of Knowledge Codification and Tacitness", *Industrial and Corporate Change*, 9: 211-253.

Crepax, N. [2002], *Storia dell'industria in Italia. Uomini, imprese e prodotti*, Bologna, Il Mulino.

de Cecco, M. [2000], *L'economia di Lucignolo: opportunità e vincoli dello sviluppo italiano*, Rome, Donzelli.

de Cecco, M. [2001a], *Piccole imprese, banche, commercialisti. Note sui protagonisti della seconda industrializzazione italiana*, in L. Cafagna, N. Crepax (eds), *Atti di intelligenza e sviluppo economico. Saggi per il bicentenario della nascita di Carlo Cattaneo,* Bologna, Il Mulino: 425-449.

de Cecco, M. [2001b], *L'economia italiana negli ultimi trent'anni,* in S. Cassese (ed.), *Ritratto dell'Italia*, Rome-Bari, Laterza: 59-94.

de Cecco, M. [2004], *L'Italia grande potenza: la realtà del mito*, in P. Ciocca, G. Toniolo (eds), *Storia economica d'Italia,* vol. 3. *Industrie, mercati, istituzioni.* 2. *I vincoli e le opportunità*, Rome-Bari, Laterza: 3-36.

Delli Gatti, D., Gallegati, M., Gallegati, M. [2003], *Sulla natura e le cause delle fluttuazioni cicliche in Italia (1861-2000)*, in P. Ciocca, G. Toniolo (eds), *Storia economica d'Italia*, vol. III: *Industrie, mercati, istituzioni*, t. I: *Le strutture dell'economia*, Rome-Bari, Laterza: 535-578.

Derossi, F. [1976], *A Profile of Italian Managers in Large Firms*, in J.J. Boddewyn (ed.), *European Industrial Managers. West and East*, White Plains, NY, International Arts and Sciences Press: 144-208.

Doria, M. [1989], *L'Ansaldo. L'impresa e lo stato*, Milan, Franco Angeli-Ciriec.

Doria, M. [1999], *Gli imprenditori tra vincoli strutturali e nuove opportunità*, in F. Amatori, D. Bigazzi, R. Giannetti, L. Segreto (eds), *Storia d'Italia. Annali 15, L'industria*, Turin, Einaudi: 617-687.

Dosi, G. [1988], "Sources, Procedures, and Microeconomic Effects of Innovation", *Journal of Economic Literature*, 26: 1120-1171.

Dosi, G., Teece, J.D., Winter, S.G. [1992], *Toward a Theory of Corporate Coherence: Preliminary Remarks*, in G. Dosi, R. Giannetti, P.A. Toninelli (eds), *Technology and Enterprise in Historical Perspective*, Oxford, Clarendon Press: 185-221.

Dringoli, A. [1995], *Struttura e sviluppo dell'impresa industriale*, Milan, McGraw-Hill.

Easterlin, R. [1981], "Why isn't the Whole World Developed?", *Journal of Economic History*, 41: 1-20.

Edwards, J.R. [1989], *A History of Financial Accounting*, London-New York, Routledge.

Encaoua, D., Jacquemin, A. [1982], "Organizational Efficiency and Monopoly Power. The Case of French Industrial Group", *European Economic Review*, 19: 25-51.

Federico, G. [1994a], *Il filo d'oro. L'industria mondiale della seta dalla restaurazione alla grande crisi*, Venice, Marsilio; Eng. trans. as *An Economic History of Silk Industry, 1830-1930*, Cambridge, Cambridge University Press, 1997.

Federico, G. (ed.), [1994b], *The Economic development of Italy since 1870*, Aldershot, Elgar.

Federico, G., Giannetti, R. [1999], *Italy: Stalling and Surpassing*, in J. Foreman Peck, G. Federico (eds), *European Industrial Policy*, Oxford, Oxford University Press: 124-151.

Federico, G. [2003], *La struttura industriale (1911-1996)*, in R. Giannetti, M. Vasta (eds), *L'impresa italiana nel Novecento*, Bologna, Il Mulino: 41-88.

Federico, G., O'Rourke, K. [2000], *Much Ado about Nothing? The Italian Trade Politcy in the 19th Century,* in J. Williamson, S. Pamuk (eds), *The Mediterranean Response to Globalization Before 1950*, London, Routledge: 269-296.

Federico, G., Tena, G. [1998], "Was Italy a Protectionist Country?", *European Review of Economic History*, 2: 73-97.

Federico, G., Tena, G. [1999], "Did Trade Policy Foster Italian Industrialization? Evidence From Effective Protection Rates 1870-1930", *Research in Economic History*, 19: 111-130.

Fenoaltea, S. [1973], *Riflessioni sull'esperienza industriale italiana dal Risorgimento alla prima Guerra Mondiale*, in G. Toniolo (ed.), *Lo sviluppo economico italiano 1861-1940*, Bari, Laterza: 121-156.

Fenoaltea, S. [1992], *Il valore aggiunto dell'industria*, in G. Rey (ed.), *I conti economici dell'Italia*, vol. II: *Una stima del valore aggiunto per rami di attività per il 1911*, Rome-Bari, Laterza: 105-190.

Fenoaltea, S. [2001], *La crescita industriale delle regioni d'Italia dall'Unità alla Grande Guerra: una prima stima per gli anni censuari*, *Quaderni dell'Ufficio Ricerche Storiche della Banca d'Italia*, no. 1.

Fenoaltea, S. [2003], *Lo sviluppo dell'industria dall'Unità alla Grande Guerra: una sintesi provvisoria* in P. Ciocca, G. Toniolo (eds), *Storia economica d'Italia*, vol. III: *Industrie, mercati, istituzioni*, t. I: *Le strutture dell'economia*, Rome-Bari, Laterza: 137-193.

Fenoaltea, S., Bardini, C. [2000], *Il valore aggiunto dell'industria*, in G. Rey (ed.), *I conti economici dell'Italia*, vol. III: *Una stima del valore aggiunto per gli anni 1891, 1938, 1951*, Rome-Bari, Laterza: 115-238.

Ferratini Tosi, F. et al. [1983], "Il ceto imprenditoriale nel primo decennio repubblicano. Anticipazioni su un campione di ricerca", *Italia contemporanea*, 153: 165-181.

Ferri, G., Trento, S. [1997], *La dirigenza delle grandi banche e delle grandi imprese: ricambio e legami*, in F. Barca (ed.), *Storia del capitalismo italiano dal dopoguerra ad oggi*, Rome, Donzelli: 405-427.

Fligstein, N. [1990], *The Transformation of Corporate Control*, Cambridge (Mass.), Harvard University Press.

Fohlin, C. [1998], "Fiduciary and Firm Liquidity Constraints: The Italian Experience with German-Style Universal Banking", *Explorations in Economic History*, 35: 83-107.

Fohlin, C. [1999], "Capital Mobilisation and Utililisation in Latecomer Economies: Germany and Italy Compared", *European Review of Economic History*, 3: 139-174.

Fontana, L. (ed.), [1997], *Le vie dell'industrializzazione europea: sistemi a confronto*, Bologna, Il Mulino.

Fortune [1972], *British top 500 Companies*.

Fortune [1992], *European top 500 Companies*.

Fortune [2002], *Fortune 5 Hundred. The Lists*.

Franks, J., Mayer, C. [1990], "Capital Markets and Corporate Control: A Study of France, Germany and the UK", *Economic Policy*, 10: 191-231.

Freeman, C., Louçã F. [2001], *As Time Goes By: From the Industrial Revolution to the Information Revolution,* Oxford, Oxford University Press.

Freeman, C., Soete, L. [1997], *The Economics of Industrial Innovation*, Cambridge (Mass.), The MIT Press.

Freeman, L.C. [1979], "Centrality in Social Networks: Conceptual Clarification", *Social Networks*, 1: 215-239.

Galbraith, J.K. [1967], *The New Industrial State*, London, Hamilton.

Galgano, F. [1974], *Le istituzioni dell'economia capitalistica*, Bologna, Il Mulino.

Galgano, F. [1993], *Lex mercatoria*, Bologna, Il Mulino.
Gallino, L. [2003], *La scomparsa dell'Italia industriale*, Turin, Einaudi.
Gallo, G. (ed.), [1990], *Sulla bocca di tutti*, Perugia, Electa Editori Umbri.
Gerowski, P.A. [1995], "What Do We Know About Entry?", *International Journal of Industrial Organization*, 13: 421-440.
Gerschenkron, A. [1962], *Economic Backwardness in Historical Perspective*, Cambridge (Mass.), Harvard University Press.
Giannetti, R. [1985], *La conquista della forza. Risorse, tecnologia ed economia nell'industria elettrica italiana (1883-1940)*, Milan, Franco Angeli.
Giannetti, R. [1996], *Imprese e politica industriale. La petrolchimica italiana negli anni '70*, in L. D'Antone (ed.), *Radici storiche ed esperienza dell'intervento straordinario nel Mezzogiorno*, Rome, Bibliopolis: 499-524.
Giannetti, R. [1998], *Tecnologia e sviluppo economico italiano 1870-1990*, Bologna, Il Mulino.
Giannetti, R. [1999], *Il progresso tecnologico*, in F. Amatori, D. Bigazzi, R. Giannetti, L. Segreto (eds), *Storia d'Italia. Annali 15, L'industria*, Turin, Einaudi: 387-440.
Giannetti, R., Federico, G., Toninelli, P.A. [1994], "Size and Strategy of Italian Industrial Enterprises: Empirical Evidences and Some Conjectures", *Industrial and Corporate Change*, 3: 491-511.
Giannetti, R., Vasta, M. [2005], *Storia dell'impresa industriale italiana*, Bologna, Il Mulino.
Gianola, R. [2000], *Luraghi, l'uomo che inventò la Giulietta*, Milan, Baldini e Castoldi.
Goldin, C., Katz, L. [1998], "The Origins of Technology-Skill Complementarity", *Quarterly Journal of Economics*, 113: 693-732.
Gort, M., Klepper, S. [1982], "Time Paths in the Diffusion of Product Innovations", *Economic Journal*, 92: 630-653.
Goto, A. [1982], "Business Groups in a Market Economy", *European Economy Review*, 19: 53-70.
Gramsci, A. [1949], *Il Risorgimento*, Turin, Einaudi.
Granovetter, M. [1998], *Coase Revisited: Business Groups in the Modern Economy*, in G. Dosi, D.J. Teece, J. Chytry (eds), *Technology. Organization, and Competitiveness*, Oxford, Oxford University Press: 67-103.
Graziani, A. [1998], *Lo sviluppo dell'economia italiana. Dalla ricostruzione alla moneta europea*, Turin, Bollati Boringhieri.
Grifone, P. [1945], *Il capitale finanziario in Italia. La politica economica del fascismo*, Turin, Einaudi.
Griliches, Z. [1969], "Capital-Skill Complementarity", *Review of Economics and Statistics*, 51: 465-468.
Gualerni, G. [1982], *Lo Stato industriale in Italia 1890-1940*, Milan, Etas libri.
Guida Monaci [various years], *Annuario generale*.

Hannah, L. [1976], *The rise of the Corporate Economy*, London, Methuen.
Hannah, L. [1991], "Scale and Scope: Towards a European Invisible Hand?", *Business History*, 33: 297-309.

Hannah, L. [1999], *Marshall's "Trees" and the Global "Forest": Were "Giant Redwoods" Different?*, in N.R. Lamoreaux, D.M. Raff, P. Temin (eds), *Learning by Doing in Markets, Firms, and Countries*, Chicago, The University of Chicago Press: 253-293.

Harrison, B. [1997], *Lean and Mean: the Changing Landscape of Corporate Power in the Age of Flexibility*, Cambridge, Cambridge University Press.

Hatzichronoglou, T. [1997], *Revision of The High-Technology Sector and Product Classification*, STI Working Papers, no. 2, Paris, OECD.

Healy, P.M., Palepu, K.G. [2003], "Fall of Enron", *Journal of Economic Perspectives*, 17: 3-26.

Hertner, P. [1993], "Gli imprenditori elettrici in una prospettiva storica", *Annali di storia dell'impresa*, Bologna, Il Mulino, 9: 8-14.

Hilferding, R. [1910], *Das Finanzkapital: eine Studie über die jüngste Entwicklung des Kapitalismus*, Wien, Verlag der Wiener Volksbuchhandlung; Eng. trans. as *Finance Capital: a Study of the Latest Phase of Capitalist Development*, London, Routledge & Kegan Paul, 1981.

Hoffmann, W. [1955], *British Industry 1700-1950*, Oxford, Blackwell.

Huberman, M. [2002], *Working Hours of the World Unite? New International evidence on Worktime, 1870-1900*, Montreal, Cirano.

Industrial census

Ministero di Agricoltura, Industria e Commercio, Direzione generale della statistica e del lavoro [1914], *Censimento degli opifici e delle imprese industriali al 10 giugno 1911*, Rome.

ISTAT [1929], *Censimento degli esercizi industriali e commerciali al 15 ottobre 1927*, Rome.

ISTAT [1940-42], *Censimento industriale e commerciale 1937-39*, Rome.

ISTAT [1957], *III Censimento generale dell'industria e del Commercio al 3 novembre 1951*, vol. XVIII: *Dati Generali riassuntivi*, Rome.

ISTAT [1964], *IV Censimento generale dell'industria e del commercio al 16 ottobre 1961*, Rome.

ISTAT [1976], *V Censimento generale dell'industria e del commercio al 25 ottobre 1971*, vol. VIII: *Dati generali riassuntivi*, Rome.

ISTAT [1985], *VI Censimento generale dell'industria, del commercio, dei servizi e dell'artigianato al 26 ottobre 1981*, vol II: *Dati sulle caratteristiche strutturali delle imprese e delle unità locali*, t. 3, Rome.

ISTAT [1996], *VII Censimento generale dell'industria e dei servizi al 21 ottobre 1991. Imprese istituzioni e unità locali. Fascicolo nazionale Italia e Imprese e unità locali, Industria*, Rome.

ISTAT [1999], *Censimento intermedio dell'industria e dei servizi al 31 dicembre 1996*, Rome.

Invernizzi, B., Revelli, R. [1993], *Small Firms in the Italian Economy: Structural Change and Evidence of Turbolence*, in Z. Acs, D.B. Audretsch (eds), *Small Firms and Entrepreneurship: An East-West Perspective*, Cambridge, Cambridge University Press: 123-153.

ISTAT [1957], "Le rilevazioni statistiche in Italia dal 1861 al 1956", *Annali di statistica*, Rome, series VIII, vol. 5.

ISTAT [1986], *Sommario di statistiche storiche italiane 1926-1985*, Rome.

ISTAT [1991], *Classificazione delle attività economiche*, Rome.

ISTAT [2002], *Annuario Statistico Italiano*, Rome.

ISTAT [2004], *Serie storiche: conto economico delle risorse e degli impieghi*, http://www.istat.it.

Kay, N.M. [1997], *Pattern in Corporate Evolution*, Oxford, Oxford University Press.

Kay, N.M. [2002], "Chandlerism in Post-War Europe: Strategic and Structural change in France, Germany and the United Kingdom", *Industrial and Corporate Change*, 11: 189-197.

Kocka, J., Dornseifer, B. [1993], "The Impact of Pre-Industrial Heritage. Reconsiderations on the German Pattern of Corporate Development in the Late 19th and the Early 20th Centuries", *Industrial and Corporate Change*, 2: 233-248.

Kreps, D., Wallis K. [1995], *Advances in Economics and Econometrics*, Cambridge, Cambridge University Press.

Kuznets, S. [1966], *Modern Economic Growth. Rate, Structure and Spread*, New Haven-London, Yale University Press.

Lancaster, T. [1990], *The Analysis of Transition Data*, New York, Cambridge University Press.

Lazonick, W.H. [1991], *Business Organization and the Myth of the Market Economy*, Cambridge, Cambridge University Press.

Legnani, M. [1987], *Prospettive di studio sui ceti dirigenti economici dell'Italia repubblicana*, in G. De Luna (ed.), *Dalla Liberazione alla Repubblica: i nuovi ceti dirigenti in Piemonte*, Milan, Franco Angeli: 57-61.

Lev, B. [2003], "Corporate Earnings: Facts and Fiction", *Journal of Economic Perspectives*, 17: 27-50.

Liang K.Y., Zeger, S.L. [1986], "Longitudinal Data Analysis Using Generalized Linear Models", *Biometrika*, 73: 13-22.

Lombardi, M. [2003], *Dinamica tecnologica ed evoluzione economico-produttiva: schemi concettuali, modelli interpretativi, strumenti di analisi*, in M. Lombardi, P.A. Mori, M. Vasta (eds), *Sistema innovativo e settori strategici: il caso della Toscana*, Milan, Franco Angeli-Ciriec: 11-46.

Lomi, A. (ed.), [1997], *L'analisi relazionale delle organizzazioni. Riflessioni teoriche ed esperienze empiriche*, Bologna, Il Mulino.

Lomi, A., Corrado, R., Sandri, S. [1997], *La struttura sociale del controllo delle imprese: condivisione dei consiglieri di amministrazione e legami societari*, in A. Lomi (ed.), *L'analisi relazionale delle organizzazioni. Riflessioni teoriche ed esperienze empiriche*, Bologna, Il Mulino: 309-345.

Louçã, F., Mendonça, S. [2002], "Steady Change: the 200 Largest US Manufacturing Firms Throughout the 20th Century", *Industrial and Corporate Change*, 11: 817-845.

Lucas, R.E. [1988], "On The Mechanism of Economic Development", *Journal of Monetary Economics*, 22: 3-42.

Lungonelli, M. [1987], "Tra industria e burocrazia: gli esordi della statistica industriale in Italia", *Studi Storici*, 28: 277-296.

Luzzatto Fegiz, P. [1928], "Il consiglio di amministrazione e l'indipendenza delle imprese", *Giornale degli economisti e rivista di statistica*, 43: 197-231.

Mac Canna, L., Brennan, N., O'Higgins, E. [1999], "National Networks of Corporate Power: An Irish Perspective", *Journal of Management and Governance*, 2: 355-377.

Maddison, A. [1991], *Dynamic Forces in Capitalist Development. A Long-Run Comparative view*, Oxford, Oxford University Press.

Maddison, A. [1995], *Monitoring the World Economy 1820-1992*, Paris, OECD.

Maifreda, G. [2000], *Gli ebrei e l'economia milanese. L'Ottocento*, Milan, Franco Angeli.

Malerba, F. [1993], *Italy*, in R.R. Nelson (ed.), *National Innovation Systems. A Comparative Analysis*, New York-Oxford, Oxford University Press: 230-259.

Malerba, F., Orsenigo, L. [1993], "Technological Regimes and Firm Behaviour", *Industrial and Corporate Change*, 2: 74-89.

Marchetti, P. [1997], *Diritto societario e disciplina della concorrenza*, in F. Barca (ed.), *Storia del capitalismo italiano dal dopoguerra ad oggi*, Rome, Donzelli: 467-499.

Marchi, A., Marchionatti, R. [1992], *Montedison 1966-1989. L'evoluzione di una grande impresa al confine tra pubblico e privato*, Milan, Franco Angeli-Ciriec.

Marris, R. [1964], *The Economic Theory of Managerial Capitalism*, London, Macmillan.

Martignone, C. [2001], *Imprenditori protestanti a Milano, 1850-1900,* Milan, Franco Angeli.

Martinelli, A., Chiesi, A.M. [1981], *Il profilo sociale e gli atteggiamenti politici*, in A. Martinelli, A.M. Chiesi, N. Dalla Chiesa (eds), *I grandi imprenditori italiani. Profilo sociale della classe dirigente economica*, Milan, Feltrinelli: 63-110.

Martinoli, G. [1971], *Trasformazioni dell'organizzazione aziendale in funzione del progresso tecnologico 1945-1960*, Bologna, Il Mulino.

Mattioli, R. [1962], "I problemi attuali del credito", *Mondo economico*, 2: 5.

Mediobanca [various years], *Calepino dell'azionista*, Milan.

Mediobanca [1981], *Le principali società italiane*, Milan.

Mediobanca [1991], *Le principali società italiane*, Milan.

Mediobanca [2000], *Le privatizzazioni in Italia dal 1992*, Milan.

Mediobanca [2001], *Le principali società italiane*, Milan.

Mellinato, G. [2001], *Crescita senza sviluppo. L'economia marittima della Venezia Giulia tra Impero asburgico ed autarchia (1914-1936)*, Monfalcone, Consorzio culturale del monfalconese.

Mintz, B., Schwartz, M. [1985], *The Power Structure of American Business*, Chicago, University of Chicago Press.

Missaggia, M.G. [1988], “Note sulle statistiche ufficiali per l’industria in Italia”, *Rivista di Storia economica*, 5: 235-254.

Momigliano, F. [1975], *Economia industriale e teoria dell’impresa*, Bologna, Il Mulino.

Mori, G. [1959], “La storia dell’industria contemporanea nei saggi, nelle ricerche e nelle pubblicazioni giubilari di questo dopoguerra”, *Annali dell’Istituto Giangiacomo Feltrinelli*, 2: 264-366.

Mori, G. [1959-60], “Premesse e implicazioni di una recente specializzazione storiografica americana, la *Entrepreneurial History*”, *Studi Storici*, 1: 755-793.

Mori, G. [1977], *Il capitalismo industriale in Italia. Processo d’industrializzazione e storia d’Italia*, Rome, Editori Riuniti.

Mori, G. [1992], *L’economia italiana dagli anni ottanta alla prima guerra mondiale*, in G. Mori (ed.), *Storia dell’industria elettrica in Italia*, vol. I: *Le origini*, Rome-Bari, Laterza: 1-106.

Mori, G. [1994], *L’economia italiana tra la fine della seconda guerra mondiale e il “secondo miracolo economico” (1945-1958)*, in *Storia dell’Italia Repubblicana*, vol. I: *Dalla caduta del fascismo agli anni Cinquanta*, Turin, Einaudi: 129-230.

Nelson, R., Winter, S.G. [1982], *An Evolutionary Theory of Economic Change*, Cambridge, Cambridge University Press.

Nightingale, P. [1998], “A Cognitive Model of Innovation”, *Research Policy*, 27: 698-709.

Nightingale, P. [2000], “Economies of Scale in Experimentation: Knowledge and Technology in Pharmaceutical R&D”, *Industrial and Corporate Change*, 9: 315-355.

Nye, J.V. [1987], “Firm Size and Economic Backwardness: A New look at the French Industrialization Debate”, *Journal of Economic History*, 47: 649-670.

Onado, M. (ed.), [1979], *Analisi finanziaria per i fidi bancari. Testi e casi*, Milan, Franco Angeli.

Onado, M. (ed.), [1986], *Sistema finanziario e industria*, Bologna, Il Mulino.

Osti, G.L. [1993], *L’industria di stato dall’ascesa al degrado: trent’anni nel gruppo Finsider. Conversazioni con Ruggero Ranieri*, Bologna, Il Mulino.

Pagano, P., Schivardi, F. [2001], *Firm Size Distribution and Growth*, Banca d’Italia, Temi e Discussione, no. 294.

Pagano, U. [2003], *Mercato. Confronto di sistemi capitalistici*, in *Enciclopedia Italiana Treccani*, Rome, *ad vocem*.

Parker, R.H. [1991], “Misleading Accounts? Pitfalls for Historians”, *Business History*, 33: 1-18.

Patel, P., Pavitt, K. [1998], *The Wide (and Increasing) Spread of Technological Competencies in the World’s Largest Firms: a Challenge to Conventional Wisdom*, in A.D. Chandler Jr, P. Hagstrom, O. Solvell (eds), *The Dynamic Firm: The Role of Technology, Strategy, Organization and Regions*, Oxford, Oxford University Press: 192-213.

Pavan, S. [1976], *Strategia e struttura delle imprese italiane,* Bologna, Il Mulino.

Pavese, C. [1986], *Le origini della società Edison e il suo sviluppo fino alla costituzione del gruppo*, in B. Bezza (ed.), *Energia e sviluppo*, Turin, Einaudi.

Pavese, C. [1993], "Carlo Esterle: grand commis della banca mista", *Annali di storia dell'impresa*, Bologna, Il Mulino, 9: 77-94.

Pavese, C. [2003], *Gli assetti proprietari e istituzionali*, in V. Castronovo (ed.), *Storia dell'Ansaldo*, vol. 9: *Un secolo e mezzo 1853-2003*, Rome-Bari, Laterza: 25-70.

Pavese, C., Toninelli, P.A. [1988], *L'andamento e la distribuzione degli investimenti industriali in Italia (1894-1914): metodologia e primi risultati*, in L. Avagliano (ed.), *L'Italia industriale nelle sue regioni: bilancio storiografico*, Napoli, ESI: 331-338.

Pavitt, K. [1984], "Sectoral Patterns of Technical Change: Towards a Taxonomy and a Theory", *Research Policy*, 13: 323-373.

Pellegrini, G. [2003], *Lo sviluppo strutturale dell'economia italiana dal dopoguerra al nuovo secolo*, in P. Ciocca, G. Toniolo (eds), *Storia economica d'Italia*, vol. III: *Industrie, mercati, istituzioni*, t. I: *Le strutture dell'economia*, Rome-Bari, Laterza: 195-224.

Pennings, J.M. [1980], *Interlocking Directorates*, San Francisco-London, Jossey Bass Publishers.

Petri, R. [1998], *Technical Change in the Italian Chemical Industry. Markets, Firms and State Intervention*, in A. Travis, H. Schroeter, E. Homburg (eds), *Political Framework, Markets and Companies, 1900-1939*, Dordrecht, Kluwer: 275-300.

Petri, R. [2002], *Storia economica d'Italia. Dalla Grande guerra al miracolo economico (1918-1963)*, Bologna, Il Mulino.

Phlips, L. [1971], *Effects of Industrial Concentration: A Cross-Section Analysis for the Common Market*, Amsterdam-London, North-Holland.

Piluso, G. [1992], "Un centauro metà pubblico e metà privato. La Bastogi da Alberto Beneduce a Mediobanca (1926-1969)", *Annali della Fondazione Luigi Einaudi*, 26: 347-392.

Piluso, G. [1999], *Gli istituti di credito speciale*, in F. Amatori, D. Bigazzi, R. Giannetti, L. Segreto (eds), *Storia d'Italia. Annali 15, L'industria*, Turin, Einaudi: 507-547.

Polese, F. (ed.), [2003], *G.B. Pirelli. Viaggio di istruzione all'estero. Diario, 1870-1871*, Venice, Marsilio.

Polese, F. [2004], *Alla ricerca di un'industria nuova. Il viaggio all'estero del giovane Pirelli e le origini di una grande impresa (1870-1877)*, Venezia, Marsilio.

Porter, M. [1980], *Competitive Strategy*, Free Press, New York.

Posen, A.S. [2002], *Japan*, in B. Steil, D.G. Victor, R.R. Nelson (eds), *Technological Innovation and Economic Performance*, Princeton, Princeton University Press: 74-111.

Posner, M., Woolf, S. [1967], *Italian Public Enterprise*, Cambridge (Mass.), Cambridge University Press.

Pozzobon, M. [1982], *L'industria padana dell'acciaio nel primo trentennio del Novecento*, in F. Bonelli (ed.), *Acciaio per l'industrializzazione*, Turin, Einaudi.

Quadrio Curzio, A., Fortis, M. (eds), [2000], *Il made in Italy oltre il 2000. Innovazione e comunità locali*, Bologna, Il Mulino.

R&S Mediobanca [2000], *CD-Rom R&S Mediobanca*, Milan.

Radar (pseudonym of E. Rienzi) [1948], *Organizzazione del capitale finanziario italiano*, Rome, Edizioni Italiane.

Ragozzino, G. [1969], "Una mappa del grande capitale in Italia", *Quaderni di rassegna sindacale*, 7: 39-73.

Raspadori, P. [2003], "Bollicine. Per una storia dell'industria delle acque minerali in Italia dalle origini agli anni Ottanta del Novecento", *Annali di storia dell'impresa*, Venice, Marsilio, 13: 357-396.

Ratnayake, R. [1999], "Industry Concentration and Competition: New Zealand experience", *International Journal of Industrial Organization*, 17: 1041-1057.

Ricciardi, A. [1985], *Teoria economica dell'impresa*, Milan, Giuffré.

Ricciardi, F. [2002], "*Business history* in Italia: una rassegna (1999-2000), *Imprese e Storia*, 25: 105-144.

Rienzi, E. [1947-48], "The Distribution of Share Capital of Italian Banking Companies", *Banca Nazionale del Lavoro Quarterly Review*, 1: 10-19.

Rinaldi, A., Vasta, M. [2003], *The Structure of Italian Capitalism, 1952-1972: New Evidence Using the Interlocking Directorates Technique*, in *Proceedings from the 6th Annual Congress of the European Business History Association. 22nd to 24th August 2002. Companies-Owners-Employees*, CD-Rom, Helsinki, CD-Linja Digital Communication Media.

Rinaldi, A., Vasta, M. [2005], "The Structure of Italian Capitalism, 1952-1972: New Evidence Using the Interlocking Directorates Technique", *Financial History Review*, 12: 173-198.

Romeo, R. [1959], *Risorgimento e capitalismo*, Bari, Laterza.

Romer, P. [1986], "Increasing Returns and Long-Run Growth", *Journal of Political Economy*, 94: 1002-1037.

Romer, P. [1994], "The Origins of Endogenous Growth", *Journal of Economic Perspectives*, 8: 3-22

Rondi Ferla, L. [1993], *Il rendimento dei capitali investiti nelle imprese elettriche*, in G. Galasso (ed.), *Storia dell'industria elettrica in Italia*, vol. III: *Espansione e oligopolio. 1926-1945*, t. I, Rome-Bari, Laterza: 247-267.

Rosenberg, N. [1976], *Problems in the Economists' Conceptualization of Technological Innovation*, in N. Rosenberg, *Perspectives on Technology*, Cambridge, Cambridge University Press: 61-84.

Rosenberg, N., Birdzell, L.E. [1986], *How the West Grew Rich. The Economic Transformation of the Industrial World*, London, Tauris & co.

Rossi, E. [1955], *I padroni del vapore*, Bari, Laterza.

Rossi, N., Sorgato, A., Toniolo, G. [1993], "I conti economici italiani: una ricostruzione statistica", *Rivista di Storia economica*, 10: 1-47.

Rossi, N., Toniolo, G. [1992], "Catching Up or Falling Behind? Italy's Economic Growth in Europe Since 1945", *Economic History Review*, 51: 537-563.

Roverato, G. [1986], *Una casa industriale. I Marzotto*, Milan, Franco Angeli.

Rumelt, R. [1986], *Strategy, Structure and Economic Performance*, Boston, Harvard Business School.

Rybczinski, T.M. [1974], "Business Finance in the EEC, USA and Japan", *Three Banks Review*, 103: 58-72.

Rybczinski, T.M. [1984], "Industrial Finance Systems in Europe, U.S. and Japan", *Journal of Economic Behavior and Organization*, 5: 276-290.

Saba, A. [1995], *Il modello italiano. La "specializzazione flessibile" e i distretti industriali*, Milan, Franco Angeli.

Saibante, A. [1926], "I profitti delle società per azioni e la concentrazione dei capitali industriali", *Metron*, vol. VI, republished in *Scritti scelti*, Rome, 1956: 74-104.

Saibante, A. [1934], *Nuovi dati statistici sulle società italiane per azioni*, in *La vita economica italiana*, republished in *Scritti scelti*, Rome, 1956: 259-270.

Salvati, M. [2000], *Occasioni mancate. Economia e politica in Italia dagli anni Sessanta ad oggi*, Rome-Bari, Laterza.

Sanders, M., ter Weel, B. [2000], "Skill-biased Technical Change: Theoretical Concepts, Empirical Problems and a Survey of the Evidence", *Merit Research Memorandum*, no. 12.

Sapelli, G. [1992], *Technical Change, Microeconomic Evolution and Growth: An Introduction View of Italian Industrial Development*, in G. Dosi, R. Giannetti, P.A. Toninelli (eds), *Technology and Enterprise in a Historical Perspective*, Oxford, Oxford University Press: 291-313.

Sapelli, G. [1997], *Storia economica dell'Italia contemporanea*, Milan, Bruno Mondadori.

Sapelli, G., Carnevali, F. [1992], *Uno sviluppo tra politica e strategia: Eni (1953-1985)*, Milan, Franco Angeli.

Saraceno, P. [1975], *Il sistema delle imprese a partecipazione statale nell'esperienza italiana*, Milan, Giuffré.

Sartori, R. [1957], *Le partecipazioni economiche dello Stato*, Rome, Studium.

Saviotti, P.P., Krafft, J. [2004], *Towards a Generalised Definition of Competition*, paper presented at the DRUID Summer Conference 2004 on Industrial Dynamics, Innovation and Development, Elsenore (Denmark), June 14th-16th.

Scalfari, E. [1963], *Storia segreta dell'industria elettrica*, Bari, Laterza.

Scalfari, E., Turani, G. [1974], *Razza padrona*, Milan, Feltrinelli.

Scherer, F.M. [1980^{2}], *Industrial Market Structure and Economic Performance*, Chicag, Rand-McNally.

Schultz, T.W. [1960], "Capital Formation by Education", *Journal of Political Economy*, 68: 571-583.

Schultz, T.W. [1962], *Rise in the Capital Stock Represented by Education in the US, 1900-1957*, in S. Mushkin (ed.), *Economics of Higher Education,* Washington, D.H.E.W.

Schumpeter, J.A. [1939], *Business Cycles,* New York, McGraw-Hill.

Scott, J. [1985], *Theoretical Framework and Research Design*, in F.S. Stokman, R. Ziegler, J. Scott (eds), *Networks of Corporate Power. A Comparative Analysis of Ten Countries*, Cambridge, Polity Press: 1-19.

Scott, J. [1991], *Social Network Analysis. A Handbook*, London, SAGE.
Scott, J. [1997], *Corporate Business and Capitalist Classes*, Oxford, Oxford University Press.
Segreto, L. [1992], *Imprenditori e finanzieri*, in G. Mori (ed.), *Storia dell'industria elettrica in Italia*, vol. I: *Le origini. 1882-1914*, t. I, Rome-Bari, Laterza: 249-331.
Sereni, E. [1966], *Capitalismo e mercato nazionale*, Rome, Editori Riuniti.
Shepard, W.G. [1982], "Caused of Increased Competition in the US Economy", *Review of Economics and Statistics*, 64: 613-626.
Siciliano, G. [2001], *Cento anni di borsa in Italia*, Bologna, Il Mulino.
Siebert, H., Stolpe, M. [2002], *Germany*, in B. Steil, D.G. Victor, R.R. Nelson (eds), *Technological Innovation and Economic Performance*, Princeton, Princeton University Press: 112-147.
Sombart, W. [1927], *Der Moderne Kapitalismus*, Munich, Duncker and Humblot.
Sori, E. [2002], "Mascalzone latino ovvero la crisi Fiat e il declino industriale dell'Italia", *Annali di storia dell'impresa*, Venice, Marsilio, 13: 495-504.
Spoerer, M. [1998], "Window-dressing in German Inter-War Balance Sheets", *Accounting, Business and Financial History*, 8: 351-370.
Stata Corporation [2002], *STATA SE/7*, College Station (Texas).
Stigler, G.J., Friedland, C. [1983], "The Literature of Economics: The Case of Berle and Means", *Journal of Law and Economics*, 26: 237-268.
Stockman, R., Leicht, R. [1994], "The Pattern of Changes in the Long-term Development of Establishment Size", *Small Business Economics*, 6: 451-463.
Stokman, F.N., Wasseur, F.W. [1985], *National Networks in 1976: A Structural Comparison*, in F.S. Stokman, R. Ziegler, J. Scott (eds), *Networks of Corporate Power. A Comparative Analysis of Ten Countries*, Cambridge, Polity Press: 20-44.
Stokman, F.N., Ziegler, R., Scott, J. (eds), [1985], *Networks of Corporate Power. A Comparative Analysis of Ten Countries*, Oxford, Polity Press.
Sutton, J. [1990], "Explaining Everything, Explaining Nothing? Game Theoretic Models in Industrial Organization", *European Economic Review*, 34: 505-512.
Sutton, J. [1998], *Technology and Market Structure: Theory and History*, Cambridge (Mass.), The MIT Press.
Sylla, R., Toniolo, G. (eds), [1991], *Patterns of European Industrialization. The Nineteenth Century*, London, Routledge.
Sylos Labini, P. [1970], *Problemi dello sviluppo economico*, Bari, Laterza.

Taccuino dell'azionista. Annuario di documentazione finanziaria industriale e di borsa, [various years], Il Sole 24 Ore-Sacip.
Tafunell, X. [1998], "Los beneficios empresariales en España, 1880-1981. Estimación de un índice anual del excedente de la gran empresa", *Revista de Historia Económica*, 16: 707-746.
Tafunell, X. [2000], "La rentabilidad financiera de la empresa española, 1880-1981: Una estimación en perspectiva sectorial", *Revista de Historia Industrial*, 18: 71-111.

Tattara, G., Toniolo, G. [1976], *L'industria manifatturiera: cicli, politiche e mutamenti di struttura*, in P. Ciocca, G. Toniolo (eds), *L'economia italiana nel periodo fascista*, Bologna, Il Mulino: 103-158.

Teece, D.J. [1980], "Economies of Scope and the Scope of the Enterprise", *Journal of Economic Behavior and Organization*, 1: 223-247.

Teece D.J., Rumelt, R., Dosi, G., Winter, S.G. [1994], "Understanding Corporate Coherence: Theory and Evidence", *Journal of Economic and Business Organization*, 23: 1-30.

Teti, R. [1999], *Imprese, imprenditori e diritto*, in F. Amatori, D. Bigazzi, R. Giannetti, L. Segreto (eds), *Storia d'Italia. Annali 15, L'industria*, Turin, Einaudi: 1215-1303.

Toninelli, P.A. [1990], *La Edison. Contabilità e bilanci in una grande impresa elettrica (1884-1916),* Bologna, Il Mulino.

Toninelli, P.A. [1999a], "Ragioneria, contabilità e storia d'impresa: alcune osservazioni in margine al caso italiano", *Annali di storia dell'impresa*, Bologna, Il Mulino, 10: 79-113.

Toninelli, P.A. [1999b], *L'evoluzione del concetto di impresa. Introduzione*, in F. Amatori, P.A. Toninelli (eds), *Un'introduzione alla storia d'impresa. Storici ed economisti a confronto*, Milan, Egea: 9-20.

Toninelli, P.A. (ed.), [2000], *The Rise and Fall of State-Owned Enterprises in the Western World*, Cambridge, Cambridge University Press.

Toninelli, P.A. [2001], *Il paradigma perduto: una riflessione sullo sviluppo economico italiano nel lungo periodo*, in L. Cafagna, N. Crepax (eds), *Atti di intelligenza e sviluppo economico. Saggi per il bicentenario della nascita di Carlo Cattaneo*, Bologna, Il Mulino: 513-569.

Toninelli, P.A. [2003], *Ascesa e declino dell'impresa pubblica in Italia (1860-2000): una nota sul ruolo dello stato nella crescita*, in A.M. Falchero, A. Giuntini, G. Nigro, L. Segreto (eds), *La storia e l'economia. Miscellanea di studi in onore di Giorgio Mori*, 2: 629-661.

Toniolo, G. [1980], *L'economia dell'Italia fascista*, Rome-Bari, 1980.

Tonizzi, M.E. [2001], *L'industria dello zucchero. La produzione saccarifera in Italia e in Europa 1800-2000*, Milan, Franco Angeli.

Traù, F. (ed.), [1999], *La "questione dimensionale" nell'industria italiana*, Bologna, Il Mulino.

Trento, S. [1994], *Il gruppo di imprese come modello di controllo nei paesi ritardatari*, in Banca d'Italia, *Il mercato della proprietà e del controllo delle imprese: aspetti teorici e istituzionali*, in *Contributi all'analisi economica*, special number: 111-136.

Turani, G. [1996], *I sogni del grande Nord*, Bologna, Il Mulino.

Vasta M. [1999a], *Innovazione tecnologica e capitale umano in Italia (1880-1914). Le traiettorie tecnologiche della seconda rivoluzione industriale*, Bologna, Il Mulino.

Vasta M. [1999b], *Capitale umano e ricerca scientifica e tecnologica*, in F. Amatori, D. Bigazzi, R. Giannetti, L. Segreto (eds) *Storia d'Italia. Annali 15, L'industria*, Turin, Einaudi: 1041-1124.

Vasta M. [2003], *The National System of Innovation in Historical Perspective: Italy from the Unification to the Present (1861-2000)*, paper presented at *Business History Conference-European Business History Association Joint Annual Meetings: "Regions, Nations and Globalization"*, Lowell (Mass.), June 2003.

Vasta M. [2006], *Patents as Quantitative Source Between Economics and History*, in *Act du Colloque Les brevets dans l'Histoire. Propriété industrielle, histoire technique et économique,* Paris, L'Harmattan, forthcoming.

Vasta, M., Baccini, A. [1997], "Bank and Industry in Italy 1911-1936: New Evidences Using *Interlocking Directorates* Technique", *Financial History Review*, 4: 139-159.

Vinci, F. [1918], "La concentrazione dei capitali nelle società ordinarie per azioni", *Rivista delle società commerciali*, 8: 195-207.

Vitali, O. [1970], *Aspetti dello sviluppo economico italiano alla luce della ricostruzione della popolazione*, Rome, Facoltà di Scienze Statistiche Demografiche e Attuariali, Università degli Studi di Roma La Sapienza, Istituto di Demografia.

Vitali, O. [1992], *Gli impieghi del reddito nell'anno 1911*, in G. Rey (ed.), *I conti economici dell'Italia*, vol. II: *Una stima del valore aggiunto per rami di attività per il 1911*, Rome-Bari, Laterza: 283-337.

Vitiello, A. [1993], *La grande famiglia degli elettrici in Italia*, in G. Galasso (ed.), *Storia dell'industria elettrica in Italia*, vol. III: *Espansione e oligopolio*, t. I, Rome-Bari, Laterza: 399-504.

Warglien, M. [1987], "Investimento industriale e instabilità finanziaria in Italia, 1878-1913", *Rivista di Storia economica*, 4: 384-439.

Wardley, P. [1991], "The Anatomy of Big Business: Aspects of Corporate Development in the Twentieth Century", *Business History*, 33: 268-296.

Wasserman, S., Faust, K. [1994], *Social Network Analysis. Methods and Applications*, Cambridge, Cambridge University Press.

White, L.J. [2002], "Trends in Aggregate Concentration in the United States", *Journal of Economic Perspectives*, 16: 137-160.

Whittington, R., Mayer, M. [2000], *The European Corporation: Strategy, Structure and Social Science,* Oxford, Oxford University Press.

Whittington, R., Mayer, M. [2002], "Response to Kay: Chandlerism in Post-War Europe. Strategic and Structural Change in France, Germany and the U.K.", *Industrial and Corporate Change*, 11: 199-205.

Whittington, R., Mayer, M., Curto, F. [1999], "Chandlerism in Post-War Europe: Strategic and Structural Change in France, Germany and the U.K.", *Industrial and Corporate Change*, 8: 519-550.

Williamson, O. [1986], *The Economic Institutions of Capitalism. Firms, Markets, relational contracting*, New York, The Free Press.

Winter, S.G. [1984], "Schumpeterian Competition in Alternative 'Technological Regimes'", *Journal of Economic Behavior and Organization*, 5: 287-320.

Zamagni, V. [1978], *Industrializzazione e squilibri regionali in Italia*, Bologna, Il Mulino.

Zamagni, V. [1987], "A Century of Change: Trends in the Composition of the Italian Labour Force, 1881-1981", *Historical Social Research*, 44: 36-97, republished in G. Federico (ed.), [1994], *The Economic Development of Italy since 1870*, Aldershot, Elgar: 210-271.

Zamagni, V. [1990a], *Dalla periferia al centro. La seconda rinascita economica dell'Italia 1861-1981*, Bologna, Il Mulino; Eng. trans. as *The Economic History of Italy, 1860-1990*, Oxford, Clarendon Press, 1993.

Zamagni, V. [1990b], *L'industria chimica in Italia dalle origini agli anni '50*, in F. Amatori, B. Bezza (eds), *Montecatini 1888-1966. Capitoli di storia di una grande impresa*, Bologna, Il Mulino: 69-148.

Zamagni, V. (ed.), [1992], *Finance and Enterprise,* London, Academic Press.

Zamagni, V. [1993], *L'offerta di istruzione in Italia 1861-1987: un fattore guida dello sviluppo o un ostacolo?*, Università di Cassino, Dipartimento di Economia e Territorio, working paper, series of Economy, no. 4.

Zamagni, V. [1994], *Alcune tesi sull'intervento dello Stato in una prospettiva di lungo periodo*, in P. Ciocca (ed.), *Il progresso economico dell'Italia. Permanenze, discontinuità, limiti,* Bologna, Il Mulino: 151-160.

Zamagni, V. [2003], "L'ENI e la chimica", *Energia*, 24: 16-24.

Zanetti, G. [1989], *Aspetti finanziari e aziendali dell'industria elettrica alla vigilia della nazionalizzazione*, in VV.AA., *La nazionalizzazione dell'energia elettrica. L'esperienza italiana e di altri paesi europei*, Rome-Bari, Laterza: 117-146.

Zanetti, G. [1996], "L'utilizzo dei dati d'impresa nella ricerca empirica: alcune esperienze italiane", *Rivista Italiana degli Economisti*, 1: 265-283.

Zanetti, G., Alzona, G. [1998], *Capire le privatizzazioni*, Bologna, Il Mulino.

Zanetti, G., Filippi, E. [1965], *Finanza e sviluppo della grande impresa in Italia*, Milan, Franco Angeli.

Zerini, E. (pseudonym of E. Rienzi) [1947a], "L'economia capitalistica e i vari aspetti delle egemonie economiche in Italia", *Critica economica*, 5: 75-102.

Zerini, E. (pseudonym of E. Rienzi) [1947b], "L'economia capitalistica e i vari aspetti delle egemonie economiche in Italia", *Critica economica*, 6: 108-142.

Zerini, E. (pseudonym of E. Rienzi) [1947c], "L'economia capitalistica e i vari aspetti delle egemonie economiche in Italia", *Critica economica*, 7: 67-98.

Zorzini, M. [1925], "L'organizzazione dell'industria idroelettrica in Italia", *Economia*, 7: 166-176.

List of figures

List of tables

List of authors

Renato Giannetti. Professor of Economic History at University of Florence, he teaches Business History at Humanities Faculty and he is member of Department of Historical and Geographical studies. His main interests are Italian economic development, history of technology and business history. He has published several essays and among the most recent *Storia dell'impresa industriale italiana* [with M. Vasta], Bologna, Il Mulino, 2005.

Michelangelo Vasta. He received a DPhil at University of Oxford. He is professor in Economic History at University of Siena (Department of Economics). He teaches Economic History and Business History. Most of his research work has dealt with Italian economic development. His main interests are: i) technical change in historical perspective; ii) business history; iii) ownership structure; iv) industrial economics. He has published several essays and among the most recent *Storia dell'impresa industriale italiana* [with R. Giannetti], Bologna, Il Mulino, 2005; "The structure of Italian capitalism, 1952-1972: new evidence using the interlocking directorates technique", *Financial History Review*, 12, 2005, [with A. Rinaldi].

Leonardo Bargigli. He received his PhD in Economics at the Department of Electronics and Telecommunications of University of Florence. His main interests are: industrial organization, technical change and innovation. He is actually junior research fellow at Department of Economics of University of Florence.

Giovanni Federico. He received his *perfezionamento* (PhD) at the Scuola Normale Superiore (Pisa) and he is actually professor of Economic History at European University Institute (EUI) of Fiesole. His main interests are: i) trade and trade policy, ii) history of agriculture; iii) history of silk industry; iv) business history. He has published several reviews and survey of literature on Italian economic development, as well as chapters in textbooks on economic growth and Italian history. Among his recent publications: *The Economic Development of Italy* [with Jon Cohen], CUP, 2001 and *Feeding the World: An Economic History of World Agriculture, 1800-2000*, PUP, 2005.

Alberto Rinaldi. He has got a PhD in Economic and Social History at Bocconi University, Milan. He is lecturer in Economic History at the University of Modena and Reggio Emilia. His research interests cover centuries XVIII to XX focusing in particular on *industrial districts* and the history of Italian capitalism. Amongst his publications: "The Emilian Model Revisited: Twenty Years After", *Business History*, 47, 2005; "The structure of Italian capitalism, 1952-1972: new evidence using the interlocking directorates technique", *Financial History Review*, 12, 2005, [with M. Vasta].

Pier Angelo Toninelli. He is professor of Contemporary History and Business History at University of Milan-Bicocca. His main interests are: i) industrial and business history of Italy; ii) history of corporate finance and accounting; iii) methodology of economic history; iv) history of state-owned enterprise. He has published various essays and he is the editor of *The Rise and Fall of State-owned Enterprise in the Western World*, CUP, 2000.

Margherita Velucchi. She received her PhD in Economics at the Department of Economics of University of Siena. Her main research interests are: econometric analysis of structural changes, Markov switching models and economic convergence. She is actually junior research fellow at Department of Statistics of University of Florence.

Index